THE *POLITICS* OF WOODROW WILSON

THE *POLITICS* OF WOODROW WILSON

Selections from His Speeches and Writings

Edited, with an Introduction, by
AUGUST HECKSCHER

Essay Index Reprint Series

BOOKS FOR LIBRARIES PRESS
FREEPORT, NEW YORK

Selections from:

COLLEGE AND STATE EDUCATIONAL, LITERARY
AND POLITICAL PAPERS (1875-1913). Copyright
1925, 1953 by Edith Bolling Wilson

LEADERS OF MEN, edited by T. S. Vail Motter.
Copyright 1952 by Edith Bolling Wilson

THE NEW DEMOCRACY, PRESIDENTIAL MESSAGES,
ADDRESSES AND OTHER PAPERS (1913-1917).
Copyright 1926, 1954 by Edith Bolling Wilson

THE NEW FREEDOM. Copyright 1919 by Doubleday & Company, Inc.

WAR AND PEACE, PRESIDENTIAL MESSAGES, AD-
DRESSES AND PUBLIC PAPERS (1917-1924). Copyright 1927, 1955 by Edith Bolling Wilson

WHEN A MAN COMES TO HIMSELF. Copyright
1901 by Harper & Brothers; copyright 1929 by
Edith Bolling Wilson

WOODROW WILSON, Life and Letters, by Ray
Stannard Baker. Vol. IV, copyright 1931 by Ray
Stannard Baker

STANDARD BOOK NUMBER:

8369-1737-5

LIBRARY OF CONGRESS CATALOG CARD NUMBER:

74-117861

PRINTED IN THE UNITED STATES OF AMERICA

Contents

Introduction

by August Heckscher

I

The word "Politics" is used in the title of this book in the sense that we speak of Aristotle's Politics; or, as the dictionary gives for one of its meanings: "political principles and opinions." It comes nearer than any other word to describing what this selection from Woodrow Wilson's works tries to do. Wilson himself cherished the idea of one day writing a magnum opus, referred to in the family circle as the P.O.P.—or more formally, "The Principles of Politics." I had hoped, when I began editing this volume, that I might by judicious selection and arrangement produce the work which Wilson had first lacked the time, and then the strength, to undertake. But that did not prove feasible. Most of Wilson's speeches and writings were shaped under the compulsion of events, with particular ends in view. They were for the day and the hour; what was permanent in them derived from the insights, from the style, and, in the end, from the enduring greatness of the cause they served. It seemed best not to try to fit the material into an analytic framework, but to let it unfold freely, more or less in accordance with the pattern of the author's life and interests.

Yet the idea remains that, taken as a whole, these selections reveal something close to a philosophy—that they reveal at least the opinions and principles which the title implies. Wilson had given much thought to the structure and character of government, long before he was called to play an active part in it. The spirit of American history and American constitutional development had preoccupied him deeply; and beyond that he had dealt with the moral, ethical, and social concepts which underlie any true philosophy of politics.

vii

Much of what he wrote in his academic years has been neglected; and much of it, in all candor, does not stand the light of modern appraisal. Like any young man seeking to find himself, to find his audience and his style, Wilson worked his way through inconsistencies and around dead ends; and in his case the perils of the journey were augmented by a tendency to over-elaboration. It is a long way from the adjectives and the inverted constructions of, say, the George Washington (none of which is included here) to the august simplicities of the war speeches. But at his best Wilson from the beginning wrote well and thought well; and he wrote and thought along lines that give meaning to the stupendous choices of his total career.

What I have done with the early Wilson is to choose freely, to exclude rigorously, and to present without apology what I believe to be the best. It is the best not only in itself but in terms of what the man later did and became. Thus from his writings on constitutional theory I have chosen those passages which reveal his thinking about the Presidency, about the need for responsible leadership in a democracy, about the nature and conditions of true statesmanship. His writings on the development of this country's history, with their emphasis on the paramount influence of the West, seemed vitally related to his later political views; and so, in a deeper and more subtle way, did the writings on religion and education. Such studies as those on Burke and Adam Smith, though interesting in themselves, seem isolated. The influence of Burke on Wilson's thought has, I believe, been over-emphasized.

The major state papers of domestic reforms and the war years are included virtually entire. These are not now easily accessible outside a library, and yet the assumptions which underlie them are constantly discussed. Wilson's foreign policy, in particular, has been under fire. The intellectual leaders and publicists of the generation immediately following the second World War have challenged the Wilsonian ideas; they have brought back the concept of the balance of power, and emphasized the constricted role of foreign policy, as opposed to the universal mission which Wilson preached. This changed outlook has been in many ways a necessary and healthful reaction. Yet the point of departure should at least be plain; and it has seemed useful to have Wilson's statements of his own ideas readily available in their original form.

An authoritative collected edition of Wilson's works, including the still unpublished letters, waits to be made. There the scholar could trace the whole involved growth of Wilson's ideas. The present collection has a more modest purpose. It seeks to recreate an image and a force in a way that will be relevant to the decade in which the world now finds itself a hundred years after his birth. It was in its day a great image and a mighty force, which those who felt its full tide still speak of with awe, and which a new generation can ill afford to neglect.

II

Wilson's career and personality are touched with pathos, the more clearly seen now that the emotions which he stirred in his lifetime have been subdued; and that pathos lies across the written and spoken word. From youth he felt himself marked for a great task. He trained himself consciously for leadership. He practiced oratory; he shaped a style; he filled his mind with the writings of the Anglo-American political and constitutional tradition. Yet the call to leadership was long deferred. And when that call came, first at Princeton and then on the larger stage of the nation and the world, the sweet moments of triumph were followed by bitter defeats.

His life was as a landscape across which sunlight and clouds passed alternately; and the climax was a storm in which the gods themselves seemed locked in conflict. The man who passed through these vicissitudes, by his gifts and ardors calling up the whirlwind, was frail in health, reserved and lonely in disposition, an unshakable spirit suffused with inner light. Despite the glory and power that came to him, despite the sternness and the pride, it was "Tommy" Wilson who went forth to meet the destiny awaiting him: aspiring, eager, as one in whom the dreams of youth live on to become mingled with the attainments of maturity.

The legend of Wilson's "coldness" has survived the testimony of his friends and the evidence of the personal letters already on the record. That he could be icy in manner is undeniable. But it would be to miss the whole point of his life and writings to assume that this was the reflection of insensitivity. He was, in fact, a man of intense, even passionate, feelings. He suffered tortures of frustration and self-doubt; he knew the elation of momentary fulfillments. To a degree that is rare even in the comparative quiet of college circles today, the young Wilson cultivated friendships, savored the intimacy of relationships developed in long conversations and idle hours, and found time for the lost art of letter-writing. Family ties were lovingly maintained, not only in the close circle of the Princeton household but among a wide group of cousins and other relatives. For various reasons Wilson came to discipline his emotions (as he disciplined his skills); but this was altogether different from not possessing them.

One of the early papers, written while he was a student in college, casts a prophetic light on the man to be. Wilson is writing of the elder Pitt. "His mind was clear and strong, his will was unwavering, his convictions were uncompromising, his imagination was powerful enough to invest all plans of national policy with a poetic charm, his confidence in himself was implicit, his love for his country was real and intense." But already there seemed to be intimations of the last great defeat: "William Pitt was a noble statesman; the Earl of Chatham was a noble ruin." Time, writes the young student, has indeed "traced out to their end all the greater lines of policy which in their beginning bore indications of the strokes of Pitt's decided hand. But he had lain in his grave many years before some of the most important measures which he had advocated were carried out in their fullness; and during his lifetime, while he was still a power in the state, even his towering influence fell powerless when he sought to force his country to follow the paths of foreign policy which he had cleared for her, and which he had known to be the only roads to honor and safety."

Later Wilson was to renew this sense at once of ominous prescience and of confident anticipation. "Who shall show us the way to this place?" he asked at the close of the climactic passage of his Sesquicentennial Address, describing "the perfect place of learning" he had in mind. Six years afterwards, as president of Princeton, the task fell to him. It was the same when he stood in 1909 at the threshold of a political career which few could then have foreseen: "I wish there were some great orator," he said, "who could go about and make men drunk with this spirit of self-sacrifice . . . whose tongue might every day carry abroad the golden accents of that creative age in which we were born a nation, accents which would ring like tones of reassurance around the whole circle of the globe." He was ready when the time came to be that orator, in days when the foundations of the civilized world seemed to be falling.

I emphasize this sense of an unfolding fate, this conviction of great deeds to be done, because without it the man and his style lose a whole dimension. At each stage of his career Wilson was what he was, as well as what he would become. As a professor the light of unfulfilled ambitions played about him. As president of Princeton he went forth to greet the alumni feeling like "a responsible minister," as he put it, "reporting to his constituents." That he should have been taken out of the academic life and made Governor of New Jersey still seems as strange as it was perhaps inevitable; and two years later he was in the White House. Wilson's personal letters make frequent references to the sense of uprooting, of lost associations and broken ties, which came to him with the sudden transformation of his life. During his first term in the White House, Ellen Axson Wilson, his wife, died. The lonely President faced the supreme tasks cut off from the early sources of inspiration, but with the fires of a disinterested passion burning the more intensely. So they flared and burned, until they consumed the physical man and left only the indestructible will.

From the beginning Wilson had been a man with a style; at the end the man, the style, and the event were merged in a classical perfection. The great speeches of the war years stand by themselves, in their way as unique as the best of Lincoln or of Churchill. I cite a single example, from the address presenting the treaty of peace to the Senate for ratification. He is speaking of the American soldiers who fought in France:

"They carried the ideals of a free people at their hearts and with that vision they were unconquerable. Their very presence brought reassurance; their fighting made victory certain.

"They were recognized as crusaders, and as their thousands swelled to millions their strength was seen to mean salvation. And they were fit men to carry such a hope and make good the assurance it foretold. Finer men never went into battle; and their officers were worthy of them. This is not the occasion upon which to utter a eulogy of the armies America sent to France, but perhaps, since I am speaking of their mission, I may speak also of the pride I shared with every American who saw or dealt with them there. They were the sort of men America would wish to be represented by, the sort of men every American would wish to claim as fellow countrymen and comrades in a great cause. They were terrible in battle, and gentle and helpful out of it, remembering the mothers and sisters, the wives and the little children at home. They were free men under arms, not forgetting their ideals of duty in the midst of tasks of violence. . . ."

The Athenian dead did not have for their epitaph a more perfect blending of pity and of pride.

But this is the ultimate note. Wilson's style at its most characteristic is that of the skilled extemporaneous speaker, warmed by a sympathetic audience so that his thoughts feed upon themselves and his phrases draw life from the moment. Those who heard Wilson speak commented upon the way he could give the impression of addressing individually each member of a gathering, his trained voice carrying through the vastest hall, in a day when electrical amplification was still unknown. Something of this intimacy survives in the printed word. There are stretches of his prose that read like one side of an animated conversation, carried on between two people who have much esteem for each other. Incandescence lights the words and a quick comprehension stirs the rhythms.

Hazards, of course, lay in such a method. Wilson himself comments, in the introduction to passages from campaign addresses, upon "the redundancy which the extemporaneous speaker apparently inevitably falls into." He spoke usually from the barest notes; he was often faultily reported, and he extended himself, unmercifully it would seem today, to reach audiences which a single broadcast would have easily given. Yet taken as a whole the level of even his least finished addresses is high. An amazing verbal resourcefulness permitted him to develop a single theme through a long series of talks, as in his campaign for preparedness or his western tour on behalf of the League, virtually without repetition.

He started as an orator. We have an early glimpse of him practicing speaking in his father's deserted church at night. Much of his first political writing was aimed at developing the conditions which would make oratory an effective influence in affairs. In between there was a period when he reconciled himself to writing as the way to influence. He went to school to the English essayists; one sees in his style the clear traces of Macaulay, Addison, Lamb; above all, both in texture and point of view, of Bagehot. There is a good deal of affectation in the writings of his early academic period, as if he were too eager to catch the ear, too anxious to please. His *History of the American People*, much admired at the time of its publication, today makes uncomfortable reading. The training, however, stood him in good stead. When later the urgency of something imperative to say took hold of him he sat down before the small typewriter he had carried with him to the White House; and the words fell into the patterns of great English speech. The mind "stripped and athletic in the acceptable exercise of power" left off what had distorted or weakened the early style. Passion stirred the utterance, but the skill in persuasion, in denunciation, in exhortation, was that of the master rhetorician.

III

Deeds and words become inseparable where such a figure is concerned. To hardly less a degree style and thought become inseparable. Wilson's liberalism has been written of as a late development; certain passages in his published works, an early mistrust of Jefferson, a love of Burke, have been cited to indicate that the reformist phrase came to him only when the road to political power opened. This interpretation misses much of the significance of Wilson's development. He was a reformer in temperament and disposition from the start, an active leader by every pull of inclination and ambition. In the educational field he first showed (to the consternation of many who fell under his goad) of what stuff he was made. It was the practical program of reform, not the spirit of reform, which was lacking until he stood at the opening of his political phase.

Wilson described himself once as "an animated conservative"; and animation, both of style and of ideas, was the essence of him. It was difficult for him to take for long the cautionary or gloomy view of things. He was not an optimist, except insofar as one can be said to be optimistic who has looked into the pit of human damnation and contrives in consequence to find the ordinary manifestations of life quite cheerful; but he was spirited by nature, and his speech and writing were marked by an intrinsic grace. It was his normal role to evoke hope and aspiration, and he then appeared too much the gentleman, too urbane and courteous, to cry them down. The effect of his style was to make the facts of life seem something less than brute facts—to make even the worst barriers seem somehow surmountable. "His mind," said one contemporary observer, "is like a light which destroys the outlines of what it plays upon; there is much illumination, but you see very little." You would see very little, that is, of the obstacles in the way; but you saw far horizons, and the varied possibilities of which the human spirit is capable.

"I do not myself," said Wilson on one occasion, "see how a scholar can be a conservative." He was stating a paradox; for the scholar with his search for the last fact, his awareness of the complexity and rootedness of things, might be expected to be conservative. But Wilson did not view it in this way. "No man can see in the least below the surface," he said, "who does not see that men press forward from stage to stage in an unending struggle for things which they have not yet obtained; that in the intellectual sphere, as in the social sphere, there is a constant, hopeful pursuit of the things that lie just beyond the touch." The Wilsonian style is unmistakable, and this style as much shapes the thought as it is shaped by it.

Some of the basic sources of his later liberalism are plainly revealed in Wilson's early political and historical writings. *Congressional Government*, the first book, is the product of a reforming zeal. The author wants to describe the working of the American constitutional system as it is, not as it has been seen through the spectacles of traditional literary theory. But beyond that, he wants to change the constitution. He wants to restore the conditions which make possible a dynamic and responsible leadership in a democracy. Great leadership must be in the service of some great end. As Wilson's preoccupation with style grips him before he has something really significant to say, so his urge to act takes hold before the substance of a political program is clear. But the instrument is ready when the time comes, sharpened and tempered by the battles at Princeton; and the materials for a valid reform program lie all around. The outcome is the Wilsonian domestic program, consistent with the man's method of action from the start, though its substance could not have been seen in more than general terms.

The preparation of the liberal leader went forward, also, through Wilson's reading of American history. A Southerner by birth and upbringing, he never identified his thinking with that of the South. More significant, he never identified it with that of the East. He was one of the first to grasp the meaning of the frontier in American history. He saw the continent in terms of its immensity, its diversity, its restless energy. He was aware of the new claims which the West was likely to make, and he was ready to recognize the legitimacy of those claims—provided they were not, like the silver issue, merely the expression of a new sectionalism. Wilson understood, moreover, the impact which the closing of the frontier was bound to have upon all aspects of American life. The country could no longer escape its problems by westward expansion but must now turn and live with itself. Social issues were bound to come to the fore; as the adjustments of life became more complex, the provision of equal opportunity became a matter of organization and deliberate action.

Lincoln symbolized for Wilson the meaning of American nationhood. At different stages in his life he turns to this figure as the reflection of his own changing concerns. In the Presidency, when Wilson faced the choice of whether to bring America into the war, he drew from Lincoln's example a tacit parallel with his own agony of decision: "There is a very holy and a very terrible isolation," he said then, "for the conscience of every man who seeks to read the destiny in affairs for others as well as himself, for a nation as well as for individuals. . . . That lonely search of the spirit for the right perhaps no man can assist." He added the unforgettable picture of "this strange child of the cabin" who "kept company with invisible things, was born into no intimacy save that of his own silently assembling and deploying thoughts." Earlier, when he waited to enter upon the political stage, Wilson pictured Lincoln as the man of the people: "He has felt beat in him . . . a universal sympathy for those who struggle, a universal understanding of the unutterable things that were in their hearts and the unbearable burdens that were upon their backs." But it is of Lincoln as the embodiment of the nation, the one historical figure capable of comprehending its breadth and variety, that Wilson wrote in the years when his ideas were in the formative stage. Lincoln alone, he believed, symbolized the true type of the American—speaking for no class, no interest, no section; yet in a profound way representing them all.

Wilson's early feeling for the organic nature of society—its complexity, the depths of its attachments and the validity of its conflicting loyalties—might have made him a genuine conservative. He knew instinctively that to push any one interest too far could mean injury to other interests of equal importance. He knew that a man "comes to himself" as he is able to put down roots in a society secure against disruption and upheaval. Living in the closely knit college community, with its vital traditions and its ideals made visible in old buildings and dedicated characters, had perhaps done as much as Burke to convince him that a doctrinaire approach not only hurts individuals but strikes at the heart of a vital social order.

Leadership in normal times must wear, he wrote, "the harness of compromise." Yet Wilson was saved from any temptation to inaction. "Once and again one of those great Influences which we call a Cause arises in the midst of the nation." So the leader in embryo discerned; and he knew that then the leader must speak out, opening his whole mind in season and out. Resistance would gather among the very people who stood to benefit most in the long run. But the leader must surely win; the masses, wrote the young Wilson, "come over to the side of reform. Resistance is left to the minority and such as will not be converted or crushed."

For such a one as Wilson, "a great Influence which we call a Cause" was never apt to be lacking. He created around himself the conditions which seemed to call out for leadership; and then he stepped forth to fulfill the need. Through changes of scene and circumstance he seemed to move amid events of supreme importance. A small New Jersey college was made the stage upon which the forces of democracy and privilege confronted each other in fateful array. The New Freedom was a battle for the liberation of a people's energies; the first World War was transformed into something bigger than a struggle of nations, as the peace was transformed into something more than a settlement of old accounts. It was Wilson's strength to enlarge and enliven all he touched; his weakness was to believe that only those resisted who had not been "converted or crushed." It can be said that he drove too hard, or confused his own purposes with a predestined cause. But he surely carried from youth the impress of a man born to lead, to act, to fight.

IV

For Wilson religion was at the heart of politics. He believed in the importance of the individual because of the individual's relationship to God; and he conceived it his task, so far as he was able, to free this individual from tyranny and oppression in all forms. The political battles against the bosses in New Jersey and against economic monopolies in the nation were given depth by Wilson's evident conviction that the fight was on behalf of man's soul. The first World War became a climactic, and as he believed decisive, chapter in an age-old struggle against tyrants.

Wilson was conscious, too, of the subtler chains upon man's freedom—subjection to partial interests, to professional concerns, even to cherished family obligations. His educational theory was in large part based upon his belief that in the liberal arts alone could students find the way out of the narrowness and specialization which corrupts what he called "the free life." For the college student he craved a period of withdrawal, where he could learn to see the world whole and come to act upon grounds of principle alone. The citizens of a democracy should afterwards carry this core of disinterestedness, capable of being appealed to in the high moments of a nation's affairs.

The emancipation of the individual was not, it should be emphasized, for the purpose of letting the individual do as he desired. The individualism of a man like Wilson was not an invitation to eccentricity; it was a call to duty and honor. For in proportion as a man is disentangled from worldly interests, his relationship with the creator becomes the more direct and unshaded. He moves freely, but he moves under the eye of God. Henceforth everything he does is at the peril of his soul, but by the same token everything that truly expresses himself is part of a divine mission.

It is a terrifying predicament. The individual must be righteous. But how can he tell what righteousness is? The test is action; it is commitment to a course from which there is no easy drawing back. As in the text which Wilson used for the sermon printed for the first time in this volume, "He that doeth righteousness, is righteous." There is no other thing to go by—no rule, no authority, nothing but what a man knows in the depth of his conscience to be right and has the courage to put into effect. And even at the best there is assurance of salvation. King David of the Old Testament, Wilson reminds us, "was a man marked in the history of mankind as the chosen instrument of God to do justice and to exalt righteousness in the people." But how does David stand forth in the Bible? There he appears "as indeed an instrument of God, but a sinful and selfish man. The verdict of the Bible," says Wilson, "is that

David, like other men, was one day to stand naked before the judgment of God and be judged not as a king but as a man."

There are leaders who are complex because they maintain a delicate intellectual balance; seeing all sides of a question, they let intimations of a larger truth creep into their most dogmatic or partisan assertions. Wilson was complex because he maintained a delicate moral balance. His emotions, his values, his whole being were suspended, one might say, between heaven and earth, between the practical and the ideal. He fell short often enough of the level at which his faculties preserved their balance. Then he could preach principles which seemed unrelated to anything attainable in this world; or he could do deeds not above those of the average politician. Yet that was not the essence of Wilson. The essence of the man was a noble ethical feeling that transfused politics with a sense of the values at stake in its issues and battles. It was a way of looking at the world which kept trivial things from seeming trivial and lit even these with the glint of an ideal hope.

V

The war of 1914 presented Wilson with the crowning challenge to his statesmanship. It is not quite true, as I think this selection from his writings will show, that Wilson had never thought about foreign policy until he found himself overwhelmed by its urgencies. "We stand at the threshold of a new age, in which, it would seem, we must lead the world"—so he had spoken in the Princeton Inaugural of 1902. The effect of the Spanish War in bringing the United States out into the wide world was a frequent theme of his early writings; and he had discerned as a political analyst how the center of gravity shifts toward the President as foreign affairs become paramount. "We can never hide our President again as a mere domestic officer," he wrote in the Columbia lectures of 1908. Yet it is plain that he had not given this field any close attention before he came to grapple with its problems. His whole tendency, when foreign policy became urgent, was to deal with it in the same spirit and by the same methods as domestic affairs.

His disposition, that is to say, was to penetrate to moral issues and to expect men and women to submerge narrow interests in pursuit of a common ideal. The 1914 message asking for repeal of the Panama Canal tolls is an example of how he applied on a broadened scale the standards of responsibility expected of an individual in a contractual relationship; and his important speech on a new Latin American policy (October 27, 1913) shows him thinking in terms of nations essentially like ourselves, subject to the same instincts and standards of conduct, which would more and more be brought into a fore-ordained harmony with the United States. How to deal with such countries if they were proven different from us, basically different in character and objectives, was the kind of problem in international relations which Wilson had not seriously confronted.

The outbreak of the European war brought him face to face with this problem. For a while neutrality provided the formula for avoiding it. But Wilson had never been a person for whom a moral vacuum was congenial, and the first stage of his thinking about the war found him justifying neutrality in terms of the service which the United States could render as a mediating force. He had sensed deeply the composite and varied nature of America, knew its strength to be that of a people drawn from many sources, speaking for many cultures and traditions. From this he derived his concept of the role it might play in a supreme crisis of Western civilization. But he thought along these lines for another reason as well. His was too subtle a mind, too well acquainted with the ironies of history and of human nature, to be easily convinced that truth, justice, and right could ever lie exclusively with one nation or with one side in a conflict. He could not at this stage believe that war was anything but an evil or that victory, whoever won it, would be anything else than an illusion. In the end, as he saw it, the only valid settlement would be negotiated among nations that accepted the ambiguities of man's condition; and he coveted for America the task of healing and reconciliation.

To the allied leaders (as to the President's faithful emissary, Colonel House) these doubts were painful to contemplate. "Peace without victory" seemed to make a mockery of the French and

British war effort. They, after all, were heroically committed; Wilson was still the detached and brooding observer. The course of German submarine warfare drew Wilson closer to belligerency; he was becoming involved in a fate which he could not escape and yet which he could not readily accept. "In Wilson," wrote Walter Lippmann of that period, "there was an unworldliness of pity and doubt and high contempt that prevented him from agreeing wholly with much of what circumstances compelled him to do." The declaration of war broke the long spell of indecision, but it could not by itself, despite its lofty appeal, provide the cause which would give meaning to the trials that America was about to endure, or compensate for the role of mediation which had been given up.

That cause, in the end, was the League of Nations. Wilson took up support of the League not merely as a desirable objective, an item on the agenda of peace-making. It was for him the one goal which could make the long carnage seem worth while. He never had to abandon his earlier reservations concerning the involved and shadowed antecedents of the struggle; he could even forget the secret treaties. All this he transcended by his espousal of the mighty instrument which was to give mankind a second chance, expunging old wrongs and obliterating former divisions. Wilson did not so much conceive of making over the world as making it new—providing the changed conditions in which every problem would be brought before the bar of an enlightened world opinion.

The struggle was fought on Wilson's terms and the victory bore his stamp. "I have uttered as the object of this great war ideals, and nothing but ideals," he said on returning from the Peace Conference; "and the war has been won by that inspiration." It was not an idle boast. But time has its own revenges. America failed to join the League and the country relapsed into a season of virtually nothing but materialism. Moreover in the wake of the second World War a generation re-examined the Wilsonian tradition, and with modesty and a sophisticated approach to the responsibilities of world leadership, concluded that morality was a dangerous intruder in foreign policy. The complexities and ambiguities which Wilson himself understood so profoundly have been taken as the reason why nothing can be achieved quickly or with finality. Wilson's sweeping methods have given way to a body of opinion which sees America's course, not in terms of a universal mission, but in terms of practical steps, commitments scrupulously adjusted to resources, and alliances re-establishing a balance of power.

The emergence of this school of thought marks the rise in the United States, for the first time, of a group of public servants skilled in the arts of diplomacy, trained to consider means as well as ends in the shaping of foreign policy. Such men could hardly fail to point out that Woodrow Wilson's diplomacy too frequently relied on moral absolutes to the exclusion of all other factors. At his best, whether in domestic or foreign affairs, Wilson had an instinctive grasp of realities which enabled him to preserve the vital balance between ideals and practice. At his best, too, he spoke for a concept of America that was deeply felt and had been given fresh substance by the new-won achievements of the post-1912 reforms. His idea of a nation born to serve mankind was based on faith, not on propaganda, and his idealism was free of the overtones of complacency which so strengthen the case of the recent critics of moralism. The danger of the Wilsonian methods must nevertheless be admitted: just below the level of this man's greatest accomplishments lay the vacuity of universal slogans and empty preaching.

It is tempting to draw the contrast between Wilson in this regard and the man who in many ways and through another war repeated his journey. Franklin Roosevelt, too, won his popularity in a period of domestic reform; and he, like Wilson, found himself called to deal with an unprecedented international crisis. The first reaction of both men was to withdraw into neutrality and isolation. Subsequently both found again the voice of leadership, applying American ideals broadly across the globe. But here the paths diverge. For Roosevelt, when his strength and energy began to wane, reverted to what seems an exaggerated concern with politics at home; at the last international conference, while the tide of wartime cooperation ebbs all around, we see him fixing his mind on keeping support of the American Poles. Wilson, on the other hand, became more fiercely idealistic as his creative energies diminished. His reliance upon abstractions was almost as pathetic as his successor's reliance upon the empty husks of domestic political considerations.

It would be wrong, however, to judge either man by the caricature of his virtues which failing health and fortune brought upon him. The point about Woodrow Wilson was that in the fullness of his intellectual and spiritual power he exhibited a kind of leadership from which the present generation may dissent but which it cannot afford to dismiss as irrelevant. He saw things as in a clear morning light. He honestly believed that men could put aside the obsessions which divided or confused them and disinterestedly pursue the common good. Roosevelt (to return to our contrast) believed in his most fertile and lively moods that out of imperfect men, out of narrow attachments and limited insights, a harmonious world could be constructed by skillful compromise and adjustment. But with Wilson the road to right action lay straight ahead. He rejoiced as a strong man to do the will of the Almighty. All around him he felt the moral impulses of regenerate human beings, ready to be fired with new heart for the struggle.

It was a perilous road; and none knew it better than the man who had been reared in the faith of Calvin. The dividing line between glory and self-glorification, between righteousness and self-righteousness, was as thin as a razor's edge. To be of the elect was to be charged with a transcendent mission. It was also to stand in a blazing relationship with an implacable God. As it was for the individual, so for the nation. Both were challenged to act. And both were under the doom which allows no action to be without fault.

This attitude could be cheapened and secularized; indeed it was part of the human condition that it should be cheapened; and when it was, there was left only the unamiable image of a man or nation so sure of being right that no disagreement could be tolerated. But deeply grasped, Wilsonism is very different from the search for simple solutions and permanent remedies which recent American statesmanship rejects. At its best it keeps the will to do in conjunction with a saving awareness of how often the deed falls short of the mark. It keeps lucidity of purpose together with an underlying humility. Such an attitude cannot be lightly dismissed in a day when a sense of the limitations on man's will comes close to condemning us to futility, and when for lack of declared and vital ideals whole races of the world begin to wonder whether America stands for anything beside material power.

The time has gone by when one-stringed appeals can suffice as a guide to this country's conduct in the world. "Self-evident truths" and "fundamental principles" do not by themselves form the basis of a viable foreign policy. Yet increasingly Americans are aware that without principles steadfastly adhered to, without the concept of enduring values, this country risks losing the advantage which it has maintained in the past over every form of imperial or aggressive power. In that realization we should be ready to turn back to a deeper study of the example of Woodrow Wilson. The lonely scholar seeking the path to action in a democracy, the upright individual condemned to find success in failure, brings a note into contemporary discussion to guide us past the twin pitfalls of expediency and despair.

THE *POLITICS* OF
WOODROW WILSON

Chapter One

THE PROBLEM OF THE CONSTITUTION

W ILSON was first of all a political scientist; and his first book, Congressional Government, made his name in this field. Selections from this work are followed by portions of an essay which is another first: written when he was an undergraduate at Princeton, "Cabinet Government in the United States" represents his initial literary effort outside of college publications. (It was published in the International Review, of which the editor was Henry Cabot Lodge, future antagonist of the future President.) Finally excerpts are given from the lectures delivered at Columbia University and published in 1908 under the title Constitutional Government in the United States. All these are representative of Wilson's academic output; yet all are filled with a preoccupation with the problems that were to mark the active political leader. How to make leadership responsible in a democracy; how to give coherence to a legislative program and significance to debate; how to make the American government a vital system and the Presidency an office of real power—these are the themes that run through the following passages. From the beginning, and in his most scholarly work, Wilson was already the shaper and reformer.

"CONGRESSIONAL GOVERNMENT," 1885

The Constitution No Longer Conforms to the Original Pattern

We of the present generation are in the first season of free, outspoken, unrestrained constitutional criticism. We are the first Americans to hear our own countrymen ask whether the Constitution is still adapted to serve the purposes for which it was intended; the first to entertain any serious doubts about the superiority of our

1

own institutions as compared with the systems of Europe; the first
to think of remodeling the administrative machinery of the federal government, and of forcing new forms of responsibility upon
Congress.

The evident explanation of this change of attitude towards the
Constitution is that we have been made conscious by the rude
shock of the [Civil] war and by subsequent developments of policy,
that there has been a vast alteration in the conditions of government; that the checks and balances which once obtained are no
longer effective; and that we are really living under a constitution
essentially different from that which we have been so long worship-
ing as our own peculiar and incomparable possession. In short, this
model government is no longer conformable with its own original
pattern. While we have been shielding it from criticism it has
slipped away from us.

The noble charter of fundamental law given us by the Convention of 1787 is still our Constitution; but it is now our *form of
government* rather in name than in reality, the form of the Constitution being one of nicely adjusted, ideal balances, whilst the
actual form of our present government is simply a scheme of congressional supremacy. National legislation, of course, takes force now
as at first from the authority of the Constitution; but it would be
easy to reckon by the score acts of Congress which can by no means
be squared with that great instrument's evident theory. We continue to think, indeed, according to long-accepted constitutional
formulæ, and it is still politically unorthodox to depart from old-
time phraseology in grave discussions of affairs; but it is plain to
those who look about them that most of the commonly received
opinions concerning federal constitutional balances and administrative arrangements are many years behind the actual practices of the
government at Washington, and that we are farther than most of
us realize from the times and the policy of the framers of the Constitution.

It is a commonplace observation of historians that, in the development of constitutions, names are much more persistent than the
functions upon which they were originally bestowed; that institu-

tions constantly undergo essential alterations of character, whilst retaining the names conferred upon them in their first estate; and the history of our own Constitution is but another illustration of this universal principle of institutional change. There has been a constant growth of legislative and administrative practice, and a steady accretion of precedent in the management of federal affairs, which have broadened the sphere and altered the functions of the government without perceptibly affecting the vocabulary of our constitutional language.

Ours is, scarcely less than the British, a living and fecund system. It does not, indeed, find its rootage so widely in the hidden soil of unwritten law; its tap-root at least is the Constitution; but the Constitution is now, like Magna Carta and the Bill of Rights, only the sap-centre of a system of government vastly larger than the stock from which it has branched,—a system some of whose forms have only very indistinct and rudimental beginnings in the simple substance of the Constitution, and which exercises many functions apparently quite foreign to the primitive properties contained in the fundamental law.

The Times Favor a Centralization of Government

What makes it the more important to understand the present mechanism of national government, and to study the methods of congressional rule in a light unclouded by theory, is that there is plain evidence that the expansion of federal power is to continue, and that there exists, consequently, an evident necessity that it should be known just what to do and how to do it, when the time comes for public opinion to take control of the forces which are changing the character of our Constitution. There are voices in the air which cannot be misunderstood. The times seem to favor a centralization of governmental functions such as could not have suggested itself as a possibility to the framers of the Constitution.

Since they gave their work to the world the whole face of that world has changed. The Constitution was adopted when it was six days' hard traveling from New York to Boston; when to cross East River was to venture a perilous voyage; when men were thankful for weekly mails; when the extent of the country's commerce was reckoned not in millions but in thousands of dollars; when the country knew few cities, and had but begun manufactures; when Indians were pressing upon near frontiers; when there were no telegraph lines, and no monster corporations. Unquestionably, the pressing problems of the present moment regard the regulation of our vast systems of commerce and manufacture, the control of giant corporations, the restraint of monopolies, the perfection of fiscal arrangements, the facilitating of economic exchanges, and many other like national concerns, amongst which may possibly be numbered the question of marriage and divorce; and the greatest of these problems do not fall within even the enlarged sphere of the federal government; some of them can be embraced within its jurisdiction by no possible stretch of construction, and the majority of them only by wresting the Constitution to strange and as yet unimagined uses. Still there is a distinct movement in favor of national control of all questions of policy which manifestly demand uniformity of treatment and power of administration such as cannot be realized by the separate, unconcerted action of the States; and it seems probable to many that, whether by constitutional amendment, or by still further flights of construction, yet broader territory will at no very distant day be assigned to the federal government.

It becomes a matter of the utmost importance, therefore, both for those who would arrest this tendency, and for those who, because they look upon it with allowance if not with positive favor, would let it run its course, to examine critically the government upon which this new weight of responsibility and power seems likely to be cast, in order that its capacity both for the work it now does and for that which it may be called upon to do may be definitely estimated.

Debate in the Congress Is Without Dramatic Significance

Why is it that many intelligent and patriotic people throughout this country, from Virginia to California,—people who, beyond all question, love their State and the Union more than they love our cousin state over sea,—subscribe for the London papers in order to devour the parliamentary debates, and yet would never think of troubling themselves to make tedious progress through a single copy of the "Congressional Record"? Is it because they are captivated by the old-world dignity of royal England with its nobility and its court pageantry, or because of a vulgar desire to appear better versed than their neighbors in foreign affairs, and to affect familiarity with British statesmen? No; of course not. It is because the parliamentary debates are interesting and ours are not.

In the British House of Commons the functions and privileges of our Standing Committees are all concentrated in the hands of the Ministry, who have, besides, some prerogatives of leadership which even our Committees do not possess, so that they carry all responsibility as well as great power, and all debate wears an intense personal and party interest. Every important discussion is an arraignment of the Ministry by the Opposition,—an arraignment of the majority by the minority; and every important vote is a party defeat and a party triumph. The whole conduct of the government turns upon what is said in the Commons, because the revelations of debate often change votes, and a Ministry loses hold upon power as it loses hold upon the confidence of the Commons. This great Standing Committee goes out whenever it crosses the will of the majority. It is, therefore, for these very simple and obvious reasons that the parliamentary debates are read on this side of the water in preference to the congressional debates. They affect the ministers, who are very conspicuous persons, and in whom, therefore, all the intelligent world is interested; and they determine the course of politics in a great empire. The season of a parliamentary debate is a great field day on which Liberals and Conservatives pit their full forces against each other, and people like to watch the issues of the contest.

Our congressional debates, on the contrary, have no tithe of this interest, because they have no tithe of such significance and importance. The committee reports, upon which the debates take place, are backed by neither party; they represent merely the recommendations of a small body of members belonging to both parties, and are quite as likely to divide the vote of the party to which the majority of the Committee belong as they are to meet with opposition from the other side of the chamber. If they are carried, it is no party triumph; if they are lost, it is no party discomfiture. They are no more than the proposals of a mixed Committee, and may be rejected without political inconvenience to either party or reproof to the Committee; just as they may be passed without compliment to the Committee or political advantage to either side of the House. Neither party has any great stake in the controversy. The only importance that can attach to the vote must hang upon its relation to the next general election. If the report concern a question which is at the time so much in the public eye that all action upon it is likely to be marked and remembered against the day of popular action, parties are careful to vote as solidly as possible on what they conceive to be the safe side; but all other reports are disposed of without much thought of their influence upon the fortunes of distant elections, because that influence is remote and problematical.

Administration and Legislation Are
Thought to Need No Special Skill

Administration is something that men must learn, not something to skill in which they are born. Americans take to business of all kinds more naturally than any other nation ever did, and the executive duties of government constitute just an exalted kind of business; but even Americans are not Presidents in their cradles. One cannot have too much preparatory training and experience who is to fill so high a magistracy. It is difficult to perceive, therefore, upon what safe ground of reason are built the opinions of those persons who regard short terms of service as sacredly and peculiarly republican in principle. If republicanism is founded upon good sense, nothing so far removed from good sense can be part and parcel of it. Efficiency is the only just foundation for confidence in a public officer, under republican institutions no less than under monarchs; and short terms which cut off the efficient as surely and inexorably as the inefficient are quite as repugnant to republican as to monarchical rules of wisdom.

Unhappily, however, this is not American doctrine. A President is dismissed almost as soon as he has learned the duties of his office, and a man who has served a dozen terms in Congress is a curiosity. We are too apt to think both the work of legislation and the work of administration easy enough to be done readily, with or without preparation, by any man of discretion and character. No one imagines that the drygoods or the hardware trade, or even the cobbler's craft, can be successfully conducted except by those who have worked through a laborious and unremunerative apprenticeship, and who have devoted their lives to perfecting themselves as tradesmen or as menders of shoes. But legislation is esteemed a thing which may be taken up with success by any shrewd man of middle age, which a lawyer may now and again advantageously combine with his practice, or of which any intelligent youth may easily catch the knack; and administration is regarded as something which an old soldier, an ex-diplomatist, or a popular politician may be trusted to take to by instinct. No man of tolerable talents need despair of having been born a Presidential candidate.

These must be pronounced very extraordinary conclusions for an eminently practical people to have accepted; and it must be received as an awakening of good sense that there is nowadays a decided inclination manifested on the part of the nation to supply training-schools for the Presidency in like minor offices, such as the governorships of the greater States. For the sort of Presidents needed under the present arrangement of our federal government, it is best to choose amongst the ablest and most experienced state governors.

Congressional Investigations Tyrannize over the Departments

The relations existing between Congress and the departments must be fatally demoralizing to both. There is and can be between them nothing like confidential and thorough coöperation. The departments may be excused for that attitude of hostility which they sometimes assume towards Congress, because it is quite human for the servant to fear and deceive the master whom he does not regard as his friend, but suspects of being a distrustful spy of his movements. Congress cannot control the officers of the executive without disgracing them. Its only whip is investigation, semi-judicial examination into corners suspected to be dirty. It must draw the public eye by openly avowing a suspicion of malfeasance, and must then magnify and intensify the scandal by setting its Committees to cross-examining scared subordinates and sulky ministers. And after all is over and the murder out, probably nothing is done. The offenders, if any one has offended, often remain in office, shamed before the world, and ruined in the estimation of all honest people, but still drawing their salaries and comfortably waiting for the short memory of the public mind to forget them. Why unearth the carcass if you cannot remove it?

Then, too, the departments frequently complain of the incessant exactions made upon them by Congress. They grumble that they are kept busy in satisfying its curiosity and in meeting the demands of its uneasy activity. The clerks have ordinarily as much as they can do in keeping afoot the usual routine business of their departments; but Congress is continually calling upon them for information which must be laboriously collected from all sorts of sources, remote and accessible. A great speech in the Senate may cost them hours of anxious toil; for the Senator who makes it is quite likely beforehand to introduce a resolution calling upon one of the Secretaries for full statistics with reference to this, that, or the other topic upon which he desires to speak. If it be finance, he must have comparative tables of taxation; if it be commerce or the tariff, he cannot dispense with any of the minutest figures of the Treasury accounts; whatever be his theme, he cannot lay his foundations more surely than upon official information, and the Senate is usually unhesitatingly ready with an easy assent to the resolution which puts the whole clerical force of the administration at his service. And of course the House too asks innumerable questions, which patient clerks and protesting Secretaries must answer to the last and most minute particular.

This is what the departmental officials testily call the tyranny of Congress, and no impartial third person can reasonably forbid them the use of the word.

Self-Government Must Be Made a
Thing of Clear Responsibility

An intelligent observer of our politics has declared that there is in the United States "a class, including thousands and tens of thousands of the best men in the country, who think it possible to enjoy the fruits of good government without working for them." Every one who has seen beyond the outside of our American life must recognize the truth of this; to explain it is to state the sum of all the most valid criticisms of congressional government. Public opinion has no easy vehicle for its judgments, no quick channels for its action. Nothing about the system is direct and simple. Authority is perplexingly subdivided and distributed, and responsibility has to be hunted down in out-of-the-way corners. So that the sum of the whole matter is that the means of working for the fruits of good government are not readily to be found.

The average citizen may be excused for esteeming government at best but a haphazard affair, upon which his vote and all of his influence can have but little effect. How is his choice of a representative in Congress to affect the policy of the country as regards the questions in which he is most interested, if the man for whom he votes has no chance of getting on the Standing Committee which has virtual charge of those questions? How is it to make any difference who is chosen President? Has the President any very great authority in matters of vital policy? It seems almost a thing of despair to get any assurance that any vote he may cast will even in an infinitesimal degree affect the essential courses of administration. There are so many cooks mixing their ingredients in the national broth that it seems hopeless, this thing of changing one cook at a time.

The charm of our constitutional ideal has now been long enough wound up to enable sober men who do not believe in political witchcraft to judge what it has accomplished, and is likely still to accomplish, without further winding. The Constitution is not honored by blind worship. The more open-eyed we become, as a nation, to its defects, and the prompter we grow in applying with the unhesitating courage of conviction all thoroughly-tested or well-considered expedients necessary to make self-government among us a straightforward thing of simple method, single, unstinted power, and clear responsibility, the nearer will we approach to the sound sense and practical genius of the great and honorable statesmen of 1787. And the first step towards emancipation from the timidity and false pride which have led us to seek to thrive despite the defects of our national system rather than seem to deny its perfection is a fearless criticism of that system. When we shall have examined all its parts without sentiment, and gauged all its functions by the standards of practical common sense, we shall have established anew our right to the claim of political sagacity; and it will remain only to act intelligently upon what our opened eyes have seen in order to prove again the justice of our claim to political genius.

"THE INTERNATIONAL REVIEW,"
AUGUST 1879

Legislation Without Discussion

At its highest development, representative government is that form which best enables a free people to govern themselves. The main object of a representative assembly, therefore, should be the discussion of public business. They should legislate as if in the presence of the whole country, because they come under the closest scrutiny and fullest criticism of all the representatives of the country speaking in open and free debate. Only in such an assembly, only in such an atmosphere of publicity, only by means of such a vast investigating machine, can the different sections of a great country learn each other's feelings and interests. It is not enough that the general course of legislation is known to all. Unless during its progress it is subjected to a thorough, even a tediously prolonged, process of public sifting, to the free comment of friend and foe alike, to the ordeal of battle among those upon whose vote its fate depends, an act of open legislation may have its real intent and scope completely concealed by its friends and undiscovered by its enemies, and it may be as fatally mischievous as the darkest measures of an oligarchy or a despot. Nothing can be more obvious than the fact that the very life of free, popular institutions is dependent upon their breathing the bracing air of thorough, exhaustive, and open discussions, or that select Congressional committees, whose proceedings must from their very nature be secret, are, as means of legislation, dangerous and unwholesome. Parliaments are forces for freedom; for "talk is persuasion, persuasion is force, the one force which can sway freemen to deeds such as those which have made England what she is," or our English stock what it is.

Congress is a deliberative body in which there is little real deliberation; a legislature which legislates with no real discussion of its business. Our Government is practically carried on by irresponsible committees. Too few Americans take the trouble to inform themselves as to the methods of Congressional management; and, as a consequence, not many have perceived that almost *absolute* power has fallen into the hands of men whose irresponsibility prevents the regulation of their conduct by the people from whom they derive their authority. The most important, most powerful man in the government of the United States in time of peace is the Speaker of the House of Representatives. Instead of being merely an executive officer, whose principal duties are those immediately connected with the administration of the rules of order, he is a potent party chief, the only chief of any real potency—and must of necessity be so.

Committee and Cabinet Government

What, then, is Cabinet government? What is the change proposed? Simply to give to the heads of the Executive departments—the members of the Cabinet—seats in Congress, with the privilege of the initiative in legislation and some part of the unbounded privileges now commanded by the Standing Committees. . . .

Such powers as a Cabinet with responsible leadership must possess are now divided among the forty-seven Standing Committees, whose prerogatives of irresponsible leadership savor of despotism, because exercised for the most part within the secret precincts of a committee room, and not under the eyes of the whole House, and thus of the whole country. These committees, too, as has been said, rule without any of that freedom of public debate which is essential to the liberties of the people. Their measures are too often mere partisan measures, and are hurried through the forms of voting by a party majority whose interest it is that all serious opposition, all debate that might develop obstructive antagonism, should be suppressed.

Under the conditions of Cabinet government, however, full and free debates are sure to take place. For what are these conditions? According as their policy stands or falls, the ministers themselves stand or fall; to the party which supports them each discussion involves a trial of strength with their opponents; upon it depends the amount of their success as a party; while to the opposition the triumph of ministerial plans means still further exclusion from office, their overthrow, accession to power. To each member of the assembly every debate offers an opportunity for placing himself, by able argument, in a position to command a place in any future Cabinet that may be formed from the ranks of his own party; each speech goes to the building up (or the tearing down) of his political fortunes. There is, therefore, an absolute certainty that every phase of every subject will be drawn carefully and vigorously, will be dwelt upon with minuteness, will be viewed from every possible standpoint. The legislative, holding full power of final decision, would find itself in immediate contact with the executive and its policy. Nor would there be room for factious government or factious opposition. Plainly, ministers must found their policies, an opposition must found its attacks, upon well-considered principles; for in this open sifting of debate, when every feature of every measure, even to the motives which prompted it, is the subject of outspoken discussion and keen scrutiny, no chicanery, no party craft, no questionable principles can long hide themselves. Party trickery, legislative jobbery, are deprived of the very air they breathe,—the air of secrecy, of concealment.

The public is still surprised whenever they find that dishonest legislation has been allowed to pass unchallenged. Why surprised? As things are, measures are determined in the interests of corporations, and the suffering people know almost nothing of them until their evil tendencies crop out in actual execution. Under lobby pressure from interested parties, they have been cunningly concocted in the closest sessions of partisan committees, and, by the all-powerful aid of party machinery, have been hurried through the stages of legislation without debate; so that even Press correspondents are often as ignorant of the real nature of such special measures as the outside public. Any searching debate of such questions would at once have brought the public eye upon them, and how could they then have stood? Lifting the lid of concealment must have been the discovery to all concerned of their unsavory character. Light would have killed them.

We are thus again brought into the presence of the cardinal fact of this discussion,—that *debate* is the essential function of a popular representative body. In the severe, distinct, and sharp enunciation of underlying principles, the unsparing examination and telling criticism of opposite positions, the careful, painstaking unravelling of all the issues involved, which are incident to the free discussion of questions of public policy we see the best, the only effective, means of educating public opinion.

Only a single glance is necessary to discover how utterly Committee government must fail to give effect to public opinion. In the first place, the exclusion of debate prevents the intelligent formation of opinion on the part of the nation at large; in the second place, public opinion, when once formed, finds it impossible to exercise any immediate control over the action of its representatives. There is no one in Congress to speak for the nation. Congress is a conglomeration of inharmonious elements; a collection of men representing each his neighborhood, each his local interest; an alarmingly large proportion of its legislation is "special"; all of it is at best only a limping compromise between the conflicting interests of the innumerable localities represented. There is no guiding or harmonizing power. Are the people in favor of a particular policy, —what means have they of forcing it upon the sovereign legislature at Washington? None but the most imperfect. If they return representatives who favor it (and this is the most they can do), these representatives being under no directing power will find a mutual agreement impracticable among so many, and will finally settle upon some policy which satisfies nobody, removes no difficulty, and makes little definite or valuable provision for the future. They must, indeed, be content with whatever measure the appropriate committee chances to introduce.

Conditions of Statesmanship

Let us, drawing light from every source within the range of our knowledge, make a little independent analysis of the conditions of statesmanship, with a view to ascertaining whether or not it is in reality true that we cannot contribute to its development, or even perchance give it a perennial growth among us. We learn from a critical survey of the past, that, so far as political affairs are concerned, great critical epochs are the man-making epochs of history, that revolutionary influences are man-making influences. And why? If this be the law, it must have some adequate reason underlying it; and we seem to find the reason a very plain and conspicuous one. Crises gave birth and a new growth to statesmanship because they are peculiarly periods of action, in which talents find the widest and the freest scope. They are periods not only of action, but also of unusual opportunity for gaining leadership and a controlling and guiding influence. It is opportunity for transcendent influence, therefore, which calls into active public life a nation's greater minds, —minds which might otherwise remain absorbed in the smaller affairs of private life.

And we thus come upon the principle,—a principle which will appear the more incontrovertible the more it is looked into and tested,—that governmental forms will call to the work of administration able minds and strong hearts constantly or infrequently, according as they do or do not afford them at all times an opportunity of gaining and retaining a commanding authority and an undisputed leadership in the nation's councils. Now it certainly needs no argument to prove that government by supreme committees, whose members are appointed at the caprice of an irresponsible party chief, by seniority, because of reputation gained in entirely different fields, or because of partisan shrewdness, is not favorable to a full and strong development of statesmanship. Certain it is that statesmanship has been steadily dying out in the United States since that stupendous crisis during which its government felt the first throbs of life. In the government of the United States there is no place found for the leadership of men of real ability. Why, then, complain that we have no leaders?

The President can seldom make himself recognized as a leader; he is merely the executor of the sovereign legislative will; his Cabinet officers are little more than chief clerks, or superintendents, in the Executive departments, who advise the President as to matters in most of which he has no power of action independently of the concurrence of the Senate. The most ambitious representative can rise no higher than the chairmanship of the Committee of Ways and Means, or the Speakership of the House. The cardinal feature of Cabinet government, on the other hand, is responsible leadership,—the leadership and authority of a small body of men who have won the foremost places in their party by a display of administrative talents, by evidence of high ability upon the floor of Congress in the stormy play of debate. None but the ablest can become leaders and masters in this keen tournament in which arguments are the weapons, and the people the judges. Clearly defined, definitely directed policies arouse bold and concerted opposition; and leaders of oppositions become in time leaders of Cabinets. Such a recognized leadership it is that is necessary to the development of statesmanship under popular, republican institutions; for only such leadership can make politics seem worthy of cultivation to men of high mind and aim.

And if party success in Congress—the ruling body of the nation—depends upon power in debate, skill and prescience in policy, successful defence of or attacks upon ruling ministries, how ill can contending parties spare their men of ability from Congress! To keep men of the strongest mental and moral fibre in Congress would become a party necessity. Party triumph would then be a matter of might in debate, not of supremacy in subterfuge. The two great national parties—and upon the existence of two great parties, with clashings and mutual jealousies and watchings, depends the health of free political institutions—are dying for want of unifying and vitalizing principles. Without leaders, they are also without policies, without aims. With leaders there must be followers, there must be parties. And with leaders whose leadership was earned in an open war of principle against principle, by the triumph of one opinion over all opposing opinions, parties must from the necessities of the case have definite policies. Platforms, then, must mean something. Broken promises will then end in broken power. A Cabinet without a policy that is finding effect in progressive legislation is, in a country of frequent elections, inviting its own defeat. Or is there, on the other hand, a determined, aggressive opposition? Then the ministry have a right to ask them what they would do under similar circumstances, were the reins of government to fall to them. And if the opposition are then silent, they cannot reasonably expect the country to intrust the government to them. Witness the situation of the Liberal party in England during the late serious crisis in Eastern affairs. Not daring to propose any policy,—having indeed, because of the disintegration of the party, no policy to propose,—their numerical weakness became a moral weakness, and the nation's ear was turned away from them.

Eight words contain the sum of the present degradation of our political parties: *No leaders, no principles; no principles, no parties.* Congressional leadership is divided infinitesimally; and with divided leadership there can be no great party units. Drill in debate, by giving scope to talents, invites talents; raises up a race of men habituated to the methods of public business, skilled parliamentary chiefs. And, more than this, it creates a much-to-be-desired class who early makes attendance upon public affairs the business of their lives, devoting to the service of their country all their better years. Surely the management of a nation's business will, in a well-ordered society, be as properly a matter of life-long training as the conduct of private affairs.

These are but meagre and insufficient outlines of some of the results which would follow upon the establishment of responsible Cabinet government in the United States. Its establishment has not wanted more or less outspoken advocacy from others; nor, of course, have there been lacking those who are ready to urge real or imaginary objections against it, and proclaim it an exotic unfit to thrive in American soil. It has certainly, in common with all other political

systems, grave difficulties and real evils connected with it. Difficulties
and evils are inseparable from every human scheme of government;
and, in making their choice, a people can do no more than adopt
that form which affords the largest measure of real liberty, whose
machinery is least imperfect, and which is most susceptible to the
control of their sovereign will.

"CONSTITUTIONAL GOVERNMENT
IN THE UNITED STATES," 1908

Institutions Sustained by the Conscious or
Habitual Preference of the People

It remains only to note what may be called the atmosphere of
constitutional government. It is the atmosphere of opinion. Opinion
is, of course, the atmosphere of every government, whatever its
forms and powers: governments are contrasted with one another
only by the degree and manner in which opinion affects them.
There is nowhere any such thing as a literally absolute government.
The veriest despot is a creature of circumstances, and the most important circumstance of all, whether he is conscious of adjusting
himself to it or not, is the disposition of those about him to obey
him or to defy him. Certain things are definitely expected of him:
there are certain privileges which he must always respect, certain
expectations of caste and of rank which he must always punctiliously
regard. Above all there is the great body of habit, the habitual frame
of the life in which his own people have been formed, which he
would throw himself against in vain. The boundaries of his authority
lie where he finds the limits of his subjects' willingness or ability to
obey him. They cannot obey him if he seeks to force upon them
rules too strange to their habit: they will not know how, and their
spirits will revolt. They will not obey him if he outrage them by
too gross a violation of the understandings which they have come
to regard as sacred and of the very essence of their life and happiness. The difference between a constitutional system and an unconstitutional is that in a constitutional system the requirements of
opinion are clearly formulated and understood, while in an unconstitutional they are vague and conjectural. The unconstitutional

ruler has to guess where his subjects will call a halt upon him, and experiment at the hazard of his throne and head; the constitutional ruler definitely knows the limits which he must not transgress and is safe in his authority so long as he does not overstep them.

But there is this radical difference between the opinion which limits the power of an unconstitutional ruler and that which limits the powers of a constitutional government: that the one is unorganized opinion, the other organized; the one hardly more than an impatient stir at any disturbance of tradition or of habit, the other a quick concert of thought, uttered by those who know how to guide both counsel and action. Indeed, there has seldom been in the case of a despotic government anything that really corresponded with what in constitutional government is known as public opinion. The wit who described the government of France as despotism tempered by epigram was really formulating one of the approaches to constitutional government. When opinion spoken in the salon begins to be a definite organ of criticism, when criticism has become concerted and powerful enough and sufficiently mixed with the passion of action to serve from time to time as a modifying, guiding, and controlling force, the development of constitutional government has begun.

It is therefore peculiarly true of constitutional government that its atmosphere is opinion, the air from which it takes its breath and vigor. The underlying understandings of a constitutional system are modified from age to age by changes of life and circumstance and corresponding alterations of opinion. It does not remain fixed in any unchanging form, but grows with the growth and is altered with the change of the nation's needs and purposes. The constitution of England, the original and typical constitutional government of the world, is unwritten except for its statement of individual right and privilege in Magna Carta, in the Bill of Rights, and in the Petition of Right; is, in other words, only a body of very definite opinion, except for occasional definitions of statute here and there. Its substance is the thought and habit of the nation, its conscious expectations and preferences; and around even a written constitution there grows up a body of practices which have no formal recognition or sanction in the written law, which even modify the written stipulations of the system in many subtle ways and become the instrument of opinion in effecting a slow transformation. If it were not so, the written document would become too stiff a garment for the living thing.

It is in this sense that institutions are the creatures of opinion. Their breath and vigor goes out of them when they cease to be sustained by the conscious or habitual preference of the people whose practice has created them; and new institutions take their place when once that practice is altered. That is what gives dignity to citizenship among a free people. Every man's thought is part of the vital substance of its institutions. With the change of his thought, institutions themselves may change. That is what constitutes citizenship so responsible and solemn a thing. Every man in a free country is, as it were, put upon his honor to be the kind of man such a polity supposes its citizens to be: a man with his thought upon the general welfare, his interest consciously linked with the interests of his fellow-citizens, his sense of duty broadened to the scope of public affairs. Every generation in a free state realizes that the perpetuation of its institutions depends upon the thought and disposition of the generations which are to follow, and busies itself to hand the impulse and the conception on by careful processes of education, stamping its thought upon young men, seeking to make its own frame of mind permanent. Old phrases spring to new significance as one's thought clears in such matters. "Eternal vigilance is the price of liberty." The threadbare phrase seems new stuff when we wear it on our understandings. The vigilance of intelligently directed opinion is indeed the very soil of liberty and of all the enlightened institutions meant to sustain it. And that will always be the freest country in which enlightened opinion abounds, in which to plant the practices of government. It is of the essence of a constitutional system that its people should think straight, maintain a consistent purpose, look before and after, and make their lives the image of their thoughts.

The President as Party Leader

What is it that a nominating convention wants in the man it is to present to the country for its suffrages? A man who will be and who will seem to the country in some sort an embodiment of the character and purpose it wishes its government to have,—a man who understands his own day and the needs of the country, and who has the personality and the initiative to enforce his views both upon the people and upon Congress. It may seem an odd way to get such a man. It is even possible that nominating conventions and those who guide them do not realize entirely what it is that they do. But in simple fact the convention picks out a party leader from the body of the nation. Not that it expects its nominee to direct the interior government of the party and to supplant its already accredited and experienced spokesmen in Congress and in its state and national committees; but it does of necessity expect him to represent it before public opinion and to stand before the country as its representative man, as a true type of what the country may expect of the party itself in purpose and principle. It cannot but be led by him in the campaign; if he be elected, it cannot but acquiesce in his leadership of the government itself. What the country will demand of the candidate will be, not that he be an astute politician, skilled and practiced in affairs, but that he be a man such as it can trust, in character, in intention, in knowledge of its needs, in perception of the best means by which those needs may be met, in capacity to prevail by reason of his own weight and integrity. Sometimes the country believes in a party, but more often it believes in a man; and conventions have often shown the instinct to perceive which it is that the country needs in a particular presidential year, a mere representative partisan, a military hero, or some one who will genuinely speak for the country itself, whatever be his training and antecedents. It is in this sense that the President has the rôle of party leader thrust upon him by the very method by which he is chosen.

He cannot escape being the leader of his party except by incapacity and lack of personal force, because he is at once the choice of the party and of the nation. He is the party nominee, and the only party nominee for whom the whole nation votes. Members of the

House and Senate are representatives of localities, are voted for only by sections of voters, or by local bodies of electors like the members of the state legislatures. There is no national party choice except that of President. No one else represents the people as a whole, exercising a national choice; and inasmuch as his strictly executive duties are in fact subordinated, so far at any rate as all detail is concerned, the President represents not so much the party's governing efficiency as its controlling ideals and principles. He is not so much part of its organization as its vital link of connection with the thinking nation. He can dominate his party by being spokesman for the real sentiment and purpose of the country, by giving direction to opinion, by giving the country at once the information and the statements of policy which will enable it to form its judgments alike of parties and of men.

For he is also the political leader of the nation, or has it in his choice to be. The nation as a whole has chosen him, and is conscious that it has no other political spokesman. His is the only national voice in affairs. Let him once win the admiration and confidence of the country, and no other single force can withstand him, no combination of forces will easily overpower him. His position takes the imagination of the country. He is the representative of no constituency, but of the whole people. When he speaks in his true character, he speaks for no special interest. If he rightly interpret the national thought and boldly insist upon it, he is irresistible; and the country never feels the zest of action so much as when its President is of such insight and calibre. Its instinct is for unified action, and it craves a single leader. It is for this reason that it will often prefer to choose a man rather than a party. A President whom it trusts can not only lead it but form it to his own views.

It is the extraordinary isolation imposed upon the President by our system that makes the character and opportunity of his office so extraordinary. In him are centred both opinion and party. He may stand, if he will, a little outside party and insist as if it were upon the general opinion. It is with the instinctive feeling that it is upon occasion such a man that the country wants that nominating conventions will often nominate men who are not their acknowledged leaders, but only such men as the country would like to see lead both its parties. The President may also, if he will, stand within the party counsels and use the advantage of his power and personal force to control its actual programs. He may be both the leader of his party and the leader of the nation, or he may be one or the other. If he lead the nation, his party can hardly resist him. His office is anything he has the sagacity and force to make it.

That is the reason why it has been one thing at one time, another at another. The Presidents who have not made themselves leaders have lived no more truly on that account in the spirit of the Constitution than those whose force has told in the determination of law and policy. No doubt Andrew Jackson overstepped the bounds meant to be set to the authority of his office. It was certainly in direct contravention of the spirit of the Constitution that he should have refused to respect and execute decisions of the Supreme Court of the United States, and no serious student of our history can righteously condone what he did in such matters on the ground that his intentions were upright and his principles pure. But the Constitution of the United States is not a mere lawyers' document: it is a vehicle of life, and its spirit is always the spirit of the age. Its prescriptions are clear and we know what they are; a written document makes lawyers of us all, and our duty as citizens should make us conscientious lawyers, reading the text of the Constitution without subtlety or sophistication; but life is always your last and most authoritative critic.

Some of our Presidents have deliberately held themselves off from using the full power they might legitimately have used, because of conscientious scruples, because they were more theorists than statesmen. They have held the strict literary theory of the Constitution, the Whig theory, the Newtonian theory, and have acted as if they thought that Pennsylvania Avenue should have been even longer than it is; that there should be no intimate communication of any kind between the Capitol and the White House; that the President as a man was no more at liberty to lead the houses of Congress by persuasion than he was at liberty as President to dominate them by authority,—supposing that he had, what he has not, authority enough to dominate them. But the makers of the Constitution were not enacting Whig theory, they were not making laws with the expectation that, not the laws themselves, but their opinions, known by future historians to lie back of them, should govern the constitutional action of the country. They were statesmen, not pedants, and their laws are sufficient to keep us to the paths they set us upon.

The President is at liberty, both in law and conscience, to be as big a man as he can. His capacity will set the limit; and if Congress be overborne by him, it will be no fault of the makers of the Constitution,—it will be from no lack of constitutional powers on its part, but only because the President has the nation behind him, and Congress has not.

The President, Henceforth, a Great Power of the World

One of the greatest of the President's powers I have not yet spoken of at all: his control, which is very absolute, of the foreign relations of the nation. The initiative in foreign affairs, which the President possesses without any restriction whatever, is virtually the power to control them absolutely. The President cannot conclude a treaty with a foreign power without the consent of the Senate, but he may guide every step of diplomacy, and to guide diplomacy is to determine what treaties must be made, if the faith and prestige of the government are to be maintained. He need disclose no step of negotiation until it is complete, and when in any critical matter it is completed the government is virtually committed. Whatever its disinclination, the Senate may feel itself committed also.

I have not dwelt upon this power of the President, because it has been decisively influential in determining the character and influence of the office at only two periods in our history; at the very first, when the government was young and had so to use its incipient force as to win the respect of the nations into whose family it had thrust itself, and in our own day when the results of the Spanish War, the ownership of distant possessions, and many sharp struggles for foreign trade make it necessary that we should turn our best talents to the task of dealing firmly, wisely, and justly with political and commercial rivals. The President can never again be the mere domestic figure he has been throughout so large a part of our history. The nation has risen to the first rank in power and resources. The other nations of the world look askance upon her, half in envy, half in fear, and wonder with a deep anxiety what she will do with her vast strength. They receive the frank professions of men like Mr. John Hay, whom we wholly trusted, with a grain of salt, and doubt what we were sure of, their truthfulness and sincerity, suspecting a hidden design under every utterance he makes. Our President must always, henceforth, be one of the great powers of the world, whether he act greatly and wisely or not, and the best statesmen we can produce will be needed to fill the office of Secretary of State. We have but begun to see the presidential office in this light; but it is the light which will more and more beat upon it, and more and more determine its character and its effect upon the politics of the nation. We can never hide our President again as a mere domestic officer.

Chapter Two

MAKING OF THE NATION

WILSON'S writings during this academic apprenticeship turned naturally from political science to history; in both he saw the same problems exemplified. The characteristic American spirit, with its changefulness and variety, had filled a continent. How could the sections be harmonized and the national spirit manifested except through responsible leadership? The restoration of the Presidency as the center of gravity in the American system was made necessary, also, by the new participation in world affairs following the Spanish-American war. The selections in this chapter are from addresses and essays between 1895 and 1902, when Wilson was a rising young professor. In their emphasis on the influences of the West on American life, on the danger of an Eastern provincialism, as well as in their glances toward the world scene, they foreshadow much that was to become dominant when Wilson finally stepped upon the political stage.

"THE FORUM,"
FEBRUARY 1894

A Hopeful and Confident Spirit

The American spirit is something more than the old, the immemorial Saxon spirit of liberty from which it sprung. It has been bred by the conditions attending the great task which we have all the century been carrying forward: the task, at once material and ideal, of subduing a wilderness and covering all the wide stretches of a vast continent with a single free and stable polity. It is, accordingly, above all things, a hopeful and confident spirit. It is progressive, optimistically progressive, and ambitious of objects of national scope and advantage. It is unpedantic, unprovincial, unspeculative, unfastidious; regardful of law, but as using it, not as being used by it or dominated by any formalism whatever; in a sense unrefined, because full of rude force; but prompted by large and generous motives, and often as tolerant as it is resolute. No one man, unless it be Lincoln, has ever proved big or various enough to embody this active and full-hearted spirit in all its qualities; and the men who have been too narrow or too speculative or too pedantic to represent it have, nevertheless, added to the strong and stirring variety of our national life, making it fuller and richer in motive and energy.

ADDRESS BEFORE THE NEW JERSEY HISTORICAL SOCIETY,
NEWARK, NEW JERSEY,
MAY 16, 1895

The Determining Movement of American History

What in fact has been the course of American history? How is it to be distingushed from European history? What features has it of its own, which give it its distinctive plan and movement? We have suffered, it is to be feared, a very serious limitation of view until recent years by having all our history written in the East. It has smacked strongly of a local flavor. It has concerned itself too exclusively with the origins and Old-World derivations of our story. Our historians have made their march from the sea with their heads over shoulder, their gaze always backward upon the landing-places and homes of the first settlers.

In spite of the steady immigration, with its persistent tide of foreign blood, they have chosen to speak often and to think always of our people as sprung after all from a common stock, bearing a family likeness in every branch, and following all the while old, familiar, family ways. The view is the more misleading because it is so large a part of the truth without being all of it. The common British stock did first make the country, and has always set the pace. There were common institutions up and down the coast; and these had formed and hardened for a persistent growth before the great westward migration began which was to re-shape and modify every element of our life. The national government itself was set up and made strong by success while yet we lingered for the most part upon the eastern coast and feared a too distant frontier.

But, the beginnings once safely made, change set in apace. Not only so; there had been slow change from the first. We have no frontier now, we are told,—except a broken fragment, it may be, here and there in some barren corner of the western lands, where some inhospitable mountain still shoulders us out, or where men are still lacking to break the baked surface of the plains and occupy them in the very teeth of hostile nature. But at first it was all frontier,—a mere strip of settlements stretched precariously upon the sea-edge of the wilds: an untouched continent in front of them, and behind them an unfrequented sea that almost never showed so much as the momentary gleam of a sail.

Every step in the slow process of settlement was but a step of the same kind as the first, an advance to a new frontier like the old. For long we lacked, it is true, that new breed of frontiersmen born in after years beyond the mountains. Those first frontiersmen had still a touch of the timidity of the Old World in their blood: they lacked the frontier heart. They were "Pilgrims" in very fact,—exiled, not at home. Fine courage they had: and a steadfastness in their bold design which it does a faint-hearted age good to look back upon. There was no thought of drawing back. Steadily, almost calmly, they extended their seats. They built homes, and deemed it certain their children would live there after them. But they did not love the rough, uneasy life for its own sake. How long did they keep, if they could, within sight of the sea! The wilderness was their refuge; but how long before it became their joy and hope! Here was their destiny cast; but their hearts lingered and held back. It was only as generations passed and the work widened about them that their thought also changed, and a new thrill sped along their blood.

Their life had been new and strange from their first landing in the wilderness. Their houses, their food, their clothing, their neighborhood dealings were all such as only the frontier brings. Insensibly they were themselves changed. The strange life became familiar; their adjustment to it was at length unconscious and without effort; they had no plans which were not inseparably a part and a product of it. But, until they had turned their backs once for all upon the sea; until they saw their western borders cleared of the French; until the mountain passes had grown familiar, and the lands beyond the central and constant theme of their hope, the goal and dream of their young men, they did not become an American people.

When they did, the great determining movement of our history began. The very visages of the people changed. That alert movement of the eye, that openness to every thought of enterprise or adventure, that nomadic habit which knows no fixed home and has plans ready to be carried any whither,—all the marks of the authentic type of the "American" as we know him came into our life. The crack of the whip and the song of the teamster, the heaving chorus of boatmen poling their heavy rafts upon the rivers, the laughter of the camp, the sound of bodies of men in the still forests, became the characteristic notes in our air. A roughened race, embrowned in the sun, hardened in manner by a coarse life of change and danger, loving the rude woods and the crack of the rifle, living to begin something new every day, striking with the broad and open hand, delicate in nothing but the touch of the trigger, leaving cities in its track as if by accident rather than design, settling again to the steady ways of a fixed life only when it must: such was the American people whose achievement it was to be to take possession of their continent from end to end ere their national government was a single century old. The picture is a very singular one! Settled life and wild side by side: civilization frayed at the edges,—taken forward in rough and ready fashion, with a song and a swagger,—not by statesmen, but by woodsmen and drovers, with axes and whips and rifles in their hands, clad in buckskin, like huntsmen. . . .

The fact that we kept always, for close upon three hundred years, a like element in our life, a frontier people always in our van, is, so far, the central and determining fact of our national history. . . .

Our political, our economic, our social life has felt this potent influence from the wild border all our history through. The "West" is the great word of our history. The "Westerner" has been the type and master of our American life. Now at length, as I have said, we have lost our frontier: our front lies almost unbroken along all the great coast line of the western sea. The Westerner, in some day soon to come, will pass out of our life, as he so long ago passed out of the life of the Old World. Then a new epoch will open for us. Perhaps it has opened already. Slowly we shall grow old, compact our people, study the delicate adjustments of an intricate society, and ponder the niceties, as we have hitherto pondered the bulks and structural framework, of government. Have we not, indeed, already come to these things? But the past we know. We can "see it steady and see it whole;" and its central movement and motive are gross and obvious to the eye.

The West Transformed Every Issue

Till the first century of the Constitution is rounded out we stand all the while in the presence of that stupendous westward movement which has filled the continent: so vast, so various, at times so tragical, so swept by passion. Through all the long time there has been a line of rude settlements along our front wherein the same tests of power and of institutions were still being made that were made first upon the sloping banks of the rivers of old Virginia and within the long sweep of the Bay of Massachusetts. The new life of the West has reacted all the while—who shall say how powerfully?—upon the older life of the East; and yet the East has moulded the West as if she sent forward to it through every decade of the long process the chosen impulses and suggestions of history. The West has taken strength, thought, training, selected aptitudes out of the old treasures of the East,—as if out of a new Orient; while the East has itself been kept fresh, vital, alert, originative by the West, her blood quickened all the while, her youth through every age renewed. . . .

Our statesmen,—strike out the names of Samuel Adams and Patrick Henry from the list, together with all like untutored spirits, who stood for the new, unreverencing ardor of a young democracy,— our statesmen were such men as might have taken their places in the House of Commons or in the Cabinet at home as naturally and with as easy an adjustment to their place and task as in the Continental Congress or in the immortal Constitutional Convention.

Think of the stately ways and the grand air and the authoritative social undersandings of the generation that set the new government afoot,—the generation of Washington and John Adams. Think, too, of the conservative tradition that guided all the early history of that government: that early line of genlemen Presidents; that steady "cabinet succession to the Presidency" which came at length to seem almost like an oligarchy to the impatient men who were shut out from it. The line ended, with a sort of chill, in stiff John Quincy Adams, too cold a man to be a people's prince after the old order of Presidents; and the year 1829, which saw Jackson come in, saw the old order go out.

The date is significant. Since the war of 1812, undertaken as if to set us free to move westward, seven States had been admitted to the Union: and the whole number of States was advanced to twenty-four. Eleven new States had come into partnership with the old thirteen.

The voice of the West rang through all our counsels; and, in Jackson, the new partners took possession of the Government. It is worth while to remember how men stood amazed at the change: how startled, chagrined, dismayed the conservative States of the East were at the revolution they saw effected, the riot of change they saw set in: and no man who has once read the singular story can forget how the eight years Jackson reigned saw the Government, and politics themselves, transformed. For long,—the story being written in the regions where the shock and surprise of the change was greatest,—the period of this momentous revolution was spoken of amongst us as a period of degeneration, the birth-time of a deep and permanent demoralization of our politics. But we see it differently now. Whether we have any taste or stomach for that rough age or not, however much we may wish that the old order might have stood, the generation of Madison and Adams have been prolonged, and the good tradition of the early days handed on unbroken and unsullied, we now know that what the nation underwent in that day of change was not degeneration, great and perilous as were the errors of the time, but regeneration.

The old order was changed, once and for all. A new nation

stepped, with a touch of swagger, upon the stage,—a nation which had broken alike with the traditions and with the wisely wrought experience of the Old World, and which, with all the haste and rashness of youth, was minded to work out a separate policy and destiny of its own. It was a day of hazards, but there was nothing sinister at the heart of the new plan. It was a wasteful experiment, to fling out, without wise guides, upon untried ways; but an abounding continent afforded enough and to spare even for the wasteful. It was sure to be so with a nation that came out of the secluded vales of a virgin continent. It was the bold frontier voice of the West sounding in affairs. The timid shivered, but the robust waxed strong and rejoiced, in the tonic air of the new day.

It was then we swung out into the main paths of our history. The new voices that called us were first silvery, like the voice of Henry Clay, and spoke old familiar words of eloquence. The first spokesmen of the West even tried to con the classics, and spoke incongruously in the phrases of politics long dead and gone to dust, as Benton did. But presently the tone changed, and it was the truculent and masterful accents of the real frontiersman that rang dominant above the rest, harsh, impatient, and with an evident dash of temper. The East slowly accustomed itself to the change; caught the movement, though it grumbled and even trembled at the pace; and managed most of the time to keep in the running. But it was always henceforth to be the West that set the pace. There is no mistaking the questions that have ruled our spirits as a nation during the present century. The public land question, the tariff question, and the question of slavery,—these dominate from first to last. It was the West that made each one of these the question that it was.

Without the free lands to which every man who chose might go, there would not have been that easy prosperity of life and that high standard of abundance which seemed to render it necessary that, if we were to have manufactures and a diversified industry at all, we should foster new undertakings by a system of protection which would make the profits of the factory as certain and as abundant as the profits of the farm. It was the constant movement of the population, the constant march of wagon trains into the West, that made it so cardinal a matter of policy whether the great national domain should be free land or not: and that was the land question. It was the settlement of the West that transformed slavery from an accepted institution into passionate matter of controversy.

Lincoln, The Type of the Nation

He would be a rash man who should say he understood Abraham Lincoln. No doubt natures deep as his, and various almost to the point of self-contradiction, can be sounded only by the judgment of men of a like sort,—if any such there be. But some things we all may see and judge concerning him. You have in him the type and flower of our growth. It is as if Nature had made a typical American, and then had added with liberal hand the royal quality of genius, to show us what the type could be. Lincoln owed nothing to his birth, everything to his growth: had no training save what he gave himself; no nurture, but only a wild and native strength. His life was his schooling, and every day of it gave to his character a new touch of development. His manhood not only, but his perception also, expanded with his life. His eyes, as they looked more and more abroad, beheld the national life, and comprehended it: and the lad who had been so rought-cut a provincial became, when grown to manhood, the one leader in all the nation who held the whole people singly in his heart:—held even the Southern people there, and would have won them back. And so we have in him what we must call the perfect development of native strength, the rounding out and nationalization of the provincial.

Andrew Jackson was a type, not of the nation, but of the West. For all the tenderness there was in the stormy heart of the masterful man, and staunch and simple loyalty to all who loved him, he learned nothing in the East; kept always the flavor of the rough school in which he had been bred; was never more than a frontier soldier and gentleman. Lincoln differed from Jackson by all the length of his unmatched capacity to learn. Jackson could understand only men of his own kind; Lincoln could understand men of all sorts and from every region of the land: seemed himself, indeed, to be all men by turns, as mood succeeded mood in his strange nature. He never ceased to stand, in his bony angles, the express image of the ungainly frontiersman. His mind never lost the vein of coarseness that had marked him grossly when a youth. And yet how he grew and strengthened in the real stuff of dignity and greatness: how nobly he could bear himself without the aid of grace! He kept always the shrewd and seeing eye of the woodsman and the hunter, and the flavor of wild life never left him: and yet how easily his view widened to great affairs; how surely he perceived the value and the significance of whatever touched him and made him neighbor to itself!

Lincoln's marvelous capacity to extend his comprehension to the measure of what he had in hand is the one distinguishing mark of the man: and to study the development of that capacity in him is little less than to study, where it is as it were perfectly registered, the national life itself. This boy lived his youth in Illinois when it was a frontier State. The youth of the State was coincident with his own: and man and State kept equal pace in their striding advance to maturity. The frontier population was an intensely political population. It felt to the quick the throb of the nation's life,—for the nation's life ran through it, going its eager way to the westward. The West was not separate from the East. Its communities were every day receiving fresh members from the East, and the fresh impulse of direct suggestion. Their blood flowed to them straight from the warmest veins of the older communities. More than that, elements which were separated in the East were mingled in the West: which displayed to the eye as it were a sort of epitome of the most active and permanent forces of the national life. In such communities as these Lincoln mixed daily from the first with men of every sort and from every quarter of the country. With them he discussed neighborhood politics, the politics of the State, the politics of the nation,—and his mind became traveled as he talked. How plainly amongst such neighbors, there in Illinois, must it have become evident that national questions were centring more and more in the West as the years went by: coming as it were to meet them.

Lincoln went twice down the Mississippi, upon the slow rafts that carried wares to its mouth, and saw with his own eyes, so used to look directly and point-blank upon men and affairs, characteristic regions of the South. He worked his way slowly and sagaciously, with that larger sort of sagacity which so marked him all his life, into the active business of state politics; sat twice in the state legislature, and then for a term in Congress,—his sensitive and seeing mind open all the while to every turn of fortune and every touch of nature in the moving affairs he looked upon. All the while, too, he continued to canvass, piece by piece, every item of politics, as of old, with his neighbors, familiarly around the stove, or upon the corners of the street, or more formally upon the stump; and kept always in direct contact with the ordinary views of ordinary men. Meanwhile he read, as nobody else around him read, and sought to gain a complete mastery over speech, with the conscious purpose to prevail in its use; derived zest from the curious study of mathematical proof, and amusement as well as strength from the practice of clean and naked statements of truth. It was all irregularly done, but strenuously, with the same instinct throughout, and with a steady access of facility and power. There was no sudden leap for this man, any more than for other men, from crudeness to finished power, from an understanding of the people of Illinois to an understanding of the people of the United States.

And thus he came at last, with infinite pains and a wonder of endurance, to his great national task with a self-trained capacity which no man could match, and made upon a scale as liberal as the life of the people. You could not then set this athlete a pace in learning or in perceiving that was too hard for him. He knew the people and their life as no other man did or could: and now stands in his place singular in all the annals of mankind, the "brave, sagacious, foreseeing, patient man" of the people, "new birth of our new soil, the first American."

We have here a national man presiding over sectional men. Lincoln understood the East better than the East understood him or the people from whom he sprung: and this is every way a very noteworthy circumstance. For my part, I read a lesson in the singular career of this great man. Is it possible the East remains sectional while the West broadens to a wider view?

> 'Be strong-backed, brown-handed, upright as your pines;
> By the scale of a hemisphere shape your designs,"

is an inspiring programme for the woodsman and the pioneer; but how are you to be brown-handed in a city office? What if you never see the upright pines? How are you to have so big a purpose on so small a part of the hemisphere?

As it has grown old, unquestionably, the East has grown sectional. There is no suggestion of the prairie in its city streets, or of the embrowned ranchman and farmer in its well-dressed men. Its ports teem with shipping from Europe and the Indies. Its newspapers run upon the themes of an Old World. It hears of the great plains of the continent as of foreign parts, which it may never think to see except from a car window. Its life is self-centred and selfish. The West, save where special interests centre (as in those pockets of silver where men's eyes catch as it were an eager gleam from the very ore itself): the West is in less danger of sectionalization. Who shall say in that wide country where one region ends and another begins, or, in that free and changing society, where one class ends and another begins?

This, surely, is the moral of our history. The East has spent and been spent for the West: has given forth her energy, her young men and her substance, for the new regions that have been a-making all the century through. But has she learned as much as she has taught, or taken as much as she has given? Look what it is that has now at last taken place. The westward march has stopped, upon the final slopes of the Pacific; and now the plot thickens. Populations turn upon their old paths; fill in the spaces they passed by neglected in their first journey in search of a land of promise; settle to a life such as the East knows as well as the West,—nay, much better. With the change, the pause, the settlement, our people draw into closer groups, stand face to face, to know each other and be known: and the time has come for the East to learn in her turn; to broaden her understanding of political and economic conditions to the scale of a hemisphere.

"THE ATLANTIC MONTHLY,"
JULY 1897

The American Nation Still Waits to Be Made

The making of our own nation seems to have taken place under our very eyes, so recent and so familiar is the story. The great process was worked out in the plain and open day of the modern world, statesmen and historians standing by to superintend, criticise, make record of what was done. The stirring narrative runs quickly into the day in which we live; we can say that our grandfathers builded the government which now holds so large a place in the world; the story seems of yesterday, and yet seems entire, as if the making of the republic had hastened to complete itself within a single hundred years. We are elated to see so great a thing done upon so great a scale, and to feel ourselves in so intimate a way actors in the moving scene.

Yet we should deceive ourselves were we to suppose the work done, the nation made. We have been told by a certain group of our historians that a nation was made when the federal Constitution was adopted; that the strong sentences of the law sufficed to transform us from a league of States into a people single and inseparable. Some tell us, however, that it was not till the War of 1812 that we grew fully conscious of a single purpose and destiny, and began to form policies as if for a nation. Others see the process complete only when the civil war struck slavery away, and gave North and South a common way of life that should make common ideals and common endeavors at last possible. Then, when all have had their say, there comes a great movement like the one which we call Populism, to remind us how the country still lies apart in sections: some at one stage of development, some at another; some with one hope and purpose for America, some with another. And we ask ourselves, Is the history of our making as a nation indeed over, or do we still wait upon the forces that shall at last unite us? Are we even now, in fact, a nation?

Clearly, it is not a question of sentiment, but a question of fact. If it be true that the country, taken as a whole, is at one and the same time in several stages of development,—not a great commercial and manufacturing nation, with here and there its broad pastures and the quiet farms from which it draws its food; not a vast agricultural community, with here and there its ports of shipment and its necessary marts of exchange; not yet a country of mines, merely, pouring their products forth into the markets of the world, to take thence whatever it may need for its comfort and convenience in living,—we still wait for its economic and spiritual union. It is many things at once. Sections big enough for kingdoms live by agriculture, and farm the wide stretches of a new land by the aid of money borrowed from other sections which seem almost like another nation, with their teeming cities, dark with the smoke of factories, quick with the movements of trade, as sensitive to the variations of exchange on London as to the variations in the crops raised by their distant fellow countrymen on the plains within the continent. Upon other great spaces of the vast continent, communities, millions strong, live the distinctive life of the miner, have all their fortune bound up and centred in a single group of industries, feel in their utmost concentration the power of economic forces elsewhere dispersed, and chafe under the unequal yoke that unites them with communities so unlike themselves as those which lend and trade and manufacture, and those which follow the plough and reap the grain that is to feed the world.

Such contrasts are nothing new in our history, and our system of government is admirably adapted to relieve the strain and soften the antagonism they might entail. All our national history through our country has lain apart in sections, each marking a stage of settlement, a stage of wealth, a stage of development, as population has advanced, as if by successive journeyings and encampments, from east to west; and always new regions have been suffered to become new States, form their own life under their own law, plan their own economy, adjust their own domestic relations, and legalize their own methods of business. States have, indeed, often been whimsically enough formed. We have left the matter of boundaries to surveyors rather than to statesmen, and have by no means managed to construct economic units in the making of States. We have joined mining communities with agricultural, the mountain with the plain, the ranch with the farm, and have left the making of uniform rules to the sagacity and practical habit of neighbors ill at ease with one another. But on the whole, the scheme, though a bit haphazard, has worked itself out with singularly little friction and no disaster, and the strains of the great structure we have erected have been greatly eased and dissipated. . . .

It is to this point we have come in the making of the nation. The old sort of growth is at an end,—the growth by mere expansion. We have now to look more closely to internal conditions, and study the means by which a various people is to be bound together in a single interest. Many differences will pass away of themselves. "East" and "West" will come together by a slow approach, as capital accumulates where now it is only borrowed, as industrial development makes its way westward in a new variety, as life gets its final elaboration and detail throughout all the great spaces of the continent, until all the scattered parts of the nation are drawn into real community of interest. Even the race problem of the South will no doubt work itself out in the slowness of time, as blacks and whites pass from generation to generation, gaining with each remove from the memories of the war a surer self-possession, an easier view of the division of labor and of social function to be arranged between them. Time is the only legislator in such a matter. But not everything can be left to drift and slow accommodation. The nation which has grown to the proportions almost of the continent within the century lies under our eyes, unfinished, unharmonized, waiting still to have its parts adjusted, lacking its last lesson in the ways of peace and concert. It required statesmanship of no mean sort to bring us to our present growth and lusty strength. It will require leadership of a much higher order to teach us the triumphs of coöperation, the self-possession and calm choices of maturity.

A New Form of Leadership for a New Day

No one who comprehends the essential soundness of our people's life can mistrust the future of the nation. He may confidently expect a safe nationalization of interest and policy in the end, whatever folly of experiment and fitful change he may fear in the meanwhile. He can only wonder that we should continue to leave ourselves so utterly without adequate means of formulating a national policy. Certainly Providence has presided over our affairs with a strange indulgence, if it is true that Providence helps only those who first seek to help themselves. The making of a nation has never been a thing deliberately planned and consummated by the counsel and authority of leaders, but the daily conduct and policy of a nation which has won its place must be so planned. So far we have had the hopefulness, the readiness, and the hardihood of youth in these matters, and have never become fully conscious of the position into which our peculiar frame of government has brought us. We have waited a whole century to observe that we have made no provision for authoritative national leadership in matters of policy. The President does not always speak with authority, because he is not always a man picked out and tested by any processes in which the people have been participants, and has often nothing but his office to render him influential. Even when the country does know and trust him, he can carry his views no further than to recommend them to the attention of Congress in a written message which the Houses would deem themselves subservient to give too much heed to. Within the Houses there is no man, except the Vice-President, to whose choice the whole country gives heed; and he is chosen, not to be a Senator, but only to wait upon the disability of the President, and preside meanwhile over a body of which he is not a member. The House of Representatives has in these latter days made its Speaker its political leader as well as its parliamentary moderator; but the country is, of course, never consulted about that beforehand, and his leadership is not the open leadership of discussion, but the undebatable leadership of the parliamentary autocrat.

This singular leaderless structure of our government never stood fully revealed until the present generation, and even now awaits general recognition. Peculiar circumstances and the practical political habit and sagacity of our people for long concealed it. The framers of the Constitution no doubt expected the President and his advisers to exercise a real leadership in affairs, and for more than a generation after the setting up of the government their expectation was fulfilled. Washington was accepted as leader no less by Congress than by the people. Hamilton, from the Treasury, really gave the government both its policy and its administrative structure. If John Adams had less authority than Washington, it was because the party he represented was losing its hold upon the country. Jefferson was the most consummate party chief, the most unchecked master of legislative policy, we have had in America, and his dynasty was continued in Madison and Monroe. But Madison's terms saw Clay and Calhoun come to the front in the House, and many another man of the new generation, ready to guide and coach the President rather than to be absolutely controlled by him. Monroe was not of the calibre of his predecessors, and no party could rally about so stiff a man, so cool a partisan, as John Quincy Adams. And so the old political function of the presidency came to an end, and it was left for Jackson to give it a new one,—instead of a leadership of counsel, a leadership and discipline by rewards and punishments. Then the slavery issue began to dominate politics, and a long season of concentrated passion brought individual men of force into power in Congress,—natural leaders of men like Clay, trained and eloquent advocates like Webster, keen debaters with a logic whose thrusts were as sharp as those of cold steel like Calhoun.

The war made the Executive of necessity the nation's leader again, with the great Lincoln at its head, who seemed to embody, with a touch of genius, the very character of the race itself. Then reconstruction came,—under whose leadership who could say?—and we were left to wonder what, henceforth, in the days of ordinary peace and industry, we were to make of a government which could in humdrum times yield us no leadership at all. . . .

It is with such machinery that we are to face the future, find a wise and moderate policy, bring the nation to a common, a cordial understanding, a real unity of life. The President can lead only as he can command the ear of both Congress and the country,—only as any other individual might who could secure a like general hearing and acquiescence. Policy must come always from the deliberations of the House committees, the debates, both secret and open, of the Senate, the compromises of committee conference between the Houses; no one man, no group of men, leading; no man, no group of men, responsible for the outcome. Unquestionably we believe in a guardian destiny! No other race could have accomplished so much with such a system; no other race would have dared risk such an experiment. We shall work out a remedy, for work it out we must. We must find or make, somewhere in our system, a group of men to lead us, who represent the nation in the origin and responsibility of their power; who shall draw the Executive, which makes choice of foreign policy and upon whose ability and good faith the honorable execution of the laws depends, into cordial coöperation with the legislature, which, under whatever form of government, must sanction law and policy. Only under a national leadership, by a national selection of leaders, and by a method of constructive choice rather than of compromise and barter, can a various nation be peacefully led.

ADDRESS BEFORE VIRGINIA STATE BAR ASSOCIATION,
AUGUST 4, 1897

A System That Prevents Official Responsibility

I have told you my own conclusion with regard to our present constitutional usage in the title I have chosen for this address. By the words "Leaderless Government" I mean to describe the government of the United States. I do not utter the words with the least touch of censoriousness or cynicism or even discouragement. In using them I am simply speaking a careful and, if I may say so, a dispassionate judgment. I do not believe it a necessary feature of our government that we should be without leaders; neither do I believe that we shall continue to be without them; but as a matter of fact we are without them, and we ought to ask ourselves, Why? I mean, of course, that we are without official leaders—without leaders who can be held immediately responsible for the action and policy of the government, alike upon its legislative and upon its administrative side. Leaders of some sort we, of course, always have; but they come and go like phantoms, put forward as if by accident, withdrawn, not by our choice, but as if upon some secret turn of fortune which we neither anticipate nor as a nation control—some local quarrel, some obscure movement of politics within a single district, some manipulation of a primary or some miscarriage in a convention. They are not of the nation, but come and go as if unbidden by any general voice. The government does not put them forward, but groups of men formed we hardly know where, planning we hardly know what; the government suffers no change when they disappear—that is the private affair of some single constituency and of the men who have supplanted them.

Look at the familiar system for a little with this matter in view, and you shall see that, as we now use it, it seems devised as if to prevent official and responsible leadership. The President cannot lead. We call his office great, say that the Queen of England has no power to be compared with his and make choice of nominees for the presidency as if our votes decided a constructive policy for the four years to come; but we know that in fact he has as little power to originate as the Queen has. He may, no doubt, stand in the way of measures with a veto very hard to overleap; and we think oftentimes with deep comfort of the laws he can kill when we are afraid of the majority in Congress. Congessional majorities are doubtless swayed, too, by what they know the President will do with the bills they send him. But they are swayed sometimes one way and sometimes the other, according to the temper of the times and state of parties. They as often make his assured veto a pretext for recklessness as a reason for self-restraint. They take a sort of irresponsible and defiant pleasure in "giving him the dare": in proposing things they know many people want and putting upon him the lonely responsibility of saying that they shall not have them. And if he stand for long in the way of any serious party purpose, they heat opinion against him and make his position more and more unpleasant, until he either yields or is finally discredited. It is a game in which he has no means of attack and few effective weapons of defence.

Of course he can send a message to Congress whenever he likes—the Constitution bids him do so "from time to time," in order to "give the Congress information of the state of the Union and recommend to their consideration such measures as he shall deem necessary and expedient"; and we know that, if he be a man of real power and statesmanlike initiative, he may often hit the wish and purpose of the nation so in the quick in what he urges upon Congress that the House will heed him promptly and seriously enough. But there is a stubborn and very natural pride in the Houses with respect to this matter. They, not he, are the nation's representatives in the making of law; and they would deem themselves subservient were they too often to permit him leadership in legislative policy. It is easy to stir their resentment by too much suggestion; and it is best that a message should be general, not special—best that it should cover a good many topics and not confine itself too narrowly to one, if a President would keep in credit with those who shape matters within the House and Senate. In all ordinary times the President recognizes this and preserves a sort of modesty, a tone as if of a chronicler merely, and setter forth of things administrative, when he addresses Congress. He makes it his study to use only a private influence and never to seem a maker of resolutions. And even when the occasion is extraordinary and his own mind definitely made up, he argues and urges—he cannot command. In short, in making suggestions to Congress the President of the United States has only this advantage over any other influential person in the nation who might choose to send to Congress a letter of information and advice. It is the duty of Congress to read what he says; all the larger newspapers will print it; and some will have letters from their Washington correspondents devoted to guessing what effect, if any, it will have upon legislation. The President can make his message a means of concentrating public opinion upon particular topics of his own choosing, and so force those topics upon the attention of the House. But that is all, and under ordinary circumstances it is not much.

Change and Diversity Challenge the Political System

Why is it that this leaderless character of our government did not disclose itself to an earlier generation as it has disclosed itself to us? The government has the same formal structure now that it always has had: why has its weakness been so long concealed? Why can it not serve the new time as well as it served the old? Because the new time is not like the old—for us or any other nation; the changes which we have witnessed have transformed us. The tasks set the government now differ both in magnitude and in kind from those set it in days gone by. It is no old man's fancy that the old days were different from those we now see. For one thing—and this can be no news to any man—an industrial revolution separates us from the times that went by no longer ago than when the war between the States came on; and that industrial revolution—like the war itself—has not affected all parts of the country alike—has left us more various and more unequal, part by part, than ever before.

We speak nowadays of a new sectionalism, and I, for one, deprecate the phrase. I rejoice to believe that there are no longer any permanent sectional lines in this country. But there is an unprecedented diversification of interests—and for the time, no doubt, differences of interest mark also differences of region and of development. And these differences of condition and of economic growth as between region and region, though temporary, are more sharply marked than they ever were before. Moreover, there is a confused variety: region differs from region in an almost incalculable number of significant details. And there is added to this everywhere a swift process of change, a shifting of elements, a perplexing vicissitude in affairs. Here and there communities have a fixed life, and are still and quiet as of old, but these lie apart from the great forces that are making the nation, and the law is change.

These things do not need demonstration; they hardly need illustration. No man is so ill-informed as not to know that the conditions which existed before the war were simple and uniform the country through, as compared with those which have sprung up since the war. And where conditions are comparatively simple and uniform, constructive leadership is little needed. Men readily see things alike and easily come to a common opinion upon the larger sort of questions: or, at any rate, to two general opinions, widespread and definite enough to form parties on. For well-nigh a generation after the war, moreover, the problems which the government of the Union had to settle were very definite problems indeed, which no man could mistake, and upon which opinion could readily be concentrated. I think the country sadly needed responsible and conscientious leadership during the period of Reconstruction, and it has suffered many things because it did not get it—things of which we still keenly feel the consequences. But the tasks, at least, were definite and unmistakable, and parties formed themselves upon sharp-cut issues.

Since then, how has the scene changed! It is not now fundamental matters of structure and franchise upon which we have to centre our choice; but those general questions of policy upon which every nation has to exercise its discretion: foreign policy, our duty to our neighbors, customs tariffs, coinage, currency, immigration, the law of corporations and of trusts, the regulation of railway traffic and of the great industries which supply the necessaries of life and the stuffs of manufacture. These are questions of economic policy chiefly; and how shall we settle questions of economic policy except upon grounds of interest? Who is to reconcile our interests and extract what is national and liberal out of what is sectional and selfish? These are not questions upon which it is easy to concentrate general opinion. It is infinitely difficult to effect a general enlightenment of the public mind in regard to their real merits and significance for the nation as a whole. Their settlement in any one way affects the several parts of the country unequally. They cannot be settled justly by a mere compounding of differences, a mere unguided interplay of rival individual forces, without leadership and the courage of definite party action. Such questions are as complex and as difficult of adequate comprehension as the now infinitely varied life of the nation itself; and we run incalculable risks in leaving their settlement to the action of a House of Representatives whose leaders are silent and do not tell us upon what principle they act, or upon what motive; to a Senate whose undisciplined members insist upon making each an individual contribution to the result; and to a President chosen by processes which have little or nothing to do with party organization or with the solution of questions of State. We can seldom in this way see a single year ahead of us.

The Executive and the Legislature Must
Be Drawn Closer Together

What would I have? I feel the embarrassment of the question. If I answer it, I make the unpleasant impression of posing as a statesman, and tempt those who wish to keep every man in his place to remind me that I am only a college professor, whom it would better become to stick to his legitimate business of describing things as they are, leaving it to men of affairs to determine what they ought to be. I have been trying to describe things as they are, and that has brought me, whether I would or no, straight upon this question of the future. I am not addressing a college class, but men of affairs, who want their doctrine in the concrete and with no shirking of hard questions. Moreover, the things I have been describing are the proper objects of my study. In lecturing upon Politics I try, indeed, not to lecture as a politician; but I try also not to lecture as a fossil. I must study affairs of the day as well as things dead and buried and all but forgot. . . .

My studies have taught me this one thing with a definiteness which cannot be mistaken: Successful governments have never been conducted safely in the midst of complex and critical affairs except when guided by those who were responsible for carrying out and bringing to an issue the measures they proposed; and the separation of the right to plan from the duty to execute has always led to blundering and inefficiency; and modern representative bodies cannot of themselves combine the two. The Roman Senate, the only efficient administrative assembly that I know of in the history of the world, was a permanent body, made up for the most part of men who had served their terms as executive officials through a long succession of offices. It undertook actually to direct the affairs of the state, as our Houses do; but its members had had varied executive experience, and—what was of still more significance—its mistakes came back upon itself. The shame of failure fell upon it, and not upon those who were merely its agents. Moreover, it was a thoroughly national power: it stood for no constituencies; in its days of success it represented, not a divided, but a thoroughly homogeneous state. If you would have the present error of our system in a word, it is this, that Congress is the motive power in the government and yet has in it nowhere any representative of the nation as a whole. Our Executive, on the other hand, is national; at any rate may be made so, and yet has no longer any place of guidance in our system. It represents no constituency, but the whole people; and yet, though it alone is national, it has no originative voice in domestic national policy.

The sum of the matter is, that we have carried the application of the notion that the powers of government must be separated to a dangerous and unheard-of length by thus holding our only national representative, the Executive, at arm's length from Congress, whose very commission it seems to be to represent, not the people, but the communities into which the people are divided. We should have Presidents and Cabinets of a different calibre were we to make it their bounden duty to act as a committee for the whole nation to choose and formulate matters for the consideration of Congress in the name of a party and an Administration. . . . And that is exactly what we ought to do. We should have not a little light thrown daily, and often when it was least expected, upon the conduct of the Departments, if the heads of the Departments had daily to face the representatives of the people, to propose, defend, explain administrative policy, upon the floor of the Houses, where such a plan would put them: and heads of departments would be happy under such a system only when they were very straightforward and honest and able men. I am not suggesting that initiative in legislation be by any means confined to the Administration—that would be radical, indeed—but only that they be given a free, though responsible, share in it—and that, I conceive, would bring the government back very nearly to the conception and practice of Washington. It would be a return to our first models of statesmanship and political custom.

I ask you to put this question to yourselves: Should we not draw the Executive and Legislature closer together? Should we not, on the one hand, give the individual leaders of opinion in Congress a better chance to have an intimate part in determining who should be President, and the President, on the other hand, a better chance to approve himself a statesman, and his advisers capable men of affairs, in the guidance of Congress? This will be done when the Executive is given an authoritative initiative in the Houses. I see no other way to create national figures in the field in which domestic policy is chosen, or to bring forward tested persons to vote for. I do not suggest methods—this is not the place or the occasion; I suggest an idea—a way out of chaos: the nationalization of the motive power of the government, to offset the economic sectionalization of the country; I suggest the addition to Congress, which represents us severally, of a power, constituted how you will, which shall represent us collectively in the proposing of laws; which shall have the right as of course to press national motives and courses of action to a vote in the Congress. This will not subordinate Congress; it may accept the proposals of the Administration or not, as it pleases (it once took a scolding from Washington himself for not accepting them); but the country will at least have a mouthpiece and not all of policy will lurk with committees and in executive sessions of the Senate.

"THE ATLANTIC MONTHLY,"
MARCH 1901

The World Looks to America

The affairs of the world stand in such a case . . . that our own private business must take its chances along with the greater business of the world at large. We dare not stand neutral. All mankind deem us the representatives of the moderate and sensible discipline which makes free men good citizens, of enlightened systems of law and a temperate justice, of the best experience in the reasonable methods and principles of self-government, of public force made consistent with individual liberty; and we shall not realize these ideals at home, if we suffer them to be hopelessly discredited amongst the peoples who have yet to see liberty and the peaceable days of order and comfortable progress. We should lose heart our-

selves, did we suffer the world to lose faith in us as the champions
of these things.

There is no masking or concealing the new order of the world. It
is not the world of the eighteenth century, nor yet of the nineteenth. A new era has come upon us like a sudden vision of things
unprophesied, and for which no polity has been prepared. Here is
straightway a new frontage for the nations,—this frontage toward
the Orient. Our almost accidental possession of the Philippines has
put us in the very presence of the forces which must make the
politics of the twentieth century radically unlike the politics of the
nineteenth; but we must have taken cognizance of them and dealt
with them in any event. They concern us as nearly as they concern
any other nation in the world. They concern all nations, for they
shall determine the future of the race. Fortunately, they have not
disclosed themselves before we were ready. I do not mean that our
thought was prepared for them; I do not mean that our domestic
affairs were in such shape as to seem fairly well ordered, so that we
might in good conscience turn from them as from things finished
and complete, and divert our energies to tasks beyond our borders.
I mean that this change in the order of the world came, so far as
we are concerned, at the natural point in our national development.
The matter is worth looking into. . . .

Until 1890 the United States had always a frontier; looked always
to a region beyond, unoccupied, unappropriated, an outlet for its
energy, a new place of settlement and of achievement for its people.
For nearly three hundred years their growth had followed a single
law,—the law of expansion into new territory. Themselves through
all their history a frontier, the English colonies in America grew
into a nation whose life poured still with strong tide along the old
channel. Over the mountains on to the long slopes that descended
to the Mississippi, across the great river into the plains, up the
plains to the crowning heights of the Rockies, beyond the Rockies
to the Pacific, slowly moved the frontier nation. England sought
colonies at the ends of the earth to set her energy free and give
vent to her enterprise; we, a like people in every impulse of mastery
and achievement, had our own vast continent and were satisfied.

There was always space and adventure enough and to spare, to satisfy the feet of our young men.

The great process put us to the making of states; kept the wholesome blood of sober and strenuous and systematic work warm within us; perpetuated in us the spirit of initiative and of practical expediency which had made of the colonies vigorous and heady states; created in us that national feeling which finally put sectionalism from the field and altered the very character of the government; gave us the question of the extension of slavery, brought on the civil war, and decided it by the weight of the West. From coast to coast across the great continent our institutions have spread, until the western sea has witnessed the application upon a great scale of what was begun upon a small scale on the shores of the Atlantic, and the drama has been played almost to its last act,—the drama of institutional construction on the vast scale of a continent. The whole European world, which gave us our materials, has been moralized and liberalized by the striking and stupendous spectacle.

No other modern nation has been schooled as we have been in big undertakings and the mastery of novel difficulties. We have become confirmed in energy, in resourcefulness, in practical proficiency, in self-confidence. We have become confirmed, also, so far as our character is concerned, in the habit of acting under an odd mixture of selfish and altruistic motives. Having ourselves a population fit to be free, making good its freedom in every sort of unhampered enterprise, determining its own destiny unguided and unbidden, moving as it pleased within wide boundaries, using institutions, not dominated by them, we have sympathized with freedom everywhere; have deemed it niggardly to deny an equal degree of freedom to any race or community that desired it; have pressed handsome principles of equity in international dealings; have rejoiced to believe that our principles might some day make every government a servant, not a master, of its people. Ease and prosperity have made us wish the whole world to be as happy and well to do as ourselves; and we have supposed that institutions and principles like our own were the simple prescription for making them so.

Every Man Now Knows That the
World Is to Be Changed

It is only just now, however, that we have awakened to our real relationship to the rest of mankind. Absorbed in our own development, we had fallen into a singular ignorance of the rest of the world. The isolation in which we lived was quite without parallel in modern history. Our only near neighbor of any consequence was like ourselves in every essential particular. The life of Canada has been unlike ours only in matters which have turned out in the long run to be matters of detail; only because she has had direct political connection with the mother country, and because she has had to work out the problem of forming a real union of life and sentiment between alien strains of French and English blood in her population. The contrast grows less and less between the two sides of the friendly border. And so we have looked upon nothing but our own ways of living, and have been formed in isolation. This has made us—not provincial, exactly; upon so big and various a continent there could not be the single pattern of thought and manners and purpose to be found cloistered in a secluded province. But if *provincial* be not the proper word, it suggests the actual fact. We have, like provincials, too habitually confined our view to the range of our own experiences. We have acquired a false self-confidence, a false self-sufficiency, because we have heeded no successes or failures but our own. . . .

We did not of deliberate choice undertake these new tasks which shall transform us. All the world knows the surprising circumstances which thrust them upon us. Sooner or later, nevertheless, they would have become inevitable. If they had not come upon us in this way, they would have come in another. They came upon us, as it was, though unexpected, with a strange opportuneness, as if part of a great preconceived plan for changing the world. Every man now knows that the world is to be changed,—changed according to an ordering of Providence hardly so much as foreshadowed until it came; except, it may be, to a few Europeans who were burrowing and plotting and dreaming in the mysterious East. The whole world had already become a single vicinage; each part had become neighbor to all the rest. No nation could live any longer to itself, the tasks and the duties of neighborhood being what they were. Whether we had had a material foothold there or not, it would have been the duty of the United States to play a part, and a leading part at that, in the opening and transformation of the East. We might not have seen our duty, had the Philippines not fallen to us by the willful fortune of war; but it would have been our duty, nevertheless, to play the part we now see ourselves obliged to play. The East is to be opened and transformed, whether we will or no; the standards of the West are to be imposed upon it; nations and peoples which have stood still the centuries through are to be quickened, and made part of the universal world of commerce and of ideas which has so steadily been a-making by the advance of European power from age to age.

The best guarantee of good government we can give the Filipinos is, that we shall be sensitive to the opinion of the world; that we shall be sensitive in what we do to our own standards, so often boasted of and proclaimed, and shall wish above all things else to live up to the character we have established, the standards we have professed. When they accept the compulsions of that character and accept those standards, they will be entitled to partnership with us, and shall have it. They shall, meanwhile, teach us, as we shall teach them. We shall teach them order as a condition precedent to liberty, self-control as a condition precedent to self-government; they shall teach us the true assessment of institutions,—that their only invaluable content is motive and character.

We shall no doubt learn that democracy and efficiency go together by no novel rule. Democracy is not so much a form of government as a set of principles. Other forms of government may be equally efficient; many forms of government are more efficient,— know better ways of integrating and purifying administration than we have yet learned, more successful methods of imparting drill and order to restless and undeveloped peoples than we are likely to hit upon of ourselves, a more telling way of getting and a more effectual way of keeping leadership in a world of competitive policies, doubtful concerts, and international rivalries. We must learn what we can, and yet scrupulously square everything that we do with the high principles we brought into the world: that justice may be done to the lowly no less than to the great; that government may serve its people, not make itself their master,—may in its service heed both the wishes and the needs of those who obey it; that authority may be for leadership, not for aggrandizement; that the people may be the state.

The reactions which such experiments in the universal validity of principle and method are likely to bring about in respect of our own domestic institutions cannot be calculated or forecast. Old principles applied in a new field may show old applications to have been clumsy and ill considered. We may ourselves get responsible leadership instead of government by mass meeting; a trained and thoroughly organized administrative service instead of administration by men privately nominated and blindly elected; a new notion of terms of office and of standards of policy. If we but keep our ideals clear, our principles steadfast, we need not fear the change.

"THE ATLANTIC MONTHLY,"
DECEMBER 1902

A Place Among the Nations

We have come to full maturity with this new century of our national existence and to full self-consciousness as a nation. And the day of our isolation is past. We shall learn much ourselves now that we stand closer to other nations and compare ourselves first with one and again with another. Moreover, the centre of gravity has shifted in the action of our federal government. It has shifted back to where it was at the opening of the last century, in that early day when we were passing from the gristle to the bone of our growth. For the first twenty-six years that we lived under our federal Constitution foreign affairs, the sentiment and policy of nations oversea, dominated our politics, and our Presidents were our leaders. And now the same thing has come about again. Once more it is our place among the nations that we think of; once more our Presidents are our leaders.

The centre of our party management shifts accordingly. We no longer stop upon questions of what this state wants or that, what this section will demand or the other, what this boss or that may do to attach his machine to the government. The scale of our thought is national again. We are sensitive to airs that come to us from off the seas. The President and his advisers stand upon our chief coign of observation, and we mark their words as we did not till this change came. And this centring of our thoughts, this looking for guidance in things which mere managing talents cannot handle, this union of our hopes, will not leave us what we were when first it came. Here is a new world for us. Here is a new life to which to adjust our ideals.

It is by the widening of vision that nations, as men, grow and are made great. We need not fear the expanding scene. It was plain destiny that we should come to this, and if we have kept our ideals clear, unmarred, commanding through the great century and the moving scenes that made us a nation, we may keep them also through the century that shall see us a great power in the world. Let us put our leading characters at the front; let us pray that vision may come with power; let us ponder our duties like men of conscience and temper our ambitions like men who seek to serve, not to subdue, the world; let us lift our thoughts to the level of the great tasks that await us, and bring a great age in with the coming of our day of strength.

Chapter Three

THE INDIVIDUAL AND SOCIETY

FRUSTRATED in his early political ambitions, Wilson turned to writing for his principal outlet. The selections that follow are from his more purely literary essays. They have a place in this collection because they are, in fact, foundation stones in his political philosophy. Here we see outlined the concept of personality which finds its expression through social relationships. As Rousseau had found the pattern of his ideal community in the Swiss canton, Wilson may be said to have found it in the American college. The lonely scholar, the sensitive individual, reached out to feel his impulses disciplined and steadied, his ideals given practical form, through participation in the life around him. Men come to themselves, he realized, in proportion as they are part of a larger whole. Beyond the maturing and civilizing circle of friends lay for Wilson the infinitely diverse life of modern America. To be a leader in this life meant, inevitably, some blurring of the finer intellectual distinctions; it meant "the act of recognition and completion," rather than of creation. The mature individual held back from the abyss thus opened—and yet found himself fascinated and drawn forward by the supreme challenge to personality.

"THE ATLANTIC MONTHLY,"
SEPTEMBER 1897

The Human Quality in Literature

"The rarest sort of a book," says Mr. Bagehot, slyly, is "a book to read"; and "the knack in style is to write like a human being." It is painfully evident, upon experiment, that not many of the books which come teeming from our presses every year are meant to be read. They are meant, it may be, to be pondered; it is hoped, no doubt, they may instruct, or inform, or startle, or arouse, or reform, or provoke, or amuse us; but we read, if we have the true reader's zest and palate, not to grow more knowing, but to be less pent up and bound within a little circle—as those who take their pleasure, and not as those who laboriously seek instruction—as a means of seeing and enjoying the world of men and affairs. We wish companionship and renewal of spirit, enrichment of thought and the full adventure of the mind; and we desire fair company, and a large world in which to find them. . . .

When you say that a book was meant to be read, you mean, for one thing, of course, that it was not meant to be studied. You do not study a good story, or a haunting poem, or a battle song, or a love ballad, or any moving narrative, whether it be out of history or out of fiction—nor any argument, even, that moves vital in the field of action. You do not have to study these things; they reveal themselves, you do not stay to see how. They remain with you, and will not be forgotten or laid by. They cling like a personal experience, and become the mind's intimates. You devour a book meant to be read, not because you would fill yourself or have an anxious care to be nourished, but because it contains such stuff as it makes the mind hungry to look upon. Neither do you read it to kill time, but to lengthen time, rather, adding to it its natural usury by living the more abundantly while it lasts, joining another's life and thought to your own. . . .

These are books written by human beings, indeed, but with no general quality belonging to the kind—with a special tone and temper, rather, a spirit out of the common, touched with a light that shines clear out of some great source of light which not every man can uncover. We call this spirit human because it moves us, quickens a like life in ourselves, makes us glow with a sort of ardor of self-discovery. It touches the springs of fancy or of action within us, and makes our own life seem more quick and vital. . . .

Say what we may of the errors and the degrading sins of our kind, we do not willingly make what is worst in us the distinguishing trait of what is human. When we declare, with Bagehot, that the author whom we love writes like a human being, we are not sneering at him; we do not say it with a leer. It is in token of admiration, rather. He makes us *like* our humankind. There is a noble passion in what he says, a wholesome humor that echoes genial comradeships; a certain reasonableness and moderation in what is thought and said; an air of the open day, in which things are seen whole and in their right colors, rather than of the close study or the academic class-room. We do not want our poetry from grammarians, nor our tales from philologists, nor our history from theorists. Their human nature is subtly transmuted into something less broad and catholic and of the general world. Neither do we want our political economy from tradesmen nor our statesmanship from mere politicians, but from those who see more and care for more than these men see or care for.

A New Capacity for a New Age

We cannot easily see the large measure and abiding purpose of the novel age in which we stand young and confused. The view that shall clear our minds and quicken us to act as those who know their task and its distant consummation will come with better knowledge and completer self-possession.

Who can doubt that man has grown more and more human with each step of that slow process which has brought him knowledge, self-restraint, the arts of intercourse, and the revelations of real joy? Man has more and more lived with his fellow-men, and it is society that has humanized him—the development of society into an infinitely various school of discipline and ordered skill. He has been made more human by schooling, by growing more self-possessed— less violent, less tumultuous; holding himself in hand, and moving always with a certain poise of spirit; not forever clapping his hand to the hilt of his sword, but preferring, rather, to play with a subtler skill upon the springs of action. This is our conception of the truly human man: a man in whom there is a just balance of faculties, a catholic sympathy—no brawler, no fanatic, no pharisee; not too credulous in hope, not too desperate in purpose; warm, but not hasty; ardent, and full of definite power, but not running about to be pleased and deceived by every new thing.

It is a genial image, of men we love—an image of men warm and true of heart, direct and unhesitating in courage, generous, magnanimous, faithful, steadfast, capable of a deep devotion and self-forgetfulness. But the age changes, and with it must change our ideals of human quality. Not that we would give up what we have loved: we would add what a new life demands. In a new age men must acquire a new capacity, must be men upon a new scale, and with added qualities. We shall need a new Renaissance, ushered in by a new "humanistic" movement, in which we shall add to our present minute, introspective study of ourselves, our jails, our slums, our nerve-centers, our shifts to live, almost as morbid as mediæval religion, a rediscovery of the round world, and of man's place in it, now that its face has changed.

We study the world, but not yet with intent to school our hearts and tastes, broaden our natures, and know our fellow-men as comrades rather than as phenomena; with purpose, rather, to build up bodies of critical doctrine and provide ourselves with theses. That, surely, is not the truly humanizing way in which to take the air of the world. Man is much more than a "rational being," and lives more by sympathies and impressions than by conclusions. It darkens his eyes and dries up the wells of his humanity to be forever in search of doctrine. We need wholesome, experiencing natures, I dare affirm, much more than we need sound reasoning.

A Sort of Robust Moral Sanity

Let us remind ourselves that to be human is, for one thing, to speak and act with a certain note of genuineness, a quality mixed of spontaneity and intelligence. This is necessary for wholesome life in any age, but particularly amidst confused affairs and shifting standards. Genuineness is not mere simplicity, for that may lack vitality, and genuineness does not. We expect what we call genuine to have pith and strength of fiber. Genuineness is a quality which we sometimes mean to include when we speak of individuality. Individuality is lost the moment you submit to passing modes or fashions, the creations of an artificial society; and so is genuineness.

No man is genuine who is forever trying to pattern his life after the lives of other people—unless, indeed, he be a genuine dolt. But individuality is by no means the same as genuineness; for individuality may be associated with the most extreme and even ridiculous eccentricity, while genuineness we conceive to be always wholesome, balanced, and touched with dignity. It is a quality that goes with good sense and self-respect. It is a sort of robust moral sanity, mixed of elements both moral and intellectual. It is found in natures too strong to be mere trimmers and conformers, too well poised and thoughtful to fling off into intemperate protest and revolt. . . .

By what means is this self-liberation to be effected—this emancipation from affectation and the bondage of being like other people? Is it open to us to choose to be genuine? I see nothing insuperable in the way, except for those who are hopelessly lacking in a sense of humor. It depends upon the range and scale of your observation whether you can strike the balance of genuineness or not. If you live in a small and petty world, you will be subject to its standards; but if you live in a large world, you will see that standards are innumerable—some old, some new, some made by the noble-minded and made to last, some made by the weak-minded and destined to perish, some lasting from age to age, some only from day to day— and that a choice must be made among them. It is then that your sense of humor will assist you. You are, you will perceive, upon a long journey, and it will seem to you ridiculous to change your life and discipline your instincts to conform to the usages of a single inn by the way. You will distinguish the essentials from the accidents, and deem the accidents something meant for your amusement.

The strongest natures do not need to wait for these slow lessons of observation, to be got by conning life: their sheer vigor makes it impossible for them to conform to fashion or care for times and seasons. But the rest of us must cultivate knowledge of the world in the large, get our offing, reach a comparative point of view, before we can become with steady confidence our own masters and pilots. The art of being human begins with the practice of being genuine, and following standards of conduct which the world has tested. If your life is not various and you cannot know the best people, who set the standards of sincerity, your reading at least can be various, and you may look at your little circle through the best books, under the guidance of writers who have known life and loved the truth.

An Alert Interest in Affairs

And then genuineness will bring serenity—which I take to be another mark of the right development of the true human being, certainly in an age passionate and confused as this in which we live. Of course serenity does not always go with genuineness. We must say of Dr. Johnson that he was genuine, and yet we know that the stormy tyrant of the Turk's Head Tavern was not serene. Carlyle was genuine (though that is not quite the *first* adjective we should choose to describe him), but of serenity he allowed cooks and cocks and every modern and every ancient sham to deprive him. Serenity is a product, no doubt, of two very different things, namely, vision and digestion. Not the eye only, but the courses of the blood must be clear, if we would find serenity. . . .

So far is serenity from being a thing of slackness or inaction that it seems bred, rather, by an equable energy, a satisfying activity. It may be found in the midst of that alert interest in affairs which is, it may be, the distinguishing trait of developed manhood. You distinguish man from the brute by his intelligent curiosity, his play of mind beyond the narrow field of instinct, his perception of cause and effect in matters to him indifferent, his appreciation of motive and calculation of results. He is interested in the world about him, and even in the great universe of which it forms a part, not merely as a thing he would use, satisfy his wants and grow great by, but as a field to stretch his mind in, for love of journeyings and excursions in the large realm of thought. Your full-bred human being loves a run afield with his understanding. With what images does he not surround himself and store his mind! With what fondness does he con travelers' tales and credit poets' fancies! With what patience does he follow science and pore upon old records, and with what eagerness does he ask the news of the day! No great part of what he learns immediately touches his own life or the course of his own affairs; he is not pursuing a business, but satisfying as he can an insatiable mind. . . .

To Emancipate Men from Narrowness

Luckily we are not the first human beings. We have come into a great heritage of interesting things, collected and piled all about us by the curiosity of past generations. And so our interest is selective. Our education consists in learning intelligent choice. Our energies do not clash or compete: each is free to take his own path to knowledge. Each has that choice, which is man's alone, of the life he shall live, and finds out first or last that the art in living is not only to be genuine and one's own master, but also to learn mastery in perception and preference. . . .

That man seems to me a little less than human who lives as if our life in the world were but just begun, thinking only of the things of sense, reckoning nothing of the infinite thronging and assemblage of affairs the great stage over, or of the old wisdom that has ruled the world. That is, if he have the choice. Great masses of our fellow-men are shut out from choosing, by reason of absorbing toil, and it is part of the enlightenment of our age that our understandings are being opened to the workingman's need of a little leisure wherein to look about him and clear his vision of the dust of the workshop. We know that there is a drudgery which is inhuman, let it but encompass the whole life, with only heavy sleep between task and task. We know that those who are so bound can have no freedom to be men, that their very spirits are in bondage. It is part of our philanthropy—it should be part of our statesmanship—to ease the burden as we can, and enfranchise those who spend and are spent for the sustenance of the race. But what shall we say of those who are free and yet choose littleness and bondage, or of those who, though they might see the whole face of society, nevertheless choose to spend all a life's space poring upon some single vice or blemish? . . .

Knowledge has come into the world in vain if it is not to emancipate those who may have it from narrowness, censoriousness, fussiness, an intemperate zeal for petty things. It would be a most pleasant, a truly humane world, would we but open our ears with a more generous welcome to the clear voices that ring in those writings upon life and affairs which mankind has chosen to keep. Not many splenetic books, not many intemperate, not many bigoted, have kept men's confidence; and the mind that is impatient, or intolerant, or hoodwinked, or shut in to a petty view shall have no part in carrying men forward to a true humanity, shall never stand as examples of the true humankind. What is truly human has always upon it the broad light of what is genial, fit to support life, cordial, and of a catholic spirit of helpfulness. . . .

When you talk with a man who has in his nature and acquirements that freedom from constraint which goes with the full franchise of humanity, he turns easily from topic to topic; does not fall silent or dull when you leave some single field of thought such as unwise men make a prison of. The men who will not be broken from a little set of subjects, who talk earnestly, hotly, with a sort of fierceness, of certain special schemes of conduct, and look coldly upon everything else, render you infinitely uneasy, as if there were in them a force abnormal and which rocked toward an upset of the mind; but from the man whose interest swings from thought to thought with the zest and poise and pleasure of the old traveler, eager for what is new, glad to look again upon what is old, you come away with faculties warmed and heartened—with the feeling of having been comrade for a little with a genuine human being. It is a large world and a round world, and men grow human by seeing all its play of force and folly.

An Age That Calls for the Human Quality

This new day in which we live cries a challenge to us. Steam and electricity have reduced nations to neighborhoods; have made travel pastime, and news a thing for everybody. Cheap printing has made knowledge a vulgar commodity. Our eyes look, almost without choice, upon the very world itself, and the word "human" is filled with a new meaning. Our ideals broaden to suit the wide day in which we live. We crave, not cloistered virtue—it is impossible any longer to keep to the cloister—but a robust spirit that shall take the air in the great world, know men in all their kinds, choose its way amid the bustle with all self-possession, with wise genuineness, in calmness, and yet with the quick eye of interest and the quick pulse of power.

It is again a day for Shakespeare's spirit—a day more various, more ardent, more provoking to valor and every large design, even than "the spacious times of great Elizabeth," when all the world seemed new; and if we cannot find another bard, come out of a new Warwickshire, to hold once more the mirror up to nature, it will not be because the stage is not set for him. The time is such an one as he might rejoice to look upon; and if we would serve it as it should be served, we should seek to be human after this wide-eyed sort. . . .

We live for our own age—an age like Shakespeare's, when an old world is passing away, a new world coming in—an age of new speculation and every new adventure of the mind; a full stage, an intricate plot, a universal play of passion, an outcome no man can foresee.

It is to this world, this sweep of action, that our understandings must be stretched and fitted; it is in this age we must show our human quality. We must measure ourselves by the task, accept the pace set for us, make shift to know what we are about. How free and liberal should be the scale of our sympathy, how catholic our understanding of the world in which we live, how poised and masterful our action in the midst of so great affairs! We should school our ears to know the voices that are genuine, our thought to take the truth when it is spoken, our spirits to feel the zest of the day. It is within our choice to be with mean company or with great, to consort with the wise or with the foolish, now that the great world has spoken to us in the literature of all tongues and voices. The best selected human nature will tell in the making of the future, and the art of being human is the art of freedom and of force.

"CENTURY MAGAZINE,"
JUNE 1901

A Healthy Process of Disillusionment

It is a very wholesome and regenerating change which a man undergoes when he "comes to himself." It is not only after periods of recklessness or infatuation, when he has played the spendthrift

or the fool, that a man comes to himself. He comes to himself after
experiences of which he alone may be aware: when he has left off
being wholly preoccupied with his own powers and interests and
with every petty plan that centers in himself; when he has cleared
his eyes to see the world as it is, and his own true place and function in it.

It is a process of disillusionment. The scales have fallen away. He
sees himself soberly, and knows under what conditions his powers
must act, as well as what his powers are. He has got rid of earlier
prepossessions about the world of men and affairs, both those which
were too favorable and those which were too unfavorable—both
those of the nursery and those of a young man's reading. He has
learned his own paces, or, at any rate, is in a fair way to learn them;
has found his footing and the true nature of the "going" he must
look for in the world; over what sorts of roads he must expect to
make his running, and at what expenditure of effort; whither his
goal lies, and what cheer he may expect by the way. It is a process
of disillusionment, but it disheartens no soundly made man. It
brings him into a light which guides instead of deceiving him; a
light which does not make the way look cold to any man whose
eyes are fit for use in the open, but which shines wholesomely,
rather upon the obvious path, like the honest rays of the frank sun,
and makes traveling both safe and cheerful.

The Part a Man Plays Among His Fellows

There is no fixed time in a man's life at which he comes to himself, and some men never come to themselves at all. It is a change
reserved for the thoroughly sane and healthy, and for those who
can detach themselves from tasks and drudgery long and often
enough to get, at any rate once and again, a view of the proportions
of life and of the stage and plot of its action. We speak often with
amusement, sometimes with distaste and uneasiness, of men who
"have no sense of humor," who take themselves too seriously, who
are intense, self-absorbed, over-confident in matters of opinion, or
else go plumed with conceit, proud of we cannot tell what, enjoying, appreciating, thinking of nothing so much as themselves. These

are men who have not suffered that wholesome change. They have not come to themselves. If they be serious men, and real forces in the world, we may conclude that they have been too much and too long absorbed; that their tasks and responsibilities long ago rose about them like a flood, and have kept them swimming with sturdy stroke the years through, their eyes level with the troubled surface— no horizon in sight, no passing fleets, no comrades but those who struggled in the flood like themselves. If they be frivolous, light-headed, men without purpose or achievement, we may conjecture, if we do not know, that they were born so, or spoiled by fortune, or befuddled by self-indulgence. It is no great matter what we think of them.

It is enough to know that there are some laws which govern a man's awakening to know himself and the right part to play. A man is the part he plays among his fellows. He is not isolated; he cannot be. His life is made up of the relations he bears to others—is made or marred by those relations, guided by them, judged by them, expressed in them. There is nothing else upon which he can spend his spirit—nothing else that we can see. It is by these he gets his spiritual growth; it is by these we see his character revealed, his purpose, and his gifts. Some play with a certain natural passion, an unstudied directness, without grace, without modulation, with no study of the masters or consciousness of the pervading spirit of the plot; others give all their thought to their costume and think only of the audience; a few act as those who have mastered the secrets of a serious art, with deliberate subordination of themselves to the great end and motive of the play, spending themselves like good servants, indulging no wilfulness, obtruding no eccentricity, lending heart and tone and gesture to the perfect progress of the action. These have "found themselves," and have all the ease of a perfect adjustment.

Adjustment is exactly what a man gains when he comes to himself. Some men gain it late, some early; some get it all at once, as if by one distinct act of deliberate accommodation; others get it by degrees and quite imperceptibly. No doubt to most men it comes by the slow processes of experience—at each stage of life a little. A college man feels the first shock of it at graduation, when the boy's life has been lived out and the man's life suddenly begins. He has measured himself with boys; he knows their code and feels the spur of their ideals of achievement. But what the world expects of him he has yet to find out, and it works, when he has discovered it, a veritable revolution in his ways both of thought and of action. He finds a new sort of fitness demanded of him, executive, thorough-going, careful of details, full of drudgery and obedience to orders. Everybody is ahead of him. Just now he was a senior, at the top of a world he knew and reigned in, a finished product and pattern of good form. Of a sudden he is a novice again, as green as in his first school year, studying a thing that seems to have no rules—at sea amid crosswinds, and a bit seasick withal. Presently, if he be made of stuff that will shake into shape and fitness, he settles to his tasks and is comfortable. He has come to himself: understands what capacity is, and what it is meant for; sees that his training was not for ornament or personal gratification, but to teach him how to use himself and develop faculties worth using. Henceforth there is a zest in action, and he loves to see his strokes tell.

The same thing happens to the lad come from the farm into the city, a big and novel field, where crowds rush and jostle, and a rustic boy must stand puzzled for a little how to use his placid and un-jaded strength. It happens, too, though in a deeper and more subtle way, to the man who marries for love, if the love be true and fit for foul weather. Mr. Bagehot used to say that a bachelor was "an amateur in life," and wit and wisdom are married in the jest. A man who lives only for himself has not begun to live—has yet to learn his use, and his real pleasure, too, in the world. It is not neces-sary he should marry to find himself out, but it is necessary he should love. Men have come to themselves serving their mothers with an unselfish devotion, or their sisters, or a cause for whose sake they forsook ease and left off thinking of themselves. It is unselfish action growing slowly into the high habit of devotion, and at last, it may be, into a sort of consecration, that teaches a man the wide meaning of his life, and makes of him a steady professional in living, if the motive be not necessity, but love. Necessity may make a mere drudge of a man, and no mere drudge ever made a professional of himself; that demands a higher spirit and a finer incentive than his.

A Man's Powers Must Begin to Play Outward

Surely a man has come to himself only when he has found the best that is in him, and has satisfied his heart with the highest achievement he is fit for. It is only then that he knows of what he is capable and what his heart demands. And, assuredly, no thoughtful man ever came to the end of his life, and had time and a little space of calm from which to look back upon it, who did not know and acknowledge that it was what he had done unselfishly and for others, and nothing else, that satisfied him in the retrospect, and made him feel that he had played the man. That alone seems to him the real measure of himself, the real standard of his manhood. And so men grow by having responsibility laid upon them, the burden of other people's business. Their powers are put out at interest, and they get usury in kind. They are like men multiplied. Each counts manifold. Men who live with an eye only upon what is their own are dwarfed beside them—seem fractions while they are integers. The trustworthiness of men trusted seems often to grow with the trust.

It is for this reason that men are in love with power and greatness: it affords them so pleasurable an expansion of faculty, so large a run for their minds, an exercise of spirit so various and refreshing; they have the freedom of so wide a tract of the world of affairs. But if they use power only for their own ends, if there be no unselfish service in it, if its object be only their personal aggrandizement, their love to see other men tools in their hands, they go out of the world small, disquieted, beggared, no enlargement of soul vouchsafed them, no usury of satisfaction. They have added nothing to themselves. Mental and physical powers alike grow by use, as every one knows; but labor for oneself alone is like exercise in a gymnasium. No healthy man can remain satisfied with it, or regard it as anything but a preparation for tasks in the open, amid the affairs of the world—not sport, but business—where there is no orderly apparatus, and every man must devise the means by which he is to make the most of himself. To make the most of himself means the multiplication of his activities, and he must turn away from himself for that. He looks about him, studies the face of business or of affairs, catches some intimation of their larger objects, is guided by the intimation, and presently finds himself part of the motive force of communities or of nations. It makes no difference how small a part, how insignificant, how unnoticed. When his powers begin to play outward, and he loves the task at hand, not because it gains him a livelihood, but because it makes him a life, he has come to himself.

Necessity is no mother to enthusiasm. Necessity carries a whip. Its method is compulsion, not love. It has no thought to make itself attractive; it is content to drive. Enthusiasm comes with the revelation of true and satisfying objects of devotion; and it is enthusiasm that sets the powers free. It is a sort of enlightenment. It shines straight upon ideals, and for those who see it the race and struggle are henceforth toward these. An instance will point the meaning. One of the most distinguished and most justly honored of our great philanthropists spent the major part of his life absolutely absorbed in the making of money—so it seemed to those who did not know him. In fact, he had very early passed the stage at which he looked upon his business as a means of support or of material comfort. Business had become for him an intellectual pursuit, a study in enterprise and increment. The field of commerce lay before him like a chess-board; the moves interested him like the manœuvers of a game. More money was more power, a greater advantage in the game, the means of shaping men and events and markets to his own ends and uses. It was his will that set fleets afloat and determined the havens they were bound for; it was his foresight that brought goods to market at the right time; it was his suggestion that made the industry of unthinking men efficacious; his sagacity saw itself justified at home not only, but at the ends of the earth. And as the money poured in, his government and mastery increased, and his mind was the more satisfied. It is so that men make little kingdoms for themselves, and an international power undarkened by diplomacy, undirected by parliaments.

The Life of Society Is the Spur to Maturity

It was once fashionable—and that not a very long time ago—to speak of political society with a certain distaste, as a necessary evil, an irritating but inevitable restriction upon the "natural" sovereignty and entire self-government of the individual. That was the dream of the egotist. It was a theory in which men were seen to strut in the proud consciousness of their several and "absolute" capacities. It would be as instructive as it would be difficult to count the errors it has bred in political thinking. As a matter of fact, men have never dreamed of wishing to do without the "trammels" of organized society, for the very good reason that those trammels are in reality no trammels at all, but indispensable aids and spurs to the attainment of the highest and most enjoyable things man is capable of. Political society, the life of men in states, is an abiding natural relationship. It is neither a mere convenience nor a mere necessity. It is not a mere voluntary association, not a mere corporation. It is nothing deliberate or artificial, devised for a special purpose. It is in real truth the eternal and natural expression and embodiment of a form of life higher than that of the individual—that common life of mutual helpfulness, stimulation, and contest which gives leave and opportunity to the individual life, makes it possible, makes it full and complete.

It is in such a scene that man looks about to discover his own place and force. In the midst of men organized, infinitely cross-related, bound by ties of interest, hope, affection, subject to authorities, to opinion, to passion, to visions and desires which no man can reckon, he casts eagerly about to find where he may enter in with the rest and be a man among his fellows. In making his place he finds, if he seek intelligently and with eyes that see, more than ease of spirit and scope for his mind. He finds himself—as if mists had cleared away about him and he knew at last his neighborhood among men and tasks.

What every man seeks is satisfaction. He deceives himself so long as he imagines it to lie in self-indulgence, so long as he deems himself the center and object of effort. His mind is spent in vain upon itself. Not in action itself, not in "pleasure," shall it find its desires satisfied, but in consciousness of right, of powers greatly and nobly spent. It comes to know itself in the motives which satisfy it, in the zest and power of rectitude. Christianity has liberated the world, not as a system of ethics, not as a philosophy of altruism, but by its revelation of the power of pure and unselfish love. Its vital principle is not its code, but its motive. Love, clear-sighted, loyal, personal, is its breath and immortality. Christ came, not to save Himself, assuredly, but to save the world. His motive, His example, are every man's key to his own gifts and happiness. The ethical code he taught may no doubt be matched, here a piece and there a piece, out of other religions, other teachings and philosophies. Every thoughtful man born with a conscience must know a code of right and of pity to which he ought to conform; but without the motive of Christianity, without love, he may be the purest altruist and yet be as sad and as unsatisfied as Marcus Aurelius.

Christianity gave us, in the fullness of time, the perfect image of right living, the secret of social and of individual well-being; for the two are not separable, and the man who receives and verifies that secret in his own living has discovered not only the best and only way to serve the world, but also the one happy way to satisfy himself. Then, indeed, has he come to himself. Henceforth he knows what his powers mean, what spiritual air they breathe, what ardors of service clear them of lethargy, relieve them of all sense of effort, put them at their best. After this fretfulness passes away, experience mellows and strengthens and makes more fit, and old age brings, not senility, not satiety, not regret, but higher hope and serene maturity.

ADDRESS AT THE UNIVERSITY OF TENNESSEE,
KNOXVILLE, JUNE 17, 1890

The Leader of Men Sees But One Side

The true leader of men is equipped by lacking certain sensibilities which the literary man, when analyzed, is found to have as a chief part of his make-up. He lacks that subtle power of sympathy that enables the men who write the great works of the imagination to put their minds under the spell of a thousand motives not their own but the living force in those whom they interpret. He could not write fiction. He could not conceive *The Ring and the Book*—the impersonation of a half score points of view. An imaginative realization of other natures and minds than his own is as impossible for him as his own commanding, dominating frame of mind and character are impossible for the sensitive seer whose imagination can give life to a thousand characters. Mr. Browning could no more be a statesman—if statesmen are to be popular leaders also—than Mr. Disraeli could write a novel. Mr. Browning can see from everybody's point of view—no intellectual sympathy comes amiss to him: Mr. Disraeli can see from no point of view but his own—and the characters he put in those works of his which were meant to be novels move as puppets to his will, as the men he governed did. They are his mouth-pieces—as little like themselves as were the Tory squires in the Commons like themselves after they became his chess-men.

One of the most interesting and suggestive criticisms made upon Mr. Gladstone's leadership during the life of his ministries was that he was not decisive in the House of Commons as Palmerston and Peel had been before him. He could not help seeing two sides of a question: the force of objections evidently told upon him, and his conclusions seemed the result of a nice balance of considerations, not the command of an unhesitating conviction. A party likes to be led by very absolute opinions: it chills it to hear it admitted that there is some reason on the other side. Mr. Peel saw both sides of some questions; but he never saw them both at once. He saw now one, and afterwards, by slow, honest conversion, the others. Mr. Gladstone's transparent honesty adds to his moral weight with the people as a leader of opposition, for in opposition only the whole attitude is significant. Particulars of position and policy tell upon a governing party, on the other hand, and for them the consistency of unhesitating opinion counts as an element of success and prestige.

That the leader of men must have such sympathetic insight as shall enable him to know quite unerringly the motives which move other men in the mass is of course self-evident; but this insight which he must have is not the Shakespearean insight. It need not pierce the particular secrets of individual men: it need only know what it is that lies waiting to be stirred in the minds and purposes of groups and masses of men. Besides it is not a sympathy that serves, but is a sympathy whose power is to command, to command by knowing its instrument.

The competent leader of men cares little for the interior niceties of other people's characters: he cares much—everything—for the external uses to which they may be put. His will seeks the lines of least resistance; but the whole question with him is a question as to the application of force. There are men to be moved: how shall he move them? He supplies the power; others supply only the materials upon which that power operates. The power will fail if it be misapplied; it will be misapplied if it be not suitable both in its character and in its method to the nature of the materials upon which it is spent; but that nature is, after all, only its means. It is the power which dictates, dominates; the materials yield. Men are as clay in the hands of the consummate leader.

The Style That Influences the Present Generation

Style has of course a great deal to do with such effects in popular oratory. Armies do not win battles by sword-fencing, but by the fierce cut of the sabre, the direct volley of musketry, the straightforward argument of artillery, the impetuous dash of cavalry. And it is in the same way that oratorical battles are won: not by the nice refinements of statement, the deft sword-play of dialectic fence, but by the straight and speedy thrusts of speech sent through and through the gross and obvious frame of a subject. It must be clear and always clear what the sentences would be about. They must be advanced with the firm tread of disciplined march. Their meaning must be clear and loud.

Men are not led by being told what they don't know. Persuasion is a force, but not information; and persuasion is accomplished by creeping into the confidence of those you would lead. Their confidence is gained by qualities which they can recognize, by arguments which they can assimilate: by the things which find easy entrance into their minds and are easily transmitted to the palms of their hands or the ends of their walking-sticks in the shape of applause. Burke's thoughts penetrate the mind and possess the heart of the quiet student; his style of saying things fills the attention as if it were finest music; but they are not thoughts to be shouted over; it is not a style to ravish the ear of the voter at the hustings. If you would be a leader of men, you must lead your own generation, not the next. Your playing must be good now, while the play is on the boards and the audience in the seats: it will not get you the repute of a great actor to have excellences discovered in you afterwards. . . .

"Burke is a wise man," said Fox, "but he is wise too soon." He was wise also too much. He went on from the wisdom of to-day to the wisdom of to-morrow, to the wisdom which is for all time: and it was impossible he should be followed so far. Men want the wisdom which they are expected to apply to be obvious and conveniently limited in amount. They want a thoroughly reliable article, with very simple adjustments and manifest present uses. Elaborate it—increase the expenditure of thought necessary to obtain it—and they will decline to listen to any propositions concerning it. You must keep it in stock for the use of the next generation.

All Growth a Matter of Compromise

Society is not a crowd, but an organism; and, like every organism, it must grow as a whole or else be deformed. The world is agreed, too, that it is an organism also in this, that it will die unless it be vital in every part. That is the only line of reasoning by which we can really establish the majority in legitimate authority. This organic whole, Society, is made up, obviously, for the most part, of the majority. It grows by the development of its aptitudes and desires, and under their guidance. The evolution of its institutions must take place by slow modification and nice all-round adjustment. And all this is but a careful and abstract way of saying that no reform may succeed for which the major thought of the nation is not prepared: that the instructed few may not be safe leaders, except insofar as they have communicated their instructions to the many, except as they have transmuted their thought into a common, a popular thought. . . .

In no case may we safely hurry the organism away from its habit: for it is held together by that habit, and by it is enabled to perform its functions completely. The constituent habit of a people inheres in its thought, and to that thought legislation—even the legislation that advances and modifies habit—must keep very near. The ear of the leader must ring with the voices of the people. He cannot be of the school of the prophets; he must be of the number of those who studiously serve the slow-paced daily need.

In what, then, does political leadership consist? It is leadership in conduct, and leadership in conduct must discern and strengthen the tendencies that make for development. The legislative leader must perceive the direction of the nation's permanent forces and must feel the speed of their operation. There is initiative here, but not novelty; there are old thoughts, but a progressive application of them. . . .

Practical leadership may not beckon to the slow masses of men from beyond some dim, unexplored space or some intervening chasm: it must daily feel the road that leads to the goal proposed, knowing that it is a slow, a very slow, evolution to wings, and that for the present, and for a very long future also, Society must walk, dependent upon practical paths, incapable of scaling sudden, precipitous heights, a road-breaker, not a fowl of the air. In the words of the Master, Burke, "to follow, not to force, the public inclination—to give a direction, a form, a technical dress, and a specific sanction, to the general sense of the community, is the true end of legislation." That general sense of the community may wait to be aroused, and the statesman must arouse it; may be inchoate and vague, and the statesman must formulate and make it explicit. But he cannot and should not, do more. The forces of the public thought may be blind: he must lend them sight; they may blunder: he must set them right. He can do something to create such forces of opinion; but it is a creation of forms, not of substance, and without such forces at his back he can do nothing effective. . . .

You may say that if all this be truth: if practical political thought may not run in straight lines, but must twist and turn through all the sinuous paths of various circumstance, then compromise is the true gospel of politics. I cannot wholly gainsay the proposition. But it depends almost altogether upon how you conceive and define compromise whether it seem hateful or not—whether it be hateful or not. I understand the biologists to say that all growth is a process of compromise: a compromise of the vital forces within the organism with the physical forces without, which constitute its environment. Yet growth is not dishonest. Neither need compromise in politics be dishonest—if only it be progressive. Is not compromise the law of Society in all things? Do we not in all dealings adjust views, compound differences, placate antagonisms? Uncompromising thought is the luxury of the closeted recluse. Untrammeled reasoning is the indulgence of the philosopher, of the dreamer of sweet dreams. We make always a sharp distinction between the literature of conduct and the literature of the imagination. "Poetic justice" we recognize as being quite out of the common run of experience.

Nevertheless, leadership does not always wear the harness of compromise. Once and again one of those great Influences which we call a Cause arises in the midst of the nation. Men of strenuous minds and high ideals come forward with a sort of gentle majesty as champions of a political or moral principle. They wear no armour; they bestride no chargers; they only speak their thought, in season and out of season. But the attacks they sustain are more cruel than the collisions of arms. Their souls are pierced with a thousand keen arrows of obloquy. Friends desert and despise them. They stand alone: and oftentimes are made bitter by their isolation. They are doing nothing less than defy public opinion, and shall they convert it by blows? Yet, presently the forces of the popular thought hesitate, waver, seem to doubt their power to subdue a half score stubborn minds. Again a little while and they have yielded. Masses come over to the side of the reform. Resistance is left to the minority and such as will not be converted are crushed. . . .

No cause is born out of its time. Every successful reform movement has had as its efficient cry some principle of equity or morality already accepted well-nigh universally, but not yet universally applied in the affairs of life. Every such movement has been the awakening of a people to see a new field for old principles. These men who stood alone at the inception of the movement and whose voices then seemed as it were the voices of men crying in the wilderness, have in reality been simply the more sensitive organs of Society—the parts first awakened to consciousness of a situation. With the start and irritation of a rude and sudden summons from sleep, Society resents the disturbance of its restful unconsciousness, and for a moment racks itself with hasty passion. But, once get it completely aroused, it will sanely meet the necessities of conduct revealed by the hour of its awakening.

Great reformers do not, indeed, observe times and circumstances. Theirs is not a service of opportunity. They have no thought for occasion, no capacity for compromise. But they are none the less produced by occasions. They are early vehicles of the Spirit of the Age. They are born of the very times that oppose them: their success is the acknowledgment of their legitimacy.

The Leader in a Complex Society

What a lesson it is in the organic wholeness of Society, this study of leadership! How subtle and delicate is the growth of the organism, and how difficult initiative in it! Where is rashness? It is excluded. And raw invention? It is discredited. How, as we look about us into the great maze of Society, see its solidarity, its complexity, its restless forces surging amidst its delicate tissues, its hazards and its exalted hopes—how can we but be filled with awe! Many are the functions that enter into its quick unresting life. There is the lonely seer, seeking the truths that shall stand permanent and endure; the poet, tracing all perfected lines of beauty, sounding full-voiced all notes of love or hope, of duty or gladness; the toilers in the world's massy stuffs, moulders of metals, forgers of steel, refiners of gold; there are the winds of commerce, the errors and despairs of war; the old things and the new: the vast things that dominate and the small things that constitute the world; passions of men, loves of women; the things that are visible and which pass away and the things which are invisible and eternal. And in the midst of all stands the leader, gathering, as best he can, the thoughts that are completed—that are perceived—that have told upon the common mind; judging also of the work that is now at length ready to be completed; reckoning the gathered gain; perceiving the fruits of toil and of war—and combining all these into words of progress, into acts of recognition and completion. Who shall say that this is not an exalted function? Who shall doubt or dispraise the title of leadership?

Shall we wonder, either, if the leader be a man open at all points to all men, ready to break into coarse laughter with the Rabelaisian vulgar; ready also to prose with the moralist and the reformer; with an eye of tolerance and shrewd appreciation for life of every mode and degree; a sort of sensitive dial registering all forces that move upon the face of Society? I do not conceive the leader a trimmer, weak to yield what clamour claims, but the deeply human man, quick to know and to do the things that the hour and his nation need.

Chapter Four

UNDER A HIGHER JUDGMENT

WILSON'S individualism, at the core of his political philosophy, rested firmly on religious grounds. The selections in this chapter show the source of much that is striking, and often puzzling, in his statesmanship. The religious man, in Wilson's view, possessed a standard of righteousness derived directly from Christ; he moved with the absoluteness of conviction but at the same time with the constant sense of being subject to a higher judgment than his own. The Christian church was not concerned with improving society but with fortifying in men this awareness of their relations with God. Wilson gave expression to this faith in addresses at religious convocations, in talks to the Princeton students, and (as the last selection in this chapter shows) as he turned aside momentarily from the preoccupations of day-to-day politics.

ADDRESS BEFORE THE MCCORMICK THEOLOGICAL
SEMINARY AT CHICAGO, NOVEMBER 2, 1909

The Role of Christianity in the World

Christianity did not come into the world merely to save the world, merely to set crooked things straight, merely to purify social motives, merely to elevate the programme according to which we live, merely to put new illuminations into the plans we form for the regeneration of the life we are living now. The end and object of Christianity is the individual, and the individual is the vehicle of Christianity. There can be no other vehicle; no organization is in any proper sense Christian; no organization can be said itself to love the person and example of Christ. No organization can hold itself in that personal relationship to the Saviour in which the individual

78

must hold himself if he would be indeed one who lives according to the Christian precepts.

You know what the distinguishing characteristic of modern society is, that it has submerged the individual as much as that is possible. In economic society particularly we see men organized in great societies and corporations and organic groups, in which each individual member feels that his own conscience is pooled and subordinated, and in coöperating with which men, as you know, constantly excuse themselves from the exercise of their own independent judgment in matters of conscience. The great danger of our own day, as it seems to me, is that men will compound their conscientious scruples on the ground that they are not free to move independently; that they are simply parts of a great whole, and that they must move with that whole, whether they wish to or not.

For they say, "The penalty will be that we shall be absolutely crushed." The organization must dictate to us, if we be members of a corporation; if we be members of a union, the union; if we be members of a society of whatever kind, the programme of the society must dominate us. It was easy in a simpler age to apply morals to individual conduct, because individuals acted separately and by a private and individual choice, but we have not adjusted our morals to the present organization of society; and whatever you may say in general terms with regard to the obligation of the individual to exercise his own conscience, you will find yourself very much put to it if a friend comes to you with an individual problem of conduct and asks you how in the circumstances you think he ought to act.

It sometimes seems like a choice between breaking up the programme of the organization and subordinating your own conscience. I have had men tell me who were in the profession to which I was originally bred—the profession of the law—that it is extremely difficult to thread their way amidst a thousand complicated difficulties in giving advice to the great bodies of men whom they are called upon to advise, and to discriminate between what is legally safe and what is morally justifiable.

It is in this age that the preacher must preach. The preacher must find the individual and enable the individual to find himself, and in order to do that he must understand and thread the intricacies of modern society. . . .

This is an age of obscured counsel about many fundamental things, and the average individual cannot unassisted know his place in the spiritual order of the universe as it is now interpreted by multitudinous and differing voices. The minister has the very difficult and responsible task of enabling the individual to find himself amidst modern thought. . . . It is also his business to enable the individual to find himself amid modern action. There are daily choices to be made, and the individual must make them at the risk of the integrity of his own soul. He must understand that he cannot shift the responsibility upon the organization. The minister must address himself to him as his counsellor and friend and spiritual companion; they must take counsel together how a man is to live with uplifted head and pure conscience in our own complicated age, not allowing the crowd to run away with or over him.

Every great age of the world of which I have ever heard was an age not characterized chiefly by coöperative effort, but characterized chiefly by the initiative of the indomitable individual. You cannot give any age distinction by the things that everybody does. Each age derives its distinction from the things that individuals choose to be singular in doing of their own choice. Every turning point in the history of mankind has been pivoted upon the choice of an individual, when some spirit that would not be dominated stood stiff in its independence and said: "I go this way. Let any man go another way who pleases."

We die separately. We do not die by corporations. We do not die by societies. We do not withdraw into our closets by companies. Every man has to live with himself privately—and it is a most uncomfortable life. He has to remember what he did during the day, the things that he yielded to, the points that he compromised, the things that he shrugged his shoulders at and let go by when he knew that he ought to have uttered a protest and stood stiff in declining to coöperate. And this lonely dying is the confession of our consciousness that we are individually and separately and personally related to the ideals which we pursue, and to the persons to whom we should stand loyal. Corporations do not and cannot love Christ. Some individuals that compose them do, but those individuals do not love him truly who coöperate in doing the things that those associated with them do that are inconsistent with the law of Christ.

The Minister Is Set Against Modern Society

I have often preached in my political utterances the doctrine of expediency, and I am an unabashed disciple of that doctrine. What I mean to say is, you cannot carry the world forward as fast as a few select individuals think. The individuals who have the vigour to lead must content themselves with a slackened pace and go only so fast as they can be followed. They must not be impracticable. They must not be impossible. They must not insist upon getting at once what they know they cannot get. But that is not inconsistent with their telling the world in very plain terms whither it is bound and what the ultimate and complete truth of the matter, as it seems to them, is. You cannot make any progress unless you know whither you are bound. . . .

Where the individual should be indomitable is in the choice of direction, saying: "I will not bow down to the golden calf of fashion. I will not bow down to the weak habit of pursuing everything that is popular, everything that belongs to the society to which I belong. I will insist on telling that society, if I think it so, that in certain fundamental principles it is wrong; but I won't be fool enough to insist that it adopt my programme at once for putting it right." What I do insist upon is, speaking the full truth to it and never letting it forget the truth; speaking the truth again and again and again with every variation of the theme, until men will wake some morning and the theme will sound familiar, and they will say, "Well, after all, is it not so?" That is what I mean by the indomitable individual. Not the defiant individual, not the impracticable individual, but the individual who does try, and cannot be ashamed, and cannot be silenced; who tries to observe the fair manner of just speech but who will not hold his tongue.

That is the duty of the preacher. I have noticed that there is one sort of preaching in simple congregations and sometimes a different sort of preaching in congregations that are not simple. Now there cannot be two gospels. There cannot be two ways in which individuals shall save themselves. And the minister ought to see to it that with infinite gentleness, but with absolute fearlessness, every man is made to conform to the standards which are set up in the gospel, even though it cost him his reputation, even though it cost him his friends, even though it cost him his life. Then will come that moral awakening which we have been so long predicting, and for which we have so long waited; that rejuvenation of morals which comes when morals are a fresh and personal and individual thing for every man and woman in every community; when the church will seem, not like an organization for the propagation of doctrine, but like an organization made up of individuals every one of whom is vital in the processes of life.

You will see, therefore, that there is a sense in which the minister is set against modern society. Modern society is collectivist. It says, "Unite." The minister must say, "Not so. You can unite for certain temporal purposes, but you cannot merge your souls; and Christianity, come what may, must be fundamentally and forever individualistic." For my part, I do not see any promise of vitality either in the church or in society except upon the true basis of individualism. A nation is strong in proportion to the variety of its originative strength, and that is in proportion to the vitality of its individuals. It is rich in direct proportion to the independence of the souls of which it is made up. And so every promising scheme that unites us must still be illuminated and checked and offset by those eternal principles of individual responsibility which are repeated not only in the gospel but in human nature, in physical nature.

You have loved some person very dearly. You have tried to merge your individuality with that person, and you have never succeeded. There is no person linked spiritually so closely to you that you can share his individuality or he can share yours. And this inexorable law, physical and spiritual, is the law which must be the guiding fact for the minister of the gospel. He must preach Christianity to men, not to society. He must preach salvation to the individual, for it is only one by one that we can love, and love is the law of life.

And the only person living through whom we shall love is our Lord and Saviour, Jesus Christ.

ADDRESS AT THE HARTFORD THEOLOGICAL
SEMINARY, HARTFORD, CONN., MAY 26, 1909

To Mediate Between Our Spirits and Our Knowledge

We live in an age when a particular thing cries out to be done which the minister must do, and there is no one else who can do it. There was a time, not many years ago, marked by an entirely different intellectual atmosphere. There was a time, which we can all remember, when men of science were content, were actually content, with a certain materialistic interpretation of the universe. Their antagonistic position with regard to spiritual matters was not a defiant position. It was a position of self-assurance and of self-content. They did not look into such matters, because they were convinced that it was vain to look into them, and that there was nothing that would come of their examination of the secret motives, of the secret springs of action among men, of the secret source of life in the world itself. But that time has gone by. Even men of science now feel that the explanation which they give of the universe is so partial an explanation, that for the benefit of their own thought—quite aside from the benefit of their own souls—it is necessary that something should be added to it. They know that there is a spiritual segment in the complete circle of knowledge which they cannot supply and which must be supplied if the whole circle is not to show its imperfection and incompleteness.

In connection with the administration of universities in our day there is an exceedingly interesting situation in the field of science. It used to be possible to draw sharp lines of division between the several fields of science. But it is no longer possible to do that. The science of physics can no longer establish a scientific frontier against the science of mathematics. The science of physics, on the other side, cannot determine with definiteness where its jurisdiction ends and the jurisdiction of chemistry begins. Chemistry, on its further borders, cannot clearly discriminate between its field and the field of organic biology. Biology knows that it shades off into that great historical biology that lies in the field of paleontology, recorded in the buried records of what the earth's surface contains. And all of these sciences are aware that, linked as they thus are together, they must have some common principle and explanation; that we cannot stop at any frontier; that the domain of knowledge, like the globe itself, is round and there is no stopping place; that what we have to do is to complete, at whatever cost, the map of knowledge, to press onward into the field where lie the unknown things both of physical knowledge and of spiritual knowledge.

We are in the presence of the absolute necessity of a spiritual coördination of the masses of knowledge which we have piled up and which we have partially explained, and the whole world waits for that vast task of intellectual mediation to be performed. Who shall mediate between our spirits and our knowledge? Who shall show our souls the tracks of life? Who shall be our guides, to tell us how we shall thread this intricate plan of the universe and connect ourselves with the purpose for which it is made?

I do not know who is to tell us if not the minister. I do not know in whom these various bits of knowledge should center and bear fruit if not in him. The world offers this leadership, this intellectual mediation, to the minister of the Gospel. It is his if he be man enough to attempt it; man enough in his knowledge, man enough in the audacity and confidence of his spirit, man enough in the connections he has made with the eternal and everlasting forces which he knows to reside in the human spirit.

The Business of the Christian Church

I believe that we have erroneously conceived the field of the Christian Church in our age. If my observation does not mislead me, the Christian Church nowadays is tempted to think of itself as chiefly a philanthropic institution, chiefly an institution which shall supply the spiritual impulse which is necessary for carrying on those great enterprises which relieve the distress, distress of body and distress of mind, which so disturbs the world and so excites our pity, among those men particularly who have not had the advantages of fortune or of economic opportunity. And yet I believe that this is only a very small part of the business of the Church. The business of the Church is not to pity men. The business of the Church is not to rescue them from their suffering by the mere means of material relief, or even by the means of spiritual reassurance. The Church cannot afford to pity men, because it knows that men, if they would but take it, have the richest and completest inheritance that it is possible to conceive, and that, rather than being deserving of pity, they are to be challenged to assert in themselves those things which will make them independent of pity. No man who has recovered the integrity of his soul is any longer the object of pity, and it is to enable him to recover that lost integrity that the Christian Church is organized. To my thinking, the Christian Church stands at the center not only of philanthropy but at the center of education, at the center of science, at the center of philosophy, at the center of politics; in short, at the center of sentiment and thinking life. And the business of the Christian Church, of the Christian minister, is to show the spiritual relations of men to the great world processes, whether they be physical or spiritual. It is nothing less than to show the plan of life and men's relation to the plan of life.

Ask the majority of men why they go to church and, if you get the same answer that I get, you will get an answer something like this: that it is decent to go to church; that it is expected of them to go to church; moreover, that they have lived in that community, men and boys, a great many years, and their fathers and mothers went to the same churches before them; they like to maintain the moral traditions and the vague spiritual connections which go with the habit of attending church. Don't believe a word of it. It is a pure sham. Every man who is not absolutely dried up is kept alive by an inexhaustible well of sentiment. It is the fashion of our age to cover the well over with concrete so that you cannot even see or guess the gleam of the waters, but they are there, creeping up in the soil and maintaining all that produces living fruit.

What the minister has to do is to blast away these concrete covers and say to men "Here are the only sustaining waters of life, here is the rediscovery of your spirits." In that wise they must reveal God to men, reveal God to them in thought and in action, re-establish the spiritual kingdom among us, by proclaiming in season and out of season that there is no explanation for anything that is not first or last a spiritual explanation, and that man cannot live by bread alone, cannot live by scientific thought alone; that he is starving, and that digestion of this dry stuff that he takes into his mouth is not possible unless it be conveyed by the living water of the spirit.

I congratulate young men who are looking forward to the ministry that this is their high and difficult function in life. I beg them not to apologize for the Scripture to any man. I beg them not to explain it away in the presence of any audience, but to proclaim its sovereignty among men, the absolute necessity of the world to know these things if it would know itself. For it is a very significant matter, in my mind, that the Gospel came into the world to save the world as well as to save individual souls. There is one sense in which I have never had very much interest in the task of saving individual souls by merely advising them to run to cover. It has never seemed to me that the isolation of the human soul, its preservation from contamination such as the Middle Ages attempted, or any modern substitute for that, was graced with any dignity at all.

If men cannot lift their fellowmen in the process of saving themselves, I do not see that it is very important that they should save themselves, because they reduce Christianity by that means to the essence of selfishness, and anything that is touched with selfishness is very far removed from the spirit of Christianity. Christianity came into the world to save the world as well as to save individual men, and individual men can afford in conscience to be saved only as part of the process by which the world itself is regenerated. Do not go about, then, with the idea that you are picking out here and there a lost thing, but go about with the consciousness that you are setting afoot a process which will lift the whole level of the world and of modern life.

BACCALAUREATE ADDRESS, PRINCETON
UNIVERSITY, JUNE 7, 1908 *

Righteousness in Modern Life

Who is he that doeth righteousness in our modern life? You know what that modern life is. You have not been closeted in school

* Copyright © 1956 by Edith Bolling Wilson.

and college. You know, at least in some degree, what is going on about you. I shall not have to lay before you any elaborate picture of the world we now live in, as preface to my moral. Men do not choose their parts in life separately and individually in our day as they did in the days of our fathers. The men are becoming rare now who have businesses of their own, undertaken upon their own individual capital and built up and conducted independently upon their own responsibility. Professional men are rare who rise to the top of their professions without attaching themselves more or less intimately to institutions or corporations of some sort, doctors to hospitals, lawyers to great corporate undertakings, men of science to the great enterprises in which science is applied. Every affair of life takes on more and more the aspect and practice of wide organization; many men are drawn together in a common discipline and body; each man finds himself a small part of some great whole, whose operation is decided by votes taken about long tables in Directors' rooms, whose morals are composite morals, a compromise combination of what the material interests of the body dictate and what the enterprise of its managers suggests, the character of every man who participates being merged in the general compound.

Each man concerned feels the range of his own choice to be very narrow and is forced to be content with seeing questions of conscience either ignored or administered by commission. It is a composite world, and its standards are for the time being sadly confused by its attempt to compound its morals with its material ambitions, to set up composite notions of righteousness and disperse virtue through the intricacies of an elaborate organization. Moral judgments have never been simple: they have always been complicated by a thousand circumstances which puzzle the will; but they have never been quite so difficult and complicated as they are now. The primary moral difficulty of every man immersed in modern business is to find himself, to make sure of his own range and necessities of choice, know where he is legitimately a fraction and where he must insist upon being an integer, whole and indivisible.

This is our peculiar and fundamental moral problem; where and how to separate the individual from the mass, lift the individual soul out of the confusion and distraction of modern societies, unions, brotherhoods, leagues, alliances, corporations, and trusts into some clear place of vision, where it may think and see apart, looking beyond the things of the day to the things that abide. "Let no man deceive you: he that doeth righteousness is righteous."

And that is not the end of the matter, nor the whole of it. This thing that we call righteousness, this essential integrity of intention and of act, is not only the standard by which we shall ultimately be judged by others, by the world about us and the world that shall speak of us when we are gone: it is also the standard by which we shall judge ourselves, by which we shall get satisfaction or disappointment, the sweet or the bitter fruits of life, the energy that sets us free to assay the world or the subtle paralysis that ultimately ensues upon deceit and indirection. You will find that you cannot pool your consciences; you had better, then, not try to pool your morals. Keep your liberty in the one and you can afford to live with the other.

I am not suggesting to you a mere philosophy of happiness. My point is not that if you are not righteous you will not be happy, though that is true enough. The point lies deeper than that. I am not sure that it is of the first importance that you should be happy. Many an unhappy man has been of deep service to the world and to himself, has guided his fellow-men and exalted his own life,— many a man, I mean, who has not had what he wanted, who has lost what he loved, who has struggled through pain and disappointment and heart-breaking strain, that he might stand erect and see the light. The captains of the world's thought and stern endeavor have not often been debonnair figures, taking life like a happy holiday, their tasks like easy sport. As often as not they have wrought by agony of soul. Their joys have been in their triumphs over themselves.

And yet perhaps it is happiness that I would suggest as the reward of integrity and high endeavor, after all, but a greater, nobler, more elemental happiness than that which men ordinarily pursue, the happiness of satisfied powers and fortified souls.

Men Who Have Judged and Acted for Themselves

Look about you with candid eye and you shall find that the malady of the age is lack of individual courage, lack of individual integrity of thought and action. We need not speak of other countries or sweep a whole age into our generalization. Let us confine our view to our own day and our own country. What is the law of life in America now? Is it that every man should form his own moral judgments and speak them fearlessly, that every man should seek to govern his own life and square it with his own independent moral judgments? Of course there never has been a time or a society in which the individuals emerged from the mass in noticeable multitudes and the air was quick with active independence. . . .

Every age has need to have righteousness preached to it, and this age is not worse than those which have preceded it. It is better. But it is to be doubted if it is clearer-sighted, if to its astonishing knowledge and its careful sanitary cleanliness it has added virtue and moral insight and the clear judgments of conscience in the same degree. And that is because by its complex business and social organization it has encouraged the individual to run to cover, to burrow into some private place of interior management, to sit comfortably at some minor function and hold his private conscience aloof from the tasks and practices of the organization to which he belongs. We have facilitated a very subtle process, the process by which the individual separates what he calls his own life and conduct, his private character, from the life of the organization of which he forms a part, making himself a mere tool in the one thing and undertaking to be a moral agent only in the other. It will not do. No man is satisfied with the practice or holds his head very high in the presence of it, except by conscious histrionic effort. No man can cut his conscience into sections. Righteousness is of the individual heart, and the sound heart must have an inviolable integrity. If it be an age of organization, of intricate association, of business on the grand scale, of the temporary submergence of the individual and the consequent confusion of moral standards and codes of responsibility, there is all the more reason why every man should assert the rights of his own soul and recognize the compulsion of duty to find himself, to identify himself, to get a new release and liberty. . . .

No doubt business looks impersonal; but it is not so. And even if it were so, what release of conscience would that bring us? We judge ourselves singly, die with the flavor of but one career on our palates, are laid away in our graves by neighbors who have known the man, not the corporation of which he formed a part. And why do I speak only of the end? Do we judge ourselves only on our death beds? Do our neighbors assess us only at our funerals? Is the daily conduct of life not a daily process of judgment, the assessment of satisfaction or deep disappointment? And is not the daily conduct of life a thing wholly of individual contribution? What laws of nature govern our moral lives, except the laws operative in our own wills? Let every man find himself and see to the integrity of his own soul. "Let no man deceive you: he that doeth righteousness is righteous." And you are not to be deceived about yourselves any more than you are to be deceived about other men: only when you do righteousness are you righteous. It is a stern code, but it is the only sufficient one; and its stern definiteness makes many things clear.

Moreover, it is the code and principle which have lain at the heart of all history. Collectivism has always to be moralized by individualism. The church was purified by the Protestant Reformation, by the most radical of all assertions of the freedom of the individual soul, its right to determine its own responsibility and establish its own spiritual connections. The too much concentrated, the too inclusive and burdensome power of the State has always, when men have ventured to create it, in the long run been rectified by the revolt of the individual. It has always been the conscience of the individual that has kept the citadels of the church and made good the triumphs of liberty and political progress. Men who judged and acted for themselves have always been the rulers and arbiters of their time. And now once again comes the old challenge, renewed in new circumstances, in a new age which is our own and which we alone can understand and rectify.

True Righteousness Coming from Christ

The tendencies of our minds, the tendencies of our age, have affected alike our standards and our conduct. We have grown very "practical." We have seen the life about us and the life of which we form a part take on a certain organization in which men were, so to say, pooled and compounded, and enormous material energy, unexampled business efficiency have been the result. We have stood amazed, with a sort of childish delight, at the work of our own hands. Success upon the grand scale has meant power upon a scale unprecedented, the power of the individual and the power of the nation. The eyes of all the world have been turned upon us in uneasy wonder and admiration, with a touch of fear as well as of amazement. We have said, "Behold, it is a good thing. Look at its tremendous efficiency. It is the glory of America, of the practical American genius, the colossal success which has crowned all the rest that preceded it. What if the individual is submerged? That is the inevitable result of the system. It may be moralized, that is controlled, as a whole by law, but it would break down under the too great self-assertion of the individual." The moralist, not infatuated by the gross material results, can only reply: "Then it will inevitably break down."

The individual conscience has never in any age been successfully digested into the mass. It is insusceptible of absorption. It will reassert itself and the system will undergo radical transformation, a transformation as complete as may be necessary in order to release the individual and give him his liberty again. It is tedious that history should be obliged to repeat the process so often, but it will repeat it as often as necessary. Our present cynicism will not last, is not lasting. The tendency to be "practical" will not conquer the tendency to be moral. The great awakening we have just had to the moral aspects of so much of modern business is but the beginning of change. The moralist will dictate both to the lawyer and to the man of business.

It is a strange and interesting thing that in this very age in which we have become so intensely "practical" we have grown also exceedingly sentimental. And yet perhaps it was natural enough. Moral sentiment was driven out of the practical field; it therefore took refuge where it could, outside the field of business, amidst that fringe of habits and practices which had little or nothing to do with the work of the world. The moral sentiments are very robust and splendid forces when they work upon the real stuff of life, but when they potter about amongst private habits, when they attempt the rôle of mere sympathy and succour, excusing the criminal, petting the degenerate, and trying to save the individual by mere corporate protection, putting him in a nursery in which he can do nothing to please himself, they are in danger of becoming very ridiculous and very dangerous. Thoughtful philanthropy, manly and sensible help to those who have fallen either into vice or into misfortune, we all believe in with all our hearts, but not sentimental excuses for those who have done wrong. We all understand how much the individual is moulded by his environment, but we know also that he will not be rescued by the mere change of his environment and that, if the proper challenge be given his will, he can override his environment. The moral tonic of personal responsibility will save him. Mere sympathy will not.

There is no more subtle dissolvent of morals than sentimentality; and there is no more hopeless method of seeking to moralize an age than beginning at the edges. Go straight to the point. Put every individual, great and small, upon a stern probation. Let him not escape your judgment because he is unfortunate and well-meaning. Be just. Distinguish what is really unrighteous from what is not really unrighteous. Go to Christ for the abiding standards of moral judgment. Be sure that you allow the individual his real liberty to live truly and serve loyally. Do not impose your private judgments upon him; but within the limits of Christian justice judge inflexibly. Let standards be standards, not sliding scales that follow your sympathies. Judge men according to their essential character, but demand that they have some essential character to be judged, and be not time-servers.

After all, it is a search for standards. The interior meaning of the text of scripture upon which I have founded this last discourse of mine to you is that every man is deceived who supposes that he is righteous when his righteousness is not the righteousness of Christ. "Let no man deceive you: he that doeth righteousness is righteous, even as He is righteous,"—he who is the model for the mass and "singly of more value than they all." We go many a long way 'roundabout to moralize the world, while the true way is very direct. There all the while has stood the figure of Christ, exquisite in its simplicity, indisputable in its example, not insistent, thundering no command, simply lifted up, like the serpent in the wilderness, to draw all who will look upon him unto himself.

BACCALAUREATE ADDRESS, PRINCETON
UNIVERSITY, JUNE 13, 1909 *

The Pleasure That Is Beyond Duty

"Duty" is a very handsome word,—is a very handsome thing,—but let every man look to it that he comprehend what it really means. It conveys an obligation from within, not merely from without. We have not done our duty, we have not even earned our wages, when we have done merely that which we were obliged to do: we have done our duty only when we have done that which we know completes the service, when we have put the best which was in us into the task, our hearts into the bargain.

There is here a whole philosophy of life. The object, the standard, you set yourself works by a strange alchemy upon the whole spirit of your life. Set out to fulfil obligations, to do what you must and to exact of others what they owe you, and all your days alike will end in weariness of spirit. The road of life will be long and very dreary. There will be no zest in the movement of the day, no refreshment when the night comes and sleep lies heavy upon you. There is no pleasure to be had from the fulfilment of obligations, from yielding to compulsions, from doing what you know you ought to do. Nothing but what you volunteer has the essence of life, the springs of pleasure in it. These are the things you do because you want to do them, the things your spirit has chosen for its satisfaction. They are done with the free spirit of the adventurer. They are the inviting by-paths of life into which you go for discovery, to get off the dusty road of mere duty into cool meadows and shadowed glades where the scene is changed and the air seems full of the tonic of freedom. Your first volunteer service will be your first discovery of yourself, your first intimation of what your spirit is for. It will be your introduction alike into the world of pleasure and into the world of power.

I beg you to look very carefully and very curiously at the world you are about to enter before you enter it, and mark some of its characteristics. I mean the world of business and of the professions here in America. A great deal more light shines upon it now than shone upon it when you entered college. The air has been cleared for you that you might see. An almost unprecedented storm of accusation and inquiry has passed over it, and as the storm draws off it draws many vapours with it; the air grows very sharp and clear. Things stand out about us in very definite outline and evident proportion.

And this is what we see. We have just passed through an era in which men kept their legal obligations as well as usual and yet came near ruining the country, piled up wealth and forgot how to use it honourably, built up business and came near to debauching a nation. It is a very remarkable thing, and should be very interesting to the author of the text I am commenting upon. I need not remind you of the various abuses in the business world which recent legislation has been more or less unsuccessfully attempting to correct, of the vast combinations by which capitalists in this, that, and the other line of enterprise have sought to control the markets of the country, of the special favours the railways have granted to some of their shippers and the manifest injustice and ruin they have imposed on others, of the incalculable values, and lacks of value, given to securities in the stock market by methods of financial manipulation long in vogue unchecked, almost unheeded,—of the thousand and one ways in which what were thought to be the business interests of the country were pushed forward without regard to anything but the profit of those immediately concerned. That profit, stated in terms of wealth, was signally well served. What was intended was accomplished,—and with the results you know.

Unprofitable Servants

You have heard the whole story many times, and with many variations, true and false. What has not been sufficiently noticed and emphasized is, that most of those colossal processes of wealth which have now fallen under our condemnation were conducted by honest men who were keeping within the bounds of the law. There were rogues among them, of course, but no more than any age will show, and they were almost always rejected by their comrades when they were found to be rogues. The whole huge game, so far as its success was substantial and lasting, was an honest man's game; no crooks or blacklegs were wittingly admitted into it. Every man served his own particular interest with extraordinary intensity and devotion and with immense success, and could have told you with frank and steady eyes that he had done that which was his duty to do.

But what unprofitable servants they were,—unprofitable even to themselves and to the business enterprises they served. Many of those enterprises are for the time being discredited, their prosperity almost fatally checked by a universal distrust and suspicion, by hostile legislation, by arrested credit. Everything that for their sake should be steady has been thrown out of poise and balance. Their very success has been questionable, if you demand of success that it bring enjoyment and content with it. Success has a heart and you should look into it. It is often of lead, sometimes of gall, sometimes of dry pith, only sometimes a source of living joy.

No mere material object gained ever brought happiness. No man lives with his possessions. He lives with his thoughts, with his impulses, with his memories, his satisfactions, and his hope. I heard a distinguished man say very wisely, the other day, that we must divest ourselves of the idea that men have souls. They are souls. They have bodies, and their bodies have material needs which must be supplied. There are bodily pleasures which they may enjoy; but those pleasures will not satisfy them unless they convey to the soul intimations and confirmations of what it desires. They are the mere vehicles of satisfaction, and it is the man himself, the soul, that must be satisfied.

The men who brought disaster upon business by success brought it because they ran with blinders upon their eyes, saw only the immediate task under their hands, volunteered no look around, paid no call of thought or wish upon their fellow men, left statesmanship to politicians and public interests to the censors of public morals, attended wholly to their own business. The business of life is a bigger thing than they thought it. Only the far-seeing eyes are the eyes that descry the real fields of success, the ultimate paths of content and pleasure. . . .

It is always the same. Whatever you do, whatever comes from the natural fire kindled in you, whatever your spirit willingly undertakes and makes a satisfaction of, that is the thing which profits you. It at once contains and enriches your life. The more you are stimulated to such action the more clearly does it appear to you that you are a sovereign spirit, put into the world, not to wear harness, but to work eagerly without it. You will be a profitable servant indeed when once you have found yourself thus, but it will not be that which interests you. You will be satisfied, you will be loved, you will have life and have it abundantly.

BACCALAUREATE ADDRESS, PRINCETON
UNIVERSITY, JUNE 12, 1910 *

What Lies Behind All Knowledge

Princeton does not consist, has never consisted, of you and your classmates. Here men come and go, the men of her faculty and trustees as well as the men of her classes, but her force is not abated. She fails not of the impressions she makes. Her men are formed from generation to generation as if by a spirit that survives all persons and all circumstances. There is a sense, a very real sense, not mystical but plain fact of experience, in which the spirit of truth, of knowledge, of hope, of revelation, dwells in a place like this, as it were inevitably, unless it be wholly decayed or demoralized. It has made some things certain for you, permanently and beyond conjecture. It has not left your minds fluid, volatile, escaping all mould and form. There must be very few of you, if there be any, who have

* This was Wilson's last address as President of Princeton.

failed to get a definite undoubting grasp of some things that have here become certitudes for you. How could you feel at home here, else? How could you love a place that had left you groping and in the dark, the puzzled plaything of conjecture and blank surmise? Mere comradeships and pleasures cannot have satisfied you. You must have been fed upon something and been nourished.

I am not now thinking of knowledge so much as of what certainly underlies all knowledge. I do not mean merely that you have acquired certain definite information here which may serve you always as the material upon which your thought will feed. Information is no great matter. It changes from age to age, is often altered, and can be made to take a thousand shapes. I am thinking, rather, of what lies behind all knowledge, gives it colour, significance, variety. Science, for example, alters its allegations of fact from decade to decade, alters even its theories and hypotheses, but it does not alter its method. You feel that solid under your feet, do you not, as you have traversed it in the classroom and in the laboratory? It has made the world for you not a place for children and for ignorant guesses, but a place of definite ascertainable phenomena to be candidly and discerningly sought out and rationally explained by careful and clarified processes of reason. You know that the mind can be used as an instrument of precision and also as an instrument of definition when once it has mastered that thing of enlightenment, the method of science. There is one certitude for you. The physical world need not remain the realm of conjecture.

You are certain also, are you not, that there are definite comprehensible practices, immutable principles of government and of right conduct in the dealing of men with one another. The narratives, whether of history or of biography, are faulty, no doubt full of errors and of circumstances misapprehended, but you cannot doubt that the main lines are drawn with substantial accuracy and truth; you cannot be uncertain how it is that men come by happiness or failure; you are sure that there is such a thing as justice and a noble force in men who are righteous and love the truth; you perceive that some governments are free, some tyrannous and cruel, that there is a way of freedom and of peace and a way of servitude and strife in the affairs of men, and that it is all a rewarding study of human life in its realities, in its actual habit as it lives,—that you have looked in the face of life, very noble, very tragical, full at once of pathos and of hope.

And the literature you have studied and the philosophy you have read under wise masters—have they not yielded you something that you will not henceforth doubt? All the great books of any language are records of the human spirit, the voices of men like yourselves who speak to you the secrets of your own souls as well as theirs. You enter a wide comradeship when you read them. You are made free of the company of all men everywhere; as you are also in your study of philosophy, where is the same thing unfolded in orderly and formal fashion, with the insight of interpretation, as if life were read for you by men of science.

Surely you cannot be bewildered now. The world can no longer be to you a place of vague conjectures and childish ifs and buts, a play whose rules are guesses. And yet this is not information. This is not knowledge. You know very little. You are a good deal at sea in respect of your facts. You are glad your definite examinations are behind you. You have been made certain only of what sort of world it is you live in and how you should handle yourselves in it. The things you have been rendered certain of are intangible, but more actual, authentic, infallible than facts themselves. They represent the human spirit in command of the facts. They are the laws and masteries of the mind. They are the spiritual processes and realities by which we are made sure of life. Life is made definite and manageable by masteries and convictions, and these are what you have acquired, if you have acquired anything.

The Ultimate Knowledge Is of God

But what is the ultimate certainty? Is your certainty piecemeal and fragmentary? Have you learned only in disconnected segments? Education is a method of enlightenment concerning your relations to the material universe and to your fellow-men: has this brought you no confidence with regard to your relations to the God and Father of us all? Are you not more certain than ever that God is

in his Heaven? Is your spirit awakened to all these other perceptions of life and reality without being vouchsafed a glimpse of the
Father of Spirits? To know these other things that only implied
Him is life, to know Him is life eternal,—eternal because perfect,
stripped of its last doubt and uncertainty, given the very spirit of
vision.

I have read in your hearing this morning the 103rd Psalm. Did
it seem to you unreal and fanciful? Had it not, on the contrary, a
reality which you would be at a loss to find anywhere else in the
whole body of great songs men have conceived, unless perhaps in
some other Psalm which speaks the same confident meaning with
the same supreme conviction? When Paul stood upon Mars Hill
facing that Athenian crowd gathered about him in skeptical curiosity, did he tell them anything that seems to you incredible, a tale
of mere credulity and superstition? He did not hesitate to call the
ignorance of the Athenians' religion; was his religion not the religion
of certitude, of knowledge? "I perceive," he said, "that in all things
you are very religious. For as I passed by, and beheld your devotions,
I found an altar with this inscription, TO AN UNKNOWN GOD. Whom
therefore you ignorantly worship, Him declare I unto you, God that
made the world and all things therein, seeing that he is Lord of
heaven and earth, dwelleth not in temples made with hands; neither
is worshipped with man's hands, as though he needed anything,
seeing he giveth to all life, and breath, and all things; and hath
made of one blood all the nations of men for to dwell on all the
face of the earth, and hath determined the times before appointed,
and the bounds of their habitation; that they should seek the Lord,
if haply they might feel after Him, and find Him, though He be
not far from every one of us: for in Him we live, and move, and
have our being; as certain of your own poets have said, For we are
also his offspring."

We have an instinctive sympathy with and comprehension of
Paul as he stands there. His voice of expostulation and interpretation seems our own. He is very natural, very inevitable. "We look
not at the things which are seen, but at the things which are not
seen." And we see deeper than did the Athenians who once stood

about Mars Hill and listened to the great apostle. We do not spend our time "in nothing else, but either to tell, or to hear some new thing." In all our studies we have seen this to be a world of law, not dead but quick with forces of which the phenomena about us are not the reality but the mere temporary embodiment. At every turn it has been life that we have studied, whether the life of nature or the life of men; only in life have we been interested. We perceive now that it is not knowledge that we have been getting, but understanding, comprehension, insight, and that what we chiefly desire to understand are ourselves and our fellow-men. And so we have seen Scripture become mere plain philosophy, the words of Christ the words of a teacher who has seen the ultimate realities and speaks them very simply, with the simplicity of utter authority.

It is plain enough to us that "man's life does not consist in the abundance of the things which he possesseth," but in his mastery of himself, of circumstance, of physical forces and of human relationships, of the spirit that is within him: that man "doth not live by bread alone," but by every word of truth, every word that proceedeth out of the mouth of God, the author of truth, however spoken. Our thought cannot stop short of these ultimate realities, is not content without them. Mysteries become plain facts, the things which are seen appear thin to our gaze like mere masks, and the things which are not seen become real.

Our experience here, as well as our formal study, becomes part of the explanation as our thought dwells upon it. The things we have been most conscious of are our comradeships, our companionships, the commerce we have had with one another, and we have become conscious, as we never were before, that life is a thing that links spirit with spirit, that it is itself personal, not abstract, and yet intangible, not material; a thing too of law, but not of law imposed, of law accepted, rather, not made up of what we must so much as of what we will. We are drawn into it by impulse and affection as well as by interest. It is a thing by which we live and move and have our conscious being. And so we are drawn on to Paul's conclusion. If life be thus personal, if it be of law, if the law of highest compulsion be the law of our own spirits, how shall we dispense with the knowledge of him who is the Father of Spirits; and yet how can we know Him whom we have not seen,—how can we know him except in the person of Christ, the express image of the Father, the Word that became flesh and "dwelt among us, full of grace and truth?"

Christ Is the Revelation

I have heard this called an age of science, in which individual choice counts for less and less and law for more than ever before. I have heard it said, by men who claimed to base their statements upon observation, that this is an age in which individual men of necessity fall into the background, an age of machinery, of combinations of individuals, of massed and aggregate power; and I marvel that the obvious facts should be so ignored. Perhaps not so many individuals are of significance as formerly, but the individuals who do tell more tremendously, wield a greater individual choice, command a power such as kings and conquerors never dreamed of in the simpler days gone by. Their sway is the sway of destiny over millions upon millions of their fellow-countrymen, over the policy and fortunes of nations. There never was a time when the spirit and character of individual men was of more imperial import and consequence than now. The whole scale of action is altered; but with the scale are magnified also the essential elements themselves.

And so the type and symbol is magnified,—Christ, the embodiment of great motive, of divine sympathy, of that perfect justice which sees into the hearts of men, and that sweet grace of love which takes the sting out of every judgment. "We look not at the things which are seen, but at the things which are not seen": we do not, we cannot, see Christ, but there he stands, the most indubitable fact of history, with a sway over the hearts and lives of men which has not been broken or interrupted these nineteen hundred years. No man can ever think of him as dead, unreal, a thing of books, a creature of theology. "The things which are seen are temporal," but He, He is the embodiment of those things which, not seen, are eternal,—the eternal force and grace and majesty, not of character, but of that which lies back of character, obedience to the informing will of the Father of our spirits.

The force and beauty of Christ seem not to have been his own, as if original. He spoke always of his father, and of himself only as doing his father's will and speaking his father's words. There dwelt in him a spirit, great and universal, as that of the round world itself, compact of law and truth, a spirit greater than the world, conveying life and vision from the source from which all worlds and existence itself must have taken origin. He is our revelation. In him is our life explained and our knowledge made comprehensible. He is the perfect elder brother of our spirits. In him we are made known to ourselves,—in him because he is God, and God is the end of our philosophy; the revelation of the thought which, if we will but obey it, shall make us free, lifting us to the planes where duty shall seem happiness, obedience liberty, life the fulfillment of the law.

Science is our intimation; literature is the imperfect voice of our fellow-men, seeking, like ourselves, an exit for their hopes; philosophy is what we would fain convince ourselves of but cannot see: in all of these the things which are unseen and real lurk, but elude us. In Christ, in the God whom he reveals, the veil is torn away. Look! Look there and have your fill of what you have sought most. You must ever seek in vain until you raise your eyes to the Christ where he is lifted up.

ADDRESS ON THE TERCENTENARY
OF THE TRANSLATION OF THE BIBLE,
DENVER, COLORADO, MAY 7, 1911 *

A Book Which Reveals Men to Themselves

I come here to-night to speak of the Bible as the book of the people, not the book of the minister of the gospel, not the special book of the priest from which to set forth some occult, unknown doctrine withheld from the common understanding of men, but a great book of revelation—the people's book of revelation.

* This address, which received at the time an immense circulation, was delivered by Wilson virtually without preparation in the midst of his Western tour of 1911. To give this version a greater coherence the marks indicating elisions have been omitted.

For this is a book which reveals men unto themselves, not as creatures in bondage, not as men under human authority, not as those bidden to take counsel and command of any human source. It reveals every man to himself as a distinct moral agent, responsible not to men, not even to those men whom he has put over him in authority, but responsible through his own conscience to his Lord and Maker. Whenever a man sees this vision he stands up a free man, whatever may be the government under which he lives.

Our present life, ladies and gentlemen, is a very imperfect and disappointing thing. We do not judge our own conduct in the privacy of our own closets by the standard of expediency by which we are daily and hourly governed. We know that there is a standard set for us in the heavens, a standard revealed to us in this book which is the fixed and eternal standard by which we judge ourselves, and as we read this book it seems to us that the pages of our own hearts are laid open before us for our own perusal.

There is a very interesting phrase that constantly comes to our lips which we perhaps do not often enough interpret in its true meaning. We see many a young man start out in life with apparently only this object in view—to make name and fame and power for himself, and there comes a time of maturity and reflection when we say of him, "He has come to himself." When may I say that I have come to myself? Only when I have come to recognize my true relations with the rest of the world. We speak of a man losing himself in a desert. If you reflect a moment you will see that is the only thing he has not lost. He himself is there. What he means when he says that he has lost himself is that he has lost all the rest of the world. He has nothing to steer by. He does not know where any human habitation lies. He does not know where any beaten path and highway is. If he could establish his relationship with anything else in the world he would have found himself. Let it serve as a picture.

A man has found himself when he has found his relation to the rest of the universe, and here is the book in which those relations are set forth. And so when you see a man going along the highways of life with his gaze lifted above the road, lifted to the sloping ways in front of him, then be careful of that man and get out of his way. He knows the kingdom for which he is bound. He has seen the revelation of himself and of his relations to mankind. He has seen the revelations of his relation to God and his Maker, and therefore he has seen his responsibility in the world. This is the revelation of life and of peace.

A Judgment Resting Upon All Men

No man can sit down and withhold his hands from the warfare against wrong and get peace out of his acquiescence. The most solid and satisfying peace is that which comes from this constant spiritual warfare, and there are times in the history of nations when they must take up the crude instruments of bloodshed in order to vindicate spiritual conceptions. For liberty is a spiritual conception, and when men take up arms to set other men free, there is something sacred and holy in the warfare. I will not cry "peace" so long as there is sin and wrong in the world. And this great book does not teach any doctrine of peace so long as there is sin to be combated and overcome in one's own heart and in the great moving force of human society.

The franchise of human liberty made the basis of a bargain with a king. There are kings upon the pages of Scripture, but do you think of any king in Scripture as anything else than a mere man? There was the great King David, of a line blessed because it was the line from which would spring our Lord and Saviour, a man marked in the history of mankind as the chosen instrument of God to do justice and exalt righteousness in the people.

But what does this Bible do for David? Does it utter eulogies upon him? Does it conceal his faults and magnify his virtues? Does it set him up as a great statesman would be set up in a modern biography? No; the book in which his annals are written strips the mask from David, strips every shred of counterfeit and concealment from him and shows him as indeed an instrument of God, but a sinful and selfish man, and the verdict of the Bible is that David, like other men, was one day to stand naked before the judgment seat of God and be judged not as a king but as a man.

Is not this the book of the people? Is there any man in this Holy Scripture who is exempted from the common standard of judgment?

The Man Whose Faith Is Rooted in the Bible

Do you wonder, therefore, that when I was asked what my theme this evening would be I said it would be "The Bible and Progress"? We do not judge progress by material standards. America is not ahead of the other nations of the world because she is rich. Nothing makes America great except her thoughts, except her ideals, except her acceptance of those standards of judgment which are written large upon these pages of revelation. America has all along claimed the distinction of setting this example to the civilized world—that men were to think of one another, that governments were to be set up for the service of the people, that men were to be judged by these moral standards which pay no regard to rank or birth or conditions, but which assess every man according to his single and individual value.

That is the reason that the Bible has stood at the back of progress. That is the reason that reform has come not from the top but from the bottom. If you are ever tempted to let a government reform itself, I ask you to look back in the pages of history and find me a government that reformed itself. If you are ever tempted to let a party attempt to reform itself, I ask you to find a party that ever reformed itself.

A tree is not nourished by its bloom and by its fruit. It is nourished by its roots, which are down deep in the common and hidden soil, and every process of purification and rectification comes from the bottom—not from the top. It comes from the masses of struggling human beings. It comes from the instinctive efforts of millions of human hearts trying to beat their way up into the light and into the hope of the future.

Parties are reformed and governments are corrected by the impulses coming out of the hearts of those who never exercised authority and never organized parties. Those are the sources of strength, and I pray God that these sources may never cease to be spiritualized by the immortal subjections of these words of inspiration of the Bible. If any statesman sunk in the practices which debase a nation will but read this single book, he will go to his prayers abashed.

And so I say let us never forget that these deep sources, these wells of inspiration, must always be our sources of refreshment and of renewal. Then no man can put unjust power upon us. We shall live in that chartered liberty in which a man sees the things unseen, in which he knows that he is bound for a country in which there are no questions mooted any longer of right or wrong.

Can you imagine a man who did not believe these words, who did not believe in the future life, standing up and doing what has been the heart and center of liberty always—standing up before the king himself and saying, "Sir, you have sinned and done wrong in the sight of God, and I am His messenger of judgment to pronounce upon you the condemnation of Almighty God. You may silence me, you may send me to my reckoning with my Maker, but you cannot silence or reverse the judgment." That is what a man feels whose faith is rooted in the Bible. And the man whose faith is rooted in the Bible knows that reform cannot be stayed, that the finger of God that moves upon the face of the nations is against every man that plots the nation's downfall or the people's deceit; that these men are simply groping and staggering in their ignorance to a fearful day of judgment; and that whether one generation witnesses it or not the glad day of revelation and of freedom will come in which men will sing by the host of the coming of the Lord in His glory, and all of those will be forgotten—those little, scheming, contemptible creatures that forgot the image of God and tried to frame men according to the image of the evil one.

Chapter Five

THE IDEALS OF EDUCATION

I N THE field of education Wilson found the first test of his ideas
and leadership. He had risen steadily in his profession and had
turned down the offer of the presidencies of three universities before
accepting the leadership of Princeton, from which he had been
graduated in 1879. He came to this office with his concepts fully
formed, and prepared to act vigorously for their fulfillment. ("I feel
like a responsible minister reporting to his constituents," he told a
gathering of alumni.) Wilson believed that the college should be
a community, shaping men's minds and spirits by its influences;
and that the aim of education was to fit men for life in the larger
and more various community of the nation. His concept of the curriculum, his battles for the preceptorial system, for the building of
residential colleges and for the placing of the graduate school at
heart of the university, all derived from this general approach to
education. In this chapter certain of Wilson's writings at the height
of the Princeton controversies are placed first; they show the leader
appealing for support to the wide public. Afterwards come the basic
Princeton writings, particularly the Sesqui-Centennial address
(which marked him as the future president of the university) and
the Inaugural.

ADDRESS BEFORE THE PHI BETA KAPPA
CHAPTER AT CAMBRIDGE, JULY 1, 1909

The Disorganization of the American College

We have fallen of late into a deep discontent with the college,
with the life and the work of the undergraduates in our universities.
It is an honourable discontent, bred in us by devotion, not by cap-
tiousness or hostility or by an unreasonable impatience to set the
world right. We are not critics, but anxious and thoughtful friends.

107

We are neither cynics nor pessimists, but honest lovers of a good thing, of whose slightest deterioration we are jealous. We would fain keep one of the finest instrumentalities of our national life from falling short of its best, and believe that by a little care and candor we can do so. . . .

The evident fact is, that we have now for a long generation devoted ourselves to promoting changes which have resulted in all but complete disorganization, and it is our plain and immediate duty to form our plans for reorganization. We must reëxamine the college, reconceive it, reorganize it. It is the root of our intellectual life as a nation. It is not only the instrumentality through which we must effect all the broad preliminary work which underlies sound scholarship; it is also our chief instrumentality of catholic enlightenment, our chief means for giving widespread stimulation to the whole intellectual life of the country and supplying ourselves with men who shall both comprehend their age and duty and know how to serve them supremely well. Without the American college our young men would be too exclusively shut in to the pursuit of individual interests, would lose the vital contacts and emulations which awaken them to those larger achievements and sacrifices which are the highest objects of education in a country of free citizens, where the welfare of the commonwealth springs out of the character and the informed purposes of the private citizen. The college will be found to lie somewhere very near the heart of American social training and intellectual and moral enlightenment.

The process is familiar to every one by which the disintegration was brought about which destroyed the old college with its fixed disciplines and ordered life and gave us our present problem of reorganization and recovery. It centred in the break-up of the old curriculum and the introduction of the principle that the student was to select his own studies from a great variety of courses, as great a variety as the resources of the college and the supply of teachers available made possible. But the change could not in the nature of things stop with the plan of study. It held at its heart a tremendous implication: the implication of full manhood on the part of the pupil, and all the untrammelled choices of manhood.

The pupil who was mature and well informed enough to study what he chose was also by necessary implication mature enough to be left free to do what he pleased, to choose his own associations and ways of life outside the curriculum without restraint or suggestion; and the varied, absorbing college life of our day sprang up as the natural offspring of the free election of studies.

There went along with the relaxation of rule as to what undergraduates should study, therefore, an almost absolute divorce between the studies and the life of the college, its business and its actual daily occupations. The teacher ceased to look upon himself as related in any responsible way to the life of his pupils, to what they should be doing and thinking of between one class exercise and another, and conceived his whole duty to have been performed when he had given his lecture and afforded those who were appointed to come the opportunity to hear and heed it if they chose. The teachers of this new régime, moreover, were most of them trained for their teaching work in German universities, or in American universities in which the methods, the points of view, the spirit, and the object of the German universities were, consciously or unconsciously, reproduced. They think of their pupils, therefore, as men already disciplined by some general training such as the German gymnasium gives, and seeking in the university special acquaintance with particular studies, as an introduction to special fields of information and inquiry. They have never thought of the university as a community of teachers and pupils: they think of it, rather, as a body of teachers and investigators to whom those may resort who seriously desire specialized kinds of knowledge. They are specialists imported into an American system which has lost its old point of view and found no new one suitable to the needs and circumstances of America. They do not think of living with their pupils and affording them the contacts of culture; they are only accessible to them at stated periods and for a definite and limited service; and their teaching is an interruption to their favorite work of research.

Meanwhile, the constituency of the college has wholly changed. It is not only the bookish classes who now send their sons to college, but also the men of business and of affairs, who expect their sons to follow in their own footsteps and do work with which books have little connection. In the old days of which I have spoken most young men who went to college expected to enter one or other of the learned professions, expected to have to do with books and some of the more serious kinds of learning all their lives. Books were their proper introduction to the work that lay before them; learning was their natural discipline and preparation. But nowadays the men who are looking forward to the learned professions are in a minority at the college. Most undergraduates come out of an atmosphere of business and wish a breeding which is consonant with it. They do not wish learning. They wish only a certain freshening of their faculties for the miscellaneous contacts of life, a general acquaint-ance with what men are doing and saying in their own generation, a certain facility in handling themselves and in getting on with their fellows. They are much more interested in the incidental associa-tions of college life than in the main intellectual occupations of the place. They want to be made men of, not scholars; and the life led at college is as serviceable for that as any of the tasks set in the class-room. If they want what the formal teaching offers them at all, it is for some definite and practical purpose connected with the calling they expect to follow, the business they expect to engage in. Such pupils are specially unsuitable for such teachers.

To Impart, Not Learning, But the Spirit of Learning

Here is the key to the whole matter: the object of the college, as we have known and used and loved it in America, is not scholarship (except for the few, and for them only by way of introduction and first orientation), but the intellectual and spiritual life. Its life and discipline are meant to be a process of preparation, not a process of information. By the intellectual and spiritual life I mean the life which enables the mind to comprehend and make proper use of the modern world and all its opportunities. The object of a liberal train-ing is not learning, but discipline and the enlightenment of the mind. The educated man is to be discovered by his point of view, by the temper of his mind, by his attitude towards life and his fair way of thinking. He can see, he can discriminate, he can combine ideas and perceive whither they lead; he has insight and comprehension. His mind is a practised instrument of appreciation. He is more apt to contribute light than heat to a discussion, and will oftener than another show the power of uniting the elements of a difficult subject in a whole view; he has the knowledge of the world which no one can have who knows only his own generation or only his own task.

What we should seek to impart in our colleges, therefore, is not so much learning itself as the spirit of learning. You can impart that to young men; and you can impart it to them in the three or four years at your disposal. It consists in the power to distinguish good reasoning from bad, in the power to digest and interpret evidence, in a habit of catholic observation and a preference for the non-partisan point of view, in an addiction to clear and logical processes of thought and yet an instinctive desire to interpret rather than to stick in the letter of the reasoning, in a taste for knowledge and a deep respect for the integrity of the human mind. It is citizenship of the world of knowledge, but not ownership of it. . . .

The processes of life, the contagions of association, are the only things that have ever got any real or permanent hold on men's minds. These are the conducting media for every effect we seek to work on the human spirit. The undergraduate should have scholars for teachers. They should hold his attention steadily upon great tested bodies of knowledge and should insist that he make himself acquainted with them, if only for the nonce. But they will give him nothing he is likely to carry with him through life if they stop with formal instruction, however thorough or exacting they may make it. Their permanent effects will be wrought upon his spirit. Their teaching will follow him through life only if they reveal to him the meaning, the significance, the essential validity of what they are about, the motives which prompt it, the processes which verify it. They will rule him, not by what they know and inform him of, but by the spirit of the things they expound. And that spirit they cannot convey in any formal manner. They can convey it only atmospherically, by making their ideals tell in some way upon the whole spirit of the place.

How shall their pupils carry their spirit away with them, or the spirit of the things they teach, if beyond the door of the class-room the atmosphere will not contain it? College is a place of initiation. Its effects are atmospheric. They are wrought by impression, by association, by emulation. The voices which do not penetrate beyond the doors of the class-room are lost, are ineffectual, are void of consequence and power. No thought will obtain or live there for the transmission of which the prevailing atmosphere is a non-conducting medium. If young gentlemen get from their years at college only manliness, *esprit de corps*, a release of their social gifts, a training in give and take, a catholic taste in men, and the standards of true sportsmen, they have gained much, but they have not gained what a college should give them. It should give them insight into the things of the mind and of the spirit, a sense of having lived and formed their friendships amidst the gardens of the mind where grows the tree of the knowledge of good and evil, a consciousness of having taken on them the vows of true enlightenment and of having undergone the discipline, never to be shaken off, of those who seek wisdom in candor, with faithful labour and travail of spirit.

These things they cannot get from the class-room unless the spirit of the class-room is the spirit of the place as well and of its life; and that will never be until the teacher comes out of the class-room and makes himself a part of that life. Contact, companionship, familiar intercourse is the law of life for the mind. The comradeships of undergraduates will never breed the spirit of learning. The circle must be widened. It must include the older men, the teachers, the men for whom life has grown more serious and to whom it has revealed more of its meanings. So long as instruction and life do not merge in our colleges, so long as what the undergraduates do and what they are taught occupy two separate, air-tight compartments in their consciousness, so long will the college be ineffectual.

Forces at Odds with the Intellectual Life

If you wish to create a college, therefore, and are wise, you will seek to create a life. We have allowed ourselves to grow very anxious and to feel very helpless about college athletics. They play too large a part in the life of the undergraduate, we say; and no doubt they do. There are many other things which play too large a part in that life, to the exclusion of intellectual interests and the dissipation of much excellent energy: amusements of all kinds, social preoccupations of the most absorbing sort, a multitude of activities which have nothing whatever to do with the discipline and enlightenment of the mind. But that is because they are left a free field. Life, at college, is one thing, the work of the college another, entirely separate and distinct. The life is the field that is left free for athletics not only, but also for every other amusement and diversion. Studies are no part of that life, and there is no competition. Study is the work which interrupts the life, introduces an embarrassing and inconsistent element into it. The faculty has no part in the life; it organizes the interruption, the interference.

This is not to say that there are not a great many undergraduates seriously interested in study, or that it is impossible or even difficult to make the majority of them, the large majority, pass the tests of the examinations. It is only saying that the studies do not spring out of the life of the place and are hindered by it, must resist its influences if they would flourish. I have no jealousy of athletics: it has put wholesome spirit into both the physical and the mental life of our undergraduates. There are fewer morbid boys in the new college which we know than there were in the old college which our fathers knew; and fewer prigs, too, no doubt. Athletics are indispensable to the normal life of young men, and are in themselves wholesome and delightful, besides. In another atmosphere, the atmosphere of learning, they could be easily subordinated and assimilated. The reason they cannot be now is that there is nothing to assimilate them, nothing by which they can be digested. They make their own atmosphere unmolested. There is no direct competition.

The same thing may be said, for it is true, of all the other amusements and all the social activities of the little college world. Their name is legion: they are very interesting; most of them are in themselves quite innocent and legitimate; many of them are thoroughly worth while. They now engross the attention and absorb the energies of most of the finest, most spirited, most gifted youngsters in the undergraduate body, men fit to be scholars and masters in many fields, and for whom these small things are too trivial a preparation. They would not do so if other things which would be certain to grip these very men were in competition with them, were known and spoken of and pervasive in the life of the college outside the class-room; but they are not. The field is clear for all these little activities, as it is clear for athletics. Athletics has no serious competitor except these amusements and petty engrossments; they have no serious competitor except athletics. The scholar is not in the game. He keeps modestly to his class-room and his study and must be looked up and asked questions if you would know what he is thinking about. His influence can be set going only by the deliberate effort of the undergraduate himself who looks him up and stirs him. He deplores athletics and all the other absorbing and non-academic pursuits which he sees drawing the attention of his pupils off from study and serious preparation for life, but he will not enter into competition with them. He has never dreamed of such a thing; and, to tell the truth, the life of the place is organized in such a way as to make it hardly possible for him to do so. He is therefore withdrawn and ineffectual.

It is the duty of university authorities to make of the college a society, of which the teacher will be as much, and as naturally, a member as the undergraduate. When that is done other things will fall into their natural places, their natural relations. Young men are capable of great enthusiasms for older men whom they have learned to know in some human, unartificial way, whose quality they have tasted in unconstrained conversation, the energy and beauty of whose characters and aims they have learned to appreciate by personal contact; and such enthusiasms are often amongst the strongest and most lasting influences of their lives. You will not gain the affection of your pupil by anything you do for him, impersonally, in the class-room. You may gain his admiration and vague appreciation, but he will tie to you only for what you have shown him personally or given him in intimate and friendly service.

My plea, then, is this: that we now deliberately set ourselves to make a home for the spirit of learning: that we reorganize our colleges on the lines of this simple conception, that a college is not only a body of studies but a mode of association; that its courses are only its formal side, its contacts and contagions its realities. It must become a community of scholars and pupils,—a free community but a very real one, in which democracy may work its reasonable triumphs of accommodation, its vital processes of union. I am not suggesting that young men be dragooned into becoming scholars or tempted to become pedants, or have any artificial compulsion whatever put upon them, but only that they be introduced into the high society of university ideals, be exposed to the hazards of stimulating friendships, be introduced into the easy comradeships of the republic of letters. By this means the class-room itself might some day come to seem a part of life.

"THE DELINEATOR,"
NOVEMBER 1909

The Awakening of the Whole Man

There is an ideal at the heart of everything American, and the ideal at heart of the American university is intellectual training, the awakening of the whole man, the thorough introduction of the student to the life of America and of the modern world, the completion of the task undertaken by the grammar and high schools of equipping him for the full duties of citizenship. It is with that idea that I have said that the college stands at the heart of the American university. The college stands for liberal training. Its object is discipline and enlightenment. The average thoughtful American does not want his son narrowed in all his gifts and thinking to a particular occupation. He wishes him to be made free of the world in which men think about and understand many things, and to know how to handle himself in it. He desires a training for him which will give him a considerable degree of elasticity and adaptability, and fit him to turn in any direction he chooses.

For men do not live in ruts in America. They do not always or of necessity follow the callings their fathers followed before them. They are ready to move this way or that as interest or occasion suggests. Versatility, adaptability, a wide range of powers, a quick and easy variation of careers, men excelling in businesses for which they never had any special preparation,—these are among the most characteristic marks of American life,—its elasticity and variety, the rapid shifting of parts, the serviceability of the same men for many different things, and the quick intelligence of men of many different kinds in the common undertakings of politics and in public affairs of all kinds. If the American college were to become a vocational school, preparing only for particular callings, it would be thoroughly un-American. It would be serving special, not general, needs and seeking to create a country of specialized men without versatility or general capacity.

The college of the ideal American university, therefore, is a place intended for general intellectual discipline and enlightenment; and not for intellectual discipline and enlightenment only, but also for moral and spiritual discipline and enlightenment. America is great, not by reason of her skill, but by reason of her spirit, her spirit of general serviceableness and intelligence.

The Ideal College Is a Community

We have misconceived and misused the college as an instrument of American life when we have organized it and used it as a place of special preparation for particular tasks and callings. It is for liberal training, for general discipline, for that preliminary general enlightenment which every man should have who enters modern life with any intelligent hope or purpose of leadership and achievement.

Its "liberalizing" influences should be got from its life, even more than from its studies. Special studies become liberal when those who are pursuing them associate constantly and familiarly with those who are pursuing other studies, studies of many kinds, pursued from many points of view. The real enlightenments of life come, not from tasks or from books, so much as from free intercourse with other persons who, in spite of you, inform and stimulate you, and make you realize how big and various the world is, how many things there are in it to think about, and how necessary it is to think about the subjects you are specially interested in in their right relation to many, many others, if you would think of them correctly and get to the bottom of what you are trying to do.

The ideal college, therefore, should be a community, a place of close, natural, intimate association, not only of the young men who are its pupils and novices in various lines of study but also of young men with older men, with maturer men, with veterans and professionals in the great undertakings of learning, of teachers with pupils, outside the classroom as well as inside of it. No one is successfully educated within the walls of any particular classroom or laboratory or museum; and no amount of association, however close and familiar and delightful, between mere beginners can ever produce the sort of enlightenment which the lad gets when first he begins to catch the infection of learning.

The trouble with most of our colleges nowadays is that the faculty of the college live one life and the undergraduates quite a different one. They are not members of the same community; they constitute two communities. The life of the undergraduate is not touched with the personal influence of the teacher; life among the teachers is not touched by the personal impressions which should come from frequent and intimate contact with undergraduates. The teacher does not often enough know what the undergraduate is thinking about, or what models he is forming his life upon, and the undergraduate does not know how human a fellow the teacher is, how delightfully he can talk, outside the classroom, of the subjects he is most interested in, how many interesting things both his life and his studies illustrate and make attractive. This separation need not exist, and in the college of the ideal university would not exist.

It is perfectly possible to organize the life of our colleges in such a way that students and teachers alike will take part in it; in such a way that a perfectly natural daily intercourse will be established between them; and it is only by such an organization that they can be given real vitality as places of serious training, be made communities in which youngsters will come fully to realize how interesting intellectual work is, how vital, how important, how closely associated with all modern achievement,—only by such an organization that study can be made to seem a part of life itself. Lectures often seem very formal and empty things; recitations generally prove very dull and unrewarding. It is in conversation and natural intercourse with scholars, chiefly, that you find how lively knowledge is, how it ties into everything that is interesting and important, how intimate a part it is of everything that is "practical" and connected with the world of affairs. Men are not always made thoughtful by books; but they are generally made thoughtful by association with men who think.

"SCRIBNER'S MAGAZINE,"
NOVEMBER 1909

What the World Needs in Its Trained Men

There is an uncommon challenge to effort in the modern world, and all the achievements to which it challenges are uncommonly difficult. Individuals are yoked together in modern enterprise by a harness which is both new and inelastic. The man who understands only some single process, some single piece of work which he has been set to do, will never do anything else, and is apt to be deprived at almost any moment of the opportunity to do even that, because processes change, industry undergoes instant revolutions. New inventions, fresh discoveries, alterations in the markets of the world throw accustomed methods and the men who are accustomed to them out of date and use without pause or pity. The man of special skill may be changed into an unskilled laborer overnight. Moreover, it is a day in which no enterprise stands alone or independent, but is related to every other and feels changes in all parts of the globe. The men with mere skill, with mere technical knowledge, will be mere servants perpetually, and may at any time become useless servants, their skill gone out of use and fashion. The particular thing they do may become unnecessary or may be so changed that they cannot comprehend or adjust themselves to the change.

These, then, are the things the modern world must have in its trained men, and I do not know where else it is to get them if not from its educated men and the occasional self-developed genius of an exceptional man here and there. It needs, at the top, not a few, but many men with the power to organize and guide. The college is meant to stimulate in a considerable number of men what would be stimulated in only a few if we were to depend entirely upon nature and circumstance. Below the ranks of generalship and guidance, the modern world needs for the execution of its varied and difficult business a very much larger number of men with great capacity and readiness for the rapid and concentrated exertion of a whole series of faculties: planning faculties as well as technical skill, the ability to handle men as well as to handle tools and correct processes, faculties of adjustment and adaptation as well as of precise execution,—men of resource as well as knowledge. There are the athletes, the athletes of faculty, of which our generation most stands in need.

All through its ranks, besides, it needs masterful men who can acquire a working knowledge of many things readily, quickly, intelligently, and with exactness,—things they had not foreseen or prepared themselves for beforehand, and for which they could not have prepared themselves beforehand. Quick apprehension, quick comprehension, quick action are what modern life puts a premium upon,—a readiness to turn this way or that and not lose force or momentum.

To me, then, the question seems to be, Shall the lad who goes to college go there for the purpose of getting ready to be a servant merely, a servant who will be nobody and who may become useless, or shall he go there for the purpose of getting ready to be a master adventurer in the field of modern opportunity?

We live in an age in which no achievement is to be cheaply had. All the cheap achievements, open to amateurs, are exhausted and have become commonplace. Adventure, for example, is no longer extraordinary: which is another way of saying that it is commonplace. Any amateur may seek and find adventure; but it has been sought and had in all its kinds. Restless men, idle men, chivalrous men, men drawn on by mere curiosity and men drawn on by love of the knowledge that lies outside books and laboratories, have crossed the whole face of the habitable globe in search of it, ferreting it out in corners even, following its bypaths and beating its coverts, and it is nowhere any longer a novelty or distinction to have discovered and enjoyed it. The whole round of pleasure, moreover, has been exhausted time out of mind, and most of it discredited as not pleasure after all, but just an expensive counterfeit; so that many rich people have been driven to devote themselves to expense regardless of pleasure. No new pleasure, I am credibly informed, has been invented within the memory of man. For every genuine thrill and satisfaction, therefore, we are apparently, in this sophisticated world, shut in to work, to modifying and quickening the life of the age. If college be one of the highways to life and achievement, it must be one of the highways to work.

The man who comes out of college into the modern world must, therefore, have got out of it, if he has not wasted four vitally significant years of his life, a quickening and a training which will make him in some degree a master among men. If he has got less, college was not worth his while.

The New Distractions of College Life

What has happened is, in general terms, this: that the work of the college, the work of its classrooms and laboratories, has become the merely formal and compulsory side of its life, and that a score of other things, lumped under the term "undergraduate activities," have become the vital, spontaneous, absorbing realities for nine out of every ten men who go to college. These activities embrace social, athletic, dramatic, musical, literary, religious, and professional organizations of every kind, besides many organized for mere amusement and some, of great use and dignity, which seek to exercise a general oversight and sensible direction of college ways and customs. Those which consume the most time are, of course, the athletic, dramatic, and musical clubs, whose practices, rehearsals, games, and performances fill the term time and the brief vacations alike. But it is the social organizations into which the thought, the energy, the initiative, the enthusiasm of the largest number of men go, and go in lavish measure.

The chief of these social organizations are residential families,—fraternities, clubs, groups of house-mates of one kind or another,—in which, naturally enough, all the undergraduate interests, all the undergraduate activities of the college have their vital centre. The natural history of their origin and development is very interesting. They grew up very normally. They were necessary because of what the college did not do.

Every college in America, at any rate every college outside a city, has tried to provide living rooms for its undergraduates, dormitories in which they can live and sleep and do their work outside the classroom and the laboratory. Very few colleges whose numbers have grown rapidly have been able to supply dormitories enough for all their students, and some have deliberately abandoned the attempt, but in many of them a very considerable proportion of the undergraduates live on the campus, in college buildings. It is a very wholesome thing that they should live thus under the direct influence of the daily life of such a place and, at least in legal theory, under the authority of the university of which the college forms a principal part. But the connection between the dormitory life and the real life of the university, its intellectual tasks and disciplines, its outlook upon the greater world of thought and action which lies beyond, far beyond, the boundaries of campus and classroom, is very meagre and shadowy indeed. It is hardly more than atmospheric, and the atmosphere is very attenuated, perceptible only by the most sensitive. . . .

Fraternity chapters were once—and that not so very long ago— merely groups of undergraduates who had bound themselves together by the vows of various secret societies which had spread their branches among the colleges. They had their fraternity rooms, their places of meeting; they were distinguished by well-known badges and formed little coteries distinguishable enough from the general body of undergraduates, as they wished to be; but in all ordinary matters they shared the common life of the place. The daily experiences of the college life they shared with their fellows of all kinds and all connections, in an easy democracy; their contacts were the common contacts of the classroom and the laboratory not only, but also of the boarding-house table and of all the usual undergraduate resorts. Members of the same fraternity were naturally enough inclined to associate chiefly with one another and were often, much too often, inclined, in matters of college "politics," to act as a unit and in their own interest; but they did not live separately. They did not hold aloof or constitute themselves separate families, living apart in their own houses, in privacy.

Now all that is changed. Every fraternity has its own house equipped as a complete home. The fraternity houses will often be the most interesting and the most beautiful buildings a visitor will be shown when he visits the college. In them members take all their meals, in them they spend their leisure hours and often do their reading—for each house has its library—and in them many of the members, as many as can be accommodated, have their sleeping rooms and live, because the college has not dormitories enough to lodge them or because they prefer lodging outside the dormitories. In colleges where there are no fraternities, clubs of one sort or another take their places, build homes of their own, enjoy a similar privacy and separateness, and constitute the centre of all that is most comfortable and interesting and attractive in undergraduate life.

Such is college life nowadays, and such its relation to college work and the all-important intellectual interests which the colleges are endowed and maintained to foster. I need not stop to argue that the main purposes of education cannot be successfully realized under such conditions. I need not stop to argue that the college was not and can never be intended for the uses it is now being put to. A young man can learn to become the manager of a football team or of a residential club, the leader of an orchestra or a glee club, the star of amateur theatricals, an oarsman or a chess player without putting himself to the trouble or his parents to the expense of four years at a college. These are innocent enough things for him to do and to learn, though hardly very important in the long run; they may, for all I know, make for efficiency in some of the simpler kinds of business; and no wise man who knows college lads would propose to shut them off from them or wish to discourage their interest in them. All work and no play makes Jack a dull boy not only, but may make him a vicious boy as well. Amusement, athletic games, the zest of contest and competition, the challenge there is in most college activities to the instinct of initiative and the gifts of leadership and achievement,—all these are wholesome means of stimulation, which keep young men from going stale and turning to things that demoralize. But they should not assume the front of the stage where more serious and lasting interests are to be served. Men cannot be prepared by them for modern life.

The college is meant for a severer, more definite discipline than this: a discipline which will fit men for the contests and achievements of an age whose every task is conditioned upon some intelligent and effective use of the mind, upon some substantial knowledge, some special insight, some trained capacity, some penetration which comes from study, not from natural readiness or mere practical experience.

The side shows need not be abolished. They need not be cast out or even discredited. But they must be subordinated. They must be put in their natural place as diversions, and ousted from their present dignity and preëminence as occupations.

ADDRESS AT THE PRINCETON SESQUI-CENTENNIAL
CELEBRATION, OCTOBER 21, 1896

The Classics, Literature, History

He is not a true man of the world who knows only the present fashions of it. In good breeding there is always the fine savor of generations of gentlemen, a tradition of courtesy, the perfect knowledge of long practice. The world of affairs is so old no man can know it who knows only that little last segment of it which we call the present. We have a special name for the man who observes only the present fashions of the world, and it is a less honorable name than that which we use to designate the grave and thoughtful gentlemen who keep so steadily to the practices that have made the world wise and at ease these hundreds of years. We cannot pretend to have formed the world, and we are not destined to reform it. We cannot even mend it and set it forward by the reasonable measures of a single generation's work if we forget the old processes or lose our mastery over them. We should have scant capital to trade on were we to throw away the wisdom we have inherited and seek our fortunes with the slender stock we have ourselves accumulated. This, it seems to me, is the real, the prevalent argument for holding every man we can to the intimate study of the ancient classics. Latin and Greek, no doubt, have a grammatical and syntactical habit which challenges the mind that would master it to a severer exercise of analytical power than the easy-going synthesis of any modern tongue demands; but substitutes in kind may be found for that drill. What you cannot find a substitute for is the classics as literature; and there can be no first-hand contact with that literature if you will not master the grammar and the syntax which convey its subtle power.

Your enlightenment depends on the company you keep. You do not know the world until you know the men who have possessed it and tried its ways before ever you were given your brief run upon it. And there is no sanity comparable with that which is schooled in the thoughts that will keep. It is such a schooling that we get from the world's literature. The books have disappeared which were not genuine,—which spoke things which, if they were worth saying at all, were not worth hearing more than once, as well as the books which spoke permanent things clumsily and without the gift of interpretation. The kind air which blows from age to age has disposed of them like vagrant leaves. There was sap in them for a little, but now they are gone, we do not know where. All literature that has lasted has this claim upon us: that it is not dead; but we cannot be quite so sure of any as we are of the ancient literature that still lives, because none has lived so long. It holds a sort of primacy in the aristocracy of natural selection.

Read it, moreover, and you shall find another proof of vitality in it, more significant still. You shall recognize its thoughts, and even its fancies, as your long-time familiars—shall recognize them as the thoughts that have begotten a vast deal of your own literature. We read the classics and exclaim, in our vanity: "How modern! it might have been written yesterday." Would it not be more true, as well as more instructive, to exclaim concerning our own ideas: "How ancient! they have been true these thousand years"? It is the general air of the world a man gets when he reads the classics, the thinking which depends upon no time but only upon human nature, which seems full of the voices of the human spirit, quick with the power which moves ever upon the face of affairs. "What Plato has thought he may think; what a saint has felt he may feel; what at any time has befallen any man he can understand." There is the spirit of a race in the Greek literature, the spirit of quite another people in the books of Virgil and Horace and Tacitus; but in all a mirror of the world, the old passion of the soul, the old hope that keeps so new, the informing memory, the persistent forecast.

It has always seemed to me an odd thing, and a thing against nature, that the literary man, the man whose citizenship and freedom are of the world of thought, should ever have been deemed an unsafe man in affairs; and yet I suppose there is not always injustice in the judgment. It is a perilously pleasant and beguiling comradeship, the company of authors. Not many men when once they are deep in it will leave its engaging thought of things gone by to find their practical duties in the present. But you are not making an undergraduate a man of letters when you keep him four short years at odd, or even at stated, hours in the company of authors. You shall have done much if you make him feel free among them.

This argument for enlightenment holds scarcely less good, of course, in behalf of the study of modern literature, and especially the literature of your own race and country. You should not belittle culture by esteeming it a thing of ornament, an accomplishment rather than a power. A cultured mind is a mind quit of its awkwardness, eased of all impediment and illusion, made quick and athletic in the acceptable exercise of power. It is a mind at once informed and just,—a mind habituated to choose its course with knowledge, and filled with full assurance, like one who knows the world and can live in it without either unreasonable hope or unwarranted fear. It cannot complain, it cannot trifle, it cannot despair. Leave pessimism to the uncultured, who do not know reasonable hope; leave fantastic hopes to the uncultured, who do not know the reasonableness of failure. Show that your mind has lived in the world ere now; has taken counsel with the elder dead who still live, as well as with the ephemeral living who cannot pass their graves. Help men, but do not delude them.

I believe, of course, that there is another way of preparing young men to be wise. I need hardly say that I believe in full, explicit instruction in history and in politics, in the experiences of peoples and the fortunes of governments, in the whole story of what men have attempted and what they have accomplished through all the changes both of form and of purpose in their organization of their common life. Many minds will receive and heed this systematic instruction which have no ears for the voice that is in the printed page of literature. But, just as it is one thing to sit here in republican America and hear a credible professor tell of the soil of allegiance in which the British monarchy grows, and quite another to live where Victoria is queen and hear common men bless her with full confession of loyalty, so it is one thing to hear of systems of government in histories and treatises and quite another to feel them in the pulses of the poets and prose writers who have lived under them.

The Pervasive Spirit of Science

It used to be taken for granted—did it not?—that colleges would be found always on the conservative side in politics (except on the question of free trade); but in this latter day a great deal has taken place which goes far toward discrediting the presumption. The college in our day lies very near indeed to the affairs of the world. It is a place of the latest experiments; its laboratories are brisk with the spirit of discovery; its lecture rooms resound with the discussion of new theories of life and novel programmes of reform. There is no radical like your learned radical, bred in the schools; and thoughts of revolution have in our time been harbored in universities as naturally as they were once nourished among the Encyclopedists. It is the scientific spirit of the age which has wrought the change.

I stand with my hat off at very mention of the great men who have made our age an age of knowledge. No man more heartily admires, more gladly welcomes, more approvingly reckons the gain and the enlightenment that have come to the world through the extraordinary advances in physical science which this great age has witnessed. He would be a barbarian and a lover of darkness who should grudge that great study any part of its triumph. But I am a student of society and should deem myself unworthy of the comradeship of great men of science should I not speak the plain truth with regard to what I see happening under my own eyes. I have no laboratory but the world of books and men in which I live; but I am much mistaken if the scientific spirit of the age is not doing us a great disservice, working in us a certain great degeneracy. Science has bred in us a spirit of experiment and a contempt for the past. It made us credulous of quick improvement, hopeful of discovering panaceas, confident of success in every new thing.

I have no indictment against what science has done: I have only a warning to utter against the atmosphere which has stolen from laboratories into lecture rooms and into the general air of the world at large. Science—our science—is new. It is a child of the nineteenth century. It has transformed the world and owes little debt of obligation to any past age. It has driven mystery out of the Universe; it has made malleable stuff of the hard world, and laid it out in its elements upon the table of every class-room. Its own masters have known its limitations: they have stopped short at the confines of the physical universe; they have declined to reckon with spirit or with the stuffs of the mind, have eschewed sense and confined themselves to sensation. But their work has been so stupendous that all other men of all other studies have been set staring at their methods, imitating their ways of thought, ogling their results.

We look in our study of the classics nowadays more at the phenomena of language than at the movement of spirit; we suppose the world which is invisible to be unreal; we doubt the efficacy of feeling and exaggerate the efficacy of knowledge; we speak of society as an organism and believe that we can contrive for it a new environment which will change the very nature of its constituent parts; worst of all, we believe in the present and in the future more than in the past, and deem the newest theory of society the likeliest. This is the disservice scientific study has done us: it has given us agnosticism in the realm of philosophy, scientific anarchism in the field of politics. It has made the legislator confident that he can create, and the philosopher sure that God cannot. Past experience is discredited and the laws of matter are supposed to apply to spirit and the make-up of society.

Let me say once more, this is not the fault of the scientist; he has done his work with an intelligence and success which cannot be too much admired. It is the work of the noxious, intoxicating gas which has somehow got into the lungs of the rest of us from out the crevices of his workshop—a gas, it would seem, which forms only in the outer air, and where men do not know the right use of their lungs. I should tremble to see social reform led by men who had breathed it; I should fear nothing better than utter destruction from a revolution conceived and led in the scientific spirit. Science has not changed the laws of social growth or betterment.

Science has not changed the nature of society, has not made history a whit easier to understand, human nature a whit easier to reform. It has won for us a great liberty in the physical world, a liberty from superstitious fear and from disease, a freedom to use nature as a familiar servant; but it has not freed us from ourselves. It has not purged us of passion or disposed us to virtue. It has not made us less covetous or less ambitious or less self-indulgent. On the contrary, it may be suspected of having enhanced our passion, by making wealth so quick to come, so fickle to stay. It has wrought such instant, incredible improvement in all the physical setting of our life, that we have grown the more impatient of the unreformed condition of the part it has not touched or bettered, and we want to get at our spirits and reconstruct them in like radical fashion by like processes of experiment.

The Perfect Place of Learning

We have broken with the past and have come into a new world.

Can any one wonder, then, that I ask for the old drill, the old memory of times gone by, the old schooling in precedent and tradition, the old keeping of faith with the past, as a preparation for leadership in days of social change? We have not given science too big a place in our education; but we have made a perilous mistake in giving it too great a preponderance in method in every other branch of study. We must make the humanities human again; must recall what manner of men we are; must turn back once more to the region of practicable ideals.

Of course, when all is said, it is not learning but the spirit of service that will give a college place in the public annals of the nation. It is indispensable, it seems to me, if it is to do its right service, that the air of affairs should be admitted to all its class-rooms. I do not mean the air of party politics, but the air of the world's transactions, the consciousness of the solidarity of the race, the sense of the duty of man toward man, of the presence of men in every problem, of the significance of truth for guidance as well as for knowledge, of the potency of ideas, of the promise and the hope that shine in the face of all knowledge. There is laid upon us the compulsion of the national life. We dare not keep aloof and closet ourselves while a nation comes to its maturity. The days of glad expansion are gone, our life grows tense and difficult; our re-source for the future lies in careful thought, providence, and a wise economy; and the school must be of the nation.

I have had sight of the perfect place of learning in my thought: a free place, and a various, where no man could be and not know with how great a destiny knowledge had come into the world—itself a little world; but not perplexed, living with a singleness of aim not known without; the home of sagacious men, hard-headed and with a will to know, debaters of the world's questions every day and used to the rough ways of democracy; and yet a place removed—calm Science seated there, recluse, ascetic, like a nun; not knowing that the world passes, not caring, if the truth but come in answer to her prayer; and Literature, walking within her open doors, in quiet chambers, with men of olden time, storied walls about her, and calm voices infinitely sweet; here "magic casements, opening on the foam of perilous seas, in faery lands forlorn," to which you may withdraw and use your youth for pleasure; there windows open straight upon the street, where many stand and talk, intent upon the world of men and business. A place where ideals are kept in heart in an air they can breathe; but no fool's paradise. A place where to hear the truth about the past and hold debate about the affairs of the present, with knowledge and without passion; like the world in having all men's life at heart, a place for men and all that concerns them; but unlike the world in its self-possession, its thorough way of talk; its care to know more than the moment brings to light; slow to take excitement, its air pure and wholesome with a breath of faith; every eye within it bright in the clear day and quick to look toward heaven for the confirmation of its hope. Who shall show us the way to this place?

INAUGURAL ADDRESS AS PRESIDENT OF PRINCETON
UNIVERSITY, NOVEMBER 1, 1902

A Mastery Beyond Technical Training

The modern world nowhere shows a closeted profession shut in to a narrow round of technical functions to which no knowledge of the outside world need ever penetrate. Whatever our calling, our thoughts must often be afield among men of many kinds, amidst interests as various as the phases of modern life. The managing minds of the world, even the efficient working minds of the world, must be equipped for a mastery whose chief characteristic is adaptability, play, an initiative which transcends the bounds of mere technical training. Technical schools whose training is not built up on the foundations of a broad and general discipline cannot impart this. The stuff they work upon must be prepared for them by processes which produce fibre and elasticity, and their own methods must be shot through with the impulses of the university.

It is this that makes our age and our task so interesting: this complex interdependence and interrelation of all the processes which prepare the mind for effectual service: this necessity that the merchant and the financier should have travelled minds, the engineer a knowledge of books and men, the lawyer a wide view of affairs, the physician a familiar acquaintance with the abstract data of science, and that the closeted scholar himself should throw his windows open to the four quarters of the world. Every considerable undertaking has come to be based on knowledge, on thoughtfulness, on the masterful handling of men and facts. The university must stand in the midst, where the roads of thought and knowledge interlace and cross, and, building upon some coign of vantage, command them all.

It has happened that throughout two long generations,—long

because filled with the industrial and social transformation of the world,—the thought of studious men has been bent upon devising methods by which special aptitudes could be developed, detailed investigations carried forward, inquiry at once broadened and deepened to meet the scientific needs of the age, knowledge extended and made various and yet exact by the minute and particular researches of men who devoted all the energies of their minds to a single task. And so we have gained much, though we have also lost much that must be recovered. We have gained immensely in knowledge but we have lost system. We have acquired an admirable, sober passion for accuracy. Our pulses have been quickened, moreover, by discovery. The world of learning has been transformed. No study has stood still. Scholars have won their fame, not by erudition, but by exploration, the conquest of new territory, the addition of infinite detail to the map of knowledge.

And so we have gained a splendid proficiency in investigation. We know the right methods of advanced study. We have made exhaustive record of the questions waiting to be answered, the doubts waiting to be resolved, in every domain of inquiry; thousands of problems once unsolved, apparently insoluble, we have reduced to their elements and settled, and their answers have been added to the commonplaces of knowledge. But, meanwhile, what of the preliminary training of specialists, what of the general foundations of knowledge, what of the general equipment of mind which all men must have who are to serve this busy, this sophisticated generation?

Probably no one is to blame for the neglect of the general into which we have been led by our eager pursuit of the particular. Every age has lain under the reproach of doing but one thing at a time, of having some one signal object for the sake of which other things were slighted or ignored. But the plain fact is, that we have so spread and diversified the scheme of knowledge in our day that it has lost coherence. We have dropped the threads of system in our teaching. And system begins at the beginning. We must find the common term for college and university; and those who have great colleges at the heart of the universities they are trying to develop are under a special compulsion to find it.

Learning is not divided. Its kingdom and government are centred, unitary, single. The processes of instruction which fit a large body of young men to serve their generation with powers released and fit for great tasks ought also to serve as the initial processes by which scholars and investigators are made. They ought to be but the first parts of the method by which the crude force of untrained men is reduced to the expert uses of civilization. There may come a day when general study will be no part of the function of a university, when it shall have been handed over, as some now talk of handing it over, to the secondary schools, after the German fashion; but that day will not be ours, and I, for one, do not wish to see it come. The masters who guide the youngsters who pursue general studies are very useful neighbors for those who prosecute detailed inquiries and devote themselves to special tasks. No investigator can afford to keep his doors shut against the comradeships of the wide world of letters and of thought.

Every Student a Man of the World

The age has hurried us, has shouldered us out of the old ways, has bidden us be moving and look to the cares of a practical generation; and we have suffered ourselves to be a little disconcerted. No doubt we were once pedants. It is a happy thing that the days have gone by when the texts we studied loomed bigger to our view than the human spirit that underlay them. But there are some principles of which we must not let go. We must not lose sight of that fine conception of a general training which led our fathers, in the days when men knew how to build great states, to build great colleges also to sustain them. No man who knows the world has ever supposed that a day would come when every young man would seek a college training. The college is not for the majority who carry forward the common labour of the world, nor even for those who work at the skilled handicrafts which multiply the conveniences and the luxuries of the complex modern life. It is for the minority who plan, who conceive, who superintend, who mediate between group and group and must see the wide stage as a whole.

Democratic nations must be served in this wise no less than those whose leaders are chosen by birth and privilege; and the college is no less democratic because it is for those who play a special part. I know that there are men of genius who play these parts of captaincy and yet have never been in the classrooms of a college, whose only school has been the world itself. The world is an excellent school for those who have vision and self-discipline enough to use it. It works in this wise, in part, upon us all. Raw lads are made men of by the mere sweep of their lives through the various schools of experience. It is this very sweep of life that we wish to bring to the consciousness of young men by the shorter processes of the college. We have seen the adaptation take place; we have seen crude boys made fit in four years to become men of the world.

Every man who plays a leading or conceiving part in any affair must somehow get this schooling of his spirit, this quickening and adaptation of his perceptions. He must either spread the process through his lifetime and get it by an extraordinary gift of insight and upon his own initiative, or else he must get it by the alchemy of mind practiced in college halls. We ought distinctly to set forth in our philosophy of this matter the difference between a man's preparation for the specific and definite tasks he is to perform in the world and that general enlargement of spirit and release of powers which he shall need if his task is not to crush and belittle him. When we insist that a certain general education shall precede all special training which is not merely mechanic in its scope and purpose, we mean simply that every mind needs for its highest serviceability a certain preliminary orientation, that it may get its bearings and release its perceptions for a wide and catholic view. We must deal in college with the spirits of men, not with their fortunes. Here, in history and philosophy and literature and science, are the experiences of the world summed up. These are but so many names which we give to the records of what men have done and thought and comprehended. If we be not pedants, if we be able to get at the spirit of the matter, we shall extract from them the edification and enlightenment as of those who have gone the long journey of experience with the race.

There are two ways of preparing a young man for his life work. One is to give him the skill and special knowledge which shall make a good tool, an excellent bread-winning tool, of him; and for thousands of young men that way must be followed. It is a good way. It is honorable, it is indispensable. But it is not for the college, and it never can be. The college should seek to make the men whom it receives something more than excellent servants of a trade or skilled practitioners of a profession. It should give them elasticity of faculty and breadth of vision, so that they shall have a surplus of mind to expend, not upon their profession only, for its liberalization and enlargement, but also upon the broader interests which lie about them, in the spheres in which they are to be, not breadwinners merely, but citizens as well, and in their own hearts, where they are to grow to the stature of real nobility. It is this free capital of mind the world most stands in need of,—this free capital that awaits investment in undertakings, spiritual as well as material, which advance the race and help all men to a better life. . . .

I should wish to see every student made, not a man of his task, but a man of the world, whatever his world may be. If it be the world of learning, then he should be a conscious and a broad-minded citizens of it. If it be the world of letters, his thought should run free upon the whole field of it. If it be the world of affairs, he should move amidst affairs like a man of thought. What we seek in education is a full liberation of the faculties, and the man who has not some surplus of thought and energy to expend outside the narrow circle of his own task and interest is a dwarfed, uneducated man. We judge the range and excellence of every man's abilities by their play outside the task by which he earns his livelihood. Does he merely work, or does he also look abroad and plan? Does he, at the least, enlarge the thing he handles? No task, rightly done, is truly private. It is part of the world's work. The subtle and yet universal connections of things are what the truly educated man, be he man of science, man of letters, or statesman, must keep always in his thought, if he would fit his work to the work of the world. His adjustment is as important as his energy.

Learning in the Nation's Service

There are other things besides mere material success with which we must supply our generation. It must be supplied with men who care more for principles than for money, for the right adjustments of life than for the gross accumulations of profit. The problems that call for sober thoughtfulness and mere devotion are as pressing as those which call for practical efficiency. We are here not merely to release the faculties of men for their own use, but also to quicken their social understanding, instruct their consciences, and give them the catholic vision of those who know their just relations to their fellow men.

Here in America, for every man touched with nobility, for every man touched with the spirit of our institutions, social service is the high law of duty, and every American university must square its standards by that law or lack its national title. It is serving the nation to give men the enlightenments of a general training; it is serving the nation to equip fit men for thorough scientific investigation and for the tasks of exact scholarship, for science and scholarship carry the truth forward from generation to generation and give the certain touch of knowledge to the processes of life. But the whole service demanded is not rendered until something is added to the mere training of the undergraduate and the mere equipment of the investigator, something ideal and of the very spirit of all action. The final synthesis of learning is in philosophy. You shall most clearly judge the spirit of a university if you judge it by the philosophy it teaches; and the philosophy of conduct is what every wise man should wish to derive from his knowledge of the thoughts and the affairs of the generations that have gone before him. We are not put into this world to sit still and know; we are put into it to act.

It is true that in order to learn men must for a little while withdraw from action, must seek some quiet place of remove from the bustle of affairs, where their thoughts may run clear and tranquil, and the heats of business be for the time put off; but that cloistered refuge is no place to dream in. It is a place for the first conspectus of the mind, for a thoughtful poring upon the map of life; and the boundaries which should emerge to the mind's eye are not more the intellectual than the moral boundaries of thought and action. I do not see how any university can afford such an outlook if its teachings be not informed with the spirit of religion and that the religion of Christ, and with the energy of a positive faith.

The argument for efficiency in education can have no permanent validity if the efficiency sought be not moral as well as intellectual. The ages of strong and definite moral impulse have been the ages of achievement; and the moral impulses which have lifted highest have come from Christian peoples,—the moving history of our own nation were proof enough of that. Moral efficiency is, in the last analysis, the fundamental argument for liberal culture. A merely literary education, got out of books and old literature, is a poor thing enough if the teacher stick at grammatical and syntactical drill; but if it be indeed an introduction into the thoughtful labors of men of all generations it may be made the prologue to the mind's emancipation: its emancipation from narrowness,—from narrowness of sympathy, of perception, of motive, of purpose, and of hope. And the deep fountains of Christian teaching are its most refreshing springs.

I have said already, let me say again, that in such a place as this we have charge, not of men's fortunes, but of their spirits. This is not the place in which to teach men their specific tasks,—except their tasks be those of scholarship and investigation; it is the place in which to teach them the relations which all tasks bear to the work of the world. Some men there are who are condemned to learn only the technical skill by which they are to live; but these are not the men whose privilege it is to come to a university. University men ought to hold themselves bound to walk the upper roads of usefulness which run along the ridges and command views of the general fields of life. This is why I believe general training, with no particular occupation in view, to be the very heart and essence of university training, and the indispensable foundation of every special development of knowledge or of aptitude that is to lift a man to his profession or a scholar to his function of investigation.

I have studied the history of America; I have seen her grow great in the paths of liberty and of progress by following after great ideals. Every concrete thing that she has done has seemed to rise out of some abstract principle, some vision of the mind. Her greatest victories have been the victories of peace and of humanity. And in days quiet and troubled alike Princeton has stood for the nation's service, to produce men and patriots. Her national tradition began with John Witherspoon, the master, and James Madison, the pupil, and has not been broken until this day. I do not know what the friends of this sound and tested foundation may have in store to build upon it; but whatever they add shall be added in that spirit, and with that conception of duty. There is no better way to build up learning and increase power. A new age is before us, in which, it would seem, we must lead the world. No doubt we shall set it an example unprecedented not only in the magnitude and telling perfection of our industries and arts but also in the splendid scale and studied detail of our university establishments: the spirit of the age will lift us to every great enterprise. But the ancient spirit of sound learning will also rule us; we shall demonstrate in our lecture rooms again and again, with increasing volume of proof, the old principles that have made us free and great; reading men shall read here the chastened thoughts that have kept us young and shall make us pure; the school of learning shall be the school of memory and of ideal hope; and the men who spring from our loins shall take their lineage from the founders of the republic.

FOUNDER'S DAY ADDRESS AT CARNEGIE INSTITUTE,
PITTSBURGH, NOVEMBER 5, 1903

A Certain Period of Withdrawal and Abstraction

Certainly no men ever stood in greater need than we do of leadership and the comprehensive thinking which interprets life. As the almost infinite complexity and unlimited scope of modern undertakings has made captains of industry necessary, and captains of labor, so also has it made it necessary that there should be captains of the mind capable of a sort of statesmanship in thinking.

We are come upon a new thirteenth century, a new age of discovery, where the voyage is not by the old seas or across unknown continents in search of fabulous cities, but out upon the great shadowy main of the mind's life, where the battle is being fought for existence in the maintenance of ideals, for the deciphering of morals, for the clearing away of doubts and alarms; where, when the battle is over, a day of high anticipations shall dawn, and men shall see again the visions of belief, feel again the certitude of hope.

This captaincy upon the great high seas of intellectual enterprise is what I mean by the statesmanship of letters, that mastery of interpretation which shall penetrate the motives and the policies of the modern mind. When all is said and done, man is a spirit, and lives not by what he does, but by what he thinks and hopes. His satisfactions, when they are not merely monetary, are of the spirit, and he has not steadied himself until he has interpreted his life in a way that will bring to him some consistent plan of achievement.

In order to achieve greatness a people must have intellectual as well as material power; and not intellectual power only, but intellectual variety as well. We confuse our minds with regard to education by insisting upon thinking of all kinds of education at once, and discussing them as if they constituted but a single theme. Undoubtedly a profound knowledge of the processes of nature is necessary to the material greatness of an industrial people; undoubtedly the education which gives them skill of hand and acquaintance with all the means by which advancements in the practical arts are to be attained, making them masters of every craft, is an indispensable necessity. Schools of technical training are not only desirable but indispensable, and the greater part of the education which a nation attempts must be of that kind, because that is the sort of education most universally needed—needed, I mean, by the largest number of persons. But we are not to stop there, and we are not to put our minds in confusion by placing that sort of education in competition or contrast with that which has for its object, not technical skill, but sheer enlargement of the mind, not training for a special occupation, but training for the more general tasks which include many callings in their single view.

The nation must have spiritual success as well as material success; and some men somewhere must devote their energies to laying before as many young minds as may be induced to resort to them the library of the world's full range of thinking and experience. The minds which they touch and enlarge will not be withdrawn from the field of practical success, but will be put into it with such a view of what lies before them as will fit them to get out of it the sort of achievement which will widen the whole aspect of every piece of business which they touch.

My conception of the higher education is a conception broad enough to embrace the whole field of thought, the whole record of experience; but what I emphasize about it is that it is withdrawal from the main motives of the world's material endeavor. I maintain that it is part of the statesmanship of mind that there should ever be a certain seclusion of mind preceding the struggle of life, a certain period of withdrawal and abstraction, when no particular skill is sought, no definite occupation studied, no single aim or ambition dwelt upon, but only a general preliminary orientation of the mind. It is a process by which the young mind is, so to say, laid alongside of the mind of the world, as nearly as may be, and enabled to receive its strength from the nourishing mother of us all, as Anteus received his strength from contact with the round earth.

America Speaks Through Her Men of Letters

I am sure that, as we look back on the history of our own nation, we are proud of nothing so much as of the high ideals which we conceive to have been a moving force in all that we have attempted and achieved. We have loved liberty, not only because we would ourselves be free, if we might, from the more vexatious trammels of government, but also because we wished to show other nations a fortunate way to happiness, a certain way by which to rid themselves of tyranny and injustice.

It may be that politicians in Washington had their own selfish interests to serve in bringing us to blows with Spain and in sweeping the foreign dominions of the Spanish Crown under our own rule; but the consciences of the vast majority of us are void of offense in that great matter. We know that our pulses beat high in that war because we truly believed ourselves to be defending peoples who were trodden upon and degraded by corrupt and selfish governors. We kept faith with Cuba, and we mean, with God's help, to keep faith also with the people of the Philippine Islands, by serving them and ameliorating their condition, by showing them the way to liberty without plundering them or making them our tools for a selfish end. It is the consciousness of such purpose that gives us self-respect and lends reality to our hopeful visions of the future. . . .

What we really love about our nation, in short, is its character, not its wealth. Wealth, even national wealth, viewed as a means to national greatness, is not an end but a means. We wish to be strong in order to show ourselves great, and our greatness lies, not in our strength, but in our use of it. It is no simple matter, therefore, that we should studiously fill the land with men who have been given a broad outlook upon the field of affairs and of thought. It is a central part of our statesmanship that we should have men constantly in training amongst us to take the broad view and be masters, not only of a single task, but also of the sort of thinking which will include past and present, and dwell as much upon the general interest as upon individual advantage.

America will be great among the nations only in proportion as she finds an adequate voice in letters for the best impulses and purposes that are in her. She will not be known until she is understood; and her wealth will not interpret her, or her physical power, or the breadth of her uncounted acres, or anything she has builded; but only such revealing speech as will hold the ear and command the heed of other nations and of her own people. Our thinkers must assist her to know herself. Her actions, even, will not speak unequivocally for her. They, too, must get their interpretation from her living voice. Her writers must inform her statesmen, and then, if her statesmen be not themselves men of letters, must in turn interpret her statesmen to herself and to the world.

There is no need that letters should be defended in America or exalted; they have ever had their due need of praise amongst us, and will always be sure of the power to which the gifts of her writers entitle them; but it is of some moment that we should once and again state to ourselves in this definite fashion exactly what part it is that our literature and our literary education, our books and our aptitude in the sort of catholic culture which produces the best books, play in our life. I have likened this part to statesmanship itself, and it is this that I mean and which I have sought to exalt as the statesmanship of letters.

ADDRESS BEFORE THE WESTERN ASSOCIATION
OF PRINCETON CLUBS, CLEVELAND, OHIO,
MAY 19, 1906

The Lure of Things Worthy to Be Loved

You have heard a great deal, I dare say, first and last, about the Preceptorial System, and most of it has been from the old point of view, namely, that it brought the teacher into personal and intimate contact with the pupil. But the point I would dwell upon is that the relationship is not so exclusively that of pupil and teacher as it used to be; that the new thing we are introducing is the independent pursuit of certain studies by men old enough to study for themselves and accorded the privilege in their studies of having the counsel of scholars older than themselves. It is not merely that they are being led, but that they are becoming what every university student ought to be, namely, reading men.

I have sometimes said to the men I knew best in the University that it did not make so very much difference with me what a man read, but it did not seem to me that any man had the title to call himself a university man who was not a reading man, who merely gathered the transitory impressions of the day in which he lived and did not put himself into the main currents of thought that flow out of the old centuries into the new, that constitute the pulse and life of the race. Men are in universities in order to come into contact with the vital forces that have always beat through the centuries in making civilization and in making thought, and if they do not voluntarily put themselves into contact with those forces, those forces are of no avail to them. For what a man reluctantly receives he does not retain, and it does not constitute any part of his life.

The thing which has pleased me most in regard to the Preceptorial System is not only the splendid fact that the alumni have given us the money to conduct the system, but the significant fact that the undergraduates have welcomed the change and have felt that it enriched their own life. It would be a very petty life to live if we were merely schoolmasters; it would not interest me for twenty-four hours to be a taskmaster in respect to the studies of a lot of youngsters. Unless I can lead them to see the beauty of the things that have seemed beautiful to me, I have mistaken my profession. It is not the whip that makes men, but the lure of things that are worthy to be loved. And so we feel that we are entitled to be full of hope in regard to the increasing intellectual life of Princeton. I am covetous for Princeton of all the glory that there is, and the chief glory of a university is always intellectual glory. The chief glory of a university is the leadership of the nation in the things that attach to the highest ambitions that nations can set themselves, those ideals which lift nations into the atmosphere of things that are permanent and do not fade from generation to generation. I do not see how any man can fail to perceive that scholarship, that education, in a country like ours, is a branch of statesmanship. It is a branch of that general work of enabling a great country to use its energies to the best advantage and to lift itself from generation to generation through stages of unbroken progress.

The Student and the True University Spirit

When I look about upon the generation in which we live, I, like every man who looks with thoughtful eyes upon it, am very much sobered by what I see; not disconcerted, not robbed of hope, not cooled even in my optimism, but nevertheless very much sobered by the seriousness of the task which confronts us.

Every age is compounded of things old and new, and the men of middle age are more involved in the things that are old than are the men in the generation that is coming on. And I always think of the change that must constantly be expected in a complex age as residing more with the younger generation than with the generation that is actually in charge of affairs. I see these young men drawing on all the complicated skeins that make up the pattern of our modern life, modifying that pattern, renewing the stuff where it is old, changing, confirming, doing all those things that draw on the forces of one age to be the forces of another. Because only they, when they are competent, can see the pattern as a whole. I believe that in spite of all the things which we deplore, and which bring the blood to our faces, there is a great deal that is splendid about the civilization of our day. The things that have been done in this country by way of its material advancement could not have been done without great gifts, without great powers, individual and corporate. There is a sense in which the individual in the modern industrial world is necessarily greater, if he be noticeable at all, than the individual of any other generation. For no man can do anything in his generation by and of himself. He must rule his fellow-men and draw them into coöperation with himself, if he would accomplish anything. There is a touch of statesmanship about every piece of modern business, about every piece of modern engineering. It is as if all the powers of the world were organized and the captains of industry were making their way forward in the ranks to be generals in command of the forces of mankind. . . .

Now, young men coming with new forces into this complicated plot, have freer hands than other men in the generation, cleaner hands and freer hands than anybody else. And when one asks one's self what sort of education these men should have in order to carry what will be the young man's burden for many a day to come, it seems to me evident that the education they receive should not be such as to catch them at once in the web of the complicated interests which they must touch without prejudice and without favor. To put it in plainer, less abstract terms, if you merely train men for business, directly for business, they are immersed in the business, so far as their thoughts are concerned, throughout their education, and are committed to the prejudices of their occupations before even they enter upon them. You cannot train men for a particular business without filling their heads with the atmosphere of that business; and we want a great body of young men going into the active affairs of this world untouched by the atmosphere of any particular interest. We must in our processes of education, somewhere, put ourselves in a position to give young men a view of life which shall not be touched by the interests which will engross them when they seek to make their living.

For there are many complications of human motive. When we speak of a man's making his living, we forget that he is also making somebody else's living in nine cases out of ten. Many a man would draw out of the business he is in, when he saw it was touching him with corruption, if it did not mean privation to a woman he loves, to children he loves; if it did not mean he was bringing upon others a kind of suffering and a sort of anxiety which he might be willing to bring upon himself singly, but is not willing to bring upon them. If men acted singly and each for himself, the aspect of affairs would be very different; and many a man is debased by some of the noblest impulses of his nature, his love for those who are not concerned in the things which have involved him. Many a man would be morally independent if he were in fact independent, but he is carrying the fortunes of others.

Look, therefore, how impossible it is for him to assess any problem in a disinterested fashion, if from the first he has been taught, in college as well as elsewhere, that the chief end of man is to make a living! If the chief end of man is to make a living, why, make a living any way you can. But if it ever has been shown to him in some quiet place where he has been withdrawn from the interests of the world, that the chief end of man is to keep his soul untouched from corrupt influences, and to see to it that his fellow-men hear the truth from his lips, he will never get that out of his consciousness again. There will always come up within him with a great resurgence, some way or other, those lessons of his youth, and there will come a voice from the conscience which will arrest the very progress of a generation. But if you never teach him any ideal except the ideal of making a living, there will be no voice within him, he will know no other ideal.

I believe, therefore, that there must be some universities in this country which undertake to teach men the life that is in them, by teaching them the disinterested truths of pure science, by teaching them the truths of pure philosophy, and that literature which is the permanent voice and song of the human spirit, letting them know that they are not going a lonesome journey, but that generations of men behind them are crying them on to do better things than they could otherwise even attempt, and that generations beyond them are beckoning them on to a day of happier things. There must sound in the halls of the true university this eternal voice of the human race that can never be drowned as long as men remember what the race has hoped and purposed.

The ideals that we talk about, the ideals that we try to translate into definite programmes of study, are not things which we can take or leave as we please, unless you believe that we can take or leave life itself as we please. There is no choice in the matter. I am not daunted by the prediction that we are going to be submerged in waves of materialism, because any man who has read ever so superficially the history of the race knows that there are certain things that cannot be absolutely submerged or crushed. If there remain any little band of men keeping the true university spirit alive, that band will, after a while, seem to be all that there is of a great nation.

Chapter Six

THE POLITICAL SCENE

W HILE Wilson was immersed in educational controversies, American politics seethed with impulses of reform. His conduct of the Princeton battles brought him into the public eye as a man dedicated to vital democratic principles. At the same time Wilson was looking freshly upon the popular issues of the day. The following selections are characteristic of his views as he stood at the threshold of a career of political action. Two major themes are dealt with: the problem of making government more genuinely representative, and the problem of controlling the rapid development of the corporation. In his address to the lawyers Wilson characteristically pleads for detachment in the profession—against the law's becoming the mere servant of business.

"THE NORTH AMERICAN REVIEW,"
MAY 1910

To Make Government Responsible and Efficient

The political discussions of recent years concerning the reform of our political methods have carried us back to where we began. We set out upon our political adventures as a nation with one distinct object, namely, to put the control of government in the hands of the people, to set up a government by public opinion thoroughly democratic in its structure and motive. We were more interested in that than in making it efficient. Efficiency meant strength; strength might mean tyranny; and we were minded to have liberty at any cost. And now, behold! when our experiment is an hundred and thirty-odd years old, we discover that we have neither efficiency nor control.

It is stated and conceded on every side that our whole representa-

tive system is in the hands of the "machine": that the people do
not in reality choose their representatives any longer, and that their
representatives do not serve the general interest unless dragooned
into doing so by extraordinary forces of agitation, but are controlled
by personal and private influences; that there is no one anywhere
whom we can hold publicly responsible, and that it is hide-and-seek
who shall be punished, who rewarded, who preferred, who rejected,
—that the processes of government amongst us, in short, are haphazard, the processes of control obscure and ineffectual. And so we
are at the beginning again.

We must, if any part of this be true, at once devote ourselves
again to finding means to make our governments, whether in our
cities, in our States, or in the nation, representative, responsible and
efficient.

Efficiency, of course, depends largely upon organization. There
must be definite authority, centred in somebody in particular whom
we can observe and control, and an organization built upon obedience and coöperation, an organization which acts together, with
system, intelligence, and energy. We were afraid of such an organization at the outset. It seemed to mean the concentration of
authority in too few hands and the setting up of a government
which might be too strong for the people. Our chief thought was
of control. We concluded that the best means of obtaining it was
to make practically every office elective, whether great or small,
superior or subordinate; to bring the structure of the government at
every point into direct contact with the people. The derivation of
every part of it we desired should be directly from the people. We
were very shy of appointments to office. We wished only elections,
frequent and direct. . . .

The old New England town meeting, for example, was an admirable instrument of actual self-government. Where neighborhoods
are small and neighbours know one another they can make actual
selection of the men they wish to put into office. Every candidate is known by everybody, and the officers of government when
elected serve a constituency of whose interests and opinions they
are keenly and intimately aware. Any community whose elements

are homogeneous and whose interests are simple can govern itself very well in this informal fashion. The people in such a case, rather than the government, are the organism. But those simple days have gone by. The people of our present communities, from one end of the country to the other, are not homogeneous, but composite, their interests varied and extended, their life complex and intricate. The voters who make them up are largely strangers to each other. Town meetings are out of the question, except for the most formal purposes, perfunctorily served; life sweeps around a thousand centres, and the old processes of selection, the old bases of responsibility, are impossible.

Officers of government used to be responsible because they were known and closely observed by neighbours of whose opinions and preferences they were familiarly aware; but now they are unknown, the servants of a political organization, not of their neighbors, irresponsible because obscure, or because defended by the very complexity of the system of which they form a part. The elective items on every voter's programme of duty have become too numerous to be dealt with separately and are, consequently, dealt with in the mass and by a new system, the system of political machinery against which we futilely cry out.

I say "futilely cry out" because the machine is both natural and indispensable in the circumstances and cannot be abolished unless the circumstances are changed, and very radically changed at that. We have given the people something so vast and complicated to do in asking them to select all the officers of government that they cannot do it. It must be done for them by professionals. There are so many men to be named for office; it is futile to name one or two unless you name a whole ticket; the offices that fill a ticket are so many and so obscure that it is impossible the thing should be done informally and offhand by direct, unassisted popular choice. There must be a preliminary process of selection, of nomination, of preparing the ticket as a whole, unless there is to be hopeless confusion, names put up at haphazard and nobody elected by a clear majority at the end. The machine is as yet an indispensable instrumentality of our politics.

Public opinion in the United States was never better informed, never more intelligent, never more eager to make itself felt in the control of government for the betterment of the nation than it is now; and yet, I venture to say, it was never more helpless to obtain its purposes by ordinary and stated means. It has to resort to convulsive, agitated, almost revolutionary means to have its way. It knows what it wants. It wants good men in office, sensible laws adjusted to existing conditions, conscience in affairs and intelligence in their direction. But it is at a loss how to get these. It flings itself this way and that, frightens this group of politicians, pets that, hopes, protests, demands, but cannot govern.

In its impatience it exaggerates the inefficiency and bad morals of its governments very grossly and is very unfair to men who would serve it if they could, who do serve it when they can, but who are caught in the same net of complicated circumstance in which opinion itself finds itself involved. There is no just ground for believing that our legislative and administrative bodies are generally corrupt. They are not. They are made up for the most part of honest men who are without leadership and without free opportunity; who try to understand the public interest and to devise measures to advance it, but who are subordinate to a political system which they cannot dominate or ignore. The machinery of the bodies to which they belong is inorganic, as decentralized as our elective processes would lead one to expect.

No one person or group of persons amongst them has been authorized by the circumstances of their election to lead them or to assume responsibility for their programme of action. They therefore parcel out initiative and responsibility in conformity with the obvious dictates of the system. They put their business in the hands of committees,—a committee for each subject they have to handle,—and give each of their members a place upon some committee. The measures proposed to them, therefore, come from the four quarters of the heaven, from members big and little, known and unknown, but never from any responsible source. There can be neither consistency nor continuity in the policies they attempt. What they do cannot be watched, and it cannot be itself organized and made a whole of. There is so much of it and it is so miscellaneous that it cannot be debated. The individual member must do the best he can amidst the confusion. He has only an occasional part and opportunity.

He is controlled, as a matter of fact, from out-of-doors,—not by the views of his constituents, but by a party organization which is intended to hold the heterogeneous elements of our extraordinary political system together.

The Privacy of Public Affairs

It is thus that the public business is managed with as careful privacy as the business of any private corporation. Corporations will, indeed, when they are well and wisely managed, often take the public more into their confidence than the managers of government do, in order to enhance the credit of the corporation and increase or steady the value of its securities in the money-market, as well as the sale of its products. But politicians are very secretive. They have become so by the habit of the system. Debate has fallen out of fashion in our legislative assemblies because the business of those assemblies is for the most part discussed and prepared by committees. The sittings of their committees are seldom public, except upon extraordinary occasions. Even when they are public few persons except those directly and privately interested attend, and the matter is too particular, too much like a mere single item of the session, to attract the attention of the ordinary newspaper. The business of legislation, therefore, like that of nomination, is for the most part conducted in private by the conference of small groups of men under party discipline. The public is not present either in fact or in thought. Committeemen get into the habit of being reticent and silent about what occurred in the committee-room and soon find themselves under the impression that it is their own private affair, anyway.

The habit spreads to the deliberative bodies themselves. Boards of Aldermen will often refuse to open their debates to reporters or to publish the names of those who voted Aye or No in the division when the debate was ended. And on the administrative side much

of what is to be done or proposed is agreed upon by private conference between the executives of our cities and States and the party
managers,—sometimes the managers who appear in public and are
known, sometimes those who keep in the background and occupy
no office, but are nevertheless omnipotent in matters of nomination
and who wish the executive business of the government to be carried
on in a way which will not embarrass them. And so, wherever we
turn, we find the intimate business of government sealed up in confidences of every kind: confidences against the people with regard
to their own affairs, confidences with regard to the way in which
their interests are to be served and safeguarded. Public discussions
are the mere formal dress parade of politics.

It was very amusing, when Mr. [Theodore] Roosevelt was President, to notice how seasoned politicians shivered when he spoke in
public,—shivered at his terrible indiscretions, his frank revelations,
whenever he chose, of what was going on inside political circles, his
nonchalant failure to keep any confidences whatever that he chose
to make public use of. He spoke of any inside matter he pleased, as
if it were the people's privilege to know what was going on within
their government. He may have chosen and chosen very astutely
which confidences to keep, which to break, but he was strong and
popular in proportion as he broke them and gave the people the
impression that he was really telling them all he knew about their
business, about the men and the motives which were retarding the
proper transaction of their business and the proper correction of the
abuses under which they were suffering at the hands of men who
enjoyed the confidence and protection of the managing politicians.

The Return to Representative Government

There is no ground for wonder that under a system under which
it is constant hide-and-seek to discover who is responsible, to find
out where public action originates and whither it is tending, this
system of confidences should have sprung up. I do not know that
any one in particular is to blame. But the situation is certainly extraordinary and makes it thoroughly worth while to inquire how
the people may be reintroduced into their own affairs.

It is high time. The people must be brought into their own again. They have been excluded from free and effective participation in their own governments too long,—so long that a universal distrust of representative methods of government has sprung up, a universal suspicion that there is nowhere any candor or honesty in the administration of public business, and we are in danger of revolutionary processes, of very radical changes which might be as futile as what we have already attempted by way of reform, while all the while a remedy, a very simple remedy, is at hand. We have not fallen upon these evil ways by any one's sinister intention or machinations, but the fact is the same. The system we are under, though nobody invented it to cheat the people, has grown up and does cheat the people and must be done away with by very definite intention.

There is no reason to despair, or even to tire, of representative government. It has not failed as some suppose, because it is representative and not direct. It has come near to breaking down only because it is not representative, only because the people of this country are prevented by the system of elections in which they have become entangled from electing representatives of their own choice. The people of other countries are not prevented. They manage to get their will very directly expressed, alike in legislation and in the administration of their governments. Foreign cities, for example, succeed excellently well, as well as it is reasonable ever to expect to succeed in matters of such magnitude and complexity, in getting their affairs administered in the way a majority of their people really wish them to be administered. Most of the badly governed cities of the civilized world are on this side of the Atlantic, most of the well governed on the other side; and the reason is not accidental. It has nothing to do with differences of capacity or of virtue or of theory, nothing to do with differences of principle or of national character. It results from differences of organization of the most fundamental and important kind which cut to the very roots of the whole matter. . . .

The short ballot is the short and open way by which we can return to representative government. It has turned out that the methods of organization which lead to efficiency in government are also the methods which give the people control. The busy owner is more effectually in control if he appoints a capable superintendent and holds him responsible for the conduct of the business than he would be if he undertook himself to choose all the subordinate agents and workmen and superintend both them and the superintendent; and the business is also better conducted,—incomparably better conducted. What the voters of the country are now attempting is not only impossible, but also undesirable if we desire good government. Such a charter as that of the city of New York, for example, is a mere system of obscurity and of inefficiency. It disperses responsibility, multiplies elective offices beyond all reason or necessity, and makes both of the government itself and of its control by the voters a game of hide-and-seek in a labyrinth. Nothing could have been devised better suited to the uses of the professional politician, nothing susceptible of being more perfectly articulated with the nominating machine. As a means of popular government, it is not worth the bother and expense of an election.

Simplicity is necessary in government as in business, for unity, for responsibility, for efficiency, and for control: these four are, indeed, as a matter of experience, almost interchangeable and equivalent words. You cannot form or execute a judgment either in business or in politics without some such system of coherence and simplicity.

Simplicity does not involve, in the case of government, a return to any of the abuses we have partially corrected. We did begin at the wrong end when we devoted the ardour and labour of years of reform to the mere reform of the existing civil service, to the introduction of a system of qualification for appointment to office by examination. We should have begun by making more offices appointive and the business of appointing so conspicuous and responsible a thing that those who undertook it could not afford to make appointments upon any principle of favoritism, could not afford to serve their own private objects in making them or any private interest whatever. But responsible officers need not object, will not object, to being themselves protected and assisted by a system of qualifying examinations for appointment. They should and probably would prefer it. It is a sensible and serviceable system and secures the public service against many a minor abuse which might creep in even if those who made appointments made them with full responsibility to public opinion,—in the fierce, revealing light that beats upon every act of personal power. The instrumentalities we have already created would prove more serviceable than ever.

It is a very interesting and very vital thing to have come back to our original problem, to be obliged thus to become once more thoughtful partisans of genuine democracy. The issue is nothing less. What we need is a radical reform of our electoral system, and the proper reform will be a return to democracy. It is the high duty of every lover of political liberty to become a partisan of such a reform if once he becomes convinced of it. Another great age of American politics will have dawned when men seek once more the means to establish the rights of the people and forget parties and private interests to serve a nation.

ADDRESS BEFORE THE AMERICAN BAR ASSOCIATION,
CHATTANOOGA, TENNESSEE, AUGUST 31, 1910

Lawyers Becoming Mere Specialists

Constitutional lawyers have fallen into the background. We have relegated them to the Supreme Court, without asking ourselves where we are to find them when vacancies occur in that great tribunal.

A new type of lawyers has been created; and that new type has come to be the prevailing type. Lawyers have been sucked into the maelstrom of the new business system of the country. That system is highly technical and highly specialized. It is divided into distinct sections and provinces, each with particular legal problems of its own. Lawyers, therefore, everywhere that business has thickened and had a large development, have become experts in some special technical field. They do not practise law. They do not handle the general, miscellaneous interests of society. They are not general counsellors of right and obligation. They do not bear the relation to the business of their neighbourhoods that the family doctor bears to the health of the community in which he lives. They do not concern themselves with the universal aspects of society. The family doctor is himself giving place to a score of specialists; and so is also what one might call the family solicitor. Lawyers are specialists, like all other men around them. The general, broad, universal field of law grows dim and yet more dim to their apprehension as they spend year after year in minute examination and analysis of a particular part of it; not a small part, it may be, perhaps the part which the courts are for the time most concerned with, but a part which has undergone a high degree of development, which is very technical and many-sided, and which requires the study and practice of years for its mastery; and yet a province apart, whose conquest necessarily absorbs them and necessarily separates them from the dwindling body of general practitioners who used to be our statesmen.

And so society has lost something, or is losing it,—something which it is very serious to lose in an age of law, when society depends more than ever before upon the lawgiver and the courts for its structural steel, the harmony and coördination of its parts, its convenience, its permanency, and its facility. In gaining new functions, in being drawn into modern business instead of standing outside of it, in becoming identified with particular interests instead of holding aloof and impartially advising all interests, the lawyer has lost his old function, is looked askance at in politics, must disavow special engagements if he would have his counsel heeded in matters of common concern. Society has suffered a corresponding loss,— at least American society has. It has lost its one-time feeling for law as the basis of its peace, its progress, its prosperity. Lawyers are not now regarded as the mediators of progress. Society was always ready to be prejudiced against them; now it finds its prejudice confirmed.

Meanwhile, look what legal questions are to be settled, how stupendous they are, how far-reaching, and how impossible it will be to settle them without the advice of learned and experienced lawyers! The country must find lawyers of the right sort and of the old spirit to advise it, or it must stumble through a very chaos of blind experiment. It never needed lawyers who are also statesmen more than it needs them now,—needs them in its courts, in its legislatures, in its seats of executive authority,—lawyers who can think in the terms of society itself, mediate between interests, accommodate right to right, establish equity, and bring the peace that will come with genuine hearty coöperation, and will come in no other way.

Law and the Modern Corporation

The specialization of business and the extraordinary development of corporate organization and administration have led to consequences well worth the lawyer's consideration. Everyone else is considering them, and considering them with deep concern. We have witnessed in modern business the submergence of the individual within the organization, and yet the increase to an extraordinary degree of the power of the individual, of the individual who happens to control the organization. Most men are individuals no longer so far as their business, its activities or its moralities, is concerned. They are not units, but fractions; with their individuality and independence of choice in matters of business they have lost also their individual choice within the field of morals. They must do what they are told to do or lose their connection with modern affairs. They are not at liberty to ask whether what they are told to do is right or wrong. They cannot get at the men who ordered it,— have no access to them. They have no voice of counsel or of protest. They are mere cogs in a machine which has men for its parts. And yet there are men here and there with whom the whole choice lies. There are men who control the machine as a whole and the men who compose it. There are men who use it with an imperial freedom of design, whose power and whose individuality overtop whole communities. There is more individual power than ever, but those who exercise it are few and formidable, and the mass of men are mere pawns in the game.

The present task of the law is nothing less than to rehabilitate the individual,—not to make the subordinate independent of the superior, not to turn corporations into debating societies, not to disintegrate what we have been at such pains to piece together in the organization of modern industrial enterprise, but to undo enough of what we have done in the development of our law of corporations to give the law direct access again to the individual,—to every individual in all his functions.

Corporations do not do wrong. Individuals do wrong, the individuals who direct and use them for selfish and illegitimate purposes, to the injury of society and the serious curtailment of private rights. Guilt, as has been very truly said, is always personal. You cannot punish corporations. Fines fall upon the wrong persons, more heavily upon the innocent than upon the guilty, as much upon those who knew nothing whatever of the transactions for which the fine is imposed as upon those who originated and carried them through,—upon the stockholders and the customers rather than upon the men who direct the policy of the business. If you dissolve the offending corporation, you throw great undertakings out of gear. You merely drive what you are seeking to check into other forms or temporarily disorganize some important business altogether, to the infinite loss of thousands of entirely innocent persons and to the great inconvenience of society as a whole. Law can never accomplish its objects in that way. It can never bring peace or command respect by such futilities.

I regard the corporation as indispensable to modern business enterprise. I am not jealous of its size or might, if you will but abandon at the right points the fatuous, antiquated, and quite unnecessary fiction which treats it as a legal person; if you will but cease to deal with it by means of your law as if it were a single individual not only, but also,—what every child may perceive it is not,—a responsible individual. Such fictions and analogies were innocent and convenient enough so long as corporations were comparatively small and only one of many quite as important instrumentalities used in business, only a minor item in the economic order of society. But it is another matter now. They span society, and the responsibilities involved in their complex organization and action must be analyzed by the law as the responsibilities of society itself, in all its other aspects, have been.

The corporation now overshadows partnerships altogether. Still more does it overshadow all individuals engaged in business on their own capital and separate responsibility. It is an arrangement by which hundreds of thousands of men who would in days gone by have set up in business for themselves put their money into a single huge accumulation and place the entire direction of its employment in the hands of men they have never seen, with whom they never confer. These men, these quite autocratic managers, are thereby made, as it were, multiple individuals. In them are concentrated the resources, the choices, the opportunities, in brief the power, of thousands. They could never of themselves, of their own effort and sagacity, have accumulated the vast capital they employ, and employ as if it were their own; and yet they have not the full legal responsibilities of those who supplied them with it. Because they have the power of thousands they have not the responsibility common to those whose power they use! It is an extraordinary anomaly!

A modern corporation is an economic society, a little economic state,—and not always little, even as compared with states. Many modern corporations wield revenues and command resources which no ancient state possessed, and which some modern bodies politic show no approach to in their budgets. The economic power of society itself is concentrated in them for the conduct of this, that, or the other sort of business. The functions of business are differentiated and divided amongst them, but the power for each function is massed. In some instances even the functions are not separated. Railroad companies have been known to buy coal mines. Manufacturing combinations have been observed to develop a score of sub- sidiary industries, to spread a network of organization over related enterprises, and sometimes even over enterprises whose relation to their main undertakings it is difficult for the lay mind to perceive. Society, in short, has discovered a new way of massing its resources and its power of enterprise, is building up bodies economic outside its bodies politic which may, if we do not find the means to prevent them, the means of disclosing the responsibilities of the men who compose them, dominate bodies politic themselves.

And these huge industrial organizations we continue to treat as legal persons, as individuals, which we must not think of as consisting of persons, within which we despair of enabling the law to pick out anybody in particular to put either its restraint or its command

upon! It is childish, it is futile, it is ridiculous [copy illegible].
As well treat society itself as a unit; insist that it impose a fine upon
itself for every wrong done, no matter how notorious it may be
who did it; suggest that it embarrass all its processes of action and
even break itself up into its constituent parts and begin all over
again when the persons whom it has trusted prove depraved or
selfish. It is not even interesting to continue such an experiment.

Society cannot afford to have individuals wield the power of
thousands without personal responsibility. It cannot afford to let its
strongest men be the only men who are inaccessible to the law.
Modern democratic society, in particular, cannot afford to constitute
its economic undertakings upon the monarchical or aristocratic principle and adopt the fiction that the kings and great men thus set
up can do no wrong which will make them personally amenable to
the law which restrains smaller men: that their kingdoms, not
themselves, must suffer for their blindness, their follies, and their
transgressions of right.

It does not redeem the situation that these kings and chiefs of
industry are not chosen upon the hereditary principle (sometimes,
alas! they are) but are men who have risen by their own capacity,
sometimes from utter obscurity, with the freedom of self-assertion
which should characterize a free society. Their power is none the
less arbitrary and irresponsible when obtained. That a peasant may
become king does not render the kingdom democratic.

The Lawyer Is Responsible to the Community

I have used the corporation merely as an illustration. It stands in
the foreground of all modern economic questions, so far as the
United States are concerned. It is society's present means of effective life in the field of industry. Society must get complete control
of its instrument or fail. But I have used it only as an illustration of
a great theme, a theme greater than any single illustration could
compass,—namely, the responsibility of the lawyer to the community he professes to serve.

You are not a mere body of expert business advisers in the fields
of civil law or a mere body of expert advocates for those who get

entangled in the meshes of the criminal law. You are servants of the public, of the state itself. You are under bonds to serve the general interest, the integrity and enlightenment of law itself, in the advice you give individuals. It is your duty also to advise those who make the laws,—to advise them in the general interest, with a view to the amelioration of every undesirable condition that the law can reach, the removal of every obstacle to progress and fair dealing that the law can remove, the lightening of every burden the law can lift and the righting of every wrong the law can rectify. The services of the lawyer are indispensable not only in the application of the accepted processes of the law, the interpretation of existing rules in the daily operations of life and business. His services are indispensable also in keeping, and in making, the law clear with regard to responsibility, to organization, to liability, and, above all, to the relation of private rights to the public interest.

The structure of modern society is a structure of law rather than of custom. The lawyer's advice is more than ever necessary to the state, therefore. Communities as well as individuals stand in constant need of his guidance. This used to be commonplace doctrine amongst us; why does it now need to be preached again? Is it mere accident that the relation of the legal profession to affairs has changed? It is merely because the greater constitutional questions seemed for a time to be settled and legal debates gave place to industrial enterprise, a great age of material following a great age of political development? Has it been merely a change of circumstances, or has it been a change of attitude and spirit as well on the part of the profession itself? Has not the lawyer allowed himself to become part of the industrial development, has he not been sucked into the channels of business, has he not changed his connections and become part of the mercantile structure rather than part of the general social structure of our commonwealths as he used to be? Has he not turned away from his former interests and duties and become narrowed to a technical function?

Whatever may be the cause, it is evident that he now regards himself as the counsel of individuals exclusively, and not of communities. He may plead this new organization of politics, which seems to exclude all counsel except that of party success and personal control; he may argue that public questions have changed, have drifted away from his field, and that his advice is no longer asked; but, whatever his explanation or excuse, the fact is the same. He does not play the part he used to play; he does not show the spirit in affairs he used to show. He does not do what he ought to do.

For there never was a time, in fact, when his advice, his disinterested and earnest advice, was more needed than it is now in the exigent processes of reform, in the busy processes of legislation through which we are passing, with so singular a mixture of hope and apprehension. I hear a great many lawyers join the cry of the business men, that it is time legislators left business alone, allowed it to recover from the confusion and distraction of regulative statutes, altered tariffs, and supervising commissions, find its natural methods again, and go forward upon a way of prosperity which will not be beset by fear and uncertainty. But the cry is futile, the impatience which gives rise to it is selfish and ignorant. Nothing is settled or can be let alone when it is known to be wrong until it is set right. We have settled nothing in our recent reform legislation. That is the reason it is so unsatisfactory, and why some prudent and thoughtful men grow tired of it. But that is only another reason for seeking out and finding what will be the happy and successful way of setting our economic interests in order. There has been no satisfactory settlement, but there must be one. Public opinion is wider awake about these matters than it has been within the memory of any man living, and it is not going to turn away from them until satisfactory reforms of the law are found. There will be no peace until a happy and honourable basis of peace has been hit upon. Lawyers may come into the settlement or stay out of it, as they please, but a settlement there must be. For one, I hope that they will not stay out. I fear that it would be disastrous for them to do so,—disastrous to them and to society. I covet for them their old and honourable leadership in public counsel.

Just because they have so buried themselves in modern business, just because they have been so intimate a part of it, they know better than any one else knows what legal adjustments have and have

not been made,—know the practices that circumvent the law, even
the existing law, and the provisions of statute and court procedure
that might put a stop to them or square them with what the interests of the whole community demands,—theirs is the special responsibility to advise remedies. Theirs has been the part of intimate
counsel in all that has been going on. The country holds them
largely responsible for it. It distrusts every "corporation lawyer." It
supposes him in league with persons whom it has learned to dread,
to whom it ascribes a degree of selfishness which in effect makes
them public enemies, whatever their motives or their private character may be. And the lawyer,—what does he do? He stands stoutly
on the defensive. He advises his client how he may make shift, no
matter how the law runs. He declares that business would go very
well and every man get his due if only legislators would keep their
hands off! He keeps his expert advice for private persons and criti-
cises those who struggle without his countenance or assistance along
the difficult road of reform. It is not a promising situation.

Law Is the Staff of Real Liberty

Our reforms must be legal reforms. It is a pity they should go
forward without the aid of those who have studied the law in its
habit as it lives, those who know what is practicable and what is
not, those who know, or should know, if anybody does, the history
of liberty.

The history of liberty is a history of law. Men are not free when
they have merely conceived what their rights should be. They are
not set free by philosophies of right. Their theories of the rights of
man may even lead them astray, may make them break their hearts
in pursuit of hopes they can never realize, objects they can never
grasp, ideals that will forever elude them. Nothing is more practical
than the actual body of liberty. It consists of definitions based upon
experience, or, rather, of practices that are the very essence of experience. A right is worth fighting for only when it can be put into
operation. It can be put into operation only when its scope and
limitation can be accurately defined in terms of legal procedure;

and even then it may amount to nothing if the legal procedure be difficult, costly, or complicated.

And it is part of its definiteness and reality that liberty is always personal, never aggregate; always a thing inhering in individuals taken singly, never in groups or corporations or communities. The indivisible unit of society is the individual. He is also the indigestible unit. He cannot be merged or put into combination without being lost to liberty, because lost to independence. Make of him a fraction instead of an integer, and you have broken his spirit, cut off the sources of his life. That is why I plead so earnestly for the individualization of responsibility within the corporation, for the establishment of the principle by law that a man has no more right to do a wrong as a member of a corporation than as an individual. Establish that principle, cut away the undergrowth of law that has sprung up so rankly about the corporation and made of it an ambush and covert, and it will give every man the right to say No again, to refuse to do wrong, no matter who orders him to do it. It will make a man of him. It is in his interest no less than in the interest of society, which must see to it that wrong-doing is put a stop to.

We are upon the eve of a great reconstruction. It calls for creative statesmanship as no age has done since that great age in which we set up the government under which we live, that government which was the admiration of the world until it suffered wrongs to grow up under it which have made many of our own compatriots question the freedom of our institutions and preach revolution against them. I do not fear revolution. I do not fear it even if it comes. I have unshaken faith in the power of America to keep its self-possession. If revolution comes, it will come in peaceful guise, as it came when we put aside the crude government of the Confederation and created the great federal state, which governed individuals, not corporations, and which has been these hundred and thirty years our vehicle of progress.

Chapter Seven

THE CHALLENGE OF ACTION

THESE selections cover the period between Wilson's inaugura-
tion as the Governor of New Jersey and his acceptance of the
Democratic nomination for the Presidency. They strike the main
notes of the New Freedom: the lifting of monopolistic control from
economic and political life; the release of the people's energies and
the coming in of a new age of accomplishment for America. The
tone and style are increasingly those of a man eager to get on with a
task; literary finish gives way to extemporaneous speech.

INAUGURAL ADDRESS AS GOVERNOR OF
NEW JERSEY, JANUARY 17, 1911

The Gate of Opportunity

The opportunity of our day in the field of politics no man can
mistake who can read any, even the most superficial, signs of the
times. We have never seen a day when duty was more plain, the
task to be performed more obvious, the way in which to accomplish
it more easy to determine. The air has in recent months cleared
amazingly about us, and thousands, hundreds of thousands, have
lifted their eyes to look about them, to see things they never saw
before, to comprehend things that once seemed vague and elusive.
The whole world has changed within the lifetime of men not yet
in their thirties; the world of business, and therefore the world of
society and the world of politics. The organization and movement
of business are new and upon a novel scale. Business has changed
so rapidly that for a long time we were confused, alarmed, bewildered, in a sort of terror of the things we had ourselves raised
up. We talked about them either in sensational articles in the maga-

zines which distorted every line of the picture, or in conservative editorials in our newspapers, which stoutly denied that anything at all had happened, or in grave discourses which tried to treat them as perfectly normal phenomena, or in legislative debates which sought to govern them with statutes which matched them neither in size nor in shape.

But, if only by sheer dint of talking about them, either to frighten or to reassure one another, or to make ourselves out wiser or more knowing than our fellows, we have at last turned them about and looked at them from almost every angle and begin to see them whole, as they are. Corporations are no longer hobgoblins which have sprung at us out of some mysterious ambush, nor yet unholy inventions of rascally rich men, nor yet the puzzling devices by which ingenious lawyers build up huge rights out of a multitude of small wrongs; but merely organizations of a perfectly intelligible sort which the law has licensed for the convenience of extensive business; organizations which have proved very useful but which have for the time being slipped out of the control of the very law that gave them leave to be and that can make or unmake them at pleasure. We have now to set ourselves to control them, soberly but effectively, and to bring them thoroughly within the regulation of the law.

There is a great opportunity here; for wise regulation, wise adjustment, will mean the removal of half the difficulties that now beset us in our search for justice and equality and fair chances of fortune for the individuals who make up our modern society. And there is a great obligation as well as a great opportunity, an imperative obligation, from which we cannot escape if we would. Public opinion is at last wide awake. It begins to understand the problems to be dealt with; it begins to see very clearly indeed the objects to be sought. It knows what has been going on. It sees where resistance has come from whenever efforts at reform have been made, and knows also the means of resistance that have been resorted to. It is watchful, insistent, suspicious. No man who wishes to enjoy the public confidence dare hold back, and, if he is wise, he will not resort to subterfuge. A duty is exacted of him which he must perform simply, directly, immediately. The gate of opportunity stands wide open. If we are foolish enough to be unwilling to pass through it, the whip of opinion will drive us through.

No wise man will say, of course, that he sees the whole problem of reform lying plain before him, or knows how to frame the entire body of law that will be necessary to square business with the general interest, and put right and fairness and public spirit in the saddle again in all the transactions of our new society; but some things are plain enough, and upon these we can act. . . .

We are servants of the people, of the whole people. Their interest should be our constant study. We should pursue it without fear or favour. Our reward will be greater than that to be obtained in any other service: the satisfaction of furthering large ends, large purposes, of being an intimate part of that slow but constant and ever hopeful force of liberty and of enlightenment that is lifting mankind from age to age to new levels of progress and achievement, and of having been something greater than successful men. For we shall have been instruments of humanity, men whose thought was not for themselves, but for the true and lasting comfort and happiness of men everywhere. It is not the foolish ardour of too sanguine or too radical reform that I urge upon you, but merely the tasks that are evident and pressing, the things we have knowledge and guidance enough to do; and to do with confidence and energy. I merely point out the present business of progressive and serviceable government, the next stage on the journey of duty. The path is as inviting as it is plain. Shall we hesitate to tread it?

ADDRESS AT KANSAS CITY,
MISSOURI, MAY 5, 1911

A Contest of Ideals

There can be no mistaking the fact that we are now face to face with political changes which may have a very profound effect upon our political life. Those who do not understand the impending change are afraid of it. Those who do understand it know that it is not a process of revolution, but a process of restoration, rather, in which there is as much healing as hurt.

The American people feel that a great many things in their economic life and in their political action are out of gear. They have been cheated by their own political machinery. They have been dominated by the very instrumentalities which they themselves created in the field of industrial action. The liberty of the individual is hampered and impaired. They desire, therefore, not a revolution, not a cutting loose from any part of their past, but a readjustment of the elements of their life, a reconsideration of what it is just to do and equitable to arrange in order that they may be indeed free, may indeed make their own choices and live their own life undominated, unafraid, unsuspicious, confident that they will be served by their public men and that the open processes of their government will bring to them justice and timely reform.

What we are witnessing now is not so much a conflict of parties as a contest of ideals, a struggle between those who, because they do not understand what is happening, blindly hold on to what is and those who, because they do see the real questions of the present and of the future in a clear, revealing light, know that there must be sober change; know that progress, none the less active and determined because it is sober and just, is necessary for the maintenance of our institutions and the rectification of our life. In both the great national parties there are men who feel this ardour of progress and of reform, and in both parties there are men who hold back, who struggle to restrain change, who do not understand it or who have reason to fear it. . . .

Both parties are of necessity breaking away from the past, whether they will or no, because our life has broken away from the past. The life of America is not the life it was twenty years ago. It is not the life it was ten years ago. We have changed our economic conditions from top to bottom, and with our economic conditions has changed also the organization of our life. The old party formulas do not fit the present problems. The old cries of the stump sound as if they belonged to a past age which men have almost forgotten. The things which used to be put into the party platforms of ten years ago would sound antiquated now. You will note, moreover, that the political audiences which nowadays gather together are not partisan audiences. They are made up of all elements and come together, not to hear parties denounced or praised, but to hear the interests of the nation discussed in new terms—the terms of the present moment.

We have so complicated our machinery of government, we have made it so difficult, so full of ambushes and hiding places, so indirect, that instead of having true representative government we have a great inextricable jungle of organization intervening between the people and the processes of their government; so that by stages, without intending it, without being aware of it, we have lost the purity and directness of representative government. What we must devote ourselves to now is, not to upsetting our institutions, but to restoring them.

Combinations of Wealth Dominate Life and Politics

Let us ask ourselves very frankly what it is that needs to be corrected. To sum it all up in one sentence, it is the control of politics and of our life by great combinations of wealth. Men sometimes talk as if it were wealth we were afraid of, as if we were jealous of the accumulation of great fortunes. Nothing of the kind is true. America has not the slightest jealousy of the legitimate accumulation of wealth. Everybody knows that there are hundreds and thousands of men of large means and large economic power who have come by it all perfectly legitimately not only, but in a way that deserves the thanks and admiration of the communities they have served and developed. But everybody knows also that some of the men who control the wealth and have built up the industry of the country seek to control politics and also to dominate the life of common men in a way in which no man should be permitted to dominate.

In the first place, there is the notorious operation of the bipartisan political machine: I mean the machine which does not represent party principle of any kind, but which is willing to enter into any combination, with whatever group of persons or of politicians, to control the offices of localities and of States and of the nation itself in order to maintain the power of those who direct it. This machine is supplied with its funds by the men who use it in order to protect themselves against legislation which they do not desire and in order to obtain the legislation which is necessary for the prosecution of their purposes.

The methods of our legislatures make the operations of such machines easy and convenient, for very little of our legislation is formed and effected by open debate upon the floor. Almost all of it is framed in lawyers' offices, discussed in committee rooms, passed without debate. Bills that the machine and its backers do not desire are smothered in committee; measures which they do desire are brought out and hurried through their passage. It happens again and again that great groups of such bills are rushed through in the hurried hours that mark the close of the legislative sessions, when every one is withheld from vigilance by fatigue and when it is possible to do secret things.

When we stand in the presence of these things and see how complete and sinister their operation has been we cry out with no little truth that we no longer have representative government. . . .

The second power we fear is the control of our life through the vast privileges of corporations which use the wealth of masses of men to sustain their enterprise. It is in connection with this danger that it is necessary to do some of our clearest and frankest thinking. It is a fundamental mistake to speak of the privileges of these great corporations as if they fell within the class of private right and of private property. Those who administer the affairs of great joint stock companies are really administering the property of communities, the property of the whole mass and miscellany of men who have bought the stock or the bonds that sustain the enterprise. The stocks and the bonds are constantly changing hands. There is no fixed partnership. Moreover, managers of such corporations are the trustees of moneys which they themselves never accumulated, but which have been drawn together out of private savings here, there, and everywhere.

What is necessary in order to rectify the whole mass of business of this kind is that those who control it should entirely change their point of view. They are trustees, not masters, of private property, not only because their power is derived from a multitude of men, but also because in its investment it affects a multitude of men. It determines the development or decay of communities. It is the means of lifting or depressing the life of the whole country. They must regard themselves as representatives of a public power.

JACKSON DAY DINNER ADDRESS,
WASHINGTON, JANUARY 8, 1912

Government and Business Privately Controlled

Now, what has been the matter? The matter has been that the Government of this country was privately controlled and that the business of this country was privately controlled; that we did not not have genuine representative government and that the people of this country did not have the control of their own affairs.

What do we stand for here to-night and what shall we stand for as long as we live? We stand for setting the Government of this country free and the business of this country free. The facts have been disputed by a good many sections of the Democratic party for the last half generation, but they were not clearly recognized.

I make the assertion that the Government was privately controlled. I mean to put it specifically that the Government of this country was managed by politicians who gained the contributions which they used by solicitation from particular groups of business interests, on the understanding, explicit or implied, that the first care of the Government was to be for those particular interests. I am not questioning either the integrity or patriotism of the men concerned. I have no right to. In most instances they were of that old belief, cropping up again and again in America, that the people of this country are not capable of perceiving their own interest and of managing their own affairs; that they have not the contact with large affairs; that they have not the variety of experience which qualifies them to take charge of their own affairs. It is the old Hamiltonian doctrine that those who have the biggest asset in the Government should be the trustees for the rest of us; that the men who conduct the biggest business transactions are the only men who should stand upon an elevation sufficient to see the whole range of our affairs, and that if we will but follow their leadership we may share in their prosperity.

That is the Republican doctrine, and I am perfectly willing, as a tribute to their honesty though not to their intelligence, to admit that they really believe it; that they really believe it is unsafe to trust such delicate matters as the complicated business of this country to the general judgment of the country. They believe only a very small coterie of gentlemen are to be trusted with the conduct of large affairs. There was a long period in New Jersey, for example, in which no commissioner of insurance was ever chosen without first consulting or getting the consent of the head of the largest insurance company in the State, and I am willing to admit, at any rate for the sake of argument, that it was supposed he, better than anyone else, knew who was qualified for the job. He did know who was qualified for the job and he had the proper point of view in demonstrating that it was mainly for the benefit of the big interests.

The other thing that has been privately controlled in this country is the business of the country. I do not mean that each man's particular business ought not to be privately controlled, but I mean that the great business transactions of this country are privately controlled by gentlemen whom I can name and whom I will name, if it is desired; men of great dignity of character; men, as I believe, of great purity of purpose, but men who have concentrated, in their own hands, transactions which they are not willing to have the rest of the country interfere with.

Now, the real difficulty in the United States, it seems to me, is not the existence of great individual combinations—that is dangerous enough in all countries—but the real danger is the combination of the combinations; the real danger is that the same groups of men control chains of banks, systems of railways, whole manufacturing enterprises, great mining projects, great enterprises for the developing of the natural water power of this country, and that threaded together in the personnel of a series of boards of directors is a community of interest more formidable than any conceivable combination in the United States.

It has been said that you cannot "unscramble eggs," and I am perfectly willing to admit it, but I can see in all cases before they are scrambled that they are not put in the same basket and entrusted to the same groups of persons.

What we have got to do—and it is a colossal task—a task not to be undertaken with a light head or without judgment—but what we have got to do is to disentangle this colossal community of interest. No matter how we may purpose dealing with a single combination in restraint of trade, you will agree with me in this that I think no combination is big enough for the United States to be afraid of; and when all the combinations are combined and this combination is not disclosed by any process of incorporation or law, but is merely the identity of personnel, then there is something for the law to pull apart, and gently, but firmly and persistently dissect.

ADDRESS AT BOSTON,
JANUARY 27, 1912

The Tariff Is a Matter of Conservation

The most pressing thing in America is the question of conservation, not merely the conservation of so much as remains of our unwasted resources—I do not mean the mere renewal of our forests; I do not mean mere preservation and a more economical use of our water power—I mean the preservation of our energies and of the genius of our people.

Questions of sanitation to me are questions of conservation; questions of morals are questions of conservation. You cannot conserve the energy of America unless you give to its exercise the proper moral environment. You cannot get the best work out of your workmen unless you make them by honest operations to believe that you regard them, not as your tools, but as your partners; and the whole conservation of America is a question of the supremacy of America, of her right thinking, and of her righteous action.

We owe it to future generations that we should not waste or destroy our resources, and we owe it still more to future generations that we should not lower the vitality of our workingwomen, check the vitality of our children, demoralize the processes of our life at any point. And yet how long is it since America troubled herself with questions of conservation? How long is it since we felt in the heyday of thoughtless youth, with so much youth at our hands, that we did not have to be careful in the economy of it; and how constantly did we rejoice that we had put ourselves in a position to be wasteful.

Almost every time public questions are discussed in this day somebody asks the question: "What is the leading question of the approaching political campaign?" Now, I don't know what is the leading question, but I know what is the central question, or at least I think I do, because I find that every road leads to that question, and that is the question of the tariff. The question of conservation leads straight to that same radical origin, to this road of the tariff, because by protecting ourselves from foreign competition—from the skill and energy and resourcefulness of other nations—we have felt ourselves at liberty to be wasteful in our own processes. I believe that it is one of the most serious consequences of the protective tariff that it has made it unnecessary that we should be careful and saving in our own industrial enterprises.

America in the Family of Nations

We are not about to change the tariff because men in this country have changed their theories about the tariff. We are going to change it because the conditions of America are going to burst through it and are now bursting through it.

You cannot fight a Spanish war and join the family of nations in international affairs and still keep your gaze directed inward upon yourself, because along with the singular change that came upon us, that notably altered or affected the very character of our Government, the Nation itself began to be a different thing.

Have you ever thought of the history of our Government, of the history of the Executive part of it? Do you not know that down to the period when we began to shut our doors tight against foreign commercial intercourse the Executive was the most important part of the Government of the United States, and then we went through a long period when, except for the civil war when there was concentrated energy to be found, the Executive counted for almost nothing and the Congress for almost everything, because every question was a neighbourhood question? It was our own. We had not any national spokesman, such as the Executive is, prepared to serve us. And then came the Spanish war, and since then do you think it is a question that the Executive has again become a conspicuous part of this Government?

So soon as a nation must act you must have a body through which it can act. So soon as it becomes a single will you have to have a lodgment for the guiding intelligence, a single will in every nation that is important in international relations—a strong guiding Executive—not because it deliberately chooses to have it, but because it has no choice—it must have it. And so while we have waited and drifted in altruistic fashion into a war for the sake of the Cubans, we altered the centre of gravity of our Government. . . .

Very well; our thoughts are concentrated upon ourselves. Now, we are changing our point of view and looking abroad upon the face of the earth, seeking to allow ourselves an outlet into the general field of competition, which includes the whole round globe. In the meantime what have we done? Do you really think that the tariff has produced efficiency? Do you believe that combinations, most of which have been made possible by the tariff, have had their chief effect efficiency and economy?

True Efficiency Depends on the Workman

There is only one thing upon which efficiency depends, and that is the whole thing. You cannot get efficiency out of your workmen if you overdrive them, any more than you can get it out of your machines if you overdrive them. Did you ever notice how much more tender and considerate of their machines some American manufacturers are than they are of the human beings they employ? Do not you know that every thoughtful manufacturer studies what his machinery will bear, and he will dismiss an employee who puts more on that machine than it can bear or than he ought to put on it? Very well; does he dismiss the same superintendent who puts more on the human muscle and spirit than it can bear? Not often. When you find a manufacturer who is considerate of the strain on his men and who makes them feel that he is taking as much care of them as of his machinery you find the most efficient establishment in the trade.

Would it not be a good idea to draw your cost sheets after a new fashion? Would it not be a good idea to have a cost sheet to show the strain put upon the men in every respect—not merely the physical strain, but a sheet which would show the strain put on them by lack of ventilation in the factory, by the lack of opportunities of amusement, by the absence of the feeling on the part of the workmen that they are really regarded as essential partners in a mutual undertaking which makes every man just as eager to make the product good as his employer could possibly be? It would be a moral balance sheet of the whole industry of the Nation. . . .

The only reason that America is efficient is that American brains are capable of entering into any competition that you can conceive of. The central thing is that so long as we keep American life relatively what we intended it to be, we have only to import a workman who earns 30 cents a day on the other side of the water and find him in an employ earning $2 a day on this side of the water. A man cannot change the dexterity of his fingers or his physical make-up in a month, but he can change his point of view. He can catch the infection of the factory in which he works. He can recognize under the intelligent supervision of the superintendent that through his participation and because he has become a constituent part of the great throbbing American machine that we call civilization he can be an infinitely better workman than he is anywhere else. . . .

You cannot afford to be narrow in the presence of change, and you cannot afford to think that your legislators and your executives are bringing change upon you. Neither can you afford to think that you can take no guiding part in the change. We are facing a new age, with new objects, new objects of American trade and manufacture, because the minute you begin to make models for foreign sale you have to change the machinery, the whole point of view. We are facing new objects with new standards, the standards of cosmopolitan intelligence instead of provincial intelligence, and with a new conception of what it means to produce wealth and produce prosperity.

ADDRESS BEFORE THE GENERAL ASSEMBLY OF
VIRGINIA, RICHMOND, FEBRUARY 1, 1912

Americans Must Learn to Live Together

Until the year 1890, every ten years when we took the census, we were able to draw a frontier in this country. It is true that in what is called the golden age, 1849, when gold was discovered in California, we sent outposts to the Pacific and settled the further slope of the Rocky Mountains. But between us and that slope, until 1890, there intervened an unoccupied space where the census map makers could draw a frontier. But when we reached the year 1890 there was no frontier discoverable in America.

What did that mean? That meant that men who found conditions intolerable in crowded America no longer had a place free where they could take up land of their own and start a new hope. That is what that meant, and as America turns upon herself her seething millions and the cauldron grows hotter and hotter, is it not the great duty of America to see that her men remain free and happy under the conditions that have now sprung up? It is true that we needed a frontier so much that after the Spanish war we annexed a new frontier some seven thousand miles off in the Pacific. But that is a long cry, and it takes the energy of a very young man to seek that outlet in the somewhat depressing climate of the Philippines.

So we now realize that Americans are not free to release themselves. We have got to live together and be happy in the family. I remember an old judge who was absolutely opposed to divorce, because he said that a man will be restless as long as he knows he can get loose; but that so soon as it is firmly settled in his mind that he has got to make the best of it, he finds a sudden current of peace and contentment. Now there is no divorce for us in our American life. We have got to put up with one another, and we have got to see to it that we so regulate and assuage one another that we will not be intolerable to each other. We have got to get a *modus vivendi* in America for happiness, and that is our new problem.

And I call you to witness it is a new problem. America never had to finish anything before; she has been at liberty to do the thing with a broad hand, quickly, improvise something and go on to the next thing; leave all sorts of waste behind her, push on, blaze trails through the forest, beat paths across the prairie. But now we have even to stop and pave our streets.

"THE NEW FREEDOM,"
1913

What This Young Country Will Do with her Strength

The first and chief need of this nation of ours to-day is to include in the partnership of government all those great bodies of unnamed men who are going to produce our future leaders and renew the future energies of America. And as I confess that, as I confess my belief in the common man, I know what I am saying. The man who is swimming against the stream knows the strength of it. The man who is in the mêlée knows what blows are being struck and what blood is being drawn. The man who is on the make is the judge of what is happening in America, not the man who has made good; not the man who has emerged from the flood; not the man who is standing on the bank looking on, but the man who is struggling for his life and for the lives of those who are dearer to him than himself. That is the man whose judgment will tell you what is going on in America; that is the man by whose judgment I, for one, wish to be guided.

We have had the wrong jury; we have had the wrong group,—no, I will not say the wrong group, but too small a group,—in control of the policies of the United States. The average man has not been consulted, and his heart had begun to sink for fear he never would be consulted again. Therefore, we have got to organize a government whose sympathies will be open to the whole body of the people of the United States, a government which will consult as large a proportion of the people of the United States as possible before it acts. Because the great problem of government is to know what the average man is experiencing and is thinking about. Most of us are average men; very few of us rise, except by fortunate accident, above the general level of the community about us; and therefore the man who thinks common thoughts, the man who has had common experiences, is almost always the man who interprets America aright. . . .

The hope of the United States in the present and in the future is the same that it has always been: it is the hope and confidence that out of unknown homes will come men who will constitute themselves the masters of industry and of politics. The average hopefulness, the average welfare, the average enterprise, the average initiative, of the United States are the only things that make it rich. We are not rich because a few gentlemen direct our industry; we are rich because of our own intelligence and our own industry. America does not consist of men who get their names into the newspapers; America does not consist politically of the men who set themselves up to be political leaders; she does not consist of the men who do most of her talking,—they are important only so far as they speak for that great voiceless multitude of men who constitute the great body and the saving force of the nation. Nobody who cannot speak the common thought, who does not move by the common impulse, is the man to speak for America, or for any of her future purposes. Only he is fit to speak who knows the thoughts of the great body of citizens, the men who go about their business every day, the men who toil from morning till night, the men who go home tired in the evenings, the men who are carrying on the things we are so proud of.

You know how it thrills our blood sometimes to think how all the nations of the earth wait to see what America is going to do with her power, her physical power, her enormous resources, her enormous wealth. The nations hold their breath to see what this young country will do with her young unspoiled strength; we cannot help but be proud that we are strong. But what has made us strong? The toil of millions of men, the toil of men who do not boast, who are inconspicuous, but who live their lives humbly from day to day; it is the great body of toilers that constitutes the might of America. It is one of the glories of our land that nobody is able to predict from what family, from what region, from what race, even, the leaders of the country are going to come.

ADDRESS AT PHILADELPHIA,
FEBRUARY 21, 1911

The Radicalism of the Times

What are we fighting for, then, in this so-called radicalism? Radicalism? Yes, because it goes to the root of the matter, but not radicalism in the sense that it is an insensate love of change, not radicalism in the sense that it is love of uprooting things. On the contrary, it is love of solidifying things and making them real instead of a sham. . . .

I like the image of the root rather than the image of the foundation, for the foundation takes nothing from the soil, whereas the root draws its whole sustenance from it, and I know the history of government too well not to know that all its vital forces come from the hidden earth, from the hidden origins, the hidden fountains that lie in the great body of the people. I have not seen in reading history the sources of strength coming from the top and flowing into the root. I have always seen them rising from the root into the branches. I have never read of any man who was really distinguished in the service of his kind, who could not either by direct origin or by the straight derivations of his sympathy, be traced back to the great heart and purpose of the people themselves.

The great men of the world have always been the men who spoke for the rest of their fellow-men; have always been the men who gave voice to what otherwise might have been without articulation or utterance; the men who summed up in themselves, in their own energies, in their own hopes, in their own visions, what slumbered in the minds and hearts and aspirations of countless multitudes of men, who, if they had not found the outlet of such representation would have been dumb and powerless.

The so-called radicalism of our time is nothing else than an effort to release the energies of our time. This great people is not bent upon any form of destruction. This great people is not in love with any kind of injustice. This great people is in love with the realization of what is equitable, pure, just, and of good repute, and it is bound by the clogs and impediments of our political machinery. What we are trying to do is to release all its generous forces. They are not forces of envy. They are not forces which would seek to imperil the prosperity of a great country, even though it be merely the material prosperity of that country, but there resides in them what is the heart of all hopeful enterprises.

Our forefathers were not uttering mere words when they spoke of the realization of happiness. Many people pile up great fortunes and fail to find happiness at the heart of them. Happiness comes with a pure heart. Happiness comes with unselfish motives. Happiness comes with the consciousness that you have served and sacrificed and done for men what you would have them do for you. It does not come, it never has come, it never can come, from the knowledge that you have trampled men under foot and spoiled human lives in order to attain it.

Release the generous energies of our people and you will come upon a time of prosperity when the hearts of men will flower, when men will see that the true happiness of life is not in devising schemes of power, but in realizing in themselves the common aspirations of the race. Just as in great literature there come to expression the great emotions of mankind, so in politics there come to realization the great actions of mankind, so that men are partners with each other in the hopeful enterprises of human perfection and the hopeful enterprises of justice to which all government is consecrated.

Let us not be jealous of the radicalism which seeks to derive all our forces from this single root of perfection.

ADDRESS ON LINCOLN'S BIRTHDAY,
CHICAGO, FEBRUARY 12, 1912

The Coming On of a New Spirit

I always remember that America was established not to create wealth—though any nation must create wealth which is going to make an economic foundation for its life—but to realize a vision, to realize an ideal. America has put itself under bonds to the earth to discover and maintain liberty among men, and if she cannot see liberty now with the clear, unerring vision she had at the outset, she has lost her title, she has lost every claim to the leadership and respect of the nations of the world. If she is going to put her material processes before her spiritual processes, then all I have to say is she has ceased to be America and should withdraw the name in order to withdraw the promise, because that name has always shown here in the West like a beacon of hope and confidence for all the nations of the world.

Men have turned their eyes towards America in order that they might release themselves from the very kind of privilege which we have permitted in some places to grow; and if we discover that we ourselves have fallen into the slough, that we ourselves have not taken the ways that lie upon firm ground, the ways that lift themselves up the long slopes that are the slopes of ultimate emancipation, then how will the hope of the world subside, how will men cry out in despair that the great light in the West has gone out. Unless we once more get in our hearts the passion for what America stands for we shall accomplish nothing.

In this age of difficulty and perplexity, how does any man relieve himself from perplexity? If he goes to bed at night arguing upon the grounds of solvency and expediency he will toss all night long on his bed, but if it is proof he desires, there is only one rule, and that is the rule of right and justice, and if he says, "I am going to stand by that, cost what it may," then sleep will come to him as it came to him when a little child and he imagined that angels were about his couch. That is the temper that makes America and I, for my part, am confident with the confidence of youth that this spirit has come back in America.

I don't profess its coming. [To follow] the great hurricane with which comment moves from one part of this country to another is to realize that it has come, that men are ready to make sacrifices in order that the public weal may be served and that there is henceforth to be a common council into which men will enter, not only that they and their individual fortunes may be served, but that the great fortunes of America may also be served. I am not speaking in my interest. No, gentlemen, you knew when you came here that you were not going to listen to a man who was going to commend himself to you. You knew you were going to listen to a man who whether he was right or wrong was going to tell you what he thought and leave it to the jury and not the private councils held with men of understanding.

In this country I am aware of the coming on of a new spirit—that old subtle cunning and sagacity that used to be the rule in America. The old idea of lie low and let the thing work itself out is disappearing. You can't lie low any more, because there is a searchlight moving everywhere. Frankness has come to be the law of life amongst us—amongst those of us who respect ourselves and respect our communities and hope for the best things in politics, and that's the reason the lines of party are being obscured; that's the reason men are about to treat them according to their right temperaments and purposes; that's the reason the standpat dam that has been built so high but of such solid, stupid masonry, is going to give way. . . .

America has come again upon a constructive age of politics where her statesmen shall talk business and her business consent to the processes of liberty and achievement.

ACCEPTANCE SPEECH, SEAGIRT, NEW JERSEY,
AUGUST 7, 1912

In the Presence of an Awakened Nation

We stand in the presence of an awakened Nation, impatient of partisan make-believe. The public man who does not realize the fact and feel its stimulation must be singularly unsusceptible to the influences that stir in every quarter about him. The Nation has awakened to a sense of neglected ideals and neglected duties; to a consciousness that the rank and file of her people find life very hard to sustain, that her young men find opportunity embarrassed, and that her older men find business difficult to renew and maintain because of circumstances of privilege and private advantage which have interlaced their subtle threads throughout almost every part of the framework of our present law. She has awakened to the knowledge that she has lost certain cherished liberties and has wasted priceless resources which she had solemnly undertaken to hold in trust for posterity and for all mankind; and to the conviction that she stands confronted with an occasion for constructive statesmanship such as has not arisen since the great days in which her Government was set up.

Plainly, it is a new age. The tonic of such a time is very exhilarating. It requires self-restraint not to attempt too much, and yet it would be cowardly to attempt too little. The path of duty soberly and bravely trod is the way to service and distinction, and many adventurous feet seek to set out upon it.

There never was a time when impatience and suspicion were more keenly aroused by private power selfishly employed; when jealousy of everything concealed or touched with any purpose not linked with general good, or inconsistent with it, more sharply or immediately displayed itself.

Nor was the country ever more susceptible to unselfish appeals or to the high arguments of sincere justice. These are the unmistakable symptoms of an awakening. There is the more need of wise counsel because the people are so ready to heed counsel if it be given honestly and in their interest.

Great Questions of Right and Justice

It is in the broad light of this new day that we stand face to face—with what? Plainly not with questions of party, not with a contest for office, not with a petty struggle for advantage, Democrat against Republican, liberal against conservative, progressive against reactionary. With great questions of right and of justice, rather— questions of national development, of the development of character and of standards of action no less than of a better business system, more free, more equitable, more open to ordinary men, practicable to live under, tolerable to work under, of a better fiscal system whose taxes shall not come out of the pockets of the many to go into the pockets of the few, and within whose intricacies special privilege may not so easily find covert. The forces of the Nation are asserting themselves against every form of special privilege and pri-

vate control, and are seeking bigger things than they have ever here-
tofore achieved. They are sweeping away what is unrighteous in
order to vindicate once more the essential rights of human life; and,
what is very serious to us, they are looking to us for guidance, disinterested guidance, at once honest and fearless. . . .

What is there to do? It is hard to sum the great task up, but
apparently this is the sum of the matter: There are two great things
to do. One is to set up the rule of justice and of right in such matters as the tariff, the regulation of the trusts, and the prevention of
monopoly, the adaptation of our banking and currency laws to the
various uses to which our people must put them, the treatment
of those who do the daily labour in our factories and mines and
throughout all our great industrial and commercial undertakings,
and the political life of the people of the Philippines, for whom we
hold governmental power in trust, for their service, not our own.
The other, the additional duty, is the great task of protecting our
people and our resources and of keeping open to the whole people
the doors of opportunity through which they must, generation by
generation, pass if they are to make conquest of their fortunes in
health, in freedom, in peace, and in contentment. In the performance of this second great duty we are face to face with questions of
conservation and of development, questions of forests and water
powers and mines and waterways, of the building of an adequate
merchant marine, and the opening of every highway and facility and
the setting up of every safeguard needed by a great, industrious,
expanding nation.

These are all great matters upon which everybody should be
heard. We have got into trouble in recent years chiefly because these
large things, which ought to have been handled by taking counsel
with as large a number of persons as possible because they touched
every interest and the life of every class and region, have in fact
been too often handled in private conference. They have been settled by very small, and often deliberately exclusive, groups of men
who undertook to speak for the whole Nation, or rather for themselves in the terms of the whole Nation—very honestly it may be
true, but very ignorantly sometimes, and very short-sightedly, too—a

poor substitute for genuine common counsel. No group of directors, economic or political, can speak for a people. They have neither the point of view nor the knowledge. Our difficulty is not that wicked and designing men have plotted against us, but that our common affairs have been determined upon too narrow a view, and by too private an initiative. Our task now is to effect a great readjustment and get the forces of the whole people once more into play. We need no revolution; we need no excited change; we need only a new point of view and a new method and spirit of counsel.

The Nation Has Been at War within Itself

We are servants of the people, the whole people. The Nation has been unnecessarily, unreasonably, at war within itself. Interest has clashed with interest when there were common principles of right and of fair dealing which might and should have bound them all together, not as rivals, but as partners. As the servants of all, we are bound to undertake the great duty of accommodation and adjustment.

We cannot undertake it except in a spirit which some find it hard to understand. Some people only smile when you speak of yourself as a servant of the people; it seems to them like affectation or mere demagoguery. They ask what the unthinking crowd knows or comprehends of great complicated matters of government. They shrug their shoulders and lift their eyebrows when you speak as if you really believed in presidential primaries, in the direct election of United States Senators, and in an utter publicity about everything that concerns government, from the sources of campaign funds to the intimate debate of the higher affairs of State.

They do not, or will not, comprehend the solemn thing that is in your thought. You know as well as they do that there are all sorts and conditions of men—the unthinking mixed with the wise, the reckless with the prudent, the unscrupulous with the fair and honest —and you know what they sometimes forget, that every class without exception affords a sample of the mixture, the learned and the fortunate no less than the uneducated and the struggling mass. But you see more than they do. You see that these multitudes of men, mixed, of every kind and quality, constitute somehow an organic and noble whole, a single people, and that they have interests which no man can privately determine without their knowledge and counsel. That is the meaning of representative government itself. Representative government is nothing more or less than an effort to give voice to this great body through spokesmen chosen out of every grade and class.

To Set Up an Unentangled Government

A presidential campaign * may easily degenerate into a mere personal contest and so lost its real dignity and significance. There is no indispensable man. The government will not collapse and go to pieces if any one of the gentlemen who are seeking to be entrusted with its guidance should be left at home. But men are instruments. We are as important as the cause we represent, and in order to be important must really represent a cause. What is our cause? The people's cause. That is easy to say, but what does it mean? The common as against any particular interest whatever? Yes, but that, too, needs translation into acts and policies. We represent the desire to set up an unentangled government, a government that cannot be used for private purposes, either in the field of business or in the field of politics; a government that will not tolerate the use of the organization of a great party to serve the personal aims and ambitions of any individual, and that will not permit legislation to be employed to further any private interest. It is a great conception, but I am free to serve it, as you also are. I could not have accepted a nomination which left me bound to any man or group of men. No man can be just who is not free; and no man who has to show favours ought to undertake the solemn responsibility of government

* The speeches of the 1912 campaign are not covered in this volume. *The New Freedom* is generally thought to represent the substance of these speeches; actually the book is in no small part composed of speeches delivered prior to this time, and it is so drastically edited as to be virtually an independent work. (Wilson, of course, approved the editing and wrote an introduction.) The campaign speeches themselves are now being brought together for the first time, many of them transcribed from the original shorthand notes, by Mr. John Davidson; and that volume will be issued shortly.

in any rank or post whatever, least of all in the supreme post of President of the United States.

To be free is not necessarily to be wise. But wisdom comes with counsel, with the frank and free conference of untrammeled men united in the common interest. Should I be entrusted with the great office of President, I would seek counsel wherever it could be had upon free terms. I know the temper of the great convention which nominated me; I know the temper of the country that lay back of that convention and spoke through it. I heed with deep thankfulness the message you bring me from it. I feel that I am surrounded by men whose principles and ambitions are those of true servants of the people. I thank God, and will take courage.

Chapter Eight

FOUNDATIONS OF REFORM

WILSON entered upon his first term as President with that clarity of purpose and depth of assurance which had made the first years as president of Princeton so triumphant a success. This chapter contains the great state papers which embodied the spirit of his reforms. The First Inaugural showed the Wilson rhetoric stripped to a new bareness, a fit prologue to deeds. His message to the Congress asking for tariff reform was delivered in person, a dramatic change in practice, symbolizing the concept of the Presidency which he had set forth in his earliest writings. In addition to the messages on the major reforms of the domestic program, this chapter contains addresses on relations with Mexico and Latin America, where the spirit of Wilson's new international policies was first set forth.

INAUGURAL ADDRESS, WASHINGTON,
MARCH 4, 1912

To Cleanse, to Reconsider, to Restore

MY FELLOW CITIZENS: There has been a change of government. It began two years ago, when the House of Representatives became Democratic by a decisive majority. It has now been completed. The Senate about to assemble will also be Democratic. The offices of President and Vice-President have been put into the hands of Democrats. What does the change mean? That is the question that is uppermost in our minds to-day. That is the question I am going to try to answer, in order, if I may, to interpret the occasion.

It means much more than the mere success of a party. The success of a party means little except when the Nation is using that party for a large and definite purpose. No one can mistake the purpose for which the Nation now seeks to use the Democratic Party.

It seeks to use it to interpret a change in its own plans and point of view. Some old things with which we had grown familiar, and which had begun to creep into the very habit of our thought and of our lives, have altered their aspect as we have latterly looked critically upon them, with fresh, awakened eyes; have dropped their disguises and shown themselves alien and sinister. Some new things, as we look frankly upon them, willing to comprehend their real character, have come to assume the aspect of things long believed in and familiar, stuff of our own convictions. We have been refreshed by a new insight into our own life.

We see that in many things that life is very great. It is incomparably great in its material aspects, in its body of wealth, in the diversity and sweep of its energy, in the industries which have been conceived and built up by the genius of individual men and the limitless enterprise of groups of men. It is great, also, very great, in its moral force.

Nowhere else in the world have noble men and women exhibited in more striking forms the beauty and the energy of sympathy and helpfulness and counsel in their efforts to rectify wrong, alleviate suffering, and set the weak in the way of strength and hope. We have built up, moreover, a great system of government, which has stood through a long age as in many respects a model for those who seek to set liberty upon foundations that will endure against fortuitous change, against storm and accident. Our life contains every great thing, and contains it in rich abundance.

But the evil has come with the good, and much fine gold has been corroded. With riches has come inexcusable waste. We have squandered a great part of what we might have used, and have not stopped to conserve the exceeding bounty of nature, without which our genius for enterprise would have been worthless and impotent, scorning to be careful, shamefully prodigal as well as admirably efficient. We have been proud of our industrial achievements, but we have not hitherto stopped thoughtfully enough to count the human cost, the cost of lives snuffed out, of energies overtaxed and broken, the fearful physical and spiritual cost to the men and women and children upon whom the dead weight and burden of it all has fallen pitilessly the years through. The groans and agony of it all had not yet reached our ears, the solemn, moving undertone of our life, coming up out of the mines and factories and out of every home where the struggle had its intimate and familiar seat. With the great Government went many deep secret things which we too long delayed to look into and scrutinize with candid, fearless eyes. The great Government we loved has too often been made use of for private and selfish purposes, and those who used it had forgotten the people.

At last a vision has been vouchsafed us of our life as a whole. We see the bad with the good, the debased and decadent with the sound and vital. With this vision we approach new affairs. Our duty is to cleanse, to reconsider, to restore, to correct the evil without impairing the good, to purify and humanize every process of our common life without weakening or sentimentalizing it. There has been something crude and heartless and unfeeling in our haste to succeed and be great. Our thought has been "Let every man look out for himself, let every generation look out for itself," while we reared giant machinery which made it impossible that any but those who stood at the levers of control should have a chance to look out for themselves. We had not forgotten our morals. We remembered well enough that we had set up a policy which was meant to serve the humblest as well as the most powerful, with an eye single to the standards of justice and fair play, and remembered it with pride. But we were very heedless and in a hurry to be great.

Some of the Things We Ought to Do

We have come now to the sober second thought. The scales of heedlessness have fallen from our eyes. We have made up our minds to square every process of our national life again with the standards we so proudly set up at the beginning and have always carried at our hearts. Our work is a work of restoration.

We have itemized with some degree of particularity the things that ought to be altered and here are some of the chief items: A tariff which cuts us off from our proper part in the commerce of the world, violates the just principles of taxation, and makes the Government a facile instrument in the hands of private interests; a banking and currency system based upon the necessity of the Government to sell its bonds fifty years ago and perfectly adapted to concentrating cash and restricting credits; an industrial system which, take it on all its sides, financial as well as administrative, holds capital in leading strings, restricts the liberties and limits the opportunities of labor, and exploits without renewing or conserving the natural resources of the country; a body of agricultural activities never yet given the efficiency of great business undertakings or served as it should be through the instrumentality of science taken directly to the farm, or afforded the facilities of credit best suited to its practical needs; watercourses undeveloped, waste places unreclaimed, forests untended, fast disappearing without plan or prospect of renewal, unregarded waste heaps at every mine. We have studied as perhaps no other nation has the most effective means of production, but we have not studied cost or economy as we should either as organizers of industry, as statesmen, or as individuals.

Nor have we studied and perfected the means by which government may be put at the service of humanity, in safeguarding the health of the Nation, the health of its men and its women and its children, as well as their rights in the struggle for existence. This is no sentimental duty. The firm basis of government is justice, not pity. These are matters of justice. There can be no equality of opportunity, the first essential of justice in the body politic, if men and women and children be not shielded in their lives, their very vitality, from the consequences of great industrial and social processes which they can not alter, control, or singly cope with. Society must see to it that it does not itself crush or weaken or damage its own constituent parts. The first duty of law is to keep sound the society it serves. Sanitary laws, pure food laws, and laws determining conditions of labor which individuals are powerless to determine for themselves are intimate parts of the very business of justice and legal efficiency.

These are some of the things we ought to do, and not leave the others undone, the old-fashioned, never-to-be-neglected, fundamental safeguarding of property and of individual right. This is the high enterprise of the new day: To lift everything that concerns our life as a Nation to the light that shines from the hearthfire of every man's conscience and vision of the right. It is inconceivable that we should do this as partisans; it is inconceivable we should do it in ignorance of the facts as they are or in blind haste. We shall restore, not destroy. We shall deal with our economic system as it is and as it may be modified, not as it might be if we had a clean sheet of paper to write upon; and step by step we shall make it what it should be, in the spirit of those who question their own wisdom and seek counsel and knowledge, not shallow self-satisfaction or the excitement of excursions whither they can not tell. Justice, and only justice, shall always be our motto.

And yet it will be no cool process of mere science. The Nation has been deeply stirred, stirred by a solemn passion, stirred by the knowledge of wrong, of ideals lost, of government too often debauched and made an instrument of evil. The feelings with which we face this new age of right and opportunity sweep across our heartstrings like some air out of God's own presence, where justice and mercy are reconciled and the judge and the brother are one. We know our task to be no mere task of politics but a task which shall search us through and through, whether we be able to understand our time and the need of our people, whether we be indeed their spokesmen and interpreters, whether we have the pure heart to comprehend and the rectified will to choose our high course of action.

This is not a day of triumph; it is a day of dedication. Here muster, not the forces of party, but the forces of humanity. Men's hearts wait upon us; men's lives hang in the balance; men's hopes call upon us to say what we will do. Who shall live up to the great trust? Who dares fail to try? I summon all honest men, all patriotic, all forward-looking men, to my side. God helping me, I will not fail them, if they will but counsel and sustain me!

The Tariff Duties Must Be Altered

GENTLEMEN OF THE CONGRESS: I am very glad indeed to have this opportunity to address the two Houses directly and to certify for myself the impression that the President of the United States is a person, not a mere department of the Government hailing Congress from some isolated island of jealous power, sending messages, not speaking naturally and with his own voice—that he is a human being trying to coöperate with other human beings in a common service. After this pleasant experience I shall feel quite normal in all our dealings with one another.

I have called the Congress together in extraordinary session because a duty was laid upon the party now in power at the recent elections which it ought to perform promptly, in order that the burden carried by the people under existing law may be lightened as soon as possible, and in order, also, that the business interests of the country may not be kept too long in suspense as to what the fiscal changes are to be to which they will be required to adjust themselves. It is clear to the whole country that the tariff duties must be altered. They must be changed to meet the radical alteration in the conditions of our economic life which the country has witnessed within the last generation. While the whole face and method of our industrial and commercial life were being changed beyond recognition the tariff schedules have remained what they were before the change began, or have moved in the direction they were given when no large circumstance of our industrial development was what it is to-day. Our task is to square them with the actual facts. The sooner that is done the sooner we shall escape from suffering from the facts and the sooner our men of business will be free to thrive by the law of nature—the nature of free business—instead of by the law of legislation and artificial arrangement.

We have seen tariff legislation wander very far afield in our day—very far indeed from the field in which our prosperity might have had a normal growth and stimulation. No one who looks the facts squarely in the face or knows anything that lies beneath the surface of action can fail to perceive the principles upon which recent tariff legislation has been based. We long ago passed beyond the modest notion of "protecting" the industries of the country and moved boldly forward to the idea that they were entitled to the direct patronage of the Government. For a long time—a time so long that the men now active in public policy hardly remember the conditions that preceded it—we have sought in our tariff schedules to give each group of manufacturers or producers what they themselves thought that they needed in order to maintain a practically exclusive market as against the rest of the world. Consciously or unconsciously, we have built up a set of privileges and exemptions from competition behind which it was easy by any, even the crudest, forms of combination to organize monopoly; until at last nothing is normal, nothing is obliged to stand the tests of efficiency and economy, in our world of big business, but everything thrives by concerted arrangement. Only new principles of action will save us from a final hard crystallization of monopoly and a complete loss of the influences that quicken enterprise and keep independent energy alive.

It is plain what those principles must be. We must abolish everything that bears even the semblance of privilege or of any kind of artificial advantage, and put our business men and producers under the stimulation of a constant necessity to be efficient, economical, and enterprising, masters of competitive supremacy, better workers and merchants than any in the world. Aside from the duties laid upon articles which we do not, and probably can not, produce, therefore, and the duties laid upon luxuries and merely for the sake of the revenues they yield, the object of the tariff duties henceforth laid must be effective competition, the whetting of American wits by contest with the wits of the rest of the world.

To Deal with the Facts of Our Own Day

It would be unwise to move toward this end headlong, with reckless haste, or with strokes that cut at the very roots of what has grown up amongst us by long process and at our own invitation. It does not alter a thing to upset it and break it and deprive it of a chance to change. It destroys it. We must make changes in our fiscal laws, in our fiscal system, whose object is development, a more free and wholesome development, not revolution or upset or confusion. We must build up trade, especially foreign trade. We need the outlet and the enlarged field of energy more than we ever did before. We must build up industry as well, and must adopt freedom in the place of artificial stimulation only so far as it will build, not pull down. In dealing with the tariff the method by which this may be done will be a matter of judgment exercised item by item. To some not accustomed to the excitements and responsibilities of greater freedom our methods may in some respects and at some points seem heroic; but remedies may be heroic and yet be remedies. It is our business to make sure that they are genuine remedies. Our object is clear. If our motive is above just challenge and only an occasional error of judgment is chargeable against us, we shall be fortunate.

We are called upon to render the country a great service in more matters than one. Our responsibility should be met and our methods should be thorough, as thorough as moderate and well considered, based upon the facts as they are, and not worked out as if we were beginners. We are to deal with the facts of our own day, with the facts of no other and to make laws which square with those facts. It is best, indeed it is necessary, to begin with the tariff. I will urge nothing upon you now at the opening of your session which can obscure that first object or divert our energies from that clearly defined duty. At a later time I may take the liberty of calling your attention to reforms which should press close upon the heels of the tariff changes, if not accompany them, of which the chief is the reform of our banking and currency laws; but just now I refrain. For the present, I put these matters on one side and think only of this one thing—of the changes in our fiscal system which may best serve to open once more the free channels of prosperity to a great people whom we would serve to the utmost and throughout both rank and file.

I sincerely thank you for your courtesy.

ADDRESS TO THE CONGRESS,
JUNE 23, 1913

On National Currency and Banking

GENTLEMEN OF THE CONGRESS: It is under the compulsion of what seems to me a clear and imperative duty that I have a second time this session sought the privilege of addressing you in person. I know, of course, that the heated season of the year is upon us, that work in these Chambers and in the committee rooms is likely to become a burden as the season lengthens, and that every consideration of personal convenience and personal comfort, perhaps, in the cases of some of us, considerations of personal health even, dictate an early conclusion of the deliberations of the session; but there are occasions of public duty when these things which touch us privately seem very small; when the work to be done is so pressing and so fraught with big consequence that we know that we are not at liberty to weigh against it any point of personal sacrifice. We are now in the presence of such an occasion. It is absolutely imperative that we should give the business men of this country a banking and currency system by means of which they can make use of the freedom of enterprise and of individual initiative which we are about to bestow upon them.

We are about to set them free; we must not leave them without the tools of action when they are free. We are about to set them free by removing the trammels of the protective tariff. Ever since the Civil War they have waited for this emancipation and for the free opportunities it will bring with it. It has been reserved for us to give it to them. Some fell in love, indeed, with the slothful security of their dependence upon the Government; some took advantage of the shelter of the nursery to set up a mimic mastery of their own within its walls. Now both the tonic and the discipline of liberty and maturity are to ensue. There will be some readjustments of purpose and point of view. There will follow a period of expansion and new enterprise, freshly conceived. It is for us to determine now whether it shall be rapid and facile and of easy accomplishment. This it can not be unless the resourceful business men who are to deal with the new circumstances are to have at hand and ready for use the instrumentalities and conveniences of free enterprise which independent men need when acting on their own initiative.

It is not enough to strike the shackles from business. The duty of statesmanship is not negative merely. It is constructive also. We must show that we understand what business needs and that we know how to supply it. No man, however casual and superficial his observation of the conditions now prevailing in the country, can fail to see that one of the chief things business needs now and will need increasingly as it gains in scope and vigor in the years immediately ahead of us is the proper means by which readily to vitalize its credit, corporate and individual, and its originative brains. What will it profit us to be free if we are not to have the best and most accessible instrumentalities of commerce and enterprise? What will it profit us to be quit of one kind of monopoly if we are to remain in the grip of another and more effective kind? How are we to gain and keep the confidence of the business community unless we show that we know how both to aid and to protect it? What shall we say if we make fresh enterprise necessary and also make it very difficult by leaving all else except the tariff just as we found it? The tyrannies of business, big and little, lie within the field of credit. We know that. Shall we not act upon the knowledge? Do we not know how to act upon it? If a man can not make his assets available at pleasure, his assets of capacity and character and resource, what satisfaction is it to him to see opportunity beckoning to him on every hand when others have the keys of credit in their pockets and treat them as all but their own private possession? It is perfectly clear that it is our duty to supply the new banking and currency system the country needs, and it will need it immediately more than it has ever needed it before.

The only question is, When shall we supply it—now or later, after the demands shall have become reproaches that we were so dull and so slow? Shall we hasten to change the tariff laws and then be laggards about making it possible and easy for the country to take advantage of the change? There can be only one answer to that question. We must act now, at whatever sacrifice to ourselves. It is a duty which the circumstances forbid us to postpone. I should be recreant to my deepest convictions of public obligation did I not press it upon you with solemn and urgent insistence.

The Principles of Financial Reform

The principles upon which we should act are also clear. The country has sought and seen its path in this matter within the last few years—sees it more clearly now than it ever saw it before—much more clearly than when the last legislative proposals on the subject were made. We must have a currency, not rigid as now, but readily, elastically responsive to sound credit, the expanding and contracting credits of everyday transactions, the normal ebb and flow of personal and corporate dealings. Our banking laws must mobilize reserves; must not permit the concentration anywhere in a few hands of the monetary resources of the country or their use for speculative purposes in such volume as to hinder or impede or stand in the way of other more legitimate, more fruitful uses. And the control of the system of banking and of issue which our new laws are to set up must be public, not private, must be vested in the Government itself, so that the banks may be the instruments, not the masters, of business and of individual enterprise and initiative.

The committees of the Congress to which legislation of this character is referred have devoted careful and dispassionate study to the means of accomplishing these objects. They have honored me by consulting me. They are ready to suggest action. I have come to you, as the head of the Government and the responsible leader of the party in power, to urge action, now while there is time to serve the country deliberately and as we should, in a clear air of common counsel. I appeal to you with a deep conviction of duty. I believe that you share this conviction. I therefore appeal to you with confidence. I am at your service without reserve to play my part in any way you may call upon me to play it in this great enterprise of exigent reform which it will dignify and distinguish us to perform and discredit us to neglect.

ADDRESS TO CONGRESS,
AUGUST 27, 1913

Present Relations with Mexico

GENTLEMEN OF THE CONGRESS: It is clearly my duty to lay before you, very fully and without reservation, the facts concerning our present relations with the Republic of Mexico. The deplorable posture of affairs in Mexico I need not describe, but I deem it my duty to speak very frankly of what this Government has done and should seek to do in fulfillment of its obligation to Mexico herself, as a friend and neighbor, and to American citizens whose lives and vital interests are daily affected by the distressing conditions which now obtain beyond our southern border.

Those conditions touch us very nearly. Not merely because they lie at our very doors. That, of course, makes us more vividly and more constantly conscious of them, and every instinct of neighborly interest and sympathy is aroused and quickened by them; but that is only one element in the determination of our duty. We are glad to call ourselves the friend of Mexico, and we shall, I hope, have many an occasion, in happier times as well as in these days of trouble and confusion, to show that our friendship is genuine and disinterested, capable of sacrifice and every generous manifestation. The peace, prosperity, and contentment of Mexico mean more, much more, to us than merely an enlarged field for our commerce and enterprise. They mean an enlargement of the field of self-government and the realization of the hopes and rights of a nation with whose best aspirations, so long suppressed and disappointed, we deeply sympathize. We shall yet prove to the Mexican people that we know how to serve them without first thinking how we shall serve ourselves.

But we are not the only friends of Mexico. The whole world desires her peace and progress; and the whole world is interested as never before. Mexico lies at last where all the world looks on. Central America is about to be touched by the great routes of the world's trade and intercourse running free from ocean to ocean at the Isthmus. The future has much in store for Mexico, as for all the States of Central America; but the best gifts can come to her

only if she be ready and free to receive them and to enjoy them
honorably. America in particular—America north and south and
upon both continents—waits upon the development of Mexico; and
that development can be sound and lasting only if it be the product
of a genuine freedom, a just and ordered government founded upon
law. Only so can it be peaceful or fruitful of the benefits of peace.
Mexico has a great and enviable future before her, if only she choose
and attain the paths of honest constitutional government.

The present circumstances of the Republic, I deeply regret to say,
do not seem to promise even the foundations of such a peace. We
have waited many months, months full of peril and anxiety, for the
conditions there to improve, and they have not improved. They
have grown worse, rather. The territory in some sort controlled by
the provisional authorities at Mexico City has grown smaller, not
larger. The prospect of the pacification of the country, even by
arms, has seemed to grow more and more remote; and its pacification by the authorities at the capital is evidently impossible by any
other means than force. Difficulties more and more entangle those
who claim to constitute the legitimate government of the Republic.
They have not made good their claim in fact. Their successes in the
field have proved only temporary. War and disorder, devastation
and confusion, seem to threaten to become the settled fortune of
the distracted country. As friends we could wait no longer for a
solution which every week seemed further away. It was our duty at
least to volunteer our good offices—to offer to assist, if we might, in
effecting some arrangement which would bring relief and peace and
set up a universally acknowledged political authority there.

Accordingly, I took the liberty of sending the Hon. John Lind,
formerly governor of Minnesota, as my personal spokesman and
representative, to the City of Mexico. . . .

The Self-Restraint of a Really Great Nation

Mr. Lind executed his delicate and difficult mission with singular
tact, firmness, and good judgment, and made clear to the authorities
at the City of Mexico not only the purpose of his visit but also the

spirit in which it had been undertaken. But the proposals he submitted were rejected. . . .

I am led to believe that they were rejected partly because the authorities at Mexico City had been grossly misinformed and misled upon two points. They did not realize the spirit of the American people in this matter, their earnest friendliness and yet sober determination that some just solution be found for the Mexican difficulties; and they did not believe that the present administration spoke through Mr. Lind, for the people of the United States. The effect of this unfortunate misunderstanding on their part is to leave them singularly isolated and without friends who can effectually aid them. So long as the misunderstanding continues we can only await the time of their awakening to a realization of the actual facts. We can not thrust our good offices upon them. The situation must be given a little more time to work itself out in the new circumstances; and I believe that only a little while will be necessary. For the circumstances are new. The rejection of our friendship makes them new and will inevitably bring its own alterations in the whole aspect of affairs. The actual situation of the authorities at Mexico City will presently be revealed.

Meanwhile, what is it our duty to do? Clearly, everything that we do must be rooted in patience and done with calm and disinterested deliberation. Impatience on our part would be childish, and would be fraught with every risk of wrong and folly. We can afford to exercise the self-restraint of a really great nation which realizes its own strength and scorns to misuse it. It was our duty to offer our active assistance. It is now our duty to show what true neutrality will do to enable the people of Mexico to set their affairs in order again and wait for a further opportunity to offer our friendly counsels. The door is not closed against the resumption, either upon the initiative of Mexico or upon our own, of the effort to bring order out of the confusion by friendly co-operative action, should fortunate occasion offer.

While we wait, the contest of the rival forces will undoubtedly for a little while be sharper than ever, just because it will be plain that an end must be made of the existing situation, and that very promptly; and with the increased activity of the contending factions will come, it is to be feared, increased danger to the non-combatants in Mexico as well as to those actually in the field of battle. The position of outsiders is always particularly trying and full of hazard where there is civil strife and a whole country is upset. We should earnestly urge all Americans to leave Mexico at once, and should assist them to get away in every way possible—not because we would mean to slacken in the least our efforts to safeguard their lives and their interests, but because it is imperative that they should take no unnecessary risks when it is physically possible for them to leave the country. We should let every one who assumes to exercise authority in any part of Mexico know in the most unequivocal way that we shall vigilantly watch the fortunes of those Americans who can not get away, and shall hold those responsible for their sufferings and losses to a definite reckoning. That can be and will be made plain beyond the possibility of a misunderstanding.

For the rest, I deem it my duty to exercise the authority conferred upon me by the law of March 14, 1912, to see to it that neither side to the struggle now going on in Mexico receive any assistance from this side the border. I shall follow the best practice of nations in the matter of neutrality by forbidding the exportation of arms or munitions of war of any kind from the United States to any part of the Republic of Mexico—a policy suggested by several interesting precedents and certainly dictated by many manifest considerations of practical expediency. We can not in the circumstances be the partisans of either party to the contest that now distracts Mexico, or constitute ourselves the virtual umpire between them.

I am happy to say that several of the great Governments of the world have given this Government their generous moral support in urging upon the provisional authorities at the City of Mexico the acceptance of our proffered good offices in the spirit in which they were made. We have not acted in this matter under the ordinary principles of international obligation. All the world expects us in such circumstances to act as Mexico's nearest friend and intimate adviser. This is our immemorial relation towards her. There is no-where any serious question that we have the moral right in the case or that we are acting in the interest of a fair settlement and of good government, not for the promotion of some selfish interest of our own. If further motive were necessary than our own good will towards a sister Republic and our own deep concern to see peace and order prevail in Central America, this consent of mankind to what we are attempting, this attitude of the great nations of the world towards what we may attempt in dealing with this distressed people at our doors, should make us feel the more solemnly bound to go to the utmost length of patience and forbearance in this painful and anxious business. The steady pressure of moral force will before many days break the barriers of pride and prejudice down, and we shall triumph as Mexico's friends sooner than we could triumph as her enemies—and how much more handsomely, with how much higher and finer satisfactions of conscience and of honor!

ADDRESS AT MOBILE, ALABAMA,
OCTOBER 27, 1913

A New Latin-American Policy

The future is going to be very different for this hemisphere from the past. These States lying to the south of us, which have always been our neighbors, will now be drawn closer to us by innumerable ties, and, I hope, chief of all, by the tie of a common understanding of each other. Interest does not tie nations together; it sometimes separates them. But sympathy and understanding does unite them, and I believe that by the new route that is just about to be opened, while we physically cut two continents asunder, we spiritually unite them. It is a spiritual union which we seek.

I wonder if you realize, I wonder if your imaginations have been filled with the significance of the tides of commerce. Your governor alluded in very fit and striking terms to the voyage of Columbus, but Columbus took his voyage under compulsion of circumstances. Constantinople had been captured by the Turks and all the routes of trade with the East had been suddenly closed. If there was not a way across the Atlantic to open those routes again, they were closed forever, and Columbus set out not to discover America, for he did not know that it existed, but to discover the eastern shores of Asia. He set sail for Cathay and stumbled upon America. With that change in the outlook of the world, what happened? England, that had been at the back of Europe with an unknown sea behind her, found that all things had turned as if upon a pivot and she was at the front of Europe; and since then all the tides of energy and enterprise that have issued out of Europe have seemed to be turned westward across the Atlantic. But you will notice that they have turned westward chiefly north of the Equator and that it is the northern half of the globe that has seemed to be filled with the media of intercourse and of sympathy and of common understanding.

Do you not see now what is about to happen? These great tides which have been running along parallels of latitude will now swing southward athwart parallels of latitude, and that opening gate at the Isthmus of Panama will open the world to a commerce that she has not known before, a commerce of intelligence, of thought and sympathy between North and South. The Latin American States, which, to their disadvantage, have been off the main lines, will now be on the main lines. I feel that these gentlemen honoring us with their presence to-day will presently find that some part, at any rate, of the center of gravity of the world has shifted. Do you realize that New York, for example, will be nearer the western coast of South America than she is now to the eastern coast of South America? Do you realize that a line drawn northward parallel with the greater part of the western coast of South America will run only about 150 miles west of New York? The great bulk of South America, if you will look at your globes (not at your Mercator's projection), lies eastward of the continent of North America. You will realize that when you realize that the canal will run southeast, not southwest, and that when you get into the Pacific you will be farther east than you were when you left the Gulf of Mexico. These things are significant, therefore, of this, that we are closing one chapter in the history of the world and are opening another, of great, unimaginable significance.

Friendship—Upon Terms of Equality

There is one peculiarity about the history of the Latin American States which I am sure they are keenly aware of. You hear of "concessions" to foreign capitalists in Latin America. You do not hear of concessions to foreign capitalists in the United States. They are not granted concessions. They are invited to make investments. The work is ours, though they are welcome to invest in it. We do not ask them to supply the capital and do the work. It is an invitation, not a privilege; and States that are obliged, because their territory does not lie within the main field of modern enterprise and action, to grant concessions are in this condition, that foreign interests are apt to dominate their domestic affairs, a condition of affairs always dangerous and apt to become intolerable.

What these States are going to see, therefore, is an emancipation from the subordination, which has been inevitable, to foreign enterprise and an assertion of the splendid character which, in spite of these difficulties, they have again and again been able to demonstrate. The dignity, the courage, the self-possession, the self-respect of the Latin American States, their achievements in the face of all these adverse circumstances, deserve nothing but the admiration and applause of the world. They have had harder bargains driven with them in the matter of loans than any other peoples in the world. Interest has been exacted of them that was not exacted of anybody else, because the risk was said to be greater; and then securities were taken that destroyed the risk—an admirable arrangement for those who were forcing the terms! I rejoice in nothing so much as in the prospect that they will now be emancipated from these conditions, and we ought to be the first to take part in assisting in that emancipation. I think some of these gentlemen have already had occasion to bear witness that the Department of State in recent months has tried to serve them in that wise. In the future they will draw closer and closer to us because of circumstances of which I wish to speak with moderation and, I hope, without indiscretion.

We must prove ourselves their friends, and champions upon terms of equality and honor. You cannot be friends upon any other terms than upon the terms of equality. You cannot be friends at all except

upon the terms of honor. We must show ourselves friends by comprehending their interest whether it squares with our own interest
or not. It is a very perilous thing to determine the foreign policy of
a nation in the terms of material interest. It not only is unfair to
those with whom you are dealing, but it is degrading as regards your
own actions.

Comprehension must be the soil in which shall grow all the fruits
of friendship, and there is a reason and a compulsion lying behind
all this which is dearer than anything else to the thoughtful men of
America. I mean the development of constitutional liberty in the
world. Human rights, national integrity, and opportunity as against
material interests—that, ladies and gentlemen, is the issue which we
now have to face. I want to take this occasion to say that the United
States will never again seek one additional foot of territory by conquest. She will devote herself to showing that she knows how to
make honorable and fruitful use of the territory she has, and she
must regard it as one of the duties of friendship to see that from
no quarter are material interests made superior to human liberty
and national opportunity. I say this, not with a single thought that
anyone will gainsay it, but merely to fix in our consciousness what
our real relationship with the rest of America is. It is the relationship of a family of mankind devoted to the development of true
constitutional liberty. We know that that is the soil out of which
the best enterprise springs. We know that this is a cause which we
are making in common with our neighbors, because we have had
to make it for ourselves.

Being True to Ourselves in Foreign Policy

Reference has been made here to-day to some of the national
problems which confront us as a Nation. What is at the heart of all
our national problems? It is that we have seen the hand of material
interest sometimes about to close upon our dearest rights and possessions. We have seen material interests threaten constitutional freedom in the United States. Therefore we will now know how to
sympathize with those in the rest of America who have to contend

with such powers, not only within their borders but from outside their borders also.

I know what the response of the thought and heart of America will be to the program I have outlined, because America was created to realize a program like that. This is not America because it is rich. This is not America because it has set up for a great population great opportunities of material prosperity. America is a name which sounds in the ears of men everywhere as a synonym with individual opportunity because a synonym of individual liberty. I would rather belong to a poor nation that was free than to a rich nation that had ceased to be in love with liberty. But we shall not be poor if we love liberty, because the nation that loves liberty truly sets every man free to do his best and be his best, and that means the release of all the splendid energies of a great people who think for themselves. A nation of employees cannot be free any more than a nation of employers can be.

In emphasizing the points which must unite us in sympathy and in spiritual interest with the Latin American peoples we are only emphasizing the points of our own life, and we should prove ourselves untrue to our own traditions if we proved ourselves untrue friends to them.

Do not think, therefore, gentlemen, that the questions of the day are mere questions of policy and diplomacy. They are shot through with the principles of life. We dare not turn from the principle that morality and not expediency is the thing that must guide us and that we will never condone iniquity because it is most convenient to do so. It seems to me that this is a day of infinite hope, of confidence in a future greater than the past has been, for I am fain to believe that in spite of all the things that we wish to correct the nineteenth century that now lies behind us has brought us a long stage toward the time when, slowly ascending the tedious climb that leads to the final uplands, we shall get our ultimate view of the duties of mankind. We have breasted a considerable part of that climb and shall presently—it may be in a generation or two—come out upon those great heights where there shines unobstructed the light of the justice of God.

ADDRESS TO THE CONGRESS,
JANUARY 20, 1914

The Great Question of Trusts and Monopolies

GENTLEMEN OF THE CONGRESS: In my report "on the state of the Union," which I had the privilege of reading to you on the 2d of December last, I ventured to reserve for discussion at a later date the subject of additional legislation regarding the very difficult and intricate matter of trusts and monopolies. The time now seems opportune to turn to that great question, not only because the currency legislation, which absorbed your attention and the attention of the country in December, is now disposed of, but also because opinion seems to be clearing about us with singular rapidity in this other great field of action. In the matter of the currency it cleared suddenly and very happily after the much-debated act was passed; in respect of the monopolies which have multiplied about us and in regard to the various means by which they have been organized and maintained, it seems to be coming to a clear and all but universal agreement in anticipation of our action, as if by way of preparation, making the way easier to see and easier to set out upon with confidence and without confusion of counsel.

Legislation has its atmosphere like everything else, and the atmosphere of accommodation and mutual understanding which we now breathe with so much refreshment is matter of sincere congratulation. It ought to make our task very much less difficult and embarrassing than it would have been had we been obliged to continue to act amidst the atmosphere of suspicion and antagonism which has so long made it impossible to approach such questions with dispassionate fairness. Constructive legislation, when successful, is always the embodiment of convincing experience and of the mature public opinion which finally springs out of that experience. Legislation is a business of interpretation, not of origination; and it is now plain what the opinion is to which we must give effect in this matter. It is not recent or hasty opinion. It springs out of the experience of a whole generation. It has clarified itself by long contest, and those who for a long time battled with it and sought to change it are now frankly and honorably yielding to it and seeking to conform their actions to it. The great business men who organized and financed monopoly and those who administered it in actual everyday transactions have, year after year until now, either denied its existence or justified it as necessary for the effective maintenance and development of the vast business processes of the country in the modern circumstances of trade and manufacture and finance; but all the while opinion has made head against them. The average business man is convinced that the ways of liberty are also the ways of peace and the ways of success as well; and at last the masters of business on the great scale have begun to yield their preference and purpose, perhaps their judgment also, in honorable surrender.

What we are purposing to do, therefore, is, happily, not to hamper or interfere with business as enlightened business men prefer to do it, or in any sense to put it under the ban. The antagonism between business and Government is over. We are now about to give expression to the best business judgment of America, to what we know to be the business conscience and honor of the land. The Government and business men are ready to meet each other halfway in a common effort to square business methods with both public opinion and the law. The best-informed men of the business world condemn the methods and processes and consequences of monopoly as we condemn them, and the instinctive judgment of the vast majority of business men everywhere goes with them. We shall now be their spokesmen. That is the strength of our position and the sure prophecy of what will ensue when our reasonable work is done.

When serious contest ends, when men unite in opinion and purpose, those who are to change their ways of business joining with those who ask for the change, it is possible to effect it in the way in which prudent and thoughtful and patriotic men would most wish to see it brought about, with as few, as slight, as easy and simple business readjustments as possible in the circumstances, nothing essential disturbed, nothing torn up by the roots, no parts rent asunder which can be left in wholesome combination. Fortunately, no measures of sweeping or novel change are necessary. It will be understood that our object is not to unsettle business or anywhere seriously to break its established courses athwart. On the contrary, we desire the laws we are now about to pass to be the bulwarks and safeguards of industry against the forces that now disturb them. What we have to do can be done in a new spirit, in quiet moderation, without revolution of any untoward kind.

A Comprehensive But Not Radical Program

We are all agreed that "private monopoly is indefensible and intolerable," and our program is founded upon that conviction. It will be a comprehensive but not a radical or unacceptable program and these are its items, the changes which opinion deliberately sanctions and for which business waits:

It waits with acquiescence, in the first place, for laws which will effectually prohibit and prevent such interlockings of the *personnel* of the directorates of great corporations—banks and railroads, industrial, commercial, and public service bodies—as in effect result in making those who borrow and those who lend practically one and the same, those who sell and those who buy but the same persons trading with one another under different names and in different combinations, and those who affect to compete in fact partners and masters of the whole field of particular kinds of business. Sufficient time should be allowed, of course, in which to effect these changes of organization without inconvenience or confusion.

Such a prohibition will work much more than a mere negative good by correcting the serious evils which have arisen because, for example, the men who have been the directing spirits of the great investment banks have usurped the place which belongs to independent industrial management working in its own behoof. It will bring new men, new energies, a new spirit of initiative, new blood, into the management of our great business enterprises. It will open the field of industrial development and origination to scores of men who have been obliged to serve when their abilities entitled them to direct. It will immensely hearten the young men coming on and will greatly enrich the business activities of the whole country.

In the second place, business men as well as those who direct public affairs now recognize, and recognize with painful clearness, the great harm and injustice which has been done to many, if not all, of the great railroad systems of the country by the way in which they have been financed and their own distinctive interests subordinated to the interests of the men who financed them and of other business enterprises which those men wished to promote. The country is ready, therefore, to accept, and accept with relief as well as approval, a law which will confer upon the Interstate Commerce Commission the power to superintend and regulate the financial operations by which the railroads are henceforth to be supplied with the money they need for their proper development to meet the rapidly growing requirements of the country for increased and improved facilities of transportation. We cannot postpone action in this matter without leaving the railroads exposed to many serious handicaps and hazards; and the prosperity of the railroads and the prosperity of the country are inseparably connected. Upon this question those who are chiefly responsible for the actual management and operation of the railroads have spoken very plainly and very earnestly, with a purpose we ought to be quick to accept. It will be one step, and a very important one, towards the necessary separation of the business of production from the business of transportation.

The business of the country awaits also, has long awaited and has suffered because it could not obtain, further and more explicit legislative definition of the policy and meaning of the existing antitrust law. Nothing hampers business like uncertainty. Nothing daunts or discourages it like the necessity to take chances, to run the risk of falling under the condemnation of the law before it can make sure just what the law is. Surely we are sufficiently familiar with the actual processes and methods of monopoly and of the many hurtful restraints of trade to make definition possible, at any rate up to the limits of what experience has disclosed. These practices, being now abundantly disclosed, can be explicitly and item by item forbidden by statute in such terms as will practically eliminate uncertainty, the law itself and the penalty being made equally plain.

And the business men of the country desire something more than that the menace of legal process in these matters be made explicit and intelligible. They desire the advice, the definite guidance, and information which can be supplied by an administrative body, an interstate trade commission.

The opinion of the country would instantly approve of such a commission. It would not wish to see it empowered to make terms with monopoly or in any sort to assume control of business, as if the Government made itself responsible. It demands such a commission only as an indispensable instrument of information and publicity, as a clearing house for the facts by which both the public mind and the managers of the great business undertakings should be guided, and as an instrumentality for doing justice to business where the processes of the courts or the natural forces of correction outside the courts are inadequate to adjust the remedy to the wrong in a way that will meet all the equities and circumstances of the case.

Producing industries, for example, which have passed the point up to which combination may be consistent with the public interest and the freedom of trade, can not always be dissected into their component units as readily as railroad companies or similar organizations can be. Their dissolution by ordinary legal process may oftentimes involve financial consequences likely to overwhelm the security market and bring upon it breakdown and confusion. There ought to be an administrative commission capable of directing and shaping such corrective processes, not only in aid of the courts but also by independent suggestion, if necessary.

Inasmuch as our object and the spirit of our action in these matters is to meet business half way in its processes of self-correction and disturb its legitimate course as little as possible, we ought to see to it, and the judgment of practical and sagacious men of affairs everywhere would applaud us if we did see to it, that penalties and punishments should fall not upon business itself, to its confusion and interruption, but upon the individuals who use the instrumentalities of business to do things which public policy and sound business practice condemn. Every act of business is done at the command or upon the initiative of some ascertainable person or group of persons. These should be held individually responsible and the punishment should fall upon them, not upon the business organization of which they make illegal use. It should be one of the main objects of our legislation to divest such persons of their corporate cloak and deal with them as with those who do not represent their corporations, but merely by deliberate intention break the law. Business men the country through would, I am sure, applaud us if we were to take effectual steps to see that the officers and directors of great business bodies were prevented from bringing them and the business of the country in general into disrepute and danger.

To Square Our Laws with the Desire of the Country

Other questions remain which will need very thoughtful and practical treatment. Enterprises in these modern days of great individual fortunes are oftentimes interlocked, not by being under the control of the same directors but by the fact that the greater part of their corporate stock is owned by a single person or group of persons who are in some way intimately related in interest. We are agreed, I take it, that holding companies should be prohibited, but what of the controlling private ownership of individuals or actually co-operative groups of individuals? Shall the private owners of capital stock be suffered to be themselves in effect holding companies? We do not wish, I suppose, to forbid the purchase of stocks by any person who pleases to buy them in such quantities as he can afford, or in any way arbitrarily to limit the sale of stocks to bona fide purchasers. Shall we require the owners of stock, when their voting power in several companies which ought to be independent of one another would constitute actual control, to make election in which of them they will exercise their right to vote? This question I venture for your consideration.

There is another matter in which imperative considerations of justice and fair play suggest thoughtful remedial action. Not only do many of the combinations effected or sought to be effected in the industrial world work an injustice upon the public in general; they also directly and seriously injure the individuals who are put out of business in one unfair way or another by the many dislodging and exterminating forces of combination. I hope that we shall agree in giving private individuals who claim to have been injured by these processes the right to found their suits for redress upon the facts and judgments proved and entered in suits by the Government where the Government has upon its own initiative sued the combinations complained of and won its suit, and that the statute of limitations shall be suffered to run against such litigants only from the date of the conclusion of the Government's action. It is not fair that the private litigant should be obliged to set up and establish again the facts which the Government has proved. He cannot afford, he has not the power, to make use of such processes of inquiry as the Government has command of. Thus shall individual justice be done while the processes of business are rectified and squared with the general conscience.

I have laid the case before you, no doubt, as it lies in your own mind, as it lies in the thought of the country. What must every candid man say of the suggestions I have laid before you, of the plain obligations of which I have reminded you? That these are new things for which the country is not prepared? No; but that they are old things, now familiar, and must of course be undertaken if we are to square our laws with the thought and desire of the country. Until these things are done, conscientious business men the country over will be unsatisfied. They are in these things our mentors and colleagues. We are now about to write the additional articles of our constitution of peace, the peace that is honor and freedom and prosperity.

Chapter Nine

THE EXERCISE OF POWER

WILSON brought to the White House a style of leadership entirely his own. It was in part his actual use of words; but more deeply it was his reliance on principle and ideas. These selections show the President exercising the prerogatives of his office—refusing an appointment, defending an appointment, summoning public support for his views, and, as he did on rare occasions, taking the public into his confidence in a discussion of the nature and burden of the Presidency. The first selection of this chapter is an interesting example of how Wilson's early thinking in the field of political science influenced his actions at a far later date. A less happy example of the same tendency to conceive the President as a sort of prime minister, the responsible head of his party, was Wilson's appeal for a Democratic Congress issued in 1917; that appears in a later chapter of this book.

LETTER TO A. MITCHELL PALMER,
WASHINGTON, FEBRUARY 5, 1913

A Second Term for Presidents

MY DEAR PALMER: Thank you warmly for your letter of February 3. It was characteristically considerate of you to ask my views with regard to the joint resolution which has just come over from the House to the Senate with regard to the presidential term.

I have not hitherto said anything about this question, because I had not observed that there was any evidence that the public was very much interested in it. I must have been mistaken in this, else the Senate would hardly have acted so promptly upon it.

It is a matter which concerns the character and conduct of the great office upon the duties of which I am about to enter. I feel therefore that in the present circumstances I should not be acting consistently with my ideals with regard to the rule of entire frankness and plain speaking that ought to exist between public servants and the public whom they serve if I did not speak out about it without reserve of any kind and without thought of the personal embarrassment.

The question is simply this: Shall our Presidents be free, so far as the law is concerned, to seek a second term of four years, or shall they be limited by constitutional amendment to a single term of four years or to a single term extended to six years?

I can approach the question from a perfectly impersonal point of view, because I shall most cheerfully abide by the judgment of my party and the public as to whether I shall be a candidate for the Presidency again in 1916. I absolutely pledge myself to resort to nothing but public opinion to decide that question.

The President ought to be absolutely deprived of every other means of deciding it. He can be. I shall use to the utmost every proper influence within my reach to see that he is, before the term to which I have been elected is out. That side of the question need disturb no one.

And yet, if he be deprived of every other means of deciding the question, what becomes of the argument for a constitutional limitation to a single term? The argument is not that it is clearly known now just how long each President should remain in office. Four years is too long a term for a President who is not the true spokesman of the people, who is imposed upon and does not lead. It is too short a term for a President who is doing, or attempting a great work of reform, and who has not had time to finish it.

To change the term to six years would increase the likelihood of its being too long, without any assurance that it would, in happy cases, be long enough. A fixed constitutional limitation to a single term of office is highly arbitrary and unsatisfactory from every point of view.

The argument for it rests upon temporary conditions which can easily be removed by law. Presidents, it is said, are effective for one-half of their term only because they devote their attention during the last two years of the term to building up the influences, and above all, the organization, by which they hope and purpose to secure a second nomination and election.

It is their illicit power, not their legitimate influence with the country, that the advocates of a constitutional change profess to be afraid of, and I heartily sympathize with them. It is intolerable that any President should be permitted to determine who should succeed him—himself or another—by patronage or coercion, or by any sort of control of the machinery by which delegates to the nominating convention are chosen.

There ought never to be another presidential nominating convention; and there need never be another. Several of the states have successfully solved that difficulty with regard to the choice of their governors, and Federal law can solve it in the same way with regard to the choice of Presidents. The nominations should be made directly by the people at the polls.

Conventions should determine nothing but party platforms and should be made up of the men who would be expected, if elected, to carry those platforms into effect. It is not necessary to attend to the people's business by constitutional amendment if you will only actually put the business into the people's own hands.

I think it may safely be assumed that that will be done within the next four years; for it can be done by statute; it need not wait for constitutional change. That being done, the question of the presidential term can be discussed on its merits.

It must be clear to everybody who has studied our political development at all that the character of the Presidency is passing through a transitional stage. We know what the office is now and what use must be made of it; but we do not know what it is going to work out into; and until we do know, we shall not know what constitutional change, if any is needed, it would be best to make.

The Abnormal Position of the Presidency

I must speak with absolute freedom and candor in this matter, or not speak at all; and it seems to me that the present position of the

Presidency in our actual system, as we use it, is quite abnormal and must lead eventually to something very different.

He is expected by the Nation to be the leader of his party as well as the Chief Executive officer of the Government, and the country will take no excuses from him. He must play the part and play it successfully or lose the country's confidence. He must be prime minister, as much concerned with the guidance of legislation as with the just and orderly execution of law, and he is the spokesman of the Nation in everything, even in the most momentous and most delicate dealings of the Government with foreign nations.

Why in such circumstances should he be responsible to no one for four long years? All the people's legislative spokesmen in the House of Representatives and one-third of their representatives in the Senate are brought to book every two years; why not the President, if he is to be the leader of the party and the spokesman of policy?

Sooner or later, it would seem, he must be made answerable to opinion in a somewhat more informal and intimate fashion—answerable, it may be, to the Houses whom he seeks to lead, either personally or through a Cabinet, as well as to the people for whom they speak. But that is a matter to be worked out—as it inevitably will be—in some natural American way which we cannot yet even predict.

The present fact is that the President is held responsible for what happens in Washington in every large matter, and so long as he is commanded to lead he is surely entitled to a certain amount of power—all the power he can get from the support and convictions and opinions of his fellow countrymen; and he ought to be suffered to use that power against his opponents until his work is done. It will be very difficult for him to abuse it. He holds it upon sufferance, at the pleasure of public opinion. Everyone else, his opponents included, has access to opinion, as he has. He must keep the confidence of the country by earning it, for he can keep it in no other way.

Put the present customary limitation of two terms into the Constitution, if you do not trust the people to take care of themselves, but make it two terms (not one, because four years is often too long), and give the President a chance to win the full service by proving himself fit for it.

If you wish to learn the result of constitutional ineligibility to re-election, ask any former governor of New Jersey, for example, what the effect is in actual experience. He will tell you how cynically and with what complacence the politicians banded against him waited for the inevitable end of his term to take their chances with his successor.

Constitutions place and can place no limitations upon their power. They may control what governors they can as long as they please and as long as they can keep their outside power and influence together. They smile at the coming and going of governors as some men in Washington have smiled at the coming and going of Presidents, as upon things ephemeral, which passed and were soon enough got rid of if you but sat tight and waited.

As things stand now the people might more likely be cheated than served by further limitations of the President's eligibility. His fighting power in their behalf would be immensely weakened. No one will fear a President except those whom he can make fear the elections.

If We Want Our Presidents to Fight Our Battles for Us

We singularly belie our own principles by seeking to determine by fixed constitutional provision what the people shall determine for themselves and are perfectly competent to determine for themselves. We cast a doubt upon the whole theory of popular government.

I believe that we should fatally embarrass ourselves if we made the constitutional change proposed. If we want our Presidents to fight our battles for us, we should give them the means, the legitimate means, the means their opponents will always have. Strip them of everything else but the right to appeal to the people, but leave them that; suffer them to be leaders; absolutely prevent them from being bosses.

We would otherwise appear to be going in two opposite directions. We are seeking in every way to extend the power of the people, but in the matter of the Presidency we fear and distrust the people and seek to bind them hand and foot by rigid constitutional provision. My own mind is not agile enough to go both ways.

I am very well aware that my position on this question will be misconstrued, but that is a matter of perfect indifference to me. The truth is much more important than my reputation for modesty and lack of personal ambition. My reputation will take care of itself, but constitutional questions and questions of policy will not take care of themselves without frank and fearless discussion.

I am not speaking for my own re-election; I am speaking to redeem my promise that I would say what I really think on every public question and take my chances in the court of public opinion.

LETTER TO JOSEPH R. WILSON,
APRIL 22, 1913

Against Affection and Temptation

MY DEAR, DEAR BROTHER: I never in my life had anything quite so hard to do as this that I must do about the Nashville Post Office. Knowing as I do that a better man could not possibly be found for the place, and sure though I am that it would meet with the general approval of the citizens of Nashville, I yet feel that it would be a very serious mistake for both you and for me if I were to appoint you to the Postmastership there. I cannot tell you how much I have worried about this or how much I have had to struggle against affection and temptation, but I am clear in the conviction that I am sure that in the long run, if not now, you will agree with me that I am deciding rightly.

I cannot write any more just now, because I feel too deeply.

With deepest love I remain

Your affectionate brother,
WOODROW WILSON

STATEMENT TO THE PRESS,
WASHINGTON, MAY 26, 1913

The Intolerable Burden of the Lobby

I think that the public ought to know the extraordinary exertions being made by the lobby in Washington to gain recognition for certain alterations of the Tariff bill. Washington has seldom seen so numerous, so industrious or so insidious a lobby. The newspapers are being filled with paid advertisements calculated to mislead the judgment of public men not only, but also the public opinion of the country itself. There is every evidence that money without limit is being spent to sustain this lobby and to create an appearance of a pressure of opinion antagonistic to some of the chief items of the Tariff bill.

It is of serious interest to the country that the people at large should have no lobby and be voiceless in these matters, while great bodies of astute men seek to create an artificial opinion and to overcome the interests of the public for their private profit. It is thoroughly worth the while of the people of this country to take knowledge of this matter. Only public opinion can check and detroy it.

The Government in all its branches ought to be relieved from this intolerable burden and this constant interruption to the calm progress of debate. I know that in this I am speaking for the members of the two houses, who would rejoice as much as I would to be released from this unbearable situation.

ADDRESS TO CONGRESS,
MARCH 5, 1914

The Large Thing Is the Only Thing to Do

GENTLEMEN OF THE CONGRESS: I have come to you upon an errand which can be very briefly performed, but I beg that you will not measure its importance by the number of sentences in which I state it. No communication I have addressed to the Congress carried with it graver or more far-reaching implications as to the interest of the country, and I come now to speak upon a matter with regard to which I am charged in a peculiar degree, by the Constitution itself, with personal responsibility.

I have come to ask you for the repeal of that provision of the Panama Canal Act of August 24, 1912, which exempts vessels engaged in the coastwise trade of the United States from payment of tolls, and to urge upon you the justice, the wisdom, and the large policy of such a repeal with the utmost earnestness of which I am capable.

In my own judgment, very fully considered and maturely formed, that exemption constitutes a mistaken economic policy from every point of view, and is, moreover, in plain contravention of the treaty with Great Britain concerning the canal concluded on November 18, 1901. But I have not come to urge upon you my personal views. I have come to state to you a fact and a situation. Whatever may be our own differences of opinion concerning this much debated measure, its meaning is not debated outside the United States. Everywhere else the language of the treaty is given but one interpretation, and that interpretation precludes the exemption I am asking you to repeal. We consented to the treaty; its language we accepted, if we did not originate it; and we are too big, too powerful, too self-respecting a nation to interpret with a too strained or refined reading the words of our own promises just because we have power enough to give us leave to read them as we please. The large thing to do is the only thing we can afford to do, a voluntary withdrawal from a position everywhere questioned and misunderstood. We ought to reverse our action without raising the question whether we were right or wrong, and so once more deserve our reputation for generosity and for the redemption of every obligation without quibble or hesitation.

I ask this of you in support of the foreign policy of the administration. I shall not know how to deal with other matters of even greater delicacy and nearer consequence if you do not grant it to me in ungrudging measure.

MESSAGE TO THE HOUSE OF REPRESENTATIVES,
JANUARY 28, 1915

Veto of the Immigration Bill

TO THE HOUSE OF REPRESENTATIVES: It is with unaffected regret that I find myself constrained by clear conviction to return this bill (H. R. 6060, "An act to regulate the immigration of aliens to and the residence of aliens in the United States") without my signature. Not only do I feel it to be a very serious matter to exercise the power of veto in any case, because it involves opposing the single judgment of the President to the judgment of a majority of both the Houses of the Congress, a step which no man who realizes his own liability to error can take without great hesitation, but also because this particular bill is in so many important respects admirable, well conceived, and desirable. Its enactment into law would undoubtedly enhance the efficiency and improve the methods of handling the important branch of the public service to which it relates. But candor and a sense of duty with regard to the responsibility so clearly imposed upon me by the Constitution in matters of legislation leave me no choice but to dissent.

In two particulars of vital consequence this bill embodies a radical departure from the traditional and long-established policy of this country, a policy in which our people have conceived the very character of their Government to be expressed, the very mission and spirit of the Nation in respect of its relations to the peoples of the world outside their borders. It seeks to all but close entirely the gates of asylum which have always been open to those who could find nowhere else the right and opportunity of constitutional agitation for what they conceived to be the natural and inalienable rights of men; and it excludes those to whom the opportunities of elementary education have been denied, without regard to their character, their purposes, or their natural capacity.

Restrictions like these, adopted earlier in our history as a Nation, would very materially have altered the course and cooled the humane ardors of our politics. The right of political asylum has brought to this country many a man of noble character and elevated purpose who was marked as an outlaw in his own less fortunate land, and who has yet become an ornament to our citizenship and to our public councils. The children and the compatriots of these illustrious Americans must stand amazed to see the representatives of their Nation now resolved, in the fullness of our national strength and at the maturity of our great institutions, to risk turning such men back from our shores without test of quality or purpose. It is difficult for me to believe that the full effect of this feature of the bill was realized when it was framed and adopted, and it is impossible for me to assent to it in the form in which it is here cast.

The People Have Not Spoken

The literacy test and the tests and restrictions which accompany it constitute an even more radical change in the policy of the Nation. Hitherto we have generously kept our doors open to all who were not unfitted by reason of disease or incapacity for self-support or such personal records and antecedents as were likely to make them a menace to our peace and order or to the wholesome and essential relationships of life. In this bill it is proposed to turn away from tests of character and of quality and impose tests which exclude and restrict; for the new tests here embodied are not tests of quality or of character or of personal fitness, but tests of opportunity. Those who come seeking opportunity are not to be admitted unless they have already had one of the chief of the opportunities they seek, the opportunity of education. The object of such provisions is restriction, not selection.

If the people of this country have made up their minds to limit the number of immigrants by arbitrary tests and so reverse the policy of all the generations of Americans that have gone before them, it is their right to do so. I am their servant and have no license to stand in their way. But I do not believe that they have. I respectfully submit that no one can quote their mandate to that effect. Has any political party ever avowed a policy of restriction in this fundamental matter, gone to the country on it, and been commissioned to control its legislation? Does this bill rest upon the conscious and universal assent and desire of the American people? I doubt it. It is because I doubt it that I make bold to dissent from it. I am willing to abide by the verdict, but not until it has been rendered. Let the platforms of parties speak out upon this policy and the people pronounce their wish. The matter is too fundamental to be settled otherwise.

I have no pride of opinion in this question. I am not foolish enough to profess to know the wishes and ideals of America better than the body of her chosen representatives know them. I only want instruction direct from those whose fortunes, with ours and all men's, are involved.

LETTER TO SENATOR C. A. CULBERSON,
WASHINGTON, MAY 5, 1916

Mr. Brandeis for the Supreme Court

There is probably no more important duty imposed upon the President in connection with the general administration of the Government than that of naming members of the Supreme Court; and I need hardly tell you that I named Mr. Brandeis as a member of that great tribunal only because I knew him to be singularly qualified by learning, by gifts, and by character for the position.

Many charges have been made against Mr. Brandeis: the report of your subcommittee has already made it plain to you and to the country at large how unfounded those charges were. They threw a great deal more light upon the character and motives of those with whom they originated than upon the qualifications of Mr. Brandeis. I myself looked into them three years ago when I desired to make Mr. Brandeis a member of my Cabinet and found that they proceeded for the most part from those who hated Mr. Brandeis because he had refused to be serviceable to them in the promotion of their own selfish interests, and from those whom they had prejudiced and misled. The propaganda in this matter has been very extraordinary and very distressing to those who love fairness and value the dignity of the great professions.

I perceived from the first that the charges were intrinsically incredible by anyone who had really known Mr. Brandeis. I have known him. I have tested him by seeking his advice upon some of the most difficult and perplexing public questions about which it was necessary for me to form a judgment. I have dealt with him in matters where nice questions of honor and fair play, as well as large questions of justice and the public benefit, were involved. In every matter in which I have made test of his judgment and point of view I have received from him counsel singularly enlightening, singularly clear-sighted and judicial, and, above all, full of moral stimulation.

He is a friend of all just men and a lover of the right; and he knows more than how to talk about the right—he knows how to set it forward in the face of its enemies. I knew from direct personal knowledge of the man what I was doing when I named him for the highest and most responsible tribunal of the nation.

Of his extraordinary ability as a lawyer no man who is competent to judge can speak with anything but the highest admiration. You will remember that in the opinion of the late Chief Justice Fuller he was the ablest man who ever appeared before the Supreme Court of the United States. "He is also," the Chief Justice added, "absolutely fearless in the discharge of his duties."

This Friend of Justice and of Men

Those who have resorted to him for assistance in settling great industrial disputes can testify to his fairness and love of justice. In the troublesome controversies between the garment workers and manufacturers of New York City, for example, he gave a truly remarkable proof of his judicial temperament and had what must have been the great satisfaction of rendering decisions which both sides were willing to accept as disinterested and even-handed.

Mr. Brandeis has rendered many notable services to the city and state with which his professional life has been identified. He successfully directed the difficult campaign which resulted in obtaining cheaper gas for the City of Boston. It was chiefly under his guidance and through his efforts that legislation was secured in Massachusetts which authorized saving banks to issue insurance policies for small sums at much reduced rates. And some gentlemen who tried very hard to obtain control by the Boston Elevated Railway Company of the subways of the city for a period of ninety-nine years can probably testify as to his ability as the people's advocate when public interests call for an effective champion. He rendered these services without compensation and earned, whether he got it or not, the gratitude of every citizen of the state and city he served. These are but a few of the services of this kind he has freely rendered. It will hearten friends of community and public rights throughout the country to see his quality signally recognized by his elevation to the Supreme Bench. For the whole country is aware of his quality and is interested in this appointment.

I did not in making choice of Mr. Brandeis ask for or depend upon "endorsements." I acted upon public knowledge and personal acquaintance with the man, and preferred to name a lawyer for this great office whose abilities and character were so widely recognized that he needed no endorsement. I did, however, personally consult many men in whose judgment I had great confidence, and am happy to say was supported in my selection by the voluntary recommendation of the Attorney General of the United States, who urged Mr. Brandeis upon my consideration independently of any suggestion from me.

Let me say by way of summing up, my dear Senator, that I nominated Mr. Brandeis for the Supreme Court because it was, and is, my deliberate judgment that, of all the men now at the bar whom it has been my privilege to observe, test, and know, he is exceptionally qualified. I cannot speak too highly of his impartial, impersonal, orderly, and constructive mind, his rare analytical powers, his deep human sympathy, his profound acquaintance with the historical roots of our institutions and insight into their spirit, or of the many evidences he has given of being imbued to the very heart with our American ideals of justice and equality of opportunity; of his knowledge of modern economic conditions and of the way they bear upon the masses of the people, or of his genius in getting persons to unite in common and harmonious action and look with frank and kindly eyes into each other's minds, who had before been heated antagonists. This friend of justice and of men will ornament the high court of which we are all so justly proud. I am glad to have had the opportunity to pay him this tribute of admiration and of confidence; and I beg that your Committee will accept this nomination as coming from me quick with a sense of public obligation and responsibility.

With warmest regard,
WOODROW WILSON

ADDRESS TO THE NATIONAL PRESS CLUB,
WASHINGTON, MAY 15, 1916

A President's Burden

The only thing that saves the world is the little handful of disinterested men that are in it.

Now, I have found a few disinterested men. I wish I had found more. I can name two or three men with whom I have conferred again and again and again, and I have never caught them by an inadvertence thinking about themselves for their own interests, and I tie to those men as you would tie to an anchor. I tie to them as you would tie to the voices of conscience if you could be sure that you always heard them. Men who have no axes to grind! Men who love America so that they would give their lives for it and never care whether anybody heard that they had given their lives for it; willing to die in obscurity if only they might serve! Those are the men, and nations like those men are the nations that are going to serve the world and save it.

There never was a time in the history of the world when character, just sheer character all by itself, told more than it does now. A friend of mine says that every man who takes office in Washington either grows or swells, and when I give a man an office, I watch him carefully to see whether he is swelling or growing. The mischief of it is that when they swell they do not swell enough to burst. . . . But the men who grow, the men who think better a year after they are put in office than they thought when they were put in office, are the balance wheel of the whole thing. They are the ballast that enables the craft to carry sail and to make port in the long run, no matter what the weather is. . . .

I have come through the fire since I talked to you last. Whether the metal is purer than it was, God only knows; but the fire has been there, the fire has penetrated every part of it, and if I may believe my own thoughts I have less partisan feeling, more impatience of party maneuver, more enthusiasm for the right thing, no matter whom it hurts, than I ever had before in my life. And I have something that it is no doubt dangerous to have, but that I cannot help having. I have a profound intellectual contempt for men who cannot see the signs of the times.

I have to deal with some men who know no more of the modern processes of politics than if they were living in the eighteenth century, and for them I have a profound and comprehensive intellectual contempt. They are blind. They are hopelessly blind; and the worst of it is I have to spend hours of my time talking to them when I know before I start as much as after I have finished that it is absolutely useless to talk to them. I am talking *in vacuo.* . . .

If I did not go off at week ends occasionally and throw off, as much as it is possible to throw off, this burden, I could not stand it. This week I went down the Potomac and up the James and substituted history for politics, and there was an infinite, sweet calm in some of those old places that reminded me of the records that were made in the days that are past; and I comforted myself with the recollection that the men we remember are the disinterested men who gave us the deeds that have covered the name of America all over with the luster of imperishable glory.

ADDRESS AT INDEPENDENCE HALL,
PHILADELPHIA, JULY 4, 1914

He Cannot Feel Lonely, He Cannot Feel Afraid

The world is becoming more complicated every day, my fellow-citizens. No man ought to be foolish enough to think that he understands it all. And, therefore, I am glad that there are some simple things in the world. One of the simple things is principle. Honesty is a perfectly simple thing. It is hard for me to believe that in most circumstances when a man has a choice of ways he does not know which is the right way and which is the wrong way. No man who has chosen the wrong way ought even to come into Independence Square; it is holy ground which he ought not to tread upon. He ought not to come where immortal voices have uttered the great sentences of such a document as this Declaration of Independence upon which rests the liberty of a whole nation. . . .

The most patriotic man is sometimes the man who goes in the direction that he thinks right even when he sees half the world against him. It is the dictate of patriotism to sacrifice yourself if you think that that is the path of honor and of duty. Do not blame others if they do not agree with you. Do not die with bitterness in your heart because you did not convince the rest of the world, but die happy because you believe that you tried to serve your country by not selling your soul. Those were grim days, the days of 1776. Those gentlemen did not attach their names to the Declaration of Independence on this table expecting a holiday on the next day, and that 4th of July was not itself a holiday. They attached their signatures to that significant document knowing that if they failed it was certain that every one of them would hang for the failure. They were committing treason in the interest of the liberty of three million people in America. All the rest of the world was against them and smiled with cynical incredulity at the audacious undertaking. Do you think that if they could see this great Nation now they would regret anything that they then did to draw the gaze of a hostile world upon them? Every idea must be started by somebody, and it is a lonely thing to start anything. Yet if it is in you, you must start it if you have a man's blood in you and if you love the country that you profess to be working for.

I am sometimes very much interested when I see gentlemen supposing that popularity is the way to success in America. The way to success in this great country with its fair judgments is to show that you are not afraid of anybody except God and his final verdict. If I did not believe that, I would not believe in democracy. If I did not believe that, I would not believe that people can govern themselves. If I did not believe that the moral judgment would be the last judgment, the final judgment, in the minds of men as well as at the tribunal of God, I could not believe in popular government. But I do believe these things, and, therefore, I earnestly believe in the democracy not only of America but of every awakened people that wishes and intends to govern and control its own affairs.

It is very inspiring to come to this that may be called the original fountain of independence and liberty in America and here drink draughts of patriotic feeling which seem to renew the very blood in one's veins. Down in Washington sometimes when the days are hot and the business presses intolerably and there are so many things to do that it does not seem possible to do anything in the way it ought to be done, it is always possible to lift one's thought above the task of the moment and, as it were, to realize that great thing of which we are all parts, the great body of American feeling and American principle. No man could do the work that has to be done in Washington if he allowed himself to be separated from that body of principle. He must make himself feel that he is a part of the people of the United States, that he is trying to think not only for them, but with them, and then he cannot feel lonely. He not only cannot feel lonely but he cannot feel afraid of anything.

My dream is that as the years go on and the world knows more and more of America it will also drink at these fountains of youth and renewal; that it also will turn to America for those moral inspirations which lie at the basis of all freedom; that the world will never fear America unless it feels that it is engaged in some enterprise which is inconsistent with the rights of humanity; and that America will come into the full light of the day when all shall know that she puts human rights above all other rights and that her flag is the flag not only of America but of humanity.

STATEMENT TO THE COUNTRY,
WASHINGTON, MARCH 4, 1917

A Little Group of Willful Men

The termination of the last session of the Sixty-fourth Congress by constitutional limitation disclosed a situation unparalleled in the history of the country, perhaps unparalleled in the history of any modern Government. In the immediate presence of a crisis fraught with more subtle and far-reaching possibilities of national danger than any other the Government has known within the whole history of its international relations, the Congress has been unable to act either to safeguard the country or to vindicate the elementary rights of its citizens. More than 500 of the 531 members of the two houses were ready and anxious to act; the House of Representatives had acted, by an overwhelming majority; but the Senate was unable to act because a little group of eleven Senators had determined that it should not.

The Senate has no rules by which debate can be limited or brought to an end, no rules by which dilatory tactics of any kind can be prevented. A single member can stand in the way of action, if he have but the physical endurance. The result in this case is a complete paralysis alike of the legislative and of the executive branches of the Government.

This inability of the Senate to act has rendered some of the most necessary legislation of the session impossible at a time when the need of it was most pressing and most evident. The bill which would have permitted such combinations of capital and of organization in the export and import trade of the country as the circumstances of international competition have made imperative—a bill which the business judgment of the whole country approved and demanded—has failed. The opposition of one or two Senators has made it impossible to increase the membership of the Interstate Commerce Commission to give it the altered organization necessary for its efficiency. The Conservation bill, which should have released for immediate use the mineral resources which are still locked up in the public lands, now that their release is more imperatively necessary than ever, and the bill which would have made the unused water power of the country immediately available for industry have both failed, though they have been under consideration throughout the sessions of two Congresses and have been twice passed by the House of Representatives. The appropriations for the army have failed, along with the appropriations for the civil establishment of the Government, the appropriations for the military Academy at West Point and the General Deficiency bill. It has proved impossible to extend the powers of the Shipping Board to meet the special needs of the new situations into which our commerce has been forced or to increase the gold reserve of our national banking system to meet the unusual circumstances of the existing financial situation.

It would not cure the difficulty to call the Sixty-fifth Congress in extraordinary session. The paralysis of the Senate would remain. The purpose and the spirit of action are not lacking now. The Congress is more definitely united in thought and purpose at this moment, I venture to say, than it has been within the memory of any men now in its membership. There is not only the most united patriotic purpose, but the objects members have in view are perfectly clear and definite. But the Senate cannot act unless its leaders can obtain unanimous consent. Its majority is powerless, helpless. In the midst of a crisis of extraordinary peril, when only definite and decided action can make the nation safe or shield it from war itself by the aggression of others, action is impossible.

Although, as a matter of fact, the Nation and the representatives of the Nation stand back of the Executive with unprecedented unanimity and spirit, the impression made abroad will, of course, be that it is not so and that other Governments may act as they please without fear that this Government can do anything at all. We cannot explain. The explanation is incredible. The Senate of the United States is the only legislative body in the world which cannot act when its majority is ready for action. A little group of willful men, representing no opinion but their own, have rendered the great Government of the United States helpless and contemptible.

The remedy? There is but one remedy. The only remedy is that the rules of the Senate shall be so altered that it can act. The country can be relied upon to draw the moral. I believe that the Senate can be relied on to supply the means of action and save the country from disaster.

Chapter Ten

THE ESSENCE OF AMERICA

THE foreign policy that was to crown Wilson's career had its
roots in a concept of America which he had stated eloquently
again and again through his life: a nation born to serve mankind.
These speeches during his Presidency develop the theme. Here are
sounded many notes which have been struck in earlier selections:
the role of the university, of the church, the special preeminence of
Lincoln. Only now the orator has the most powerful office in the
world for his rostrum, and a deepening sense of what ideals cost
when put to the test of action.

ADDRESS DELIVERED AT GETTYSBURG,
JULY 4, 1913

After Fifty Years

I need not tell you what the Battle of Gettysburg meant. These
gallant men in blue and gray sit all about us here.* Many of them
met upon this ground in grim and deadly struggle. Upon these famous fields and hillsides their comrades died about them. In their
presence it were an impertinence to discourse upon how the battle
went, how it ended, what it signified! But fifty years have gone by
since then, and I crave the privilege of speaking to you for a few
minutes of what those fifty years have meant.

What have they meant? They have meant peace and union and
vigour, and the maturity and might of a great nation. How wholesome and healing the peace has been! We have found one another
again as brothers and comrades in arms, enemies no longer, generous
friends rather, our battles long past, the quarrel forgotten—except
that we shall not forget the splendid valour, the manly devotion of

* Survivors of the Battle of Gettysburg were in the President's audience.

the men then arrayed against one another, now grasping hands and smiling into each other's eyes. How complete the union has become and how dear to all of us, how unquestioned, how benign and majestic, as State after State has been added to this our great family of free men! How handsome the vigour, the maturity, the might of the great Nation we love with undivided hearts; how full of large and confident promise that a life will be wrought out that will crown its strength with gracious justice and with a happy welfare that will touch all alike with deep contentment! We are debtors to those fifty crowded years; they have made us heirs to a mighty heritage.

But do we deem the Nation complete and finished? These venerable men crowding here to this famous field have set us a great example of devotion and utter sacrifice. They were willing to die that the people might live. But their task is done. Their day is turned into evening. They look to us to perfect what they established. Their work is handed on to us, to be done in another way, but not in another spirit. Our day is not over; it is upon us in full tide.

The Appeal to the Moral Judgment of Mankind

Have affairs paused? Does the Nation stand still? Is what the fifty years have wrought since those days of battle finished, rounded out, and completed? Here is a great people, great with every force that has ever beaten in the lifeblood of mankind. And it is secure. There is no one within its borders, there is no power among the nations of the earth, to make it afraid. But has it yet squared itself with its own great standards set up at its birth, when it made that first noble, naïve appeal to the moral judgment of mankind to take notice that a government had now at last been established which was to serve men, not masters? It is secure in everything except the satisfaction that its life is right, adjusted to the uttermost to the standards of righteousness and humanity. The days of sacrifice and cleansing are not closed. We have harder things to do than were done in the heroic days of war, because harder to see clearly, requiring more vision, more calm balance of judgment, a more candid searching of the very springs of right.

Look around you upon the field of Gettysburg! Picture the array, the fierce heats and agony of battle, column hurled against column, battery bellowing to battery! Valour? Yes! Greater no man shall see in war; and self-sacrifice, and loss to the uttermost; the high reckless-ness of exalted devotion which does not count the cost. We are made by these tragic, epic things to know what it costs to make a nation—the blood and sacrifice of multitudes of unknown men lifted to a great stature in the view of all generations by knowing no limit to their manly willingness to serve. In armies thus marshaled from the ranks of free men you will see, as it were, a nation embat-tled, the leaders and the led, and may know, if you will, how little except in form its action differs in days of peace from its action in days of war.

May we break camp now and be at ease? Are the forces that fight for the Nation dispersed, disbanded, gone to their homes forgetful of the common cause? Are our forces disorganized, without consti-tuted leaders and the might of men consciously united because we contend, not with armies, but with principalities and powers and wickedness in high places? Are we content to lie still? Does our union mean sympathy, our peace contentment, our vigour right action, our maturity self-comprehension and a clear confidence in choosing what we shall do? War fitted us for action, and action never ceases.

In the Light That Streams from Great Days Gone By

I have been chosen the leader of the Nation. I cannot justify the choice by any qualities of my own, but so it has come about, and here I stand. Whom do I command? The ghostly hosts who fought upon these battle fields long ago and are gone? These gallant gentle-men stricken in years whose fighting days are over, their glory won? What are the orders for them, and who rallies them? I have in my mind another host, whom these set free of civil strife in order that they might work out in days of peace and settled order the life of a great Nation. That host is the people themselves, the great and the small, without class or difference of kind or race or origin; and un-divided in interest, if we have but the vision to guide and direct them and order their lives aright in what we do. Our constitutions are their articles of enlistment. The orders of the day are the laws upon our statute books. What we strive for is their freedom, their right to lift themselves from day to day and behold the things they have hoped for, and so make way for still better days for those whom they love who are to come after them. The recruits are the little children crowding in. The quartermaster's stores are in the mines and forests and fields, in the shops and factories. Every day something must be done to push the campaign forward; and it must be done by plan and with an eye to some great destiny.

How shall we hold such thoughts in our hearts and not be moved? I would not have you live even today wholly in the past, but would wish to stand with you in the light that streams upon us now out of that great day gone by. Here is the nation God has builded by our hands. What shall we do with it? Who stands ready to act again and always in the spirit of this day of reunion and hope and patriotic fervor? The day of our country's life has but broadened into morning. Do not put uniforms by. Put the harness of the present on. Lift your eyes to the great tracts of life yet to be conquered in the interest of righteous peace, of that prosperity which lies in a people's hearts and outlasts all wars and errors of men. Come, let us be comrades and soldiers yet to serve our fellow men in quiet counsel, where the blare of trumpets is neither heard nor heeded and where the things are done which make blessed the nations of the world in peace and righteousness and love.

ADDRESS AT SWARTHMORE COLLEGE,
OCTOBER 25, 1913

The University a Nursery of Principle and Honor

No one can stand in the presence of a gathering like this, on a day suggesting the memories which this day suggests, without asking himself what a college is for. There have been times when I have suspected that certain undergraduates did not know. I remember that in days of discouragement as a teacher I gratefully recalled the sympathy of a friend of mine in the Yale faculty, who said that after 20 years of teaching he had come to the conclusion that the human mind had infinite resources for resisting the introduction of knowledge. Yet I have my serious doubts as to whether the main object of a college is the introduction of knowledge. It may be the transmission of knowledge through the human system, but not much of it sticks. Its introduction is temporary; it is for the discipline of the hour. Most of what a man learns in college he assiduously forgets afterwards. Not because he purposes to forget it, but because the crowding events of the days that follow seem somehow to eliminate it.

What a man ought never to forget with regard to a college is that it is a nursery of principle and of honor. I can not help thinking of William Penn as a sort of spiritual knight who went out upon his adventures to carry the torch that had been put in his hands, so that other men might have the path illuminated for them which led to justice and to liberty. I can not admit that a man establishes his right to call himself a college graduate by showing me his diploma. The only way he can prove it is by showing that his eyes are lifted to some horizon which other men less instructed than he have not been privileged to see. Unless he carries freight of the spirit he has not been bred where spirits are bred.

This man Penn, representing the sweet enterprise of the quiet and powerful sect that called themselves Friends, proved his right to the title by being the friend of mankind. He crossed the ocean, not merely to establish estates in America, but to set up a free commonwealth in America and to show that he was of the lineage of those who had been bred in the best traditions of the human spirit. I would not be interested in celebrating the memory of William Penn if his conquest had been merely a material one. Sometimes we have been laughed at—by foreigners in particular—for boasting of the size of the American Continent, the size of our own domain as a nation; for they have, naturally enough, suggested that we did not make it. But I claim that every race and every man is as big as the thing that he takes possession of, and that the size of America is in some sense a standard of the size and capacity of the American people. And yet the mere extent of the American conquest is not what gives America distinction in the annals of the world, but the professed purpose of the conquest which was to see to it that every foot of this land should be the home of free, self-governed people, who should have no government whatever, which did not rest upon the consent of the governed. I would like to believe that all this hemisphere is devoted to the same sacred purpose and that nowhere can any government endure which is stained by blood or supported by anything but the consent of the governed.

The Only Glory of America

The spirit of Penn will not be stayed. You can not set limits to such knightly adventurers. After their own day is gone their spirits stalk the world, carrying inspiration everywhere that they go and reminding men of the lineage, the fine lineage, of those who have sought justice and right. It is no small matter, therefore, for a college to have as its patron saint a man who went out upon such a conquest. What I would like to ask you young people today is: How many of you have devoted yourselves to the like adventure? How many of you will volunteer to carry these spiritual messages of liberty to the world? How many of you will forego anything except your allegiance to that which is just and that which is right? We die but once, and we die without distinction if we are not willing to die the death of sacrifice. Do you covet honor? You will never get it by serving yourself. Do you covet distinction? You will get it only as the servant of mankind. Do not forget, then, as you walk these classic places, why you are here. You are not here merely to prepare to make a living. You are here in order to enable the world to live more amply, with greater vision, with a finer spirit of hope and achievement. You are here to enrich the world, and you impoverish yourself if you forget the errand.

It seems to me that there is no great difference between the ideals of the college and the ideals of the State. Can you not translate the one into the other? Men have not had to come to college, let me remind you, to quaff the fountains of this inspiration. You are merely more privileged than they. Men out of every walk of life, men without advantages of any kind, have seen the vision, and you, with it written large upon every page of your studies, are the more

blind if you do not see it when it is pointed out. You could not be
forgiven for overlooking it. They might have been. But they did not
await instruction. They simply drew the breath of life into their
lungs, felt the aspirations that must come to every human soul,
looked out upon their brothers, and felt their pulses beat as their
fellows' beat, and then sought by counsel and action to move forward to common ends that would be crowned with honor and
achievement. This is the only glory of America.

ADDRESS AT THE BROOKLYN NAVY YARD,
MAY 11, 1914

The Heroes of Vera Cruz

Duty is not an uncommon thing. Men are performing it in the
ordinary walks of life all around us all the time, and they are making
great sacrifices to perform it. What gives men like these peculiar
distinction is not merely that they did their duty, but that their
duty had nothing to do with them or their own personal and peculiar interests. They did not give their lives for themselves. They gave
their lives for us, because we called upon them as a Nation to perform an unexpected duty. That is the way in which men grow distinguished, and that is the only way, by serving somebody else than
themselves. And what greater thing could you serve than a Nation
such as this we love and are proud of? Are you sorry for these lads?
Are you sorry for the way they will be remembered? Does it not
quicken your pulses to think of the list of them? I hope to God
none of you may join the list, but if you do you will join an immortal company.

So, while we are profoundly sorrowful, and while there goes out
of our hearts a very deep and affectionate sympathy for the friends
and relatives of these lads who for the rest of their lives shall mourn
them, though with a touch of pride, we know why we do not go
away from this occasion cast down, but with our heads lifted and
our eyes on the future of this country, with absolute confidence of
how it will be worked out. Not only upon the mere vague future of
this country, but upon the immediate future. We have gone down
to Mexico to serve mankind if we can find out the way. We do not

want to fight the Mexicans. We want to serve the Mexicans if we can, because we know how we would like to be free, and how we would like to be served if there were friends standing by in such case ready to serve us. A war of aggression is not a war in which it is a proud thing to die, but a war of service is a thing in which it is a proud thing to die.

Notice how truly these men were of our blood. I mean of our American blood, which is not drawn from any one country, which is not drawn from any one stock, which is not drawn from any one language of the modern world; but free men everywhere have sent their sons and their brothers and their daughters to this country in order to make that great compounded Nation which consists of all the sturdy elements and of all the best elements of the whole globe. I listened again to this list of the dead with a profound interest because of the mixture of the names, for the names bear the marks of the several national stocks from which these men came. But they are not Irishmen or Germans or Frenchmen or Hebrews or Italians any more. They were not when they went to Vera Cruz; they were Americans, every one of them, and with no difference in their Americanism because of the stock from which they came. They were in a peculiar sense of our blood, and they proved it by showing that they were of our spirit—that no matter what their derivation, no matter where their people came from, they thought and wished and did the things that were American; and the flag under which they served was a flag in which all the blood of mankind is united to make a free Nation.

ADDRESS AT COLUMBUS, OHIO,
DECEMBER 10, 1915

The Devotion of the Spirit to Something Nobler than Itself

There are a great many arguments about Christianity. There are a great many things which we spiritually assert which we can not prove in the ordinary, scientific sense of the word "prove"; but there are some things which we can show. The proof of Christianity is written in the biography of the saints, and by the saints I do not mean the technical saints, those whom the church or the world has picked out to label "saints," for they are not very numerous, but the people whose lives, whose individual lives, have been transformed by Christianity. It is the only force in the world that I have ever heard of that does actually transform the life, and the proof of that transformation is to be found all over the Christian world and is multiplied and repeated as Christianity gains fresh territory in the heathen world. Men begin suddenly to erect great spiritual standards over the little personal standards which they theretofore professed and will walk smiling to the stake in order that their souls may be true to themselves. There is nothing else that does that. There is something that is analogous to it, and that is patriotism. Men will go into the fire of battle and freely give their lives for something greater than themselves, their duty to their country; and there is a pretty fine analogy between patriotism and Christianity. It is the devotion of the spirit to something greater and nobler than itself. These are the transforming influences. All the transforming influences in the world are unselfish. There is not a single selfish force in the world that is not touched with sinister power, and the church is the only embodiment of the things that are entirely unselfish, the principles of self-sacrifice and devotion.

The reason that I am proud to be an American is because America was given birth to by such conceptions as these; that its object in the world, its only reason for existence as a Government, was to show men the paths of liberty and of mutual serviceability, to lift the common man out of the paths, out of the sloughs of discouragement and even despair; set his feet upon firm ground; tell him, "Here is the high road upon which you are as much entitled to walk as we are, and, we will see that there is a free field and no favor, and that as your moral qualities are and your physical powers so will your success be. We will not let any man make you afraid, and we will not let any man do you an injustice."

Those are the ideals of America. We have not always lived up to them. No community has always lived up to them, but we are dignified by the fact that those are the things we live for and sail by; America is great in the world, not as she is a successful Government merely, but as she is the successful embodiment of a great ideal of unselfish citizenship. That is what makes the world feel America draw it like a lodestone. That is the reason why the ships that cross the sea have so many hopeful eyes lifted from their humbler quarters toward the shores of the new world. That is the reason why men, after they have been for a little while in America and go back for a visit to the old country, have a new light in their faces—the light that has kindled there in the country where they have seen some of their objects fulfilled. That is the light that shines from America. God grant that it may always shine and that in many a humble hearth, in quiet country churches, the flames may be lighted by which this great light is kept alive.

ACCEPTANCE OF THE LINCOLN MEMORIAL,
HODGENVILLE, KENTUCKY, SEPTEMBER 4, 1916

The Authentic Proofs of Democracy

How eloquent this little house within this shrine is of the vigor of democracy! There is nowhere in the land any home so remote, so humble, that it may not contain the power of mind and heart and conscience to which nations yield and history submits its processes. Nature pays no tribute to aristocracy, subscribes to no creed of caste, renders fealty to no monarch or master of any name or kind. Genius is no snob. It does not run after titles or seek by preference the high circles of society. It affects humble company as well as great. It pays no special tribute to universities or learned societies or conventional standards of greatness, but serenely chooses its own comrades, its own haunts, its own cradle even, and its own life of adventure and of training. Here is proof of it.

This little hut was the cradle of one of the great sons of men, a man of singular, delightful, vital genius who presently emerged upon the great stage of the nation's history, gaunt, shy, ungainly, but dominant and majestic, a natural ruler of men, himself inevitably the central figure of the great plot. No man can explain this, but every man can see how it demonstrates the vigor of democracy, where every door is open, in every hamlet and countryside, in city and wilderness alike, for the ruler to emerge when he will and claim his leadership in the free life. Such are the authentic proofs of the validity and vitality of democracy.

Here, no less, hides the mystery of democracy. Who shall guess this secret of nature and providence and a free polity? Whatever the vigor and vitality of the stock from which he sprang, its mere vigor and soundness do not explain where this man got his great heart that seemed to comprehend all mankind in its catholic and benignant sympathy, the mind that sat enthroned behind those brooding, melancholy eyes, whose vision swept many an horizon which those about him dreamed not of, that mind that comprehended what it had never seen, and understood the language of affairs with the ready ease of one to the manner born—or that nature which seemed in its varied richness to be the familiar of men of every way of life. This is the sacred mystery of democracy, that its richest fruits spring up out of soils which no man has prepared and in circumstances amidst which they are the least expected. This is a place alike of mystery and of reassurance.

It is likely that in a society ordered otherwise than our own Lincoln could not have found himself or the path of fame and power upon which he walked serenely to his death. In this place it is right that we should remind ourselves of the solid and striking facts upon which our faith in democracy is founded. Many another man besides Lincoln has served the nation in its highest places of counsel and of action whose origins were as humble as his. Though the greatest example of the universal energy, richness, stimulation, and force of democracy, he is only one example among many. The permeating and all-pervasive virtue of the freedom which challenges us in America to make the most of every gift and power we possess every page of our history serves to emphasize and illustrate. Standing here in this place, it seems almost the whole of the stirring story.

The Lonely Search of the Spirit for the Truth

Here Lincoln had his beginnings. Here the end and consummation of that great life seem remote and a bit incredible. And yet there was no break anywhere between beginning and end, no lack of natural sequence anywhere. Nothing really incredible happened.

Lincoln was unaffectedly as much at home in the White House as he was here. Do you share with me the feeling, I wonder, that he was permanently at home nowhere? It seems to me that in the case of a man—I would rather say of a spirit—like Lincoln the question where he was is of little significance, that it is always what he was that really arrests our thought and takes hold of our imagination. It is the spirit always that is sovereign.

Lincoln, like the rest of us, was put through the discipline of the world—a very rough and exacting discipline for him, an indispensable discipline for every man who would know what he is about in the midst of the world's affairs; but his spirit got only its schooling there. It did not derive its character or its vision from the experiences which brought it to its full revelation. The test of every American must always be, not where he is, but what he is. That, also, is of the essence of democracy, and is the moral of which this place is most gravely expressive.

We would like to think of men like Lincoln and Washington as typical Americans, but no man can be typical who is so unusual as these great men were. It was typical of American life that it should produce such men with supreme indifference as to the manner in which it produced them, and as readily here in this hut as amidst the little circle of cultivated gentlemen to whom Virginia owed so much in leadership and example. And Lincoln and Washington were typical Americans in the use they made of their genius. But there will be few such men at best, and we will not look into the mystery of how and why they come. We will only keep the door open for them always, and a hearty welcome—after we have recognized them.

I have read many biographies of Lincoln; I have sought out with the greatest interest the many intimate stories that are told of him, the narratives of nearby friends, the sketches at close quarters, in which those who had the privilege of being associated with him have tried to depict for us the very man himself "in his habit as he lived"; but I have nowhere found a real intimate of Lincoln's. I nowhere get the impression in any narrative or reminiscence that the writer had in fact penetrated to the heart of his mystery, or that any man could penetrate to the heart of it. That brooding spirit had no real familiars. I get the impression that it never spoke out in complete self-revelation, and that it could not reveal itself completely to anyone.

It was a very lonely spirit that looked out from underneath those shaggy brows and comprehended men without fully communing with them, as if, in spite of all its genial efforts at comradeship, it dwelt apart, saw its visions of duty where no man looked on. There is a very holy and very terrible isolation for the conscience of every man who seeks to read the destiny in affairs for others as well as for himself, for a nation as well as for individuals. That privacy no man can intrude upon. That lonely search of the spirit for the right perhaps no man can assist. This strange child of the cabin kept company with invisible things, was born into no intimacy but that of its own silently assembling and deploying thoughts.

I have come here today, not to utter a eulogy on Lincoln; he stands in need of none, but to endeavor to interpret the meaning of this gift to the nation of the place of his birth and origin. Is not this an altar upon which we may forever keep alive the vestal fire of democracy as upon a shrine at which some of the deepest and most sacred hopes of mankind may from age to age be rekindled? For these hopes must constantly be rekindled, and only those who live can rekindle them. The only stuff that can retain the life-giving heat is the stuff of living hearts. And the hopes of mankind cannot be kept alive by words merely, by constitutions and doctrines of right and codes of liberty. The object of democracy is to transmute these into the life and action of society, the self-denial and self-sacrifice of heroic men and women willing to make their lives an embodiment of right and service and enlightened purpose. The commands of democracy are as imperative as its privileges and opportunities are wide and generous. Its compulsion is upon us. It will be great and lift a great light for the guidance of the nations only if we are great and carry that light high for the guidance of our own feet. We are not worthy to stand here unless we ourselves be in deed and in truth real democrats and servants of mankind, ready to give our very lives for the freedom and justice and spiritual exaltation of the great Nation which shelters and nurtures us.

Chapter Eleven

FROM NEUTRALITY TO LEADERSHIP

WITH the outbreak of war in Europe began a long period of soul-searching for the United States and for its President. The speeches and statements in this chapter suggest Wilson's deep spiritual torment, a torment which only here and there breaks through on the surface, and takes on, when it does, the nature of paradoxes that outrage prevailing concepts. "Too proud to fight," "peace without victory"—these were outcroppings of a profound and tragic sense of the dilemma in which the country found itself. To reconcile the idea of neutrality with the idea of service to mankind was Wilson's task. In the concept of the League of Nations, first set forth here, and in the principles of the great speech of January 22, 1917, he found a purpose essentially noble and disinterested, giving meaning to America's position. But to have a purpose was, inevitably, to be ready to fight for it; and by January 1917, fighting was only a few months off.

STATEMENT TO THE NATION,
WASHINGTON, AUGUST 19, 1914

The Appeal for Neutrality

MY FELLOW COUNTRYMEN: I suppose that every thoughtful man in America has asked himself, during these last troubled weeks, what influence the European war may exert upon the United States, and I take the liberty of addressing a few words to you in order to point out that it is entirely within our own choice what its effects upon us will be and to urge very earnestly upon you the sort of speech and conduct which will best safeguard the Nation against distress and disaster.

The effect of the war upon the United States will depend upon what American citizens say and do. Every man who really loves America will act and speak in the true spirit of neutrality, which is the spirit of impartiality and fairness and friendliness to all concerned. The spirit of the Nation in this critical matter will be determined largely by what individuals and society and those gathered in public meetings do and say, upon what newspapers and magazines contain, upon what ministers utter in their pulpits, and men proclaim as their opinions on the street.

The people of the United States are drawn from many nations, and chiefly from the nations now at war. It is natural and inevitable that there should be the utmost variety of sympathy and desire among them with regard to the issues and circumstances of the conflict. Some will wish one nation, others another, to succeed in the momentous struggle. It will be easy to excite passion and difficult to allay it. Those responsible for exciting it will assume a heavy responsibility, responsibility for no less a thing than that the people of the United States, whose love of their country and whose loyalty to its Government should unite them as Americans all, bound in honor and affection to think first of her and her interests, may be divided in camps of hostile opinion, hot against each other, involved in the war itself in impulse and opinion if not in action.

Such divisions amongst us would be fatal to our peace of mind and might seriously stand in the way of the proper performance of our duty as the one great nation at peace, the one people holding itself ready to play a part of impartial mediation and speak the counsels of peace and accommodation, not as a partisan, but as a friend.

I venture, therefore, my fellow countrymen, to speak a solemn word of warning to you against that deepest, most subtle, most essential breach of neutrality which may spring out of partisanship, out of passionately taking sides. The United States must be neutral in fact as well as in name during these days that are to try men's souls. We must be impartial in thought as well as in action, must put a curb upon our sentiments as well as upon every transaction that might be construed as a preference of one party to the struggle before another.

My thought is of America. I am speaking, I feel sure, the earnest wish and purpose of every thoughtful American that this great country of ours, which is, of course, the first in our thoughts and in our hearts, should show herself in this time of peculiar trial a Nation fit beyond others to exhibit the fine poise of undisturbed judgment, the dignity of self-control, the efficiency of dispassionate action; a Nation that neither sits in judgment upon others nor is disturbed in her own counsels and which keeps herself fit and free to do what is honest and disinterested and truly serviceable for the peace of the world.

Shall we not resolve to put upon ourselves the restraints which will bring to our people the happiness and the great and lasting influence for peace we covet for them?

ADDRESS BEFORE THE ANNUAL CONFERENCE
OF THE METHODIST PROTESTANT CHURCH,
WASHINGTON, APRIL 9, 1915

The Great War

These are days of very great perplexity, when a great cloud of trouble hangs and broods over the greater part of the world. It seems as if great, blind material forces had been released, which had for long been held in leash and restraint. And yet, underneath that you can see the strong impulses of great ideals.

It would be impossible for men to go through what men are going through on the battlefields of Europe—to go through the present dark night of their terrible struggle—if it were not that they saw, or thought that they saw, the broadening of light where the morning sun should come up, and believed that they were standing, each on his side of the contest, for some eternal principle of right.

Then, all about them, all about us, there sits the silent, waiting tribunal which is going to utter the ultimate judgment upon this struggle, the great tribunal of the opinion of the world, and I fancy I see, I hope that I see, I pray that it may be that I do truly see great spiritual forces lying waiting for the outcome of this thing to assert themselves, and asserting themselves even now, to enlighten our judgment and steady our spirits. No man is wise enough to pronounce judgment, but we can all hold our spirits in readiness to accept the truth when it dawns on us and is revealed to us in the outcome of this titanic struggle.

You will see that it is only in such general terms that one can speak in the midst of a confused world, because, as I have already said, no man has the key to this confusion, no man can see the outcome, but every man can keep his own spirit prepared to contribute to the net result when the outcome displays itself.

ADDRESS AT NEW YORK,
APRIL 20, 1915

The Mediating Nation of the World

Do you realize that, roughly speaking, we are the only great Nation at present disengaged? I am not speaking, of course, with disparagement of the greatness of those nations in Europe which are not parties to the present war, but I am thinking of their close neighborhood to it. I am thinking how their lives much more than ours touch the very heart and stuff of the business, whereas we have rolling between us and those bitter days across the water 3,000 miles of cool and silent ocean. Our atmosphere is not yet charged with those disturbing elements which must permeate every nation of Europe. Therefore, is it not likely that the nations of the world will some day turn to us for the cooler assessment of the elements engaged? I am not now thinking so preposterous a thought as that we should sit in judgment upon them—no nation is fit to sit in judgment upon any other nation—but that we shall some day have to assist in reconstructing the processes of peace. Our resources are untouched, we are more and more becoming by the force of circumstances the mediating Nation of the world in respect of its finance. We must make up our minds what are the best things to do and what are the best ways to do them. We must put our money, our energy, our enthusiasm, our sympathy into these things, and we must have our judgments prepared and our spirits chastened against the coming of that day.

So that I am not speaking in a selfish spirit when I say that our whole duty, for the present at any rate, is summed up in this motto,

"America first." Let us think of America before we think of Europe, in order that America may be fit to be Europe's friend when the day of tested friendship comes. The test of friendship is not now sympathy with the one side or the other, but getting ready to help both sides when the struggle is over. The basis of neutrality, gentlemen, is not indifference; it is not self-interest. The basis of neutrality is sympathy for mankind. It is fairness, it is good will, at bottom. It is impartiality of spirit and of judgment.

We are the mediating Nation of the world. I do not mean that we undertake not to mind our own business and to mediate where other people are quarreling. I mean the word in a broader sense. We are compounded of the nations of the world; we mediate their blood, we mediate their traditions, we mediate their sentiments, their tastes, their passions; we are ourselves compounded of those things. We are, therefore, able to understand all nations; we are able to understand them in the compound, not separately, as partisans, but unitedly as knowing and comprehending and embodying them all. It is in that sense that I mean that America is a mediating Nation. The opinion of America, the action of America, is ready to turn, and free to turn, in any direction. Did you ever reflect upon how almost every other nation has through long centuries been headed in one direction? That is not true of the United States. The United States has no racial momentum. It has no history back of it which makes it run all its energies and all its ambitions in one particular direction.

And America is particularly free in this, that she has no hampering ambitions as a world power. We do not want a foot of anybody's territory. If we have been obliged by circumstances, or have considered ourselves to be obliged by circumstances, in the past, to take territory which we otherwise would not have thought of taking, I believe I am right in saying that we have considered it our duty to administer that territory, not for ourselves but for the people living in it, and to put this burden upon our consciences—not to think that this thing is ours for our use, but to regard ourselves as trustees of the great business for those to whom it does really belong, trustees ready to hand it over to the cestui que trust at any time when the business seems to make that possible and feasible. That is what I mean by saying we have no hampering ambitions. We do not want anything that does not belong to us. Is not a nation in that position free to serve other nations, and is not a nation like that ready to form some part of the assessing opinion of the world?

My interest in the neutrality of the United States is not the petty desire to keep out of trouble. . . . I am interested in neutrality because there is something so much greater to do than fight; there is a distinction waiting for this Nation that no nation has ever yet got. That is the distinction of absolute self-control and self-mastery. Whom do you admire most among your friends? The irritable man? The man out of whom you can get a "rise" without trying? The man who will fight at the drop of the hat, whether he knows what the hat is dropped for or not? Don't you admire and don't you fear, if you have to contest with him, the self-mastered man who watches you with calm eye and comes in only when you have carried the thing so far that you must be disposed of? That is the man you respect. That is the man who, you know, has at bottom a much more fundamental and terrible courage than the irritable, fighting man. Now, I covet for America this splendid courage of reserve moral force. . . .

ADDRESS AT PHILADELPHIA,
MAY 10, 1915

The Example of America Must Be a Special Example

It is a very interesting circumstance to me, in thinking of those of you who have just sworn allegiance to this great Government, that you were drawn across the ocean by some beckoning finger of hope, by some belief, by some vision of a new kind of justice, by some expectation of a better kind of life. No doubt you have been disappointed in some of us. Some of us are very disappointing. No doubt you have found that justice in the United States goes only with a pure heart and a right purpose as it does everywhere else in the world. No doubt what you found here did not seem touched for you, after all, with the complete beauty of the ideal which you had conceived beforehand. But remember this: If we had grown at all poor in the ideal, you brought some of it with you. A man does not go out to seek the thing that is not in him. A man does not hope for the thing that he does not believe in, and if some of us have forgotten what America believed in, you, at any rate, imported in your own hearts a renewal of the belief.

That is the reason that I, for one, make you welcome. If I have in any degree forgotten what America was intended for, I will thank God if you will remind me. I was born in America. You dreamed dreams of what America was to be, and I hope you brought the dreams with you. No man that does not see visions will ever realize any high hope or undertake any high enterprise. Just because you brought dreams with you, America is more likely to realize dreams such as you brought. You are enriching us if you came expecting us to be better than we are. . . .

A nation that is not constantly renewed out of new sources is apt to have the narrowness and prejudice of a family; whereas, America must have this consciousness, that on all sides it touches elbows and touches hearts with all the nations of mankind. The example of America must be a special example. The example of America must be the example not merely of peace because it will not fight, but of peace because peace is the healing and elevating influence of the world and strife is not. There is such a thing as a man being too proud to fight. There is such a thing as a nation being so right that it does not need to convince others by force that it is right.

ADDRESS AT NEW YORK,
MAY 17, 1915

The Navy and the Nation

These quiet ships lying in the river have no suggestion of bluster about them, no intimation of aggression. They are commanded by men thoughtful of the duty of citizens as well as the duty of officers, men acquainted with the traditions of the great service to which they belong, men who know by touch with the people of the United States what sort of purposes they ought to entertain and what sort of discretion they ought to exercise in order to use those engines of force as engines to promote the interests of humanity.

The interesting and inspiring thing about America is that she asks nothing for herself except what she has a right to ask for humanity itself. We want no nation's property. We mean to question no nation's honor. We do not wish to stand selfishly in the way of the development of any nation. We want nothing that we cannot get by our own legitimate enterprise and by the inspiration of our own example; and, standing for these things, it is not pretension on our part to say that we are privileged to stand for what every nation would wish to stand for, and speak for those things which all humanity must desire.

When I think of the flag which those ships carry, the only touch of color about them, the only thing that moves as if it had a subtle spirit in it in their solid structure, it seems to me that I see alternate strips of parchment upon which are written the rights of liberty and justice, and stripes of blood spilt to vindicate those rights; and, then, in the corner a prediction of the blue serene into which every nation may swim which stands for these things.

The mission of America is the only thing that a sailor or a soldier should think about. He has nothing to do with the formulation of her policy. He is to support her policy whatever it is; but he is to support her policy in the spirit of herself, and the strength of our polity is that we who for the time being administer the affairs of this Nation do not originate her spirit. We attempt to embody it; we attempt to realize it in action; we are dominated by it, we do not dictate it.

So with every man in arms who serves the Nation; he stands and waits to do the thing which the Nation desires. Those who represent America sometimes seem to forget her programs, but the people never forget them. It is as startling as it is touching to see how whenever you touch a principle you touch the hearts of the people of the United States. They listen to your debates of policy, they determine which party they will prefer to power, they choose and prefer as between men, but their real affection, their real force, their real irresistible momentum is for the ideas which men embody. I never go on the streets of a great city without feeling that somehow

I do not confer elsewhere than on the streets with the great spirit
of the people themselves, going about their business, attending to
the things which immediately concern them, and yet carrying a
treasure at their hearts all the while, ready to be stirred not only as
individuals but as members of a great union of hearts that constitutes a patriotic people. This sight in the river touches me merely
as a symbol of all this; and it quickens the pulse of every man who
realizes these things to have anything to do with them. When a
crisis occurs in this country, gentlemen, it is as if you put your hand
on the pulse of a dynamo, it is as if the things that you were in
connection with were spiritually bred, as if you had nothing to do
with them except, if you listen truly, to speak the things that you
hear.

These things now brood over the river; this spirit now moves with
the men who represent the Nation in the Navy; these things will
move upon the waters in the maneuvers—no threat lifted against
any man, against any nation, against any interests, but just a great
solemn evidence that the force of America is the force of moral
principle, that there is nothing else that she loves, and that there
is nothing else for which she will contend.

ADDRESS AT CHICAGO,
JANUARY 31, 1916

Out of This Red Flame of Light

When I speak of preparation for national defense I am speaking
of something intangible and visionary; I am looking at a vision of
the mind. America has never seen its destiny with the physical eye.
The destiny of America lies written in the lines of poets, in the
characters of self-sacrificing soldiers, in the conceptions and ambitions of her greatest statesmen; lies written in the teachings of her
school rooms, in all those ideals of service of humanity and of liberty
for the individual which are to be found written in the very school-
books of the boys and girls whom we send to be taught to be Americans. The destiny of America is an ideal destiny. America has no
reason for being unless her destiny and her duty be ideal. It is her

incumbent privilege to declare and stand for the rights of men. Nothing less is worth fighting for, nothing less is worth sacrificing for. The men and women of the American Colonies were physically comfortable. Even the much complained of arrangements of trade in those days were not unfair in the sense that they did not bring prosperity. America was offended and restless under the mere suggestion that she was not allowed to get her prosperity in her own way and under the guidance of her own spirit and purpose, and the American Revolution was fought for an ideal. We would have been as prosperous under the British Crown, but we should not have been as happy and we should not have respected ourselves as much.

Therefore, what America is bound to fight for when the time comes is nothing more nor less than her self-respect. There is no immediate prospect that her material interests may be seriously affected, but there is constant danger, every day of the week, that her spiritual interests may suffer serious affront, and it is in order that they may be safeguarded, in order that America may show that the old conceptions of liberty are ready to translate themselves in her hands into conceptions and manifestations of power at any time that it is necessary so to transform them, that we must make ourselves ready. You have not sent your representatives to Washington, ladies and gentlemen, to represent your business merely, to represent your ideals of material life. You have sent them there to represent you in your character as a Nation, and it is only from that point of view that they counsel you; it is only upon that footing that they can appeal to you. . . .

It is probably a fortunate circumstance, therefore, that America has been cried awake by these voices in the disturbed and reddened night, when fire sweeps sullenly from continent to continent; and it may be that in this red flame of light there will rise again that ideal figure of America holding up the hand of hope and of guidance to the people of the world and saying, "I stand ready to counsel and to help; I stand ready to assert whenever the flame is quenched those infinite principles of rectitude and peace which alone can bring happiness and liberty to mankind."

GRIDIRON DINNER ADDRESS,
WASHINGTON, FEBRUARY 26, 1916

The Sense of Humanity and Justice

America ought to keep out of this war. She ought to keep out of this war at the sacrifice of everything except this single thing upon which her character and history are founded, her sense of humanity and justice. If she sacrifices that, she has ceased to be America; she has ceased to entertain and to love the traditions which have made us proud to be Americans, and when we go about seeking safety at the expense of humanity, then I for one will believe that I have always been mistaken in what I have conceived to be the spirit of American history.

You never can tell your direction except by long measurements. You can not establish a line by two posts; you have got to have three at least to know whether they are straight with anything, and the longer your line the more certain your measurement. There is only one way in which to determine how the future of the United States is going to be projected, and that is by looking back and see-ing which way the lines ran which led up to the present moment of power and of opportunity. There is no doubt about that. There is no question what the roll of honor in America is. The roll of honor consists of the names of men who have squared their conduct by ideals of duty. There is no one else upon the roster; there is no one else whose name we care to remember when we measure things upon a national scale.

I wish that whenever an impulse of impatience comes upon us, whenever an impulse to settle a thing some short way tempts us, we might close the door and take down some old stories of what Ameri-can idealists and statesmen did in the past, and not let any counsel in that does not sound in the authentic voice of American tradition. Then we shall be certain what the lines of the future are, because we shall know we are steering by the lines of the past. We shall know that no temporary convenience, no temporary expediency, will lead us either to be rash or to be cowardly. I would be just as much ashamed to be rash as I would to be a coward. Valor is self-respect-ing. Valor is circumspect. Valor strikes only when it is right to

strike. Valor withholds itself from all small implications and entanglements and waits for the great opportunity when the sword
will flash as if it carried the light of heaven upon its blade.

ADDRESS BEFORE THE LEAGUE TO ENFORCE PEACE,
WASHINGTON, MAY 27, 1916

The Idea of a League of Nations

This great war that broke so suddenly upon the world two years
ago, and which has swept within its flame so great a part of the
civilized world, has affected us very profoundly, and we are not only
at liberty, it is perhaps our duty, to speak very frankly of it and of
the great interests of civilization which it affects.

With its causes and its objects we are not concerned. The obscure
fountains from which its stupendous flood has burst forth we are
not interested to search for or explore. But so great a flood, spread
far and wide to every quarter of the globe, has of necessity engulfed
many a fair province of right that lies very near to us. Our own
rights as a Nation, the liberties, the privileges, and the property of
our people have been profoundly affected. We are not mere disconnected lookers-on. The longer the war lasts, the more deeply do
we become concerned that it should be brought to an end and the
world be permitted to resume its normal life and course again. And
when it does come to an end we shall be as much concerned as
the nations at war to see peace assume an aspect of permanence,
give promise of days from which the anxiety of uncertainty shall
be lifted, bring some assurance that peace and war shall always
hereafter be reckoned part of the common interest of mankind. We
are participants, whether we would or not, in the life of the world.
The interests of all nations are our own also. We are partners with
the rest. What affects mankind is inevitably our affair as well as the
affair of the nations of Europe and of Asia.

One observation on the causes of the present war we are at liberty
to make, and to make it may throw some light forward upon the
future, as well as backward upon the past. It is plain that this war
could have come only as it did, suddenly and out of secret counsels,

without warning to the world, without discussion, without any of the deliberate movements of counsel with which it would seem natural to approach so stupendous a contest. It is probable that if it had been foreseen just what would happen, just what alliances would be formed, just what forces arrayed against one another, those who brought the great contest on would have been glad to substitute conference for force. If we ourselves had been afforded some opportunity to apprise the belligerents of the attitude which it would be our duty to take, of the policies and practices against which we would feel bound to use all our moral and economic strength, and in certain circumstances even our physical strength also, our contribution to the counsel which might have averted the struggle would have been considered worth weighing and regarding.

And the lesson which the shock of being taken by surprise in a matter so deeply vital to all the nations of the world has made poignantly clear is, that the peace of the world must henceforth depend upon a new and more wholesome diplomacy. Only when the great nations of the world have reached some sort of agreement as to what they hold to be fundamental to their common interest, and as to some feasible method of acting in concert when any nation or group of nations seeks to disturb those fundamental things, can we feel that civilization is at last in a way of justifying its existence and claiming to be finally established. It is clear that nations must in the future be governed by the same high code of honor that we demand of individuals.

The Rejection of Arbitrary Force

We must, indeed, in the very same breath with which we avow this conviction admit that we have ourselves upon occasion in the past been offenders against the law of diplomacy which we thus forecast; but our conviction is not the less clear, but rather the more clear, on that account. If this war has accomplished nothing else for the benefit of the world, it has at least disclosed a great moral necessity and set forward the thinking of the statesmen of the world by a whole age. Repeated utterances of the leading statesmen of most of the great nations now engaged in war have made it plain that their thought has come to this, that the principle of public right must henceforth take precedence over the individual interests of particular nations, and that the nations of the world must in some way band themselves together to see that that right prevails as against any sort of selfish aggression; that henceforth alliance must not be set up against alliance, understanding against understanding, but that there must be a common agreement for a common object, and that at the heart of that common object must lie the inviolable rights of peoples and of mankind. The nations of the world have become each other's neighbors. It is to their interest that they should understand each other. In order that they may understand each other, it is imperative that they should agree to co-operate in a common cause, and that they should so act that the guiding principle of that common cause shall be even-handed and impartial justice.

This is undoubtedly the thought of America. This is what we ourselves will say when there comes proper occasion to say it. In the dealings of nations with one another arbitrary force must be rejected and we must move forward to the thought of the modern world, the thought of which peace is the very atmosphere. That thought constitutes a chief part of the passionate conviction of America.

We believe these fundamental things: First, that every people has a right to choose the sovereignty under which they shall live. Like other nations, we have ourselves no doubt once and again offended against that principle when for a little while controlled by selfish passion as our franker historians have been honorable enough to admit; but it has become more and more our rule of life and action. Second, that the small states of the world have a right to enjoy the same respect for their sovereignty and for their territorial integrity that great and powerful nations expect and insist upon. And, third, that the world has a right to be free from every disturbance of its peace that has its origin in aggression and disregard of the rights of peoples and nations.

So sincerely do we believe in these things that I am sure that I speak the mind and wish of the people of America when I say that the United States is willing to become a partner in any feasible association of nations formed in order to realize these objects and make them secure against violation.

There is nothing that the United States wants for itself that any other nation has. We are willing, on the contrary, to limit ourselves along with them to a prescribed course of duty and respect for the rights of others which will check any selfish passion of our own, as it will check any aggressive impulse of theirs.

If it should ever be our privilege to suggest or initiate a movement for peace among the nations now at war, I am sure that the people of the United States would wish their Government to move along these lines: First, such a settlement with regard to their own immediate interests as the belligerents may agree upon. We have nothing material of any kind to ask for ourselves, and are quite aware that we are in no sense or degree parties to the present quarrel. Our interest is only in peace and its future guarantees. Second, an universal association of the nations to maintain the inviolate security of the highway of the seas for the common and unhindered use of all the nations of the world, and to prevent any war begun either contrary to treaty covenants or without warning and full submission of the causes to the opinion of the world—a virtual guarantee of territorial integrity and political independence.

But I did not come here, let me repeat, to discuss a programme. I came only to avow a creed and give expression to the confidence I feel that the world is even now upon the eve of a great consummation, when some common force will be brought into existence which shall safeguard right as the first and most fundamental interest of all peoples and all governments, when coercion shall be summoned not to the service of political ambition or selfish hostility, but to the service of a common order, a common justice, and a common peace. God grant that the dawn of that day of frank dealing and of settled peace, concord, and co-operation may be near at hand!

ADDRESS TO THE UNITED STATES SENATE,
JANUARY 22, 1917

To Guarantee Peace and Justice Throughout the World

GENTLEMEN OF THE SENATE: I have sought this opportunity to address you because I thought that I owed it to you as the counsel associated with me in the final determination of our international obligations, to disclose to you without reserve the thought and purpose that have been taking form in my mind in regard to the duty of our Government in the days to come when it will be necessary to lay afresh and upon a new plan the foundations of peace among the nations.

It is inconceivable that the people of the United States should play no part in that great enterprise. To take part in such a service will be the opportunity for which they have sought to prepare themselves by the very principles and purposes of their polity and the approved practices of their Government ever since the days when they set up a new nation in the high and honorable hope that it might in all that it was and did show mankind the way to liberty. They cannot in honor withhold the service to which they are now about to be challenged. They do not wish to withhold it. But they owe it to themselves and to the other nations of the world to state the conditions under which they will feel free to render it.

That service is nothing less than this, to add their authority and their power to the authority and force of other nations to guarantee peace and justice throughout the world. Such a settlement cannot now be long postponed. It is right that before it comes this Government should frankly formulate the conditions upon which it would feel justified in asking our people to approve its formal and solemn adherence to a League for Peace. I am here to attempt to state those conditions.

The present war must first be ended; but we owe it to candor and to a just regard for the opinion of mankind to say that, so far as our participation in guarantees of future peace is concerned, it makes a great deal of difference in what way and upon what terms it is ended. The treaties and agreements which bring it to an end must embody terms which will create a peace that is worth guaranteeing and preserving, a peace that will win the approval of mankind, not merely a peace that will serve the several interests and immediate aims of the nations engaged. We shall have no voice in determining what those terms shall be, but we shall, I feel sure, have a voice in determining whether they shall be made lasting or not by the guarantees of a universal covenant, and our judgment upon what is fundamental and essential as a condition precedent to permanency should be spoken now, not afterwards when it may be too late.

No covenant of co-operative peace that does not include the peoples of the New World can suffice to keep the future safe against war; and yet there is only one sort of peace that the peoples of America could join in guaranteeing. The elements of that peace must be elements that engage the confidence and satisfy the principles of the American governments, elements consistent with their political faith and with the practical convictions which the peoples of America have once for all embraced and undertaken to defend.

I do not mean to say that any American government would throw any obstacle in the way of any terms of peace the governments now at war might agree upon, or seek to upset them when made, whatever they might be. I only take it for granted that mere terms of peace between the belligerents will not satisfy even the belligerents themselves. Mere agreements may not make peace secure. It will be absolutely necessary that a force be created as a guarantor of the permanency of the settlement so much greater than the force of any nation now engaged or any alliance hitherto formed or projected that no nation, no probable combination of nations could face or withstand it. If the peace presently to be made is to endure, it must be a peace made secure by the organized major force of mankind.

The terms of the immediate peace agreed upon will determine whether it is a peace for which such a guarantee can be secured. The question upon which the whole future peace and policy of the world depends is this: Is the present war a struggle for a just and secure peace, or only for a new balance of power? If it be only a struggle for a new balance of power, who will guarantee, who can guarantee the stable equilibrium of the new arrangement? Only a tranquil Europe can be a stable Europe. There must be, not a balance of power, but a community of power; not organized rivalries, but an organized common peace.

A Peace Without Victory

Fortunately we have received very explicit assurances on this point. The statesmen of both of the groups of nations now arrayed against one another have said, in terms that could not be misinterpreted, that it was no part of the purpose they had in mind to crush their antagonists. But the implications of these assurances may not be equally clear to all—may not be the same on both sides of the water. I think it will be serviceable if I attempt to set forth what we understand them to be.

They imply, first of all, that it must be a peace without victory. It is not pleasant to say this. I beg that I may be permitted to put my own interpretation upon it and that it may be understood that no other interpretation was in my thought. I am seeking only to face realities and to face them without soft concealments. Victory would mean peace forced upon the loser, a victor's terms imposed upon the vanquished. It would be accepted in humiliation, under duress, at an intolerable sacrifice, and would leave a sting, a resentment, a bitter memory upon which terms of peace would rest, not permanently, but only as upon quicksand. Only a peace between equals can last. Only a peace the very principle of which is equality and a common participation in a common benefit. The right state of mind, the right feeling between nations, is as necessary for a lasting peace as is the just settlement of vexed questions of territory or of racial and national allegiance.

The equality of nations upon which peace must be founded if it is to last must be an equality of rights; the guarantees exchanged must neither recognize nor imply a difference between big nations and small, between those that are powerful and those that are weak. Right must be based upon the common strength, not upon the individual strength, of the nations upon whose concert peace will depend. Equality of territory or of resources there of course cannot be; nor any other sort of equality not gained in the ordinary peaceful and legitimate development of the peoples themselves. But no one asks or expects anything more than an equality of rights. Mankind is looking now for freedom of life, not for equipoises of power.

Conditions of Peace

And there is a deeper thing involved than even equality of right among organized nations. No peace can last, or ought to last, which does not recognize and accept the principle that governments derive all their just powers from the consent of the governed, and that no right anywhere exists to hand peoples about from sovereignty to sovereignty as if they were property. I take it for granted, for instance, if I may venture upon a single example, that statesmen everywhere are agreed that there should be a united, independent, and autonomous Poland, and that henceforth inviolable security of life, of worship, and of industrial and social development should be guaranteed to all peoples who have lived hitherto under the power of governments devoted to a faith and purpose hostile to their own.

I speak of this, not because of any desire to exalt an abstract political principle which has always been held very dear by those who have sought to build up liberty in America, but for the same reason that I have spoken of the other conditions of peace which seem to me clearly indispensable—because I wish frankly to uncover realities. Any peace which does not recognize and accept this principle will inevitably be upset. It will not rest upon the affections or the convictions of mankind. The ferment of spirit of whole populations will fight subtly and constantly against it, and all the world will sympathize. The world can be at peace only if its life is stable, and there can be no stability where the will is in rebellion, where there is not tranquillity of spirit and a sense of justice, of freedom, and of right.

So far as practicable, moreover, every great people now struggling towards a full development of its resources and of its powers should be assured a direct outlet to the great highways of the sea. Where this can not be done by the cession of territory, it can no doubt be done by the neutralization of direct rights of way under the general guarantee which will assure the peace itself. With a right comity of arrangement no nation need be shut away from free access to the open paths of the world's commerce.

And the paths of the sea must alike in law and in fact be free. The freedom of the seas is the *sine qua non* of peace, equality, and co-operation. No doubt a somewhat radical reconsideration of many of the rules of international practice hitherto thought to be established may be necessary in order to make the seas indeed free and common in practically all circumstances for the use of mankind, but the motive for such changes is convincing and compelling. There can be no trust or intimacy between the peoples of the world without them. The free, constant, unthreatened intercourse of nations is an essential part of the process of peace and of development. It need not be difficult either to define or to secure the freedom of the seas if the governments of the world sincerely desire to come to an agreement concerning it.

It is a problem closely connected with the limitation of naval armaments and the co-operation of the navies of the world in keeping the seas at once free and safe. And the question of limiting naval armaments opens the wider and perhaps more difficult question of the limitation of armies and of all programs of military preparation. Difficult and delicate as these questions are, they must be faced with the utmost candor and decided in a spirit of real accommodation if peace is to come with healing in its wings, and come to stay. Peace cannot be had without concession and sacrifice. There can be no sense of safety and equality among the nations if great preponderating armaments are henceforth to continue here and there to be built up and maintained. The statesmen of the world must plan for peace and nations must adjust and accommodate their policy to it as they have planned for war and made ready for pitiless contest and rivalry. The question of armaments, whether on land or sea, is the most immediately and intensely practical question connected with the future fortunes of nations and of mankind.

For the Silent Mass of Mankind Everywhere

I have spoken upon these great matters without reserve and with the utmost explicitness because it has seemed to me to be necessary

f the world's yearning desire for peace was anywhere to find free
voice and utterance. Perhaps I am the only person in high authority
amongst all the peoples of the world who is at liberty to speak and
hold nothing back. I am speaking as an individual, and yet I am
speaking also, of course, as the responsible head of a great government, and I feel confident that I have said what the people of the
United States would wish me to say. May I not add that I hope and
believe that I am in effect speaking for liberals and friends of humanity in every nation and of every program of liberty? I would fain
believe that I am speaking for the silent mass of mankind everywhere who have as yet had no place or opportunity to speak their
real hearts out concerning the death and ruin they see to have come
already upon the persons and the homes they hold most dear.

And in holding out the expectation that the people and Government of the United States will join the other civilized nations of the
world in guaranteeing the permanence of peace upon such terms as
I have named, I speak with the greater boldness and confidence because it is clear to every man who can think that there is in this
promise no breach in either our traditions or our policy as a nation,
but a fulfilment, rather, of all that we have professed or striven for.

I am proposing, as it were, that the nations should with one
accord adopt the doctrine of President Monroe as the doctrine of
the world: that no nation should seek to extend its polity over any
other nation or people, but that every people should be left free to
determine its own polity, its own way of development, unhindered,
unthreatened, unafraid, the little along with the great and powerful.

I am proposing that all nations henceforth avoid entangling
alliances which would draw them into competitions of power; catch
them in a net of intrigue and selfish rivalry, and disturb their own
affairs with influences intruded from without. There is no entangling alliance in a concert of power. When all unite to act in the
same sense and with the same purpose all act in the common interest and are free to live their own lives under a common protection.

I am proposing government by the consent of the governed; that
freedom of the seas which in international conference after conference representatives of the United States have urged with the

eloquence of those who are the convinced disciples of liberty; and that moderation of armaments which makes of armies and navies a power for order merely, not an instrument of aggression or of selfish violence.

These are American principles, American policies. We could stand for no others. And they are also the principles and policies of forward looking men and women everywhere, of every modern nation, of every enlightened community. They are the principles of mankind and must prevail.

Chapter Twelve

INTO WAR

THE second Inaugural Address, though still seeing America standing apart from the European struggle, set the stage for great and somber decisions. Less than a month later Wilson asked Congress to declare the nation at war. The time of brooding and indecision was over. These selections are upon the theme of force—force as the instrument of a higher good. In the speech to the Congress of December 4, 1917, Wilson declared with unsurpassed eloquence the retribution that was to fall upon the guilty. But the insistence on a just peace was not absent, and was to become an increasing preoccupation as the war drew toward its close.

SECOND INAUGURAL ADDRESS,
WASHINGTON, MARCH 5, 1917

The War Has Set Its Mark upon Us

The four years which have elapsed since last I stood in this place have been crowded with counsel and action of the most vital interest and consequence. Perhaps no equal period in our history has been so fruitful of important reforms in our economic and industrial life or so full of significant changes in the spirit and purpose of our political action. We have sought very thoughtfully to set our house in order, correct the grosser errors and abuses of our industrial life, liberate and quicken the processes of our national genius and energy, and lift our politics to a broader view of the people's essential interests. It is a record of singular variety and singular distinction. But I shall not attempt to review it. It speaks for itself and will be of increasing influences as the years go by. This is not the time for retrospect. It is time, rather, to speak our thoughts and purposes concerning the present and the immediate future.

Although we have centered counsel and action with such unusual concentration and success upon the great problems of domestic legislation to which we addressed ourselves four years ago, other matters have more and more forced themselves upon our attention, matters lying outside our own life as a nation and over which we had no control, but which, despite our wish to keep free of them, have drawn us more and more irresistibly into their own current and influence.

It has been impossible to avoid them. They have affected the life of the whole world. They have shaken men everywhere with a passion and an apprehension they never knew before. It has been hard to preserve calm counsel while the thought of our own people swayed this way and that under their influence. We are a composite and cosmopolitan people. We are of the blood of all the nations that are at war. The currents of our thoughts as well as the currents of our trade run quick at all seasons back and forth between us and them. The war inevitably set its mark from the first alike upon our minds, our industries, our commerce, our politics, and our social action. To be indifferent to it or independent of it was out of the question.

And yet all the while we have been conscious that we were not part of it. In that consciousness, despite many divisions, we have drawn closer together. We have been deeply wronged upon the seas, but we have not wished to wrong or injure in return; have retained throughout the consciousness of standing in some sort apart, intent upon an interest that transcended the immediate issues of the war itself. As some of the injuries done us have become intolerable we have still been clear that we wished nothing for ourselves that we were not ready to demand for all mankind,—fair dealing, justice, the freedom to live and be at ease against organized wrong.

It is in this spirit and with this thought that we have grown more and more aware, more and more certain that the part we wished to play was the part of those who mean to vindicate and fortify peace. We have been obliged to arm ourselves to make good our claim to a certain minimum of right and of freedom of action. We stand firm in armed neutrality since it seems that in no other way we can demonstrate what it is we insist upon and cannot forego. We may even be drawn on, by circumstances, not by our own purpose or desire, to a more active assertion of our rights as we see them and a more immediate association with the great struggle itself. But nothing will alter our thought or our purpose. They are too clear to be obscured. They are too deeply rooted in the principles of our national life to be altered. We desire neither conquest nor advantage. We wish nothing that can be had only at the cost of another people. We have always professed unselfish purpose and we covet the opportunity to prove that our professions are sincere.

With the Whole World for Stage

There are many things still to do at home, to clarify our own politics and give new vitality to the industrial processes of our own life, and we shall do them as time and opportunity serve; but we realize that the greatest things that remain to be done must be done with the whole world for stage and in coöperation with the wide and universal forces of mankind, and we are making our spirits ready for those things. They will follow in the immediate wake of the war itself and will set civilization up again. We are provincials no longer. The tragical events of the thirty months of vital turmoil through which we have just passed have made us citizens of the world. There can be no turning back. Our own fortunes as a nation are involved, whether we would have it so or not.

And yet we are not the less Americans on that account. We shall be the more American if we but remain true to the principles in which we have been bred. They are not the principles of a province or of a single continent. We have known and boasted all along that they were the principles of a liberated mankind. These, therefore, are the things we shall stand for, whether in war or in peace:

That all nations are equally interested in the peace of the world and in the political stability of free peoples, and equally responsible for their maintenance;

That the essential principle of peace is the actual equality of nations in all matters of right or privilege;

That peace cannot securely or justly rest upon an armed balance of power;

That governments derive all their just powers from the consent of the governed and that no other powers should be supported by the common thought, purpose, or power of the family of nations;

That the seas should be equally free and safe for the use of all peoples, under rules set up by common agreement and consent, and that, so far as practicable, they should be accessible to all upon equal terms;

That national armaments should be limited to the necessities of national order and domestic safety;

That the community of interest and of power upon which peace must henceforth depend imposes upon each nation the duty of seeing to it that all influences proceeding from its own citizens meant to encourage or assist revolution in other states should be sternly and effectually suppressed and prevented.

A New Dignity for the Nation

I need not argue these principles to you, my fellow countrymen: they are your own, part and parcel of your own thinking and your own motive in affairs. They spring up native amongst us. Upon this as a platform of purpose and of action we can stand together.

And it is imperative that we should stand together. We are being forged into a new unity amidst the fires that now blaze throughout the world. In their ardent heat we shall, in God's providence, let us hope, be purged of faction and division, purified of the errant humors of party and of private interest, and shall stand forth in the days to come with a new dignity of national pride and spirit. Let each man see to it that the dedication is in his own heart, the high purpose of the Nation in his own mind, ruler of his own will and desire.

I stand here and have taken the high and solemn oath to which you have been audience because the people of the United States have chosen me for this august delegation of power and have by their gracious judgment named me their leader in affairs. I know now what the task means. I realize to the full the responsibility which it involves. I pray God I may be given the wisdom and the prudence to do my duty in the true spirit of this great people. I am their servant and can succeed only as they sustain and guide me by their confidence and their counsel. The thing I shall count upon, the thing without which neither counsel nor action will avail, is the unity of America,—an America united in feeling, in purpose, and in its vision of duty, of opportunity, and of service. We are to beware of all men who would turn the tasks and the necessities of the Nation to their own private profit or use them for the building up of private power; beware that no faction or disloyal intrigue break the harmony or embarrass the spirit of our people; beware that our Government be kept pure and incorrupt in all its parts. United alike in the conception of our duty and in the high resolve to perform it in the face of all men, let us dedicate ourselves to the great task to which we must now set our hand. For myself I beg your tolerance, your countenance, and your united aid. The shadows that now lie dark upon our path will soon be dispelled and we shall walk with the light all about us if we be but true to ourselves,—to ourselves as we have wished to be known in the counsels of the world and in the thought of all those who love liberty and justice and the right exalted.

ADDRESS TO THE CONGRESS,
APRIL 2, 1917

For a Declaration of War

GENTLEMEN OF THE CONGRESS: I have called the Congress into extraordinary session because there are serious, very serious, choices of policy to be made, and made immediately, which it was neither right nor constitutionally permissible that I should assume the responsibility of making.

On the third of February last I officially laid before you the extraordinary announcement of the Imperial German Government that on and after the first day of February it was its purpose to put aside all restraints of law or of humanity and use its submarines to sink every vessel that sought to approach either the ports of Great Britain and Ireland or the western coasts of Europe or any of the ports controlled by the enemies of Germany within the Mediterranean. That had seemed to be the object of the German submarine warfare earlier in the war, but since April of last year the Imperial Government had somewhat restrained the commanders of its undersea craft in conformity with its promise then given to us that passenger boats should not be sunk and that due warning would be given to all other vessels which its submarines might seek to destroy, when no resistance was offered or escape attempted, and care taken that their crews were given at least a fair chance to save their lives in their open boats. The precautions taken were meager and haphazard enough, as was proved in distressing instance after instance in the progress of the cruel and unmanly business, but a certain degree of restraint was observed. The new policy has swept every restriction aside. Vessels of every kind, whatever their flag, their character, their cargo, their destination, their errand, have been ruthlessly sent to the bottom without warning and without thought of help or mercy for those on board, the vessels of friendly neutrals along with those of belligerents. Even hospital ships and ships carrying relief to the sorely bereaved and stricken people of Belgium, though the latter were provided with safe conduct through the proscribed areas by the German Government itself and were distinguished by unmistakable marks of identity, have been sunk with the same reckless lack of compassion or of principle.

I was for a little while unable to believe that such things would in fact be done by any government that had hitherto subscribed to the humane practices of civilized nations. International law had its origin in the attempt to set up some law which would be respected and observed upon the seas, where no nation had right of dominion and where lay the free highways of the world. By painful stage after stage has that law been built up, with meager enough results, indeed, after all was accomplished that could be accomplished, but always with a clear view, at least, of what the heart and conscience of mankind demanded. This minimum of right the German Government has swept aside under the plea of retaliation and necessity and because it has no weapons which it could use at sea except these which it is impossible to employ as it is employing them without throwing to the winds all scruples of humanity or of respect for the understandings that were supposed to underlie the intercourse of the world. I am not now thinking of the loss of property involved, immense and serious as that is, but only of the wanton and wholesale destruction of the lives of non-combatants, men, women, and children, engaged in pursuits which have always, even in the darkest periods of modern history, been deemed innocent and legitimate. Property can be paid for; the lives of peaceful and innocent people cannot be. The present German submarine warfare against commerce is a warfare against mankind.

It is a war against all nations. American ships have been sunk, American lives taken, in ways which it has stirred us very deeply to learn of, but the ships and people of other neutral and friendly nations have been sunk and overwhelmed in the waters in the same way. There has been no discrimination. The challenge is to all mankind. Each nation must decide for itself how it will meet it. The choice we make for ourselves must be made with a moderation of counsel and a temperateness of judgment befitting our character and our motives as a nation. We must put excited feeling away. Our motive will not be revenge or the victorious assertion of the physical might of the nation, but only the vindication of right, of human right, of which we are only a single champion.

When I addressed the Congress on the twenty-sixth of February last I thought that it would suffice to assert our neutral rights with arms, our right to use the seas against unlawful interference, our right to keep our people safe against unlawful violence. But armed neutrality, it now appears, is impracticable. Because submarines are in effect outlaws when used as the German submarines have been used against merchant shipping, it is impossible to defend ships against their attacks as the law of nations has assumed that merchantmen would defend themselves against privateers or cruisers, visible craft giving chase upon the open sea. It is common prudence in such circumstances, grim necessity indeed, to endeavor to destroy them before they have shown their own intention. They must be dealt with upon sight, if dealt with at all. The German Government denies the right of neutrals to use arms at all within the areas of the sea which it has proscribed, even in the defense of rights which no modern publicist has ever before questioned their right to defend. The intimation is conveyed that the armed guards which we have placed on our merchant ships will be treated as beyond the pale of law and subject to be dealt with as pirates would be. Armed neutrality is ineffectual enough at best; in such circumstances and in the face of such pretensions it is worse than ineffectual: it is likely only to produce what it was meant to prevent; it is practically certain to draw us into the war without either the rights or the effectiveness of belligerents. There is one choice we cannot make, we are incapable of making: we will not choose the path of submission and suffer the most sacred rights of our Nation and our people to be ignored or violated. The wrongs against which we now array ourselves are no common wrongs; they cut to the very roots of human life.

With a profound sense of the solemn and even tragical character of the step I am taking and of the grave responsibilities which it involves, but in unhesitating obedience to what I deem my constitutional duty, I advise that the Congress declare the recent course of the Imperial German Government to be in fact nothing less than war against the government and people of the United States; that it formally accept the status of belligerent which has thus been thrust upon it; and that it take immediate steps not only to put the country in a more thorough state of defense but also to exert all its power and employ all its resources to bring the Government of the German Empire to terms and end the war. . . .

To Vindicate the Principles of Peace and Justice

While we do these things, these deeply momentous things, let us be very clear, and make very clear to all the world what our motives and our objects are. My own thought has not been driven from its habitual and normal course by the unhappy events of the last two months, and I do not believe that the thought of the Nation has been altered or clouded by them. I have exactly the same things in mind now that I had in mind when I addressed the Senate on the twenty-second of January last; the same that I had in mind when I addressed the Congress on the third of February and on the twenty-sixth of February. Our object now, as then, is to vindicate the principles of peace and justice in the life of the world as against selfish and autocratic power and to set up amongst the really free and self-governed peoples of the world such a concert of purpose and of action as will henceforth insure the observance of those principles. Neutrality is no longer feasible or desirable where the peace of the world is involved and the freedom of its peoples, and the menace to that peace and freedom lies in the existence of autocratic governments backed by organized force which is controlled wholly by their will, not by the will of their people. We have seen the last of neutrality in such circumstances. We are at the beginning of an age in which it will be insisted that the same standards of conduct and of responsibility for wrong done shall be observed among nations and their governments that are observed among the individual citizens of civilized states.

We have no quarrel with the German people. We have no feeling towards them but one of sympathy and friendship. It was not upon their impulse that their government acted in entering this war. It was not with their previous knowledge or approval. It was a war determined upon as wars used to be determined upon in the old, unhappy days when peoples were nowhere consulted by their rulers and wars were provoked and waged in the interest of dynasties or of little groups of ambitious men who were accustomed to use their fellow men as pawns and tools. Self-governed nations do not fill their neighbor states with spies or set the course of intrigue to bring about some critical posture of affairs which will give them an opportunity to strike and make conquest. Such designs can be successfully worked out only under cover and where no one has the right to ask questions. Cunningly contrived plans of deception or aggression, carried, it may be, from generation to generation, can be worked out and kept from the light only within the privacy of courts or behind the carefully guarded confidences of a narrow and privileged class. They are happily impossible where public opinion commands and insists upon full information concerning all the nation's affairs.

A steadfast concert for peace can never be maintained except by a partnership of democratic nations. No autocratic government could be trusted to keep faith within it or observe its covenants. It must be a league of honor, a partnership of opinion. Intrigue would eat its vitals away; the plottings of inner circles who could plan what they would and render account to no one would be a corruption seated at its very heart. Only free peoples can hold their purpose and their honor steady to a common end and prefer the interests of mankind to any narrow interest of their own. . . .

We are accepting this challenge of hostile purpose because we know that in such a Government, following such methods, we can never have a friend; and that in the presence of its organized power, always lying in wait to accomplish we know not what purpose, there can be no assured security for the democratic Governments of the world. We are now about to accept gage of battle with this natural foe to liberty and shall, if necessary, spend the whole force of the Nation to check and nullify its pretensions and its power. We are glad, now that we see the facts with no veil of false pretense about them, to fight thus for the ultimate peace of the world and for the liberation of its peoples, the German peoples included: for the rights of nations great and small and the privilege of men everywhere to choose their way of life and of obedience. The world must be made safe for democracy. Its peace must be planted upon the tested foundations of political liberty. We have no selfish ends to serve. We desire no conquest, no dominion. We seek no indemnities for ourselves, no material compensation for the sacrifices we shall freely make. We are but one of the champions of the rights of mankind. We shall be satisfied when those rights have been made as secure as the faith and the freedom of nations can make them.

It is a distressing and oppressive duty, Gentlemen of the Congress, which I have performed in thus addressing you. There are, it may be, many months of fiery trial and sacrifice ahead of us. It is a fearful thing to lead this great peaceful people into war, into the most terrible and disastrous of all wars, civilization itself seeming to be in the balance. But the right is more precious than peace, and we shall fight for the things which we have always carried nearest our hearts, —for democracy, for the right of those who submit to authority to have a voice in their own Governments, for the rights and liberties of small nations, for a universal dominion of right by such a concert of free peoples as shall bring peace and safety to all nations and make the world itself at last free. To such a task we can dedicate our lives and our fortunes, everything that we are and everything that we have, with the pride of those who know that the day has come when America is privileged to spend her blood and her might for the principles that gave her birth and happiness and the peace which she has treasured. God helping her, she can do no other.

MEMORIAL DAY ADDRESS AT ARLINGTON CEMETERY,
MAY 30, 1917

America Was Born to Serve Mankind

Any Memorial Day of this sort is, of course, a day touched with sorrowful memory, and yet I for one do not see how we can have any thought of pity for the men whose memory we honor to-day. I do not pity them. I envy them, rather; because theirs is a great work for liberty accomplished and we are in the midst of a work unfinished, testing our strength where their strength has already been tested.

There is a touch of sorrow, but there is a touch of reassurance also in a day like this, because we know how the men of America have responded to the call of the cause of liberty and it fills our minds with a perfect assurance that that response will come again in equal measure, with equal majesty, and with a result which will hold the attention of all mankind.

When you reflect upon it, these men who died to preserve the Union died to preserve the instrument which we are now using to serve the world—a free Nation espousing the cause of human liberty. In one sense the great struggle into which we have now entered is an American struggle, because it is in defense of American honor and American rights, but it is something even greater than that; it is a world struggle. It is a struggle of men who love liberty everywhere, and in this cause America will show herself greater than ever because she will rise to a greater thing.

We have said in the beginning that we planned this great Government that men who wished freedom might have a place of refuge and a place where their hope could be realized, and now, having established such a Government, having preserved such a Government, having vindicated the power of such a Government, we are saying to all mankind, "We did not set this Government up in order that we might have a selfish and separate liberty, for we are now ready to come to your assistance and fight out upon the field of the world the cause of human liberty."

In this thing America attains her full dignity and the full fruition of her great purpose.

No man can be glad that such things have happened as we have witnessed in these last fateful years, but perhaps it may be permitted to us to be glad that we have an opportunity to show the principles that we profess to be living, principles that live in our hearts, and to have a chance by the pouring out of our blood and treasure to vindicate the thing which we have professed. For, my friends, the real fruition of life is to do the thing we have said we wished to do. There are times when words seem empty and only action seems great. Such a time has come, and in the providence of God America will once more have an opportunity to show to the world that she was born to serve mankind.

ADDRESS TO CONFEDERATE VETERANS,
WASHINGTON, JUNE 5, 1917

An Instrument in the Hands of God

There are many memories of the Civil War that thrill along the blood and make one proud to have been sprung of a race that could produce such bravery and constancy; and yet the world does not live on memories. The world is constantly making its toilsome way forward into new and different days, and I believe that one of the things that contributes satisfaction to a reunion like this and a welcome like this is that this is also a day of oblivion. There are some things that we have thankfully buried, and among them are the great passions of division which once threatened to rend this Nation in twain. The passion of admiration we still entertain for the heroic figures of those old days, but the passion of separation, the passion

of difference of principle, is gone—gone out of our minds, gone out
of our hearts; and one of the things that will thrill this country as
it reads of this reunion is that it will read also of a rededication on
the part of all of us to the great Nation which we serve in common.

These are days of oblivion as well as of memory, for we are forgetting the things that once held us asunder. Not only that, but
they are days of rejoicing, because we now at last see why this great
Nation was kept united, for we are beginning to see the great world
purpose which it was meant to serve. Many men I know, particularly
of your own generation, have wondered at some of the dealings of
Providence, but the wise heart never questions the dealings of Providence, because the great long plan as it unfolds has a majesty about
it and a definiteness of purpose, an elevation of ideal, which we
were incapable of conceiving as we tried to work things out with
our short sight and weak strength. And now that we see ourselves
part of a Nation united, powerful, great in spirit and in purpose,
we know the great ends which God in His mysterious Providence
wrought through our instrumentality, because at the heart of the
men of the North and of the South there was the same love of self-
government and of liberty, and now we are to be an instrument in
the hands of God to see that liberty is made secure for mankind.

At the day of our greatest division there was one common passion
amongst us, and that was the passion for human freedom. We did
not know that God was working out in His own way the method
by which we should best serve human freedom—by making this
Nation a great united, indivisible, indestructible instrument in His
hands for the accomplishment of these great things. . . .

There are not many things that one desires about war, my fellow
citizens, but you have come through war, you know how you have
been chastened by it, and there comes a time when it is good for a
Nation to know that it must sacrifice if need be everything that it
has to vindicate the principles which it professes. We have pros-
pered with a sort of heedless and irresponsible prosperity. Now we
are going to lay all our wealth, if necessary, and spend all our blood,
if need be, to show that we were not accumulating that wealth
selfishly, but were accumulating it for the service of mankind. Men

all over the world have thought of the United States as a trading and money-getting people, whereas we who have lived at home know the ideals with which the hearts of this people have thrilled; we know the sober convictions which have lain at the basis of our life all the time; and we know the power and devotion which can be spent in heroic wise for the service of those ideals that we have treasured. We have been allowed to become strong in the Providence of God that our strength might be used to prove, not our selfishness, but our greatness, and if there is any ground for thankfulness in a day like this, I am thankful for the privilege of self-sacrifice, which is the only privilege that lends dignity to the human spirit.

FLAG DAY ADDRESS,
WASHINGTON, JUNE 14, 1917

What Purpose We Seek to Serve

We meet to celebrate Flag Day because this flag which we honor and under which we serve is the emblem of our unity, our power, our thought and purpose as a Nation. It has no other character than that which we give it from generation to generation. The choices are ours. It floats in majestic silence above the hosts that execute those choices, whether in peace or in war. And yet, though silent, it speaks to us,—speaks to us of the past, of the men and women who went before us and of the records they wrote upon it. We celebrate the day of its birth; and from its birth until now it has witnessed a great history, has floated on high the symbol of great events, of a great plan of life worked out by a great people. We are about to carry it into battle, to lift it where it will draw the fire of our enemies. We are about to bid thousands, hundreds of thousands, it may be millions, of our men, the young, the strong, the capable men of the Nation, to go forth and die beneath it on fields of blood far away,—for what? For some unaccustomed thing? For something for which it has never sought the fire before? American armies were never before sent across the seas. Why are they sent now? For some new purpose, for which this great flag has never been carried before, or for some old, familiar, heroic purpose for which it has seen men, its own men, die on every battlefield upon which Americans have borne arms since the Revolution?

These are questions which must be answered. We are Americans. We in our turn serve America, and can serve her with no private purpose. We must use her flag as she has always used it. We are accountable at the bar of history and must plead in utter frankness what purpose it is we seek to serve.

The War Was Begun by the Military Masters of Germany

It is plain enough how we were forced into the war. The extraordinary insults and aggressions of the Imperial German Government left us no self-respecting choice but to take up arms in defense of our rights as a free people and of our honor as a sovereign government. The military masters of Germany denied us the right to be neutral. They filled our unsuspecting communities with vicious spies and conspirators and sought to corrupt the opinion of our people in their own behalf. When they found that they could not do that, their agents diligently spread sedition amongst us and sought to draw our own citizens from their allegiance,—and some of those agents were men connected with the official Embassy of the German Government itself here in our own capital. They sought by violence to destroy our industries and arrest our commerce. They tried to incite Mexico to take up arms against us and to draw Japan into a hostile alliance with her,—and that, not by indirection, but by direct suggestion from the Foreign Office in Berlin. They impudently denied us the use of the high seas and repeatedly executed their threat that they would send to their death any of our people who ventured to approach the coasts of Europe. And many of our own people were corrupted. Men began to look upon their own neighbors with suspicion and to wonder in their hot resentment and surprise whether there was any community in which hostile intrigue did not lurk. What great nation in such circumstances would not have taken up arms? Much as we had desired peace, it was denied us, and not of our own choice. This flag under which we serve would have been dishonored had we withheld our hand.

But that is only part of the story. We know now as clearly as we knew before we were ourselves engaged that we are not the enemies of the German people and that they are not our enemies. They did not originate or desire this hideous war or wish that we should be drawn into it; and we are vaguely conscious that we are fighting their cause, as they will some day see it, as well as our own. They are themselves in the grip of the same sinister power that has now at last stretched its ugly talons out and drawn blood from us. The whole world is at war because the whole world is in the grip of that power and is trying out the great battle which shall determine whether it is to be brought under its mastery or fling itself free.

The war was begun by the military masters of Germany, who proved to be also the masters of Austria-Hungary. These men have never regarded nations as peoples, men, women, and children of like blood and frame as themselves, for whom governments existed and in whom governments had their life. They have regarded them merely as serviceable organizations which they could by force or intrigue bend or corrupt to their own purpose. They have regarded the smaller states, in particular, and the peoples who could be overwhelmed by force, as their natural tools and instruments of domination. Their purpose has long been avowed. The statesmen of other nations, to whom that purpose was incredible, paid little attention; regarded what German professors expounded in their classrooms and German writers set forth to the world as the goal of German policy as rather the dream of minds detached from practical affairs, as preposterous private conceptions of German destiny, than as the actual plans of responsible rulers; but the rulers of Germany themselves knew all the while what concrete plans, what well-advanced intrigues lay back of what the professors and the writers were saying, and were glad to go forward unmolested, filling the thrones of Balkan states with German princes, putting German officers at the service of Turkey to drill her armies and make interest with her government, developing plans of sedition and rebellion in India and Egypt, setting their fires in Persia. The demands made by Austria upon Serbia were a mere single step in a plan which compassed Europe and Asia, from Berlin to Bagdad. They hoped those demands might not arouse Europe, but they meant to press them

whether they did or not, for they thought themselves ready for the
final issue of arms.

Their plan was to throw a broad belt of German military power
and political control across the very center of Europe and beyond
the Mediterranean into the heart of Asia; and Austria-Hungary was
to be as much their tool and pawn as Serbia or Bulgaria or Turkey
or the ponderous states of the East. Austria-Hungary, indeed, was
to become part of the central German Empire, absorbed and dominated by the same forces and influences that had originally cemented
the German states themselves. The dream had its heart at Berlin.
It could have had a heart nowhere else! It rejected the idea of solidarity of race entirely. The choice of peoples played no part in it
at all. It contemplated binding together racial and political units
which could be kept together only by force,—Czechs, Magyars,
Croats, Serbs, Rumanians, Turks, Armenians,—the proud states of
Bohemia and Hungary, the stout little commonwealths of the Balkans, the indomitable Turks, the subtile peoples of the East. These
peoples did not wish to be united. They ardently desired to direct
their own affairs, would be satisfied only by undisputed independ-
dence. They could be kept quiet only by the presence or the constant threat of armed men. They would live under a common power
only by sheer compulsion and await the day of revolution. But the
German military statesmen had reckoned with all that and were
ready to deal with it in their own way.

And they have actually carried the greater part of that amazing
plan into execution! Look how things stand. Austria is at their
mercy. It has acted, not upon its own initiative or upon the choice
of its own people, but at Berlin's dictation ever since the war began.
Its people now desire peace, but cannot have it until leave is granted
from Berlin. The so-called Central Powers are in fact but a single
Power. Serbia is at its mercy, should its hands be but for a moment
freed. Bulgaria has consented to its will, and Rumania is overrun.
The Turkish armies, which Germans trained, are serving Germany,
certainly not themselves, and the guns of German warships lying
in the harbor at Constantinople remind Turkish statesmen every

day that they have no choice but to take their orders from Berlin. From Hamburg to the Persian Gulf the net is spread.

The Point to Which Fate Has Brought the Germans

Is it not easy to understand the eagerness for peace that has been manifested from Berlin ever since the snare was set and sprung? Peace, peace, peace has been the talk of her Foreign Office for now a year and more; not peace upon her own initiative, but upon the initiative of the nations over which she now deems herself to hold the advantage. A little of the talk has been public, but most of it has been private. Through all sorts of channels it has come to me, and in all sorts of guises, but never with the terms disclosed which the German Government would be willing to accept. That government has other valuable pawns in its hands besides those I have mentioned. It still holds a valuable part of France, though with slowly relaxing grasp, and practically the whole of Belgium. Its armies press close upon Russia and overrun Poland at their will. It cannot go further; it dare not go back. It wishes to close its bargain before it is too late and it has little left to offer for the pound of flesh it will demand.

The military masters under whom Germany is bleeding see very clearly to what point Fate has brought them. If they fall back or are forced back an inch, their power both abroad and at home will fall to pieces like a house of cards. It is their power at home they are thinking about now more than their power abroad. It is that power which is trembling under their very feet; and deep fear has entered their hearts. They have but one chance to perpetuate their military power or even their controlling political influence. If they can secure peace now with the immense advantages still in their hands which they have up to this point apparently gained, they will have justified themselves before the German people: they will have gained by force what they promised to gain by it: an immense expansion of German power, an immense enlargement of German industrial and commercial opportunities. Their prestige will be secure, and with their prestige their political power. If they fail, their people will thrust them aside; a government accountable to the people themselves will be set up in Germany as it has been in England, in the United States, in France, and in all the great countries of the modern time except Germany. If they succeed they are safe and Germany and the world are undone; if they fail Germany is saved and the world will be at peace. If they succeed, America will fall within the menace. We and all the rest of the world must remain armed, as they will remain, and must make ready for the next step in their aggression; if they fail, the world may unite for peace and Germany may be of the union. . . .

The sinister intrigue is being no less actively conducted in this country than in Russia and in every country in Europe to which the agents and dupes of the Imperial German Government can get access. That Government has many spokesmen here, in places high and low. They have learned discretion. They keep within the law. It is opinion they utter now, not sedition. They proclaim the liberal purposes of their masters; declare this a foreign war which can touch America with no danger to either her lands or her institutions; set England at the center of the stage and talk of her ambition to assert economic dominion throughout the world; appeal to our ancient tradition of isolation in the politics of the nations; and seek to undermine the Government with false professions of loyalty to its principles.

A Peoples' War

But they will make no headway. The false betray themselves always in every accent. It is only friends and partisans of the German Government whom we have already identified who utter these thinly disguised disloyalties. The facts are patent to all the world, and nowhere are they more plainly seen than in the United States, where we are accustomed to deal with facts and not with sophistries; and the great fact that stands out above all the rest is that this is a People's War, a war for freedom and justice and self-government amongst all the nations of the world, a war to make the world safe for the peoples who live upon it and have made it their own, the German people themselves included; and that with us rests the choice to break through all these hypocrises and patent cheats and masks of brute force and help set the world free, or else stand aside and let it be dominated a long age through by sheer weight of arms, and the arbitrary choices of self-constituted masters, by the nation which can maintain the biggest armies and the most irresistible armaments,—a power to which the world has afforded no parallel and in the face of which political freedom must wither and perish.

For us there is but one choice. We have made it. Woe be to the man or group of men that seeks to stand in our way in this day of high resolution when every principle we hold dearest is to be vindicated and made secure for the salvation of the nations. We are ready to plead at the bar of history, and our flag shall wear a new luster. Once more we shall make good with our lives and fortunes the great faith to which we were born, and a new glory shall shine in the face of our people.

LETTER TO THE SOLDIERS AND SAILORS
OF THE UNITED STATES, AUGUST 1917

The Key to Duty

The Bible is the word of life. I beg that you will read it and find this out for yourselves—read, not little snatches here and there, but long passages that will really be the road to the heart of it. You will find it full of real men and women not only, but also of things you have wondered about and been troubled about all your life, as men have been always; and the more you read the more it will become plain to you what things are worth while and what are not, what things make men happy—loyalty, right dealings, speaking the truth, readiness to give everything for what they think their duty, and, most of all, the wish that they may have the real approval of the Christ, who gave everything for them—and the things that are guaranteed to make men unhappy—selfishness, cowardice, greed, and everything that is low and mean. When you have read the Bible you will know that it is the Word of God, because you will have found it the key to your own heart, your own happiness, and your own duty.

Peace by the Overcoming of Evil

GENTLEMEN OF THE CONGRESS: Eight months have elapsed since I last had the honor of addressing you. They have been months crowded with events of immense and grave significance for us. I shall not undertake to retail or even to summarize those events. The practical particulars of the part we have played in them will be laid before you in the reports of the Executive Departments. I shall discuss only our present outlook upon these vast affairs, our present duties, and the immediate means of accomplishing the objects we shall hold always in view. . . .

I believe that it is necessary to say plainly what we here at the seat of action consider the war to be for and what part we mean to play in the settlement of its searching issues. We are the spokesmen of the American people and they have a right to know whether their purpose is ours. They desire peace by the overcoming of evil, by the defeat once for all of the sinister forces that interrupt peace and render it impossible, and they wish to know how closely our thought runs with theirs and what action we propose. They are impatient with those who desire peace by any sort of compromise,—deeply and indignantly impatient,—but they will be equally impatient with us if we do not make it plain to them what our objectives are and what we are planning for in seeking to make conquest of peace by arms.

I believe that I speak for them when I say two things: First, that this intolerable Thing of which the masters of Germany have shown us the ugly face, this menace of combined intrigue and force which we now see so clearly as the German power, a Thing without conscience or honor or capacity for covenanted peace, must be crushed and, if it be not utterly brought to an end, at least shut out from the friendly intercourse of the nations; and, second, that when this Thing and its power are indeed defeated and the time comes that we can discuss peace,—when the German people have spokesmen whose word we can believe and when those spokesmen are ready in the name of their people to accept the common judgment of the nations as to what shall henceforth be the bases of law and of covenant for the life of the world,—we shall be willing and glad to pay the full price for peace, and pay it ungrudgingly. We know what that price will be. It will be full, impartial justice,—justice done at every point and to every nation that the final settlement must affect, our enemies as well as our friends.

You catch, with me, the voices of humanity that are in the air. They grow daily more audible, more articulate, more persuasive, and they come from the hearts of men everywhere. They insist that the war shall not end in vindictive action of any kind; that no nation or people shall be robbed or punished because the irresponsible rulers of a single country have themselves done deep and abominable wrong. It is this thought that has been expressed in the formula "No annexations, no contributions, no punitive indemnities." Just because this crude formula expresses the instinctive judgment as to right of plain men everywhere it has been made diligent use of by the masters of German intrigue to lead the people of Russia astray— and the people of every other country their agents could reach, in order that a premature peace might be brought about before autocracy has been taught its final and convincing lesson, and the people of the world put in control of their own destinies.

But the fact that a wrong use has been made of a just idea is no reason why a right use should not be made of it. It ought to be brought under the patronage of its real friends. Let it be said again that autocracy must first be shown the utter futility of its claims to power or leadership in the modern world. It is impossible to apply any standard of justice so long as such forces are unchecked and undefeated as the present masters of Germany command. Not until that has been done can Right be set up as arbiter and peace-maker among the nations. But when that has been done,—as, God willing, it assuredly will be,—we shall at last be free to do an unprecedented thing, and this is the time to avow our purpose to do it. We shall be free to base peace on generosity and justice, to the exclusion of all selfish claims to advantage even on the part of the victors.

The Task Is to Win the War

Let there be no misunderstanding. Our present and immediate task is to win the war, and nothing shall turn us aside from it until it is accomplished. Every power and resource we possess, whether of men, of money, or of materials, is being devoted and will continue to be devoted to that purpose until it is achieved. Those who desire to bring peace about before that purpose is achieved I counsel to carry their advice elsewhere. We will not entertain it. We shall regard the war as won only when the German people say to us, through properly accredited representatives, that they are ready to agree to a settlement based upon justice and the reparation of the wrongs their rulers have done. They have done a wrong to Belgium which must be repaired. They have established a power over other lands and peoples than their own,—over the great Empire of Austria-Hungary, over hitherto free Balkan states, over Turkey, and within Asia,—which must be relinquished.

Germany's success by skill, by industry, by knowledge, by enterprise we did not grudge or oppose, but admired, rather. She had built up for herself a real empire of trade and influence, secured by the peace of the world. We were content to abide the rivalries of manufacture, science, and commerce that were involved for us in her success and stand or fall as we had or did not have the brains and the initiative to surpass her. But at the moment when she had conspicuously won her triumphs of peace she threw them away, to establish in their stead what the world will no longer permit to be established, military and political domination by arms, by which to oust where she could not excel the rivals she most feared and hated. The peace we make must remedy that wrong. It must deliver the once fair lands and happy peoples of Belgium and northern France from the Prussian conquest and the Prussian menace, but it must also deliver the peoples of Austria-Hungary, the peoples of the Balkans, and the peoples of Turkey, alike in Europe and in Asia, from the impudent and alien dominion of the Prussian military and commercial autocracy.

We Intend No Wrong Against the German Empire

We owe it, however, to ourselves to say that we do not wish in any way to impair or to re-arrange the Austro-Hungarian Empire. It is no affair of ours what they do with their own life, either industrially or politically. We do not purpose or desire to dictate to them in any way. We only desire to see that their affairs are left in their own hands, in all matters, great or small. We shall hope to secure for the peoples of the Balkan peninsula and for the people of the Turkish Empire the right and opportunity to make their own lives safe, their own fortunes secure against oppression or injustice and from the dictation of foreign courts or parties.

And our attitude and purpose with regard to Germany herself are of a like kind. We intend no wrong against the German Empire, no interference with her internal affairs. We should deem either the one or the other absolutely unjustifiable, absolutely contrary to the principles we have professed to live by and to hold most sacred throughout our life as a nation.

The people of Germany are being told by the men whom they now permit to deceive them and to act as their masters that they are fighting for the very life and existence of their Empire, a war of desperate self-defense against deliberate aggression. Nothing could be more grossly or wantonly false, and we must seek by the utmost openness and candor as to our real aims to convince them of its falseness. We are in fact fighting for their emancipation from fear, along with our own,—from the fear as well as from the fact of unjust attack by neighbors or rivals or schemers after world empire. No one is threatening the existence or the independence or the peaceful enterprise of the German Empire.

The worst that can happen to the detriment of the German people is this, that if they should still, after the war is over, continue to be obliged to live under ambitious and intriguing masters interested to disturb the peace of the world, men or classes of men whom the other peoples of the world could not trust, it might be impossible to admit them to the partnership of nations which must henceforth guarantee the world's peace. That partnership must be a partnership of peoples, not a mere partnership of governments. It might be impossible, also, in such untoward circumstances to admit Germany to the free economic intercourse which must inevitably spring out of the other partnerships of a real peace. But there would be no aggression in that; and such a situation, inevitable because of distrust, would in the very nature of things sooner or later cure itself, by processes which would assuredly set in.

The wrongs, the very deep wrongs, committed in this war will have to be righted. That of course. But they cannot and must not be righted by the commission of similar wrongs against Germany and her allies. The world will not permit the commission of similar wrongs as a means of reparation and settlement. Statesmen must by this time have learned that the opinion of the world is everywhere wide awake and fully comprehends the issues involved. No representative of any self-governed nation will dare disregard it by attempting any such covenants of selfishness and compromise as were entered into at the Congress of Vienna. The thought of the plain people here and everywhere throughout the world, the people who enjoy no privilege and have very simple and unsophisticated standards of right and wrong, is the air all governments must henceforth breathe if they would live. It is in the full disclosing light of that thought that all policies must be conceived and executed in this midday hour of the world's life. German rulers have been able to upset the peace of the world only because the German people were not suffered under their tutelage to share the comradeship of the other peoples of the world either in thought or in purpose. They were allowed to have no opinion of their own which might be set up as a rule of conduct for those who exercised authority over them. But the congress that concludes this war will feel the full strength of the tides that run now in the hearts and conscience of free men everywhere. Its conclusions will run with those tides.

The Cause Is Just and Holy

What shall we do, then, to push this great war of freedom and justice to its righteous conclusion? We must clear away with a thorough hand all impediments to success and we must make every adjustment of law that will facilitate the full and free use of our whole capacity and force as a fighting unit. . . . What I am perfectly clear about is that in the present session of the Congress our whole attention and energy should be concentrated on the vigorous, rapid, and successful prosecution of the great task of winning the war.

We can do this with all the greater zeal and enthusiasm because we know that for us this is a war of high principle, debased by no selfish ambition of conquest or spoliation; because we know, and all the world knows, that we have been forced into it to save the very institutions we live under from corruption and destruction. The purposes of the Central Powers strike straight at the very heart of everything we believe in; their methods of warfare outrage every principle of humanity and of knightly honor; their intrigue has corrupted the very thought and spirit of many of our people; their sinister and secret diplomacy has sought to take our very territory away from us and disrupt the Union of the States. Our safety would be at an end, our honor forever sullied and brought into contempt were we to permit their triumph. They are striking at the very existence of democracy and liberty.

It is because it is for us a war of high, disinterested purpose, in which all the free peoples of the world are banded together for the vindication of right, a war for the preservation of our Nation and of all that it has held dear of principle and of purpose, that we feel ourselves doubly constrained to propose for its outcome only that which is righteous and of irreproachable intention, for our foes as well as for our friends. The couse being just and holy, the settlement must be of like motive and quality. For this we can fight, but for nothing less noble or less worthy of our traditions. For this cause we entered the war and for this cause will we battle until the last gun is fired.

I have spoken plainly because this seems to me the time when it is most necessary to speak plainly, in order that all the world may know that even in the heat and ardor of the struggle and when our whole thought is of carrying the war through to its end we have not forgotten any ideal or principle for which the name of America has been held in honor among the nations and for which it has been our glory to contend in the great generations that went before us. A supreme moment of history has come. The eyes of the people have been opened and they see. The hand of God is laid upon the nations. He will show them favors, I devoutly believe, only if they rise to the clear heights of His own justice and mercy.

Chapter Thirteen

TOWARD PEACE

O NCE Wilson had presented a clear view of the aims for which America and the Allies were fighting, he could be adamant against compromise. His Message to the Pope and his famous speeches embodying the Fourteen and the Four Points were as a face of flint turned toward a premature peace, while they appealed seductively to the struggling and weary peoples of the belligerent nations. At the height of his power, Wilson slipped. The appeal for a Democratic Congress, understandable in the light of his political philosophy but ill-timed and misconceived, set the stage for the defeats that were to come.

REPLY TO THE COMMUNICATION OF THE POPE
TO THE BELLIGERENT GOVERNMENTS,
AUGUST 27, 1917

His Holiness Proposes a Return to the Status Quo Ante

TO HIS HOLINESS BENEDICTUS XV, POPE:

Every heart that has not been blinded and hardened by this terrible war must be touched by this moving appeal of His Holiness the Pope, must feel the dignity and force of the humane and generous motives which prompted it, and must fervently wish that we might take the path of peace he so persuasively points out. But it would be folly to take it if it does not in fact lead to the goal he proposes. Our response must be based upon the stern facts and upon nothing else. It is not a mere cessation of arms he desires; it is a stable and enduring peace. This agony must not be gone through with again, and it must be a matter of very sober judgment what will insure us against it.

His Holiness in substance proposes that we return to the status quo *ante bellum,* and that then there be a general condonation, disarmament, and a concert of nations based upon an acceptance of the principle of arbitration; that by a similar concert freedom of the seas be established; and that the territorial claims of France and Italy, the perplexing problems of the Balkan states, and the restitution of Poland be left to such conciliatory adjustments as may be possible in the new temper of such a peace, due regard being paid to the aspirations of the peoples whose political fortunes and affiliations will be involved.

It is manifest that no part of this program can be successfully carried out unless the restitution of the *status quo ante* furnishes a firm and satisfactory basis for it. The object of this war is to deliver the free peoples of the world from the menace and the actual power of a vast military establishment controlled by an irresponsible government which, having secretly planned to dominate the world, proceeded to carry the plan out without regard either to the sacred obligations of treaty or the long-established practices and long-cherished principles of international action and honor; which chose its own time for the war; delivered its blow fiercely and suddenly; stopped at no barrier either of law or of mercy; swept a whole continent within the tide of blood,—not the blood of soldiers only, but the blood of innocent women and children also and of the helpless poor; and now stands balked but not defeated, the enemy of four-fifths of the world. This power is not the German people. It is the ruthless master of the German people. It is no business of ours how that great people came under its control or submitted with temporary zest to the domination of its purpose; but it is our business to see to it that the history of the rest of the world is no longer left to its handling.

To deal with such a power by way of peace upon the plan proposed by His Holiness the Pope would, so far as we can see, involve a recuperation of its strength and a renewal of its policy; would make it necessary to create a permanent hostile combination of nations against the German people, who are its instruments; and would result in abandoning the new-born Russia to the intrigue, the manifold subtle interference, and the certain counter-revolution

which would be attempted by all the malign influences to whic
the German Government has of late accustomed the world. Ca
peace be based upon a restitution of its power or upon any word c
honor it could pledge in a treaty of settlement and accommodation

Peace Based upon the Faith of All the Peoples

Responsible statesmen must now everywhere see, if they neve
saw before, that no peace can rest securely upon political or ecc
nomic restrictions meant to benefit some nations and cripple o
embarrass others, upon vindictive action of any sort, or any kind o
revenge or deliberate injury. The American people have suffered in
tolerable wrongs at the hands of the Imperial German Government
but they desire no reprisal upon the German people, who have
themselves suffered all things in this war, which they did not choose
They believe that peace should rest upon the rights of peoples, not
the rights of governments,—the rights of peoples great or small,
weak or powerful,—their equal right to freedom and security and
self-government and to a participation upon fair terms in the economic opportunities of the world,—the German people of course
included, if they will accept equality and not seek domination.

The test, therefore, of every plan of peace is this: Is it based upon
the faith of all the peoples involved or merely upon the word of an
ambitious and intriguing government, on the one hand, and of a
group of free peoples, on the other? This is a test which goes to the
root of the matter; and it is the test which must be applied.

The purposes of the United States in this war are known to the
whole world,—to every people to whom the truth has been permitted to come. They do not need to be stated again. We seek no
material advantage of any kind. We believe that the intolerable
wrongs done in this war by the furious and brutal power of the
Imperial German Government ought to be repaired, but not at the
expense of the sovereignty of any people,—rather in vindication of
the sovereignty both of those that are weak and those that are
strong. Punitive damages, the dismemberment of empires, the establishment of selfish and exclusive economic leagues, we deem inex-
pedient and in the end worse than futile, no proper basis for a peace

of any kind, least of all for an enduring peace. That must be based upon justice and fairness and the common rights of mankind.

We cannot take the word of the present rulers of Germany as a guarantee of anything that is to endure, unless explicitly supported by such conclusive evidences of the will and purpose of the German people themselves as the other peoples of the world would be justified in accepting. Without such guarantees treaties of settlement, agreements for disarmament, covenants to set up arbitration in the place of force, territorial adjustments, reconstitutions of small nations, if made with the German Government, no man, no nation could now depend on. We must wait some new evidence of the purposes of the great peoples of the Central Empires. God grant it may be given soon and in a way to restore the confidence of all peoples everywhere in the faith of nations and the possibility of a covenanted peace.

ADDRESS TO THE CONGRESS,
JANUARY 8, 1918

Parleys Have Been in Progress

Once more, as repeatedly before, the spokesmen of the Central Empires have indicated their desire to discuss the objects of the war and the possible bases of a general peace. Parleys have been in progress at Brest-Litovsk between representatives of the Central Powers to which the attention of all the belligerents has been invited for the purpose of ascertaining whether it may be possible to extend these parleys into a general conference with regard to terms of peace and settlement. The Russian representatives presented not only a perfectly definite statement of the principles upon which they would be willing to conclude peace but also an equally definite program of the concrete application of those principles. The representatives of the Central Powers, on their part, presented an outline of settlement which, if much less definite, seemed susceptible of liberal interpretation until their specific program of practical terms was added. That program proposed no concessions at all either to the sovereignty of Russia or to the preferences of the populations with whose fortunes it dealt, but meant, in a word, that the Central Empires were to keep every foot of territory their armed forces had occupied,—every province, every city, every point of vantage,— as a permanent addition to their territories and their power. It is a reasonable conjecture that the general principles of settlement which they at first suggested originated with the more liberal states- men of Germany and Austria, the men who have begun to feel the force of their own peoples' thought and purpose, while the concrete terms of actual settlement came from the military leaders who have no thought but to keep what they have got. The negotiations have been broken off. The Russian representatives were sincere and in earnest. They cannot entertain such proposals of conquest and domination.

The whole incident is full of significance. It is also full of per- plexity. With whom are the Russian representatives dealing? For whom are the representatives of the Central Empires speaking? Are they speaking for the majorities of their respective parliaments or for the minority parties, that military and imperialistic minority which has so far dominated their whole policy and controlled the affairs of Turkey and of the Balkan states which have felt obliged to become their associates in this war? The Russian representatives have insisted, very justly, very wisely, and in the true spirit of mod- ern democracy, that the conferences they have been holding with the Teutonic and Turkish statesmen should be held within open, not closed, doors, and all the world has been audience, as was de- sired. To whom have we been listening, then? To those who speak the spirit and intention of the Resolutions of the German Reichstag of the ninth of July last, the spirit and intention of the liberal leaders and parties of Germany, or to those who resist and defy that spirit and intention and insist upon conquest and subjugation? Or are we listening, in fact, to both, unreconciled and in open and hopeless contradiction? These are very serious and pregnant ques- tions. Upon the answer to them depends the peace of the world.

A Challenge to State the Objects of the War

But, whatever the results of the parleys at Brest-Litovsk, whatever the confusions of counsel and of purpose in the utterances of the spokesmen of the Central Empires, they have again attempted to acquaint the world with their objects in the war and have again challenged their adversaries to say what their objects are and what sort of settlement they would deem just and satisfactory. There is no good reason why that challenge should not be responded to, and responded to with the utmost candor. We did not wait for it. Not once, but again and again, we have laid our whole thought and purpose before the world, not in general terms only, but each time with sufficient definition to make it clear what sort of definitive terms of settlement must necessarily spring out of them. Within the last week Mr. Lloyd George has spoken with admirable candor and in admirable spirit for the people and Government of Great Britain. There is no confusion of counsel among the adversaries of the Central Powers, no uncertainty of principle, no vagueness of detail. The only secrecy of counsel, the only lack of fearless frankness, the only failure to make definite statement of the objects of the war, lies with Germany and her Allies. The issues of life and death hang upon these definitions. No statesman who has the least conception of his responsibility ought for a moment to permit himself to continue this tragical and appalling outpouring of blood and treasure unless he is sure beyond a peradventure that the objects of the vital sacrifice are part and parcel of the very life of Society and that the people for whom he speaks think them right and imperative as he does.

There is, moreover, a voice calling for these definitions of principle and of purpose which is, it seems to me, more thrilling and more compelling than any of the many moving voices with which the troubled air of the world is filled. It is the voice of the Russian people. They are prostrate and all but helpless, it would seem, before the grim power of Germany, which has hitherto known no relenting and no pity. Their power, apparently, is shattered. And yet their soul is not subservient. They will not yield either in principle or in action. Their conception of what is right, of what it is humane and honorable for them to accept, has been stated with a frankness, a largeness of view, a generosity of spirit, and a universal human sympathy which must challenge the admiration of every friend of mankind; and they have refused to compound their ideals or desert others that they themselves may be safe. They call to us to say what it is that we desire, in what, if in anything, our purpose and our spirit differ from theirs; and I believe that the people of the United States would wish me to respond, with utter simplicity and frankness. Whether their present leaders believe it or not, it is our heartfelt desire and hope that some way may be opened whereby we may be privileged to assist the people of Russia to attain their utmost hope of liberty and ordered peace.

It will be our wish and purpose that the processes of peace, when they are begun, shall be absolutely open and that they shall involve and permit henceforth no secret understandings of any kind. The day of conquest and aggrandizement is gone by; so is also the day of secret covenants entered into in the interest of particular governments and likely at some unlooked-for moment to upset the peace of the world. It is this happy fact, now clear to the view of every public man whose thoughts do not still linger in an age that is dead and gone, which makes it possible for every nation whose purposes are consistent with justice and the peace of the world to avow now or at any other time the objects it has in view.

The Fourteen Points

We entered this war because violations of right had occurred which touched us to the quick and made the life of our own people impossible unless they were corrected and the world secured once for all against their recurrence. What we demand in this war, therefore, is nothing peculiar to ourselves. It is that the world be made fit and safe to live in; and particularly that it be made safe for every peace-loving nation which, like our own, wishes to live its own life, determine its own institutions, be assured of justice and fair dealing by the other peoples of the world as against force and selfish aggression. All the peoples of the world are in effect partners in this interest, and for our own part we see very clearly that unless justice be done to others it will not be done to us. The program of the world's peace, therefore, is our program; and that program, the only possible program, as we see it, is this:

I. Open covenants of peace, openly arrived at, after which there shall be no private international understandings of any kind but diplomacy shall proceed always frankly and in the public view.

II. Absolute freedom of navigation upon the seas, outside territorial waters, alike in peace and in war, except as the seas may be closed in whole or in part by international action for the enforcement of international covenants.

III. The removal, so far as possible, of all economic barriers and the establishment of an equality of trade conditions among all the nations consenting to the peace and associating themselves for its maintenance.

IV. Adequate guarantees given and taken that national armaments will be reduced to the lowest point consistent with domestic safety.

V. A free, open-minded, and absolutely impartial adjustment of all colonial claims, based upon a strict observance of the principle that in determining all such questions of sovereignty the interests of the populations concerned must have equal weight with the equitable claims of the government whose title is to be determined.

VI. The evacuation of all Russian territory and such a settlement of all questions affecting Russia as will secure the best and freest coöperation of the other nations of the world in obtaining for her an unhampered and unembarrassed opportunity for the independent determination of her own political development and national policy and assure her of a sincere welcome into the society of free nations under institutions of her own choosing; and, more than a welcome, assistance also of every kind that she may need and may herself desire. The treatment accorded Russia by her sister nations in the months to come will be the acid test of their good will, of their comprehension of her needs as distinguished from their own interests, and of their intelligent and unselfish sympathy.

VII. Belgium, the whole world will agree, must be evacuated and restored, without any attempt to limit the sovereignty which she enjoys in common with all other free nations. No other single act will serve as this will serve to restore confidence among the nations in the laws which they have themselves set and determined for the government of their relations with one another. Without this heal-ing act the whole structure and validity of international law is for-ever impaired.

VIII. All French territory should be freed and the invaded por-tions restored, and the wrong done to France by Prussia in 1871 in the matter of Alsace-Lorraine, which has unsettled the peace of the world for nearly fifty years, should be righted, in order that peace may once more be made secure in the interest of all.

IX. A readjustment of the frontiers of Italy should be effected along clearly recognizable lines of nationality.

X. The peoples of Austria-Hungary, whose place among the nations we wish to see safeguarded and assured, should be accorded the freest opportunity of autonomous development.

XI. Rumania, Serbia, and Montenegro should be evacuated; occupied territories restored; Serbia accorded free and secure access to the sea; and the relations of the several Balkan states to one another determined by friendly counsel along historically established lines of allegiance and nationality; and international guarantees of the political and economic independence and territorial integrity of the several Balkan states should be entered into.

XII. The Turkish portions of the present Ottoman Empire should be assured a secure sovereignty, but the other nationalities which are now under Turkish rule should be assured an undoubted security of life and an absolutely unmolested opportunity of auton-omous development, and the Dardanelles should be permanently opened as a free passage to the ships and commerce of all nations under international guarantees.

XIII. An independent Polish state should be erected which should include the territories inhabited by indisputably Polish popu-lations, which should be assured a free and secure access to the sea, and whose political and economic independence and territorial integrity should be guaranteed by international covenant.

XIV. A general association of nations must be formed under specific covenants for the purpose of affording mutual guarantees of political independence and territorial integrity to great and small states alike.

In regard to these essential rectifications of wrong and assertions of right we feel ourselves to be intimate partners of all the governments and peoples associated together against the Imperialists. We cannot be separated in interest or divided in purpose. We stand together until the end.

A Place of Equality for Germany

For such arrangements and covenants we are willing to fight and to continue to fight until they are achieved; but only because we wish the right to prevail and desire a just and stable peace such as can be secured only by removing the chief provocations to war, which this program does remove. We have no jealousy of German greatness, and there is nothing in this program that impairs it. We grudge her no achievement or distinction of learning or of pacific enterprise such as have made her record very bright and very enviable. We do not wish to injure her or to block in any way her legitimate influence or power. We do not wish to fight her either with arms or with hostile arrangements of trade if she is willing to associate herself with us and the other peace-loving nations of the world in covenants of justice and law and fair dealing. We wish her only to accept a place of equality among the peoples of the world,—the new world in which we now live,—instead of a place of mastery.

Neither do we presume to suggest to her any alteration or modification of her institutions. But it is necessary, we must frankly say, and necessary as a preliminary to any intelligent dealings with her on our part, that we should know whom her spokesmen speak for when they speak to us, whether for the Reichstag majority or for the military party and the men whose creed is imperial domination.

We have spoken now, surely, in terms too concrete to admit of any further doubt or question. An evident principle runs through the whole program I have outlined. It is the principle of justice to all peoples and nationalities, and their right to live on equal terms of liberty and safety with one another, whether they be strong or weak. Unless this principle be made its foundation no part of the structure of international justice can stand. The people of the United States could act upon no other principle; and to the vindication of this principle they are ready to devote their lives, their honor, and everything that they possess. The moral climax of this the culminating and final war for human liberty has come, and they are ready to put their own strength, their own highest purpose, their own integrity and devotion to the test.

ADDRESS AT BALTIMORE, MARYLAND,
APRIL 6, 1918

The Enemy Seeks, Not Justice, But Dominion

This is the anniversary of our acceptance of Germany's challenge to fight for our right to live and be free, and for the sacred rights of free men everywhere. The Nation is awake. There is no need to call to it. We know what the war must cost, our utmost sacrifice, the lives of our fittest men and, if need be, all that we possess. . . .

The reasons for this great war, the reason why it had to come, the need to fight it through, and the issues that hang upon its outcome, are more clearly disclosed now than ever before. It is easy to see just what this particular loan means because the Cause we are fighting for stands more sharply revealed than at any previous crisis of the momentous struggle. The man who knows least can now see plainly how the cause of Justice stands and what the imperishable thing is he is asked to invest in. Men in America may be more sure than they ever were before that the cause is their own, and that, if it should be lost, their own great Nation's place and mission in the world would be lost with it.

I call you to witness, my fellow countrymen, that at no stage of this terrible business have I judged the purposes of Germany intemperately. I should be ashamed in the presence of affairs so grave, so fraught with the destinies of mankind throughout all the world, to speak with truculence, to use the weak language of hatred or vindictive purpose. We must judge as we would be judged. I have sought to learn the objects Germany has in this war from the mouths of her own spokesmen, and to deal as frankly with them as I wished them to deal with me. I have laid bare our own ideals, our own purposes, without reserve or doubtful phrase, and have asked them to say as plainly what it is that they seek.

We have ourselves proposed no injustice, no aggression. We are ready, whenever the final reckoning is made, to be just to the German people, deal fairly with the German power, as with all others. There can be no difference between peoples in the final judgment, if it is indeed to be a righteous judgment. To propose anything but justice, even-handed and dispassionate justice, to Germany at any time, whatever the outcome of the war, would be to renounce and dishonor our own cause. For we ask nothing that we are not willing to accord.

It has been with this thought that I have sought to learn from those who spoke for Germany whether it was justice or dominion and the execution of their own will upon the other nations of the world that the German leaders were seeking. They have answered, answered in unmistakable terms. They have avowed that it was not justice but dominion and the unhindered execution of their own will.

The German Military Have Avowed Their Purpose

The avowal has not come from Germany's statesmen. It has come from her military leaders, who are her real rulers. Her statesmen have said that they wished peace, and were ready to discuss its terms whenever their opponents were willing to sit down at the conference table with them. Her present Chancellor has said,—in indefinite and uncertain terms, indeed, and in phrases that often seem to deny their own meaning, but with as much plainness as he thought prudent,—that he believed that peace should be based upon the principles which we had declared would be our own in the final settlement. At Brest-Litovsk her civilian delegates spoke in similar terms; professed their desire to conclude a fair peace and accord to the peoples with whose fortunes they were dealing the right to choose their own allegiances. But action accompanied and followed the profession. Their military masters, the men who act for Germany and exhibit her purpose in execution, proclaimed a very different conclusion. We cannot mistake what they have done,—in Russia, in Finland, in the Ukraine, in Rumania. The real test of their justice and fair play has come. From this we may judge the

rest. They are enjoying in Russia a cheap triumph in which no brave
or gallant nation can long take pride. A great people, helpless by
their own act, lies for the time at their mercy. Their fair professions
are forgotten. They nowhere set up justice, but everywhere impose
their power and exploit everything for their own use and aggrandizement; and the peoples of conquered provinces are invited to be free
under their dominion!

Are we not justified in believing that they would do the same
things at their western front if they were not there face to face with
armies whom even their countless divisions cannot overcome? If,
when they have felt their check to be final, they should propose
favorable and equitable terms with regard to Belgium and France
and Italy, could they blame us if we concluded that they did so
only to assure themselves of a free hand in Russia and the East?

Their purpose is undoubtedly to make all the Slavic peoples, all
the free and ambitious nations of the Baltic peninsula, all the lands
that Turkey has dominated and misruled, subject to their will and
ambition and build upon that dominion an empire of force upon
which they fancy that they can then erect an empire of gain and
commercial supremacy,—an empire as hostile to the Americas as
to the Europe which it will overawe,—an empire which will ultimately master Persia, India, and the peoples of the Far East. In
such a program our ideals, the ideals of justice and humanity and
liberty, the principle of the free self-determination of nations upon
which all the modern world insists, can play no part. They are
rejected for the ideals of power, for the principle that the strong
must rule the weak, that trade must follow the flag, whether those
to whom it is taken welcome it or not, that the peoples of the
world are to be made subject to the patronage and overlordship of
those who have the power to enforce it.

That program once carried out, America and all who care or dare
to stand with her must arm and prepare themselves to contest the
mastery of the world, a mastery in which the rights of common
men, the rights of women and of all who are weak, must for the
time being be trodden under foot and disregarded, and the old,

age-long struggle for freedom and right begin again at its beginning. Everything that America has lived for and loved and grown great to vindicate and bring to a glorious realization will have fallen in utter ruin and the gates of mercy more pitilessly shut upon mankind!

The Challenge Accepted

The thing is preposterous and impossible; and yet is not that what the whole course and action of the German armies has meant wherever they have moved? I do not wish, even in this moment of utter disillusionment, to judge harshly or unrighteously. I judge only what the German arms have accomplished with unpitying thoroughness throughout every fair region they have touched.

What, then, are we to do? For myself, I am ready, ready still, ready even now, to discuss a fair and just and honest peace at any time that it is sincerely purposed,—a peace in which the strong and the weak shall fare alike. But the answer, when I proposed such a peace, came from the German commanders in Russia, and I cannot mistake the meaning of the answer.

I accept the challenge. I know that you accept it. All the world shall know that you accept it. It shall appear in the utter sacrifice and self-forgetfulness with which we shall give all that we love and all that we have to redeem the world and make it fit for free men like ourselves to live in. This now is the meaning of all that we do. Let everything that we say, my fellow countrymen, everything that we henceforth plan and accomplish, ring true to this response till the majesty and might of our concerted power shall fill the thought and utterly defeat the force of those who flout and misprize what we honor and hold dear. Germany has once more said that force, and force alone, shall decide whether Justice and peace shall reign in the affairs of men, whether Right as America conceives it or Dominion as she conceives it shall determine the destinies of mankind. There is, therefore, but one response possible from us: Force, Force to the utmost, Force without stint or limit, the righteous and triumphant Force which shall make Right the law of the world, and cast every selfish dominion down in the dust.

ADDRESS AT MOUNT VERNON,
JULY 4, 1918

The Faith and Purpose with Which We Act

GENTLEMEN OF THE DIPLOMATIC CORPS AND MY FELLOW CITIZENS:
I am happy to draw apart with you to this quiet place of old counsel in order to speak a little of the meaning of this day of
our Nation's independence. The place seems very still and remote.
It is as serene and untouched by the hurry of the world as it was
in those great days long ago when General Washington was here
and held leisurely conference with the men who were to be associated with him in the creation of a nation. From these gentle slopes
they looked out upon the world and saw it whole, saw it with the
light of the future upon it, saw it with modern eyes that turned
away from a past which men of liberated spirits could no longer
endure. It is for that reason that we cannot feel, even here, in the
immediate presence of this sacred tomb, that this is a place of death.
It was a place of achievement. A great promise that was meant for
all mankind was here given plan and reality. The associations by
which we are here surrounded are the inspiriting associations of
that noble death which is only a glorious consummation. From this
green hillside we also ought to be able to see with comprehending
eyes the world that lies about us and should conceive anew the
purposes that must set men free.

It is significant,—significant of their own character and purpose
and of the influences they were setting afoot,—that Washington
and his associates, like the barons at Runnymede, spoke and acted,
not for a class, but for a people. It has been left for us to see to it
that it shall be understood that they spoke and acted, not for a
single people only, but for all mankind. They were thinking, not of
themselves and of the material interests which centered in the little
groups of landholders and merchants and men of affairs with whom
they were accustomed to act, in Virginia and the colonies to the
north and south of her, but of a people which wished to be done
with classes and special interests and the authority of men whom
they had not themselves chosen to rule over them. They entertained
no private purpose, desired no peculiar privilege. They were con-

sciously planning that men of every class should be free and America
a place to which men out of every nation might resort who wished
to share with them the rights and privileges of free men. And we
take our cue from them,—do we not? We intend what they intended. We here in America believe our participation in this present
war to be only the fruitage of what they planted. Our case differs
from theirs only in this, that it is our inestimable privilege to concert with men out of every nation what shall make not only the
liberties of America secure but the liberties of every other people as
well. We are happy in the thought that we are permitted to do
what they would have done had they been in our place. There must
now be settled once for all what was settled for America in the
great age upon whose inspiration we draw to-day. This is surely a
fitting place from which calmly to look out upon our task, that we
may fortify our spirits for its accomplishment. And this is the appropriate place from which to avow, alike to the friends who look
on and to the friends with whom we have the happiness to be
associated in action, the faith and purpose with which we act.

Our Conception of the Struggle

This, then, is our conception of the great struggle in which we
are engaged. The plot is written plain upon every scene and every
act of the supreme tragedy. On the one hand stand the peoples of
the world,—not only the peoples actually engaged, but many others
also who suffer under mastery but cannot act; peoples of many races
and in every part of the world,—the people of stricken Russia still,
among the rest, though they are for the moment unorganized and
helpless. Opposed to them, masters of many armies, stand an isolated, friendless group of governments who speak no common purpose but only selfish ambitions of their own by which none can
profit but themselves, and whose peoples are fuel in their hands;
governments which fear their people and yet are for the time their
sovereign lords, making every choice for them and disposing of their
lives and fortunes as they will, as well as of the lives and fortunes
of every people who fall under their power,—governments clothed
with the strange trappings and the primitive authority of an age that

is altogether alien and hostile to our own. The Past and the Present are in deadly grapple and the peoples of the world are being done to death between them.

There can be but one issue. The settlement must be final. There can be no compromise. No halfway decision would be tolerable. No halfway decision is conceivable. These are the ends for which the associated peoples of the world are fighting and which must be conceded them before there can be peace:

I. The destruction of every arbitrary power anywhere that can separately, secretly, and of its single choice disturb the peace of the world; or, if it cannot be presently destroyed, at the least its reduction to virtual impotence.

II. The settlement of every question, whether of territory, of sovereignty, of economic arrangement, or of political relationship, upon the basis of the free acceptance of that settlement by the people immediately concerned, and not up on the basis of the material interest or advantage of any other nation or people which may desire a different settlement for the sake of its own exterior influence or mastery.

III. The consent of all nations to be governed in their conduct towards each other by the same principles of honor and of respect for the common law of civilized society that govern the individual citizens of all modern states in their relations with one another; to the end that all promises and covenants may be sacredly observed, no private plots or conspiracies hatched, no selfish injuries wrought with impunity, and a mutual trust established upon the handsome foundation of a mutual respect for right.

IV. The establishment of an organization of peace which shall make it certain that the combined power of free nations will check every invasion of right and serve to make peace and justice the more secure by affording a definite tribunal of opinion to which all must submit and by which every international readjustment that cannot be amicably agreed upon by the peoples directly concerned shall be sanctioned.

These great objects can be put into a single sentence. What we seek is the reign of law, based upon the consent of the governed and sustained by the organized opinion of mankind.

These great ends cannot be achieved by debating and seeking to reconcile and accommodate what statesmen may wish, with their projects for balances of power and of national opportunity. They can be realized only by the determination of what the thinking peoples of the world desire, with their longing hope for justice and for social freedom and opportunity.

I can fancy that the air of this place carries the accents of such principles with a peculiar kindness. Here were started forces which the great nation against which they were primarily directed at first regarded as a revolt against its rightful authority but which it has long since seen to have been a step in the liberation of its own people as well as of the people of the United States; and I stand here now to speak,—speak proudly and with confident hope,—of the spread of this revolt, this liberation, to the great stage of the world itself! The blinded rulers of Prussia have roused forces they knew little of,—forces which, once roused, can never be crushed to earth again; for they have at their heart an inspiration and a purpose which are deathless and of the very stuff of triumph!

STATEMENT ISSUED OCTOBER 25, 1918

Appeal for a Democratic Congress

MY FELLOW COUNTRYMEN:—The Congressional elections are at hand. They occur in the most critical period our country has ever faced or is likely to face in our time. If you have approved of my leadership and wish me to continue to be your unembarrassed spokesman in affairs at home and abroad, I earnestly beg that you will express yourselves unmistakably to that effect by returning a Democratic majority to both the Senate and the House of Representatives. I am your servant and will accept your judgment without cavil, but my power to administer the great trust assigned me by the Constitution would be seriously impaired should your judgment be adverse, and I must frankly tell you so because so many critical issues depend upon your verdict. No scruple of taste must in grim times like these be allowed to stand in the way of speaking the plain truth.

I have no thought of suggesting that any political party is paramount in matters of patriotism. I feel too keenly the sacrifices which have been made in this war by all our citizens, irrespective of party affiliations, to harbor such an idea. I mean only that the difficulties and delicacies of our present task are of a sort that makes it imperatively necessary that the Nation should give its undivided support to the Government under a unified leadership, and that a Republican Congress would divide the leadership.

The leaders of the minority in the present Congress have unquestionably been pro war, but they have been anti-administration. At almost every turn, since we entered the war they have sought to take the choice of policy and the conduct of the war out of my hands and put it under the control of instrumentalities of their own choosing. This is no time either for divided counsel or for divided leadership. Unity of command is as necessary now in civil action as it is upon the field of battle. If the control of the House and Senate should be taken away from the party now in power an opposing majority could assume control of legislation and oblige all action to be taken amidst contest and obstruction.

The return of a Republican majority to either House of the Congress would, moreover, certainly be interpreted on the other side of the water as a repudiation of my leadership. Spokesmen of the Republican Party are urging you to elect a Republican Congress in order to back up and support the President, but even if they should in this way impose upon some credulous voters on this side of the water, they would impose on no one on the other side. It is well understood there as well as here that the Republican leaders desire not so much to support the President as to control him. The peoples of the allied countries with whom we are associated against Germany are quite familiar with the significance of elections. They would find it very difficult to believe that the voters of the United States had chosen to support their President by electing to the Congress a majority controlled by those who are not in fact in sympathy with the attitude and action of the administration.

I need not tell you, my fellow countrymen, that I am asking your support not for my own sake or for the sake of a political party, but for the sake of the Nation itself, in order that its inward unity of purpose may be evident to all the world. In ordinary times I would not feel at liberty to make such an appeal to you. In ordinary times divided counsels can be endured without permanent hurt to the country. But these are not ordinary times. If in these critical days it is your wish to sustain me with undivided minds, I beg that you will say so in a way which it will not be possible to misunderstand either here at home or among our associates on the other side of the sea. I submit my difficulties and my hopes to you.

STATEMENT ISSUED NOVEMBER 11, 1918

The Armistice Signed

MY FELLOW COUNTRYMEN: The armistice was signed this morning. Everything for which America fought has been accomplished. It will now be our fortunate duty to assist by example, by sober, friendly counsel and by material aid in the establishment of just democracy throughout the world.

ADDRESS TO CONGRESS,
NOVEMBER 11, 1918

The Humane Intention of the Victorious Governments

The war thus comes to an end; for, having accepted these terms of armistice, it will be impossible for the German command to renew it.

It is not now possible to assess the consequences of this great consummation. We know only that this tragical war, whose consuming flames swept from one nation to another until all the world was on fire, is at an end and that it was the privilege of our own people to enter it at its most critical juncture in such fashion and in such force as to contribute in a way of which we are all deeply proud to the great result. We know, too, that the object of the war is attained; the object upon which all free men had set their hearts; and attained with a sweeping completeness which even now we do not realize. Armed imperialism such as the men conceived who were

but yesterday the masters of Germany is at an end, its illicit aml
tions engulfed in black disaster. Who will now seek to revive i
The arbitrary power of the military caste of Germany which on
would secretly and of its own single choice disturb the peace of tl
world is discredited and destroyed. And more than that,—mu
more than that,—has been accomplished. The great nations whic
associated themselves to destroy it have now definitely united in tl
common purpose to set up such a peace as will satisfy the longir
of the whole world for disinterested justice, embodied in settl
ments which are based upon something much better and muc
more lasting than the selfish competitive interests of powerful state
There is no longer conjecture as to the objects the victors have i
mind. They have a mind in the matter, not only, but a heart als
Their avowed and concerted purpose is to satisfy and protect tl
weak as well as to accord their just rights to the strong.

The humane temper and intention of the victorious Gover
ments has already been manifested in a very practical way. The
representatives in the Supreme War Council at Versailles have l
unanimous resolution assured the peoples of the Central Empire
that everything that is possible in the circumstances will be done t
supply them with food and relieve the distressing want that is in s
many places threatening their very lives; and steps are to be take
immediately to organize these efforts at relief in the same systemati
manner that they were organized in the case of Belgium. By th
use of the idle tonnage of the Central Empires it ought presently t
be possible to lift the fear of utter misery from their oppresse
populations and set their minds and energies free for the great an
hazardous tasks of political reconstruction which now face them o
every hand. Hunger does not breed reform; it breeds madness an
all the ugly distempers that make an ordered life impossible.

For with the fall of the ancient governments which rested like a
incubus upon the peoples of the Central Empires has come politica
change not merely, but revolution; and revolution which seems a
yet to assume no final and ordered form but to run from one flui
change to another, until thoughtful men are forced to ask them
selves, With what Governments, and of what sort, are we about t

deal in the making of the covenants of peace? With what authority will they meet us, and with what assurance that their authority will abide and sustain securely the international arrangements into which we are about to enter? There is here matter for no small anxiety and misgiving. When peace is made, upon whose promises and engagements besides our own is it to rest?

Let us be perfectly frank with ourselves and admit that these questions cannot be satisfactorily answered now or at once. But the moral is not that there is little hope of an early answer that will suffice. It is only that we must be patient and helpful and mindful above all of the great hope and confidence that lie at the heart of what is taking place. Excesses accomplish nothing. Unhappy Russia has furnished abundant recent proof of that. Disorder immediately defeats itself. If excesses should occur, if disorder should for a time raise its head, a sober second thought will follow and a day of constructive action, if we help and do not hinder.

The Discipline of Freedom

The present and all that it holds belongs to the nations and the peoples who preserve their self-control and the orderly processes of their governments; the future to those who prove themselves the true friends of mankind. To conquer with arms is to make only a temporary conquest; to conquer the world by earning its esteem is to make permanent conquest. I am confident that the nations that have learned the discipline of freedom and that have settled with self-possession to its ordered practice are now about to make conquest of the world by the sheer power of example and of friendly helpfulness.

The peoples who have but just come out from under the yoke of arbitrary government and who are now coming at last into their freedom will never find the treasures of liberty they are in search of if they look for them by the light of the torch. They will find that every pathway that is stained with the blood of their own brothers leads to the wilderness, not to the seat of their hope. They are now face to face with their initial test. We must hold the light steady until they find themselves. And in the meantime, if it be possible, we must establish a peace that will justly define their place among the nations, remove all fear of their neighbors and of their former masters, and enable them to live in security and contentment when they have set their own affairs in order. I, for one, do not doubt their purpose or their capacity. There are some happy signs that they know and will choose the way of self-control and peaceful accommodation. If they do, we shall put our aid at their disposal in every way that we can. If they do not, we must await with patience and sympathy the awakening and recovery that will assuredly come at last.

Chapter Fourteen

THE GREAT HOUR

THE war over, Wilson informed the Congress that he would sail
to take part in the peace conference. His arrival in Europe was
the signal for an unprecedented outpouring of popular emotion;
men and women saw in him the symbol of their long-frustrated
hopes. Selections from the speeches Wilson made in Europe before
the start of the peace conference form the body of this chapter.
Brief, extemporaneously spoken, they show the exalted mood of
that hour—not only the mood of the American President but of the
peoples whose feelings he sensitively reflected. The speech at
Carlisle, in his grandfather's church, could stand alone in its perfection as the expression of a great but irretrievable hour in the world's
history.

ANNUAL MESSAGE TO THE CONGRESS,
DECEMBER 2, 1918

A Year of Great Events

GENTLEMEN OF THE CONGRESS: The year that has elapsed since I
last stood before you to fulfill my constitutional duty to give to the
Congress from time to time information on the state of the Union
has been so crowded with great events, great processes and great
results that I cannot hope to give you an adequate picture of its
transactions or of the far-reaching changes which have been wrought
in the life of our nation and of the world. You have yourselves
witnessed these things, as I have. It is too soon to assess them; and
we who stand in the midst of them and are part of them are less
qualified than men of another generation will be to say what they
mean, or even what they have been. But some great outstanding
facts are unmistakable and constitute, in a sense, part of the public

business with which it is our duty to deal. To state them is to set the stage for the legislative and executive action which must grow out of them and which we have yet to shape and determine.

A year ago we had sent 145,918 men overseas. Since then we have sent 1,950,513, an average of 162,542 each month, the number in fact rising, in May last to 245,951, in June to 278,760, in July to 307,182, and continuing to reach similar figures in August and September,—in August 289,570 and in September 257,438. No such movement of troops ever took place before, across three thousand miles of sea, followed by adequate equipment and supplies, and carried safely through extraordinary dangers of attack,—dangers which were alike strange and infinitely difficult to guard against. In all this movement only seven hundred and fifty-eight men were lost by enemy attack,—six hundred and thirty of whom were upon a single English transport which was sunk near the Orkney Islands.

I need not tell you what lay back of this great movement of men and material. It is not invidious to say that back of it lay a supporting organization of the industries of the country and of all its productive activities more complete, more thorough in method and effective in result, more spirited and unanimous in purpose and effort than any other great belligerent had been able to effect. We profited greatly by the experience of the nations which had already been engaged for nearly three years in the exigent and exacting business, their every resource and every executive proficiency taxed to the utmost. We were their pupils. But we learned quickly and acted with a promptness and a readiness of coöperation that justify our great pride that we were able to serve the world with unparalleled energy and quick accomplishment.

The Spirit of the Nation

But it is not the physical scale and executive efficiency of preparation, supply, equipment and dispatch that I would dwell upon, but the mettle and quality of the officers and men we sent over and of the sailors who kept the seas, and the spirit of the nation that stood behind them. No soldiers or sailors ever proved themselves more quickly ready for the test of battle or acquitted themselves with

more splendid courage and achievement when put to the test. Those
of us who played some part in directing the great processes by which
the war was pushed irresistibly forward to the final triumph may
now forget all that and delight our thoughts with the story of what
our men did. Their officers understood the grim and exacting task
they had undertaken and performed it with an audacity, efficiency
and unhesitating courage that touch the story of convoy and battle
with imperishable distinction at every turn, whether the enterprise
were great or small,—from their great chiefs, Pershing and Sims,
down to the youngest lieutenant; and their men were worthy of
them,—such men as hardly need to be commanded, and go to their
terrible adventure blithely and with the quick intelligence of those
who know just what it is they would accomplish. I am proud to be
the fellow countryman of men of such stuff and valor. Those of us
who stayed at home did our duty; the war could not have been won
or the gallant men who fought it given their opportunity to win
it otherwise; but for many a long day we shall think ourselves
'accurs'd we were not there, and hold our manhoods cheap while
any speaks that fought" with these at St. Mihiel or Thierry. The
memory of those days of triumphant battle will go with these fortunate men to their graves; and each will have his favorite memory.
'Old men forget; yet all shall be forgot, but he'll remember with
advantages what feats he did that day!"

What we all thank God for with deepest gratitude is that our
men went in force into the line of battle just at the critical moment
when the whole fate of the world seemed to hang in the balance
and threw their fresh strength into the ranks of freedom in time to
turn the whole tide and sweep of the fateful struggle,—turn it once
for all, so that thenceforth it was back, back, back for their enemies,
always back, never again forward! After that it was only a scant four
months before the commanders of the Central Empires knew themselves beaten; and now their very empires are in liquidation!

And throughout it all how fine the spirit of the Nation was: what
unity of purpose, what untiring zeal! What elevation of purpose
ran through all its splendid display of strength, its untiring accomplishment. I have said that those of us who stayed at home to do

the work of organization and supply will always wish that we had
been with the men whom we sustained by our labor; but we can
never be ashamed. It has been an inspiring thing to be here in the
midst of fine men who had turned aside from every private interest
of their own and devoted the whole of their trained capacity to the
tasks that supplied the sinews of the whole great undertaking! The
patriotism, the unselfishness, the thoroughgoing devotion and distinguished capacity that marked their toilsome labors, day after day,
month after month, have made them fit mates and comrades of the
men in the trenches and on the sea. And not the men here in
Washington only. They have but directed the vast achievement.
Throughout innumerable factories, upon innumerable farms, in the
depths of coal mines and iron mines and copper mines, wherever
the stuffs of industry were to be obtained and prepared, in the ship-
yards, on the railways, at the docks, on the sea, in every labor that
was needed to sustain the battle lines, men have vied with each
other to do their part and do it well. They can look any man-at-arms
in the face, and say, We also strove to win and gave the best that
was in us to make our fleets and armies sure of their triumph!

The Peace Settlements Now to Be Agreed Upon

The allied Governments have accepted the bases of peace which
I outlined to the Congress on the eighth of January last, as the Central Empires also have, and very reasonably desire my personal
counsel in their interpretation and application, and it is highly desirable that I should give it in order that the sincere desire of our
Government to contribute without selfish purpose of any kind to
settlements that will be of common benefit to all the nations concerned may be made fully manifest. The peace settlements which
are now to be agreed upon are of transcendent importance both to
us and to the rest of the world, and I know of no business or interest which should take precedence of them. The gallant men of
our armed forces on land and sea have consciously fought for the
ideals which they knew to be the ideals of their country; I have
sought to express those ideals; they have accepted my statements of
them as the substance of their own thought and purpose, as the

associated Governments have accepted them; I owe it to them to see to it, so far as in me lies, that no false or mistaken interpretation is put upon them, and no possible effort omitted to realize them. It is now my duty to play my full part in making good what they offered their life's blood to obtain. I can think of no call to service which could transcend this.

I shall be in close touch with you and with affairs on this side the water, and you will know all that I do. At my request, the French and English Governments have absolutely removed the censorship of cable news which until within a fortnight they had maintained and there is now no censorship whatever exercised at this end except upon attempted trade communications with enemy countries. It has been necessary to keep an open wire constantly available between Paris and the Department of State and another between France and the Department of War. In order that this might be done with the least possible interference with the other uses of the cables, I have temporarily taken over the control of both cables in order that they may be used as a single system. I did so at the advice of the most experienced cable officials, and I hope that the results will justify my hope that the news of the next few months may pass with the utmost freedom and with the least possible delay from each side of the sea to the other.

May I not hope, Gentlemen of the Congress, that in the delicate tasks I shall have to perform on the other side of the sea, in my efforts truly and faithfully to interpret the principles and purposes of the country we love, I may have the encouragement and the added strength of your united support? I realize the magnitude and difficulty of the duty I am undertaking; I am poignantly aware of its grave responsibilities. I am the servant of the Nation. I can have no private thought or purpose of my own in performing such an errand. I go to give the best that is in me to the common settlements which I must now assist in arriving at in conference with the other working heads of the associated Governments. I shall count upon your friendly countenance and encouragement. I shall not be inaccessible. The cables and the wireless will render me available for any counsel or service you may desire of me, and I shall be happy in the thought that I am constantly in touch with the weighty matters of domestic policy with which we shall have to deal. I shall make my absence as brief as possible and shall hope to return with the happy assurance that it has been possible to translate into action the great ideals for which America has striven.

RESPONSE TO THE WELCOMING ADDRESS
OF PRESIDENT POINCARÉ OF FRANCE,
DECEMBER 14, 1918

The Quick Contact of Sympathy

MR. PRESIDENT: I am deeply indebted to you for your gracious greeting. It is very delightful to find myself in France and to feel the quick contact of sympathy and unaffected friendship between the representatives of the United States and the representatives of France. You have been very generous in what you were pleased to say about myself, but I feel that what I have said and what I have tried to do has been said and done only in an attempt to speak the thought of the people of the United States truly and to carry that thought out in action. From the first the thought of the people of the United States turned toward something more than the mere winning of this war. It turned to the establishment of eternal principles of right and justice. It realized that merely to win the war was not enough; that it must be won in such a way and the questions raised by it settled in such a way as to insure the future peace of the world and lay the foundation for the freedom and happiness of its many peoples and nations.

Never before has war worn so terrible a visage or exhibited more grossly the debasing influence of illicit ambitions. I am sure that I shall look upon the ruin wrought by the armies of the Central Empires with the same repulsion and deep indignation that it stirs in the hearts of the men of France and Belgium, and I appreciate, as you do, sir, the necessity of such action in the final settlement of the issues of the war as will not only rebuke such acts of terror and spoliation, but make men everywhere aware that they cannot be ventured upon without the certainty of just punishment.

I know with what ardor and enthusiasm the soldiers and sailors of the United States have given the best that was in them to this war of redemption. They have expressed the true spirit of America. They believe their ideals to be acceptable to free peoples everywhere and are rejoiced to have played the part they have played in giving reality to those ideals in coöperation with the armies of the Allies. We are proud of the part they have played and we are happy that they should have been associated with such comrades in a common cause.

It is with peculiar feelings, Mr. President, that I find myself in France joining with you in rejoicing over the victory that has been won. The ties that bind France and the United States are peculiarly close. I do not know in what other comradeship we could have fought with more zest or enthusiasm. It will daily be a matter of pleasure with me to be brought into consultation with the statesmen of France and her Allies in concerting the measures by which we may secure permanence for these happy relations of friendship and coöperation, and secure for the world at large such safety and freedom in its life as can be secured only by the constant association and coöperation of friends.

I greet you, sir, not only with deep personal respect but as the representative of the great people of France, and beg to bring you the greetings of another great people to whom the fortunes of France are of profound and lasting interest.

I raise my glass to the health of the President of the French Republic and to Madame Poincaré, and to the prosperity of France.

ADDRESS AT THE UNIVERSITY OF PARIS,
DECEMBER 21, 1918

A Great Wind Moving Through the World

MR. PRESIDENT, MR. RECTEUR: I feel very keenly the distinguished honor which has been conferred upon me by the great University of Paris, and it is very delightful to me also to have the honor of being inducted into the great company of scholars whose life and fame have made the history of the University of Paris a thing admired among men of cultivation in all parts of the world.

By what you have said, sir, of the theory of education which has been followed in France, and which I have tried to promote in the United States, I am tempted to venture upon a favorite theme.

I have always thought, sir, that the chief object of education was to awaken the spirit, and that inasmuch as literature whenever it touched its great and higher notes was an expression of the spirit of mankind, the best induction into education was to feel the pulses of humanity which had beaten from age to age through the utterances of men who had penetrated to the secrets of the human spirit. And I agree with the intimation which has been conveyed to-day that the terrible war through which we have just passed has not been only a war between nations, but that it has been also a war between systems of culture—the one system, the aggressive system, using science without conscience, stripping learning of its moral restraints, and using every faculty of the human mind to do wrong to the whole race; the other system reminiscent of the high traditions of men, reminiscent of all those struggles, some of them obscure but others clearly revealed to the historian, of men of indomitable spirit everywhere struggling toward the right and seeking above all things else to be free. The triumph of freedom in this war means that spirits of that sort now dominate the world. There is a great wind of moral force moving through the world, and every man who opposes himself to that wind will go down in disgrace. The task of those who are gathered here, or will presently be gathered here, to make the settlements of this peace is greatly simplified by the fact that they are masters of no one; they are the servants of mankind, and if we do not heed the mandates of mankind we shall make ourselves the most conspicuous and deserved failures in the history of the world.

My conception of the League of Nations is just this, that it shall operate as the organized moral force of men throughout the world, and that whenever or wherever wrong and aggression are planned or contemplated, this searching light of conscience will be turned upon them and men everywhere will ask, "What are the purposes that you hold in your heart against the fortunes of the world?" Just a little exposure will settle most questions. If the Central powers had dared to discuss the purposes of this war for a single fortnight, it never would have happened, and if, as should be, they were forced to discuss it for a year, war would have been inconceivable.

So I feel that this war is, as has been said more than once to-day, intimately related with the university spirit. The university spirit is intolerant of all the things that put the human mind under restraint. It is intolerant of everything that seeks to retard the advancement of ideals, the acceptance of the truth, the purification of life; and every university man can ally himself with the forces of the present time with the feeling that now at last the spirit of truth, the spirit to which universities have devoted themselves, has prevailed and is triumphant. If there is one point of pride that I venture to entertain, it is that it has been my privilege in some measure to interpret the university spirit in the public life of a great nation, and I feel that in honoring me today in this unusual and conspicuous manner you have first of all honored the people whom I represent. The spirit that I try to express I know to be their spirit, and in proportion as I serve them I believe that I advance the cause of freedom.

I, therefore, wish to thank you, sir, from the bottom of my heart for a distinction which has in a singular way crowned my academic career.

ADDRESS AT BUCKINGHAM PALACE,
DECEMBER 27, 1918

We Have Used the Great Words

YOUR MAJESTY: I am deeply complimented by the gracious words which you have uttered. The welcome which you have given me and Mrs. Wilson has been so warm, so natural, so evidently from the heart that we have been more than pleased; we have been touched by it, and I believe that I correctly interpret that welcome as embodying not only your own generous spirit towards us personally, but also as expressing for yourself and the great nation over which you preside that same feeling for my people, for the people of the United States. For you and I, sir—I temporarily—embody the spirit of two great nations; and whatever strength I have, and whatever authority, I possess only so long and so far as I express the spirit and purpose of the American people.

Any influence that the American people have over the affairs of the world is measured by their sympathy with the aspirations of free men everywhere. America does love freedom, and I believe that she loves freedom unselfishly. But if she does not, she will not and cannot help the influence to which she justly aspires. I have had the privilege, sir, of conferring with the leaders of your own Government and with the spokesmen of the Governments of France and of Italy, and I am glad to say that I have the same conceptions that they have of the significance and scope of the duty upon which we have met. We have used great words, all of us, we have used the great words "right" and "justice," and now we are to prove whether or not we understand those words and how they are to be applied to the particular settlements which must conclude this war. And we must not only understand them, but we must have the courage to act upon our understanding.

Yet, after I have uttered the word "courage," it comes into my mind that it would take more courage to resist the great moral tide now running in the world than to yield to it, than to obey it. There is a great tide running in the hearts of men. The hearts of men have never beaten so singularly in unison before. Men have never before been so conscious of their brotherhood. Men have never before realized how little difference there was between right and justice in one latitude and in another, under one sovereignty and under another; and it will be our high privilege, I believe, sir, not only to apply the moral judgments of the world to the particular settlements which we shall attempt, but also to organize the moral force of the world to preserve those settlements, to steady the forces of mankind and to make the right and the justice to which great nations like our own have devoted themselves the predominant and controlling force of the world.

There is something inspiriting in knowing that this is the errand that we have come on. Nothing less than this would have justified me in leaving the important tasks which fall upon me upon the other side of the sea, nothing but the consciousness that nothing else compares with this in dignity and importance. Therefore it is the more delightful to find myself in the company of a body of men united in ideal and in purpose, to feel that I am privileged to unite my thought with yours in carrying forward those standards which we are so proud to hold high and to defend.

REPLY TO A CHURCH COMMITTEE,
LONDON, DECEMBER 28, 1918

The Sanctions of Religion

GENTLEMEN: I am very much honored, and might say touched, by this beautiful address that you have just read, and it is very delightful to feel the comradeship of spirit which is indicated by a gathering like this.

You are quite right, sir, in saying that I do recognize the sanctions of religion in these times of perplexity with matters so large to settle that no man can feel that his mind can compass them. I think one would go crazy if he did not believe in Providence. It would be a maze without a clue. Unless there were some supreme guidance we would despair of the results of human counsel. So that it is with genuine sympathy that I acknowledge the spirit and thank you for the generosity of your address.

ADDRESS AT THE GUILD HALL,
LONDON, DECEMBER 28, 1918

Peace by Agreement of Minds

I have not yet been to the actual battlefields, but I have been with many of the men who have fought the battles, and the other day I had the pleasure of being present at a session of the French Academy when they admitted Marshal Joffre to their membership. The sturdy, serene soldier stood and uttered, not the words of triumph, but the simple words of affection for his soldiers; and the conviction which he summed up, in a sentence which I will not try accurately to quote but reproduce in its spirit, was that France must always remember that the small and the weak could never live free in the world unless the strong and the great always put their power and strength in the service of right. That is the afterthought—the thought that something must be done now not only to make the just settlements, that of course, but to see that the settlements remained and were observed and that honor and justice prevailed in the world. And as I have conversed with the soldiers, I have been more and more aware that they fought for something that not all of them had defined, but which all of them recognized the moment you stated it to them.

They fought to do away with an old order and to establish a new one, and the center and characteristic of the old order was that unstable thing which we used to call the "balance of power"—a thing in which the balance was determined by the sword which was thrown in the one side or the other; a balance which was determined by the unstable equilibrium of competitive interests; a balance which was maintained by jealous watchfulness and an antagonism of interests which, though it was generally latent, was always deep-seated. The men who have fought in this war have been the men from free nations who were determined that that sort of thing should end now and forever.

It is very interesting to me to observe how from every quarter, from every sort of mind, from every concert of counsel, there comes the suggestion that there must now be, not a balance of power, not one powerful group of nations set off against another, but a single overwhelming, powerful group of nations who shall be the trustee of the peace of the world. It has been delightful in my conferences with the leaders of your Government to find how our minds moved along exactly the same line, and how our thought was always that the key to the peace was the guarantee of the peace, not the items of it; that the items would be worthless unless there stood back of them a permanent concert of power for their maintenance. That is the most reassuring thing that has ever happened in the world.

When this war began the thought of a League of Nations was indulgently considered as the interesting thought of closeted students. It was thought of as one of those things that it was right to characterize by a name which as a university man I have always resented; it was said to be academic, as if that in itself were a condemnation, something that men could think about but never get. Now we find the practical leading minds of the world determined to get it. No such sudden and potent union of purpose has ever been witnessed in the world before. Do you wonder, therefore, gentlemen, that in common with those who represent you I am eager to get at the business and write the sentences down; and that I am particularly happy that the ground is cleared and the foundations laid—for we have already accepted the same body of principles? Those principles are clearly and definitely enough stated to make their application a matter which should afford no fundamental difficulty. And back of us is that imperative yearning of the world to have all disturbing questions quieted, to have all threats against peace silenced, to have just men everywhere come together for a common object. The peoples of the world want peace and they want it now, not merely by conquest of arms, but by agreement of mind.

ADDRESS AT HIS GRANDFATHER'S CHURCH,
CARLISLE, ENGLAND, DECEMBER 29, 1918

To Return to the Paths of Duty

It is with unaffected reluctance that I project myself into this solemn service. I remember my grandfather very well, and, remembering him as I do, I am confident that he would not approve of it. I remember how much he required. I remember the stern lessons of duty he spoke to me. I remember also painfully the things which he expected me to know which I did not know. I know there has come a change of times when a layman like myself is permitted to speak in a congregation. But I was reluctant because the feelings that have been excited in me are too intimate and too deep to permit of public expression. The memories that have come to me to-day of the mother who was born here are very affecting, and her quiet character, her sense of duty and dislike of ostentation, have come back to me with increasing force as those years of duty have accumulated. Yet perhaps it is appropriate that in a place of worship I should acknowledge my indebtedness to her and to her remarkable father, because, after all, what the world is now seeking to do is to return to the paths of duty, to turn away from the savagery of interest to the dignity of the performance of right. And I believe that as this war has drawn the nations temporarily together in a combination of physical force we shall now be drawn together in a combination of moral force that will be irresistible.

It is moral force that is irresistible. It is moral force as much as physical that has defeated the effort to subdue the world. Words have cut as deep as the sword. The knowledge that wrong was being attempted has aroused the nations. They have gone out like men upon a crusade. No other cause could have drawn so many nations together. They knew that an outlaw was abroad who purposed unspeakable things. It is from quiet places like this all over the world that the forces accumulate which presently will overbear any attempt to accomplish evil on a large scale. Like the rivulets gathering into the river and the river into the seas, there come from communities like this streams that fertilize the consciences of men, and it is the conscience of the world that we are trying to place upon the throne which others would usurp.

ADDRESS TO THE ITALIAN PARLIAMENT,
ROME, JANUARY 3, 1919

At the Opening of a New Age

We cannot stand in the shadow of this war without knowing that there are things awaiting us which are in some senses more difficult than those we have undertaken. While it is easy to speak of right and justice, it is sometimes difficult to work them out in practice, and there will require a purity of motive and disinterestedness of object which the world has never witnessed before in the councils of nations. It is for that reason that it seems to me that you will forgive me if I lay some of the elements of the new situation before you for a moment. The distinguishing fact of this war is that great empires have gone to pieces, and the characteristic of those empires was that they held different peoples reluctantly together under the coercion of force and the guidance of intrigue. The great difficulty among such States as those of the Balkans has been that they were always accessible to secret influence; that they were always being penetrated by intrigue of one sort and another; and that north of them lay disturbed populations which were held together, not by sympathy and friendship, but by the coercive force of a military power. Now the intrigue is checked and the bands are broken, and what are we going to do to provide a new cement to hold these people together? They have not been accustomed to being independent. They must now be independent. I am sure that you recognize the principle as I do that it is not our privilege to say what sort of government they shall set up, but we are friends of these people and it is our duty as their friends to see to it that some kind of protection is thrown around them, something supplied which will hold them together. There is only one thing that holds nations together, if you exclude force, and that is friendship and good will. The only thing that binds men together is friendship and by the same token the only thing that binds nations together is friendship.

Therefore, our task at Paris is to organize the friendship of the world, to see to it that all the moral forces that make for right and justice and liberty are united and are given a vital organization to which the peoples of the world will readily and gladly respond. In other words, our task is no less colossal than this, to set up a new international psychology, to have a new atmosphere. I am happy to say that in my dealings with the distinguished gentlemen who lead your nation and those who lead France and England, I feel that atmosphere gathering, that desire to do justice, that desire to establish friendliness, that desire to make peace rest upon right; and with this common purpose no obstacle need be formidable. The only use of an obstacle is to be overcome. All that an obstacle does with brave men is, not to frighten them, but to challenge them. So that it ought to be our pride to overcome everything that stands in the way.

We know that there cannot be another balance of power. That has been tried and found wanting, for the best of all reasons that it does not stay balanced inside itself, and a weight which does not hold together cannot constitute a makeweight in the affairs of men. Therefore, there must be something substituted for the balance of power, and I am happy to find everywhere in the air of these great nations the conception that that thing must be a thoroughly united league of nations. What men once considered theoretical and idealistic turns out to be practical and necessary. We stand at the opening of a new age in which a new statesmanship will, I am confident, lift mankind to new levels of endeavor and achievement.

ADDRESS AT THE UNIVERSITY OF TURIN,
JANUARY 6, 1919

A Human Web No Power Can Destroy

MR. RECTOR, GENTLEMEN OF THE FACULTIES OF THE UNIVERSITY, LADIES AND GENTLEMEN: It is with a feeling of being in very familiar scenes that I come here today. So soon as I entered the quadrangle and heard the voices of the students it seemed to me as if the greater part of my life had come back to me, and I am particularly honored that this distinguished university should have received me among its sons. . . .

When I think seriously of the significance of a ceremony like this, some very interesting reflections come to my mind, because, after all, the comradeships of letters, the intercommunications of thought, are among the permanent things of the world. There was a time when scholars, speaking in the beautiful language in which the last address was made, were the only international characters of the world; when there was only one international community: the community of scholars. As ability to read and write has extended, international intercommunication has extended. But one permanent common possession has remained, and that is the validity of sound thinking. When men have thought along the lines of philosophy, have had revealed to them the visions of poetry, have worked out in their studies the permanent lines of law, have realized the great impulses of humanity, and then begun to advance human life materially by the instrumentalities of science, they have been weaving a human web which no power can permanently tear and destroy. And so in being taken into the comradeship of this university I feel that I am being taken into one of those things which will always bind the nations together. After all, when we are seeking peace, we are seeking nothing else than this, that men shall think the same thoughts, govern their conduct by the same ideals, entertain the same purposes, love their own people, but also love humanity, and above all else, love that great and indestructible thing which we call justice and right.

These things are greater than we are. These are our real masters, for they dominate our spirits, and the universities will have forgotten their duty when they cease to weave this immortal web. It is one of the chief griefs of this great war that the universities of the Central Empires used the thoughts of science to destroy mankind. It is the duty of the great universities of Italy and of the rest of the world to redeem science from this disgrace, to show that the pulse of humanity beats in the classroom, that the pulse of humanity also beats in the laboratory, and that there are sought out, not the secrets of death but the secrets of life.

Chapter Fifteen

IMAGE OF THE LEAGUE

WILSON had seized upon the League of Nations as the cause that could give meaning to America's entrance into the war. At Paris he faced the task of turning the ideal into reality. This chapter contains his speeches to the Peace Conference, in which the concept of the League was set forth. But exposition was soon mixed with defense. A brief return to America in February 1918 saw Wilson already confronting opposition; and the great speech on Memorial Day at Suresnes Cemetery, near Paris, reflected a grim awareness that "the airs of an older day" were beginning to stir again.

ADDRESS BEFORE THE PEACE CONFERENCE,
PARIS, JANUARY 25, 1919

A Machinery to Maintain Peace

MR. CHAIRMAN: I consider it a distinguished privilege to be permitted to open the discussion in this conference on the League of Nations. We have assembled for two purposes, to make the present settlements which have been rendered necessary by this war, and also to secure the peace of the world, not only by the present settlements, but by the arrangements we shall make at this conference for its maintenance. The League of Nations seems to me to be necessary for both of these purposes. There are many complicated questions connected with the present settlements which perhaps cannot be successfully worked out to an ultimate issue by the decisions we shall arrive at here. I can easily conceive that many of these settlements will need subsequent reconsideration, that many of the decisions we make shall need subsequent alteration in some degree;

for, if I may judge by my own study of some of these questions, they are not susceptible of confident judgments at present.

It is, therefore, necessary that we should set up some machinery by which the work of this conference should be rendered complete. We have assembled here for the purpose of doing very much more than making the present settlements. We are assembled under very peculiar conditions of world opinion. I may say without straining the point that we are not representatives of Governments, but representatives of peoples. It will not suffice to satisfy governmental circles anywhere. It is necessary that we should satisfy the opinion of mankind. The burdens of this war have fallen in an unusual degree upon the whole population of the countries involved. I do not need to draw for you the picture of how the burden has been thrown back from the front upon the older men, upon the women, upon the children, upon the homes of the civilized world, and how the real strain of the war has come where the eye of government could not reach, but where the heart of humanity beats. We are bidden by these people to make a peace which will make them secure. We are bidden by these people to see to it that this strain does not come upon them again, and I venture to say that it has been possible for them to bear this strain because they hoped that those who represented them could get together after this war and make such another sacrifice unnecessary.

It is a solemn obligation on our part, therefore, to make permanent arrangements that justice shall be rendered and peace maintained. This is the central object of our meeting. Settlements may be temporary, but the action of the nations in the interest of peace and justice must be permanent. We can set up permanent processes. We may not be able to set up permanent decisions. Therefore, it seems to me that we must take, so far as we can, a picture of the world into our minds. Is it not a startling circumstance, for one thing, that the great discoveries of science, that the quiet studies of men in laboratories, that the thoughtful developments which have taken place in quiet lecture rooms, have now been turned to the destruction of civilization? The powers of destruction have not so much multiplied as gained facility. The enemy whom we have just overcome had at his seats of learning some of the principal centers of scientific study and discovery, and he used them in order to make destruction sudden and complete; and only the watchful, continuous coöperation of men can see to it that science, as well as armed men, is kept within the harness of civilization.

The Fortunes of Mankind Are in the Hands of the Plain People

In a sense the United States is less interested in this subject than the other nations here assembled. With her great territory and her extensive sea borders, it is less likely that the United States should suffer from the attacks of enemies than that many of the other nations here should suffer; and the ardor of the United States—for it is a very deep and genuine ardor—for the society of nations is not an ardor springing out of fear or apprehension, but an ardor springing out of the ideals which have come to consciousness in this war. In coming into this war the United States never for a moment thought that she was intervening in the politics of Europe or the politics of Asia or the politics of any part of the world. Her thought was that all the world had now become conscious that there was a single cause which turned upon the issues of this war. That was the cause of justice and of liberty for men of every kind and place. Therefore, the United States should feel that its part in this war had been played in vain if there ensued upon it merely a body of European settlements. It would feel that it could not take part in guaranteeing those European settlements unless that guarantee involved the continuous superintendence of the peace of the world by the associated nations of the world.

Therefore, it seems to me that we must concert our best judgment in order to make this League of Nations a vital thing—not merely a formal thing, not an occasional thing, not a thing sometimes called into life to meet an exigency, but always functioning in watchful attendance upon the interests of the nations—and that its continuity should be a vital continuity; that it should have functions that are continuing functions and that do not permit an intermission of its watchfulness and of its labor; that it should be the eye of the nations to keep watch upon the common interest, an eye that does not slumber, an eye that is everywhere watchful and attentive.

And if we do not make it vital, what shall we do? We shall disappoint the expectations of the peoples. This is what their thought centers upon. I have had the very delightful experience of visiting several nations since I came to this side of the water, and every time the voice of the body of the people reached me through any representative, at the front of its plea stood the hope for the League of Nations. Gentlemen, the select classes of mankind are no longer the governors of mankind. The fortunes of mankind are now in the hands of the plain people of the whole world. Satisfy them, and you have justified their confidence not only, but established peace. Fail to satisfy them, and no arrangement that you can make will either set up or steady the peace of the world.

You can imagine, gentlemen, I dare say, the sentiments and the purpose with which representatives of the United States support this great project for a League of Nations. We regard it as the keystone of the whole program which expressed our purposes and ideals in this war and which the associated nations have accepted as the basis of the settlement. If we returned to the United States without having made every effort in our power to realize this program, we should return to meet the merited scorn of our fellow citizens. For they are a body that constitutes a great democracy. They expect their leaders to speak their thoughts and no private purpose of their own. They expect their representatives to be their servants. We have no choice but to obey their mandate. . . .

To Attain the Ends for Which We Fought

I hope, Mr. Chairman, that when it is known, as I feel confident it will be known, that we have adopted the principle of the League of Nations and mean to work out that principle in effective action, we shall by that single thing have lifted a great part of the load of anxiety from the hearts of men everywhere. We stand in a peculiar case. As I go about the streets here I see everywhere the American uniform. Those men came into the war after we had uttered our purposes. They came as crusaders, not merely to win a war, but to win a cause; and I am responsible to them, for it fell to me to formulate the purposes for which I asked them to fight, and I, like them, must be a crusader for these things, whatever it costs and whatever it may be necessary to do, in honor, to accomplish the object for which they fought. I have been glad to find from day to day that there is no question of our standing alone in this matter, for there are champions of this cause upon every hand. I am merely avowing this in order that you may understand why, perhaps, it fell to us, who are disengaged from the politics of this great continent and of the Orient, to suggest that this was the keystone of the arch and why it occurred to the generous mind of our president to call upon me to open this debate. It is not because we alone represent this idea, but because it is our privilege to associate ourselves with you in representing it.

I have only tried in what I have said to give you the fountains of the enthusiasm which is within us for this thing, for those fountains spring, it seems to me, from all the ancient wrongs and sympathies of mankind, and the very pulse of the world seems to beat to the surface in this enterprise.

ADDRESS TO THE FRENCH CHAMBER OF DEPUTIES,
PARIS, FEBRUARY 3, 1919

The Comradeship of Freedom

I am keenly aware of the unusual and distinguished honor you are paying me by permitting me to meet you in this place and address you from this historic platform. Indeed, sir, as day follows day, and week has followed week, in this hospitable land of France, I have felt the sense of comradeship every day become more and more vivid; the thrill of sympathy every day become more and more intimate, and it has seemed to me that the meaning of history was being singularly made clear. We knew before this war began that France and America were united in affection. We knew the occasion which drew the two nations together in those years, which now seem so far away, when the world was first beginning to thrill with the impulse of human liberty, when soldiers of France came to help the struggling little Republic of America to get to its feet and proclaim one of the first victories of freedom.

We have never forgotten that, but we did not see the full meaning of it. A hundred years and more went by and the spindles were slowly weaving the web of history. We did not see the pattern until the threads began to come together; we did not see it to be complete, the whole art of the designer to be made plain. For look what has happened. In that far-off day when France came to the assistance of America, America was fighting Great Britain, and now she is linked as closely to Great Britain as she is to France. We see now how these apparently diverging lines of history are coming together. The nations which once stood in battle array against one another are now shoulder and shoulder facing a common enemy. It was a long time before we saw that, and in the last four years something has happened that is unprecedented in the history of mankind. It is nothing less than this, that bodies of men on both sides of the sea and in all parts of the world have come to realize their comradeship in freedom.

France, in the meantime, as we have so often said, stood at the frontier of freedom. Her lines ran along the very lines that divided the home of freedom from the home of military despotism: Hers was the immediate peril. Hers was the constant dread. Hers was the most pressing necessity of preparation; and she had constantly to ask herself this question, "If the blow falls, who will come to our assistance?" And the question was answered in the most unexpected way. Her allies came to her assistance, but many more than her allies. The free peoples of the world came to her assistance. And then America paid her debt of gratitude to France by sending her sons to fight upon the soil of France. She did more. She assisted in drawing the forces of the world together in order that France might never again feel her isolation, in order that France might never again feel that hers was a lonely peril, would never again have to ask the question who would come to her assistance.

France Stands as a Frontier

For the alternative is a terrible alternative for France. I do not need to point out to you that east of you in Europe the future is full of questions. Beyond the Rhine, across Germany, across Poland, across Russia, across Asia, there are questions unanswered, and they may be for the present unanswerable. France still stands at a frontier. France still stands in the presence of those threatening and unanswerable questions,—threatening because unanswered,—stands waiting for the solution of matters which touch her directly and intimately and constantly. And if she must stand alone, what must she do? She must be constantly armed. She must put upon her people a constant burden of taxation. She must undergo a sacrifice that may become intolerable. And not only she, but the other nations of the world, must do the like. They must stand armed cap-à-pie. They must be ready for any terrible incident of injustice. The thing is not conceivable. I visited the other day a portion of the devastated regions of France. I saw the noble city of Rheims in ruin, and I could not help saying to myself, "Here is where the blow fell, because the rulers of the world did not sooner see how to prevent it." The rulers of the world have been thinking of the relations of governments and forgetting the relations of peoples. They have been thinking of the maneuvers of international dealings, when what they ought to have been thinking of was the fortunes of men and women and the safety of homes, and the care that they should take that their people should be happy because they were safe. They now know that the only way to do it is to make it certain that the same thing will happen always that happened this time, that there shall never be any doubt or waiting or surmise, but that whenever France or any other free people is threatened, the whole world will be ready to vindicate its liberty.

It is for that reason, I take it, that I find such a warm and intelligent enthusiasm in France for the society of nations. The society of nations, France with her keen vision, France with her prophetic vision, sees to be not only the need of France, but the need of mankind. And she sees that the sacrifices which are necessary for the establishment of the society of nations are not to be compared with the sacrifices that will be necessary if she does not have the society. A little abatement of independence of action is not to be compared with the constant dread of another catasrophe.

The whole world's heart has bled that the catastrophe should have fallen on the fair cities and areas of France. There was no more beautiful country. There was no more prosperous country. There was no more free-spirited people in it. All the world admired France, and none of the world grudged France her greatness and her prosperity, except those who grudged her her liberty. And it profited us, terrible as the cost has been, to witness what has happened, to see with the physical eye what has happened because injustice was wrought. The President of the Chamber has pictured as I cannot picture the appalling sufferings, the terrible tragedy of France, but it is a tragedy which need not be repeated. As the pattern of history has disclosed itself, it has disclosed the hearts of men drawing towards one another. Comradeships have become vivid. The purpose of association has become evident. The nations of the world are about to consummate a brotherhood which will make it unnecessary in the future to maintain those crushing armaments which make the peoples suffer almost as much in peace as they suffer in war.

ADDRESS BEFORE THE PEACE CONFERENCE,
PARIS, FEBRUARY 14, 1919

A Living Thing Is Born

Armed force is in the background in this program, but it *is* in the background, and if the moral force of the world will not suffice, the physical force of the world shall. But that is the last resort, because this is intended as a constitution of peace, not as a league of war.

The simplicity of the document seems to me to be one of its chief virtues, because, speaking for myself, I was unable to foresee the variety of circumstances with which this League would have to deal. I was unable, therefore, to plan all the machinery that might be necessary to meet differing and unexpected contingencies. Therefore, I should say of this document that it is not a straitjacket, but a vehicle of life. A living thing is born, and we must see to it that the clothes we put upon it do not hamper it—a vehicle of power, but a vehicle in which power may be varied at the discretion of those who exercise it and in accordance with the changing circumstances of the time. And yet, while it is elastic, while it is general in its terms, it is definite in the one thing that we were called upon to make definite. It is a definite guarantee of peace. It is a definite guarantee by word against aggression. It is a definite guarantee against the things which have just come near bringing the whole structure of civilization into ruin. Its purposes do not for a moment lie vague. Its purposes are declared and its powers made unmistakable.

It is not in contemplation that this should be merely a League to secure the peace of the world. It is a League which can be used for coöperation in any international matter. That is the significance of the provision introduced concerning labor. There are many ameliorations of labor conditions which can be effected by conference and discussion. I anticipate that there will be a very great usefulness in the bureau of labor which it is contemplated shall be set up by the League. While men and women and children who work have been in the background through long ages, and sometimes seemed to be forgotten, while Governments have had their watchful and suspicious eyes upon the maneuvers of one another, while the thought of statesmen has been about structural action and the large transactions of commerce and of finance, now, if I may believe the picture which I see, there comes into the foreground the great body of the laboring people of the world, the men and women and children upon whom the great burden of sustaining the world must from day to day fall, whether we wish it to do so or not; people who go to bed tired and wake up without the stimulation of lively hope. These people will be drawn into the field of international consultation and help, and will be among the wards of the combined Governments of the world. There is, I take leave to say, a very great step in advance in the mere conception of that.

Then, as you will notice, there is an imperative article concerning the publicity of all international agreements. Henceforth no member of the League can claim any agreement valid which it has not registered with the secretary general, in whose office, of course, it will be subject to the examination of anybody representing a member of the League. And the duty is laid upon the secretary general to publish every document of that sort at the earliest possible time.

I suppose most persons who have not been conversant with the business of foreign offices do not realize how many hundreds of these agreements are made in a single year, and how difficult it might be to publish the more unimportant of them immediately—how uninteresting it would be to most of the world to publish them immediately—but even they must be published just so soon as it is possible for the secretary general to publish them.

For the Helpless and Undeveloped Peoples of the World

Then there is a feature about this covenant which to my mind is one of the greatest and most satisfactory advances that has been made. We are done with annexations of helpless people, meant in some instances by some powers to be used merely for exploitation. We recognize in the most solemn manner that the helpless and undeveloped peoples of the world, being in that condition, put an obligation upon us to look after their interest primarily before we use them for our interest; and that in all cases of this sort hereafter it shall be the duty of the League to see that the nations who are assigned as the tutors and advisers and directors of those peoples shall look to their interest and to their development before they look to the interests and material desires of the mandatory nation itself. There has been no greater advance than this, gentlemen. If you look back upon the history of the world you will see how helpless peoples have too often been a prey to powers that had no conscience in the matter. It has been one of the many distressing revelations of recent years that the great power which has just been happily defeated put intolerable burdens and injustices upon the helpless people of some of the colonies which it annexed to itself; that its interest was rather their extermination than their development; that the desire was to possess their land for European purposes, and not to enjoy their confidence in order that mankind might be lifted in those places to the next higher level. Now, the world, expressing its conscience in law, says there is an end of that. Our consciences shall be applied to this thing. States will be picked out which have already shown that they can exercise a conscience in this matter, and under their tutelage the helpless peoples of the world will come into a new light and into a new hope.

So I think I can say of this document that it is at one and the same time a practical document and a humane document. There is a pulse of sympathy in it. There is a compulsion of conscience throughout it. It is practical, and yet it is intended to purify, to rectify, to elevate. And I want to say that, so far as my observation instructs me, this is in one sense a belated document. I believe that the conscience of the world has long been prepared to express itself in some such way. We are not just now discovering our sympathy for these people and our interest in them. We are simply expressing it, for it has long been felt, and in the administration of the affairs of more than one of the great States represented here—so far as I know, of all the great States that are represented here—that humane impulse has already expressed itself in their dealings with their colonies whose peoples were yet at a low stage of civilization. We have had many instances of colonies lifted into the sphere of complete self-government. This is not the discovery of a principle. It is the universal application of a principle. It is the agreement of the great nations which have tried to live by these standards in their separate administrations to unite in seeing that their common force and their common thought and intelligence are lent to this great and humane enterprise. I think it is an occasion, therefore, for the most profound satisfaction that this humane decision should have been reached in a matter for which the world has long been waiting and until a very recent period thought that it was still too early to hope.

Many terrible things have come out of this war, gentlemen, but some very beautiful things have come out of it. Wrong has been defeated, but the rest of the world has been more conscious than it ever was before of the majesty of right. People that were suspicious of one another can now live as friends and comrades in a single family, and desire to do so. The miasma of distrust, of intrigue, is cleared away. Men are looking eye to eye and saying, "We are brothers and have a common purpose. We did not realize it before, but now we do realize it, and this is our covenant of fraternity and of friendship."

ADDRESS ON RETURN TO AMERICA,
BOSTON, FEBRUARY 24, 1919

The Conference Seems to Go Slowly

The proudest thing I have to report to you is that this great country of ours is trusted throughout the world. I have not come to report the proceedings or results of the proceedings of the peace conference—that would be premature. I can say that I have received very happy impressions from this conference, impressions that while there are many differences of judgment, while there are some divergencies of object, there is nevertheless a common spirit and a common realization of the necessity of setting up a new standard of right in the world. Because the men who are in conference in Paris realize as keenly as any American can realize that they are not masters of their people, that they are servants of their people, and that the spirit of their people has awakened to a new purpose and a new conception of their power to realize that purpose, and that no man dare go home from that conference and report anything less noble than was expected of it.

The conference seems to you to go slowly; from day to day in Paris it seems to go slowly, but I wonder if you realize the complexity of the task which is undertaken. It seems as if the settlements of this war affect, and affect directly, every great, and I sometimes think every small, nation in the world. And no one decision can prudently be made which is not properly linked in with the great series of other decisions which must accompany it, and it must be reckoned in with the final result if the real quality and character of that result is to be properly judged.

What we are doing is to hear the whole case, hear it from the mouths of the men most interested, hear it from those who are officially commissioned to state it, hear the rival claims, hear the claims that affect new nationalities, that affect new areas of the world, that affect new commercial and economic connections that have been established by the great world war through which we have gone. And I have been struck by the moderateness of those who have represented national claims. I can testify that I have nowhere seen the gleam of passion. I have seen earnestness, I have seen tears come to the eyes of men who plead for downtrodden people whom they were privileged to speak for, but they were not tears of anger, they were tears of ardent hope; and I do not see how any man can fail to have been subdued by these pleas, subdued to this feeling that he was not there to assert an individual judgment of his own but to try to assist the cause of humanity.

If America Were to Fail the World

I met a group of scholars when I was in Paris. Some gentlemen from one of the Greek universities who had come to see me and in whose presence, or rather in the presence of the traditions of learning, I felt very young, indeed. And I told them that I had had one of the delightful revenges that sometimes come to men. All my life I have heard men speak with a sort of condescension of ideals and of idealists, and particularly of those separated, encloistered persons whom they choose to term academic, who were in the habit of uttering ideals in a free atmosphere when they clash with nobody in particular. And I said I have had this sweet revenge. Speaking with perfect frankness in the name of the people of the United States I have uttered as the objects of this great war ideals, and nothing but ideals, and the war has been won by that inspiration.

Men were fighting with tense muscle and lowered head until they came to realize those things, feeling they were fighting for their lives and their country, and when these accents of what it was all about reached them from America they lifted their heads, they raised their eyes to heaven, then they saw men in khaki coming across the sea in the spirit of crusaders, and they found these were strange men, reckless of danger not only, but reckless because they seemed to see something that made that danger worth while. Men have testified to me in Europe that our men were possessed by something that they could only call religious fervor. They were not like any of the other soldiers. They had vision; they had dream, and they were fighting in dream; and fighting in dream they turned the whole tide of battle, and it never came back. And now do you realize that this confidence we have established throughout the world imposes a burden upon us—if you choose to call it a burden. It is one of those burdens which any nation ought to be proud to carry. Any man who resists the present tides that run in the world will find himself thrown upon a shore so high and barren that it will seem as if he had been separated from his human kind forever.

Europe that I left the other day was full of something that it had never felt fill its heart so full before. It was full of hope. The Europe of the second year of the war—the Europe of the third year of the war—was sinking to a sort of stubborn desperation. They did not see any great thing to be achieved even when the war should be won. They hoped there would be some salvage; they hoped they could clear their territories of invading armies; they hoped they could set up their homes and start their industries afresh. But they thought it would simply be a resumption of the old life that Europe had led—led in fear; led in anxiety; led in constant suspicion and watchfulness. They never dreamed that it would be a Europe of settled peace and justified hope. And now these ideals have wrought this new magic that all the peoples of Europe are buoyed up and confident in the spirit of hope, because they believe that we are at the eve of a new age in the world, when nations will understand one another; when nations will support one another in every just cause; when nations will unite every moral and every physical strength to see that right shall prevail. If America were at this juncture to fail the world, what would come of it?

I do not mean any disrespect to any other great people when I say that America is the hope of the world. And if she does not justify that hope results are unthinkable. Men will be thrown back upon bitterness of disappointment not only but bitterness of despair. All nations will be set up as hostile camps again; men at the peace conference will go home with their heads upon their breasts, knowing they have failed—for they were bidden not to come home from there until they did something more than sign the treaty of peace. Suppose we sign the treaty of peace and that it is the most satisfactory treaty of peace that the confusing elements of the modern world will afford and go home and think about our labors. We will know that we have left written upon the historic table at Versailles, upon which Vergennes and Benjamin Franklin wrote their names, nothing but a modern scrap of paper, no nations united to defend it, no great forces combined to make it good, no assurance given to the downtrodden and fearful people of the world that they shall be safe. Any man who thinks that America will take part in giving the world any such rebuff and disappointment as that does not know America. I invite him to test the sentiments of the Nation. . . .

Arrangements of the present peace cannot stand a generation unless they are guaranteed by the united forces of the civilized world. And if we do not guarantee them can you not see the picture? Your hearts have instructed you where the burden of this war fell. It did not fall upon national treasuries; it did not fall upon the instruments of administration; it did not fall upon the resources of nations. It fell upon the voiceless homes everywhere, where women were toiling in hope that their men would come back. When I think of the homes upon which dull despair would settle if this great hope is disappointed, I should wish for my part never to have had America play any part whatever in this attempt to emancipate the world.

But I talk as if there were any question. I have no more doubt of the verdict of America in this matter than I have doubt of the blood that is in me. And so, my fellow citizens, I have come back to report progress, and I do not believe that progress is going to stop short of the goal. The nations of the world have set their heads now to do a great thing, and they are not going to slacken their purpose. And when I speak of the nations of the world I do not speak of the governments of the world. I speak of peoples who constitute the nations of the world. They are in the saddle, and they are going to see to it that if their present governments do not do their will some other governments shall. The secret is out, and present governments know it.

Messengers of Hope

When I was in Italy, a little limping group of wounded Italian soldiers sought an interview with me. I could not conjecture what it was they were going to say to me, and with the greatest simplicity, with touching simplicity, they presented me with a petition in favor of the League of Nations.

Their wounded limbs, their impaired vitality, were the only argument they brought with them. It was a simple request that I lend all the influence that I might happen to have to relieve future generations of the sacrifices that they had been obliged to make. That appeal has remained in my mind as I have ridden along the streets in European capitals and heard cries of the crowd, cries for the League of Nations from lips of people who, I venture to say, had no particular notion of how it was to be done, who were not ready to propose a plan for a League of Nations, but whose hearts said that something by way of a combination of all men everywhere must come out of this. As we drove along country roads weak old women would come out and hold flowers to us. Why should they hold flowers up to strangers from across the Atlantic? Only because they believed that we were the messengers of friendship and of hope, and these flowers were their humble offerings of gratitude that friends from so great a distance should have brought them so great a hope.

It is inconceivable that we should disappoint them, and we shall not. The day will come when men in America will look back with swelling hearts and rising pride that they should have been privileged to make the sacrifice which it was necessary to make in order to combine their might and their moral power with the cause of justice for men of every kind everywhere.

They Gave the Greatest of All Gifts

No one with a heart in his breast, no American, no lover of humanity, can stand in the presence of these graves without the most profound emotion. These men who lie here are men of a unique breed. Their like has not been seen since the far days of the Crusades. Never before have men crossed the seas to a foreign land to fight for a cause which they did not pretend was peculiarly their own, but knew was the cause of humanity and of mankind. And when they came, they found fit comrades for their courage and their devotion. They found armies of liberty already in the field—men who, though they had gone through three years of fiery trial, seemed only to be just discovering, not for a moment losing, the high temper of the great affair, men seasoned in the bloody service of liberty. Joining hands with these, the men of America gave that greatest of all gifts, the gift of life and the gift of spirit.

It will always be a treasured memory on the part of those who knew and loved these men that the testimony of everybody who saw them in the field of action was of their unflinching courage, their ardor to the point of audacity, their full consciousness of the high cause they had come to serve, and their constant vision of the issue. It is delightful to learn from those who saw these men fight and saw them waiting in the trenches for the summons to the fight that they had a touch of the high spirit of religion, that they knew they were exhibiting a spirit as well as a physical might, and those of us who know and love America know that they were discovering to the whole world the true spirit and devotion of their motherland. It was America who came in the person of these men and who will forever be grateful that she was so represented.

And it is the more delightful to entertain these thoughts because we know that these men, though buried in a foreign, are not buried in an alien soil. They are at home, sleeping with the spirits of those who thought the same thoughts and entertained the same aspirations. The noble women of Suresnes have given evidence of the loving sense with which they received these dead as their own, for they have cared for their graves, they have made it their interest, their loving interest, to see that there was no hour of neglect, and that constantly through all the months that have gone by, the mothers at home should know that there were mothers here who remembered and honored their dead.

You have just heard in the beautiful letter from Monsieur Clemenceau what I believe to be the real message of France to us on a day like this, a message of genuine comradeship, a message of genuine sympathy, and I have no doubt that if our British comrades were here, they would speak in the same spirit and in the same language. For the beauty of this war is that it has brought a new partnership and a new comradeship and a new understanding into the field of the effort of the nations.

But it would be no profit to us to eulogize these illustrious dead if we did not take to heart the lesson which they have taught us. They are dead; they have done their utmost to show their devotion to a great cause, and they have left us to see to it that that cause shall not be betrayed, whether in war or in peace. It is our privilege and our high duty to consecrate ourselves afresh on a day like this to the objects for which they fought. It is not necessary that I should rehearse to you what those objects were. These men did not come across the sea merely to defeat Germany and her associated powers in the war. They came to defeat forever the things for which the Central powers stood, the sort of power they meant to assert in the world, the arrogant, selfish dominance which they meant to establish; and they came, moreover, to see to it that there should never be a war like this again. It is for us, particularly for us who are civilians, to use our proper weapons of counsel and agreement to see to it that there never is such a war again. The nation that should now fling out of this common concord of counsel would betray the human race.

The Airs of an Older Day are Beginning to Stir Again

So it is our duty to take and maintain the safeguards which will see to it that the mothers of America and the mothers of France and England and Italy and Belgium and all the other suffering nations should never be called upon for this sacrifice again. This can be done. It must be done. And it will be done. The thing that these men left us, though they did not in their counsels conceive it, is the great instrument which we have just erected in the League of Nations. The League of Nations is the covenant of governments that these men shall not have died in vain. I like to think that the dust of those sons of America who were privileged to be buried in their mother country will mingle with the dust of the men who fought for the preservation of the Union, and that as those men gave their lives in order that America might be united, these men have given their lives in order that the world might be united. Those men gave their lives in order to secure the freedom of a nation. These men have given theirs in order to secure the freedom of mankind; and I look forward to an age when it will be just as impossible to regret the results of their labor as it is now impossible to regret the result of the labor of those who fought for the Union of the States. I look for the time when every man who now puts his counsel against the united service of mankind under the League of Nations will be just as ashamed of it as if he now regretted the Union of the States.

You are aware, as I am aware, that the airs of an older day are beginning to stir again, that the standards of an old order are trying to assert themselves again. There is here and there an attempt to insert into the counsel of statesmen the old reckonings of selfishness and bargaining and national advantage which were the roots of this war, and any man who counsels these things advocates the renewal of the sacrifice which these men have made; for if this is not the final battle for right, there will be another that will be final. Let these gentlemen not suppose that it is possible for them to accomplish this return to an order of which we are ashamed and that we are ready to forget. They cannot accomplish it. The peoples of the world are awake and the peoples of the world are in the saddle. Private counsels of statesmen cannot now and cannot hereafter determine the destinies of nations. If we are not the servants of the opinion of mankind, we are of all men the littlest, the most contemptible, the least gifted with vision. If we do not know our age, we cannot accomplish our purpose, and this age is an age which looks forward, not backward; which rejects the standards of national selfishness that once governed the counsels of nations and demands that they shall give way to a new order of things in which the only questions will be, "Is it right?" "Is it just?" "Is it in the interest of mankind?"

We Have Listened to the Challenge

This is a challenge that no previous generation ever dared to give ear to. So many things have happened, and they have happened so fast, in the last four years, that I do not think many of us realize what it is that has happened. Think how impossible it would have been to get a body of responsible statesmen seriously to entertain the idea of the organization of a League of Nations four years ago! And think of the change that has taken place! I was told before I came to France that there would be confusion of counsel about this thing, and I found unity of counsel. I was told that there would be opposition, and I found union of action. I found the statesmen with whom I was about to deal united in the idea that we must have a League of Nations, that we could not merely make a peace settlement and then leave it to make itself effectual, but that we must conceive some common organization by which we should give our common faith that this peace would be maintained and the conclusions at which we had arrived should be made as secure as the united counsels of all the great nations that fought against Germany could make them. We have listened to the challenge, and that is the proof that there shall never be a war like this again.

Ladies and gentlemen, we all believe, I hope, that the spirits of these men are not buried with their bodies. Their spirits live. I hope—I believe—that their spirits are present with us at this hour. I hope that I feel the compulsion of their presence. I hope that I realize the significance of their presence. Think, soldiers, of those comrades of yours who are gone. If they were here, what would they say? They would not remember what you are talking about to-day. They would remember America which they left with their high hope and purpose. They would remember the terrible field of battle. They would remember what they constantly recalled in times of danger, what they had come for and how worth while it was to give their lives for it. And they would say, "Forget all the little circumstances of the day. Be ashamed of the jealousies that divide you. We command you in the name of those who, like ourselves, have died to bring the counsels of men together, and we remind you what America said she was born for. She was born, she said, to show mankind the way to liberty. She was born to make this great gift a common gift. She was born to show men the way of experience by which they might realize this gift and maintain it, and we adjure you in the name of all the great traditions of America to make yourselves soldiers now once for all in this common cause, where we need wear no uniform except the uniform of the heart, clothing ourselves with the principles of right and saying to men everywhere, 'You are our brothers and we invite you into the comradeship of liberty and of peace.'"

Let us go away hearing these unspoken mandates of our dead comrades.

If I may speak a personal word, I beg you to realize the compulsion that I myself feel that I am under. By the Constitution of our great country I was the commander-in-chief of these men. I advised the Congress to declare that a state of war existed. I sent these lads over here to die. Shall I—can I—ever speak a word of counsel which is inconsistent with the assurances I gave them when they came over? It is inconceivable. There is something better, if possible, that a man can give than his life, and that is his living spirit to a service that is not easy, to resist counsels that are hard to resist, to stand against purposes that are difficult to stand against, and to say, "Here stand I, consecrated in spirit to the men who were once my comrades and who are now gone, and who have left me under eternal bonds of fidelity."

CABLEGRAM TO THE AMERICAN PEOPLE,
JUNE 28, 1919

The Charter for a New World Order

The treaty of peace has been signed. If it is ratified and acted upon in full and sincere execution of its terms it will furnish the charter for a new order of affairs in the world. It is a severe treaty in the duties and penalties it imposes upon Germany, but it is severe only because great wrongs done by Germany are to be righted and repaired; it imposes nothing that Germany cannot do; and she can regain her rightful standing in the world by the prompt and honorable fulfillment of its terms. And it is much more than a treaty of peace with Germany. It liberates great peoples who have never before been able to find the way to liberty. It ends once for all, an old and intolerable order under which small groups of selfish men could use the peoples of great empires to serve their own ambition for power and dominion. It associates the free Governments of the world in a permanent league in which they are pledged to use their united power to maintain peace by maintaining right and justice. It makes international law a reality supported by imperative sanctions. It does away with the right of conquest and rejects the policy of annexation and substitutes a new order under which backward nations—populations which have not yet come to political consciousness and peoples who are ready for independence but not yet quite prepared to dispense with protection and guidance—shall no more be subjected to the domination and exploitation of a stronger nation, but shall be put under the friendly direction and afforded the helpful assistance of governments which undertake to be responsible to the opinion of mankind in the execution of their task by accepting the direction of the League of Nations. It recognizes the inalienable rights of nationality; the rights of minorities and the sanctity of religious belief and practice. It lays the basis for conventions which shall free the commercial intercourse of the world from unjust and vexatious restrictions and for every sort of international coöperation that will serve to cleanse the life of the world and facilitate its common action in beneficent service of every kind. It furnishes guarantees such as were never given or even contemplated before for the fair treatment of all who labor at the daily tasks of the world. It is for this reason that I have spoken of it as a great charter for a new order of affairs. There is ground here for deep satisfaction, universal reassurance, and confident hope.

Chapter Sixteen

THE LOST BATTLE

THE selections of this chapter go from Wilson's return to this country, after the signing of the Treaty, to his appeal—a man broken in body but not in spirit—to make the election of 1920 "a great and solemn referendum" upon America's joining the League. The presentation of the treaty to the Senate is one of Wilson's finest state papers. The Pueblo speech was the last delivered on his western tour, just before he was stricken. Its closing passages, reprinted here, are full of the nobility and pathos of a lost cause.

ADDRESS IN CARNEGIE HALL,
NEW YORK, JULY 9, 1919

I Have Come Back with My Heart Full

We have had our eyes very close upon our tasks at times, but whenever we lifted them we were accustomed to lift them to a distant horizon. We were aware that all the peoples of the earth had turned their faces toward us as those who were the friends of freedom and of right, and whenever we thought of national policy and of its reaction upon the affairs of the world we knew we were under bonds to do the large thing and the right thing. It is a privilege, therefore, beyond all computation for a man, whether in a great capacity or a small, to take part in the counsels and in the resolutions of a people like this.

I am afraid some people, some persons, do not understand that vision. They do not see it. They have looked too much upon the ground. They have thought too much of the interests that were near them and they have not listened to the voices of their neighbors. I have never had a moment's doubt as to where the heart and purpose of this people lay. When any one on the other side of the water has raised the question, "Will America come in and help?" I have said, "Of course America will come in and help." She cannot do anything else. She will not disappoint any high hope that has been formed of her. Least of all will she in this day of new-born liberty all over the world fail to extend her hand of support and assistance to those who have been made free.

I wonder if at this distance, you can have got any conception of the tragic intensity of the feeling of those peoples in Europe who have just had yokes thrown off them. Have you reckoned up in your mind how many peoples, how many nations, were held unwillingly under the yoke of the Austro-Hungarian Empire, under the yoke of Turkey, under the yoke of Germany? These yokes have been thrown off. These peoples breathe the air and look around to see a new day dawn about them, and whenever they think of what is going to fill that day with action they think first of us. They think first of the friends who through the long years have spoken for them, who were privileged to declare that they came into the war to release them, who said that they would not make peace upon any other terms than their liberty, and they have known that America's presence in the war and in the conference was the guarantee of the result. . . .

I have come back with my heart full of enthusiasm for throwing everything that I can, by way of influence or action, in with you to see that the peace is preserved—that when the long reckoning comes men may look back upon this generation of America and say, "They were true to the vision which they saw at their birth."

ADDRESS TO THE SENATE,
WASHINGTON, JULY 10, 1919

Presenting the Treaty for Ratification

The United States entered the war upon a different footing from every other nation except our associates on this side the sea. We entered it, not because our material interests were directly threatened or because any special treaty obligations to which we were parties had been violated, but only because we saw the supremacy, and even the validity, of right everywhere put in jeopardy and free government likely to be everywhere imperiled by the intolerable aggression of a power which respected neither right nor obligation and whose very system of government flouted the rights of the citizen as against the autocratic authority of his governors. And in the settlements of the peace we have sought no special reparation for ourselves, but only the restoration of right and the assurance of liberty everywhere that the effects of the settlement were to be felt. We entered the war as the disinterested champions of right and we interested ourselves in the terms of the peace in no other capacity.

The hopes of the nations allied against the Central Powers were at a very low ebb when our soldiers began to pour across the sea. There was everywhere amongst them, except in their stoutest spirits, a somber foreboding of disaster. The war ended in November, eight months ago, but you have only to recall what was feared in midsummer last, four short months before the armistice, to realize what it was that our timely aid accomplished alike for their morale and their physical safety. That first, never-to-be-forgotten action at Chateau-Thierry had already taken place. Our redoubtable soldiers and marines had already closed the gap the enemy had succeeded in opening for their advance upon Paris,—had already turned the tide of battle back towards the frontiers of France and begun the rout that was to save Europe and the world. Thereafter the Germans were to be always forced back, back, were never to thrust successfully forward again. And yet there was no confident hope. Anxious men and women, leading spirits of France, attended the celebration of the Fourth of July last year in Paris out of generous courtesy,— with no heart for festivity, little zest for hope. But they came away with something new at their hearts; they had themselves told us so. The mere sight of our men—of their vigor, of the confidence that showed itself in every movement of their stalwart figures and every turn of their swinging march, in their steady comprehending eyes and easy discipline, in the indomitable air that added spirit to everything they did,—made everyone who saw them that memorable day realize that something had happened that was much more than a mere incident in the fighting, something very different from the mere arrival of fresh troops. A great moral force had flung itself into the struggle. The fine physical force of those spirited men spoke of something more than bodily vigor. They carried the great ideals of a free people at their hearts and with that vision were unconquerable. Their very presence brought reassurance; their fighting made victory certain.

Ideals in the Midst of Violence

They were recognized as crusaders, and as their thousands swelled to millions their strength was seen to mean salvation. And they were fit men to carry such a hope and make good the assurance it forecast. Finer men never went into battle; and their officers were worthy of them. This is not the occasion upon which to utter a eulogy of the armies America sent to France, but perhaps, since I am speaking of their mission, I may speak also of the pride I shared with every American who saw or dealt with them there. They were the sort of men America would wish to be represented by, the sort of men every American would wish to claim as fellow countrymen and comrades in a great cause. They were terrible in battle, and gentle and helpful out of it, remembering the mothers and the sisters, the wives and the little children at home. They were free men under arms, not forgetting their ideals of duty in the midst of tasks of violence. I am proud to have had the privilege of being associated with them and of calling myself their leader.

But I speak now of what they meant to the men by whose sides they fought and to the people with whom they mingled with such utter simplicity, as friends who asked only to be of service. They were for all the visible embodiment of America. What they did made America and all that she stood for a living reality in the thoughts not only of the people of France but also of tens of millions of men and women throughout all the toiling nations of a world standing everywhere in peril of its freedom and of the loss of everything it held dear, in deadly fear that its bonds were never to be loosed, its hopes forever to be mocked and disappointed.

And the compulsion of what they stood for was upon us who represented America at the peace table. It was our duty to see to it that every decision we took part in contributed, so far as we were able to influence it, to quiet the fears and realize the hopes of the peoples who had been living in that shadow, the nations that had come by our assistance to their freedom. It was our duty to do everything that it was within our power to do to make the triumph of freedom and of right a lasting triumph in the assurance of which men might everywhere live without fear.

The Tasks of the Conference

Old entanglements of every kind stood in the way,—promises which Governments had made to one another in the days when might and right were confused and the power of the victor was without restraint. Engagements which contemplated any dispositions of territory, any extensions of sovereignty that might seem to be to the interest of those who had the power to insist upon them, had been entered into without thought of what the peoples concerned might wish or profit by; and these could not always be honorably brushed aside. It was not easy to graft the new order of ideas on the old, and some of the fruits of the grafting may, I fear, for a time be bitter. But, with very few exceptions, the men who sat with us at the peace table desired as sincerely as we did to get away from the bad influences, the illegitimate purposes, the demoralizing ambitions, the international counsels and expedients out of which the sinister designs of Germany had sprung as a natural growth.

It had been our privilege to formulate the principles which were accepted as the basis of the peace, but they had been accepted, not because we had come in to hasten and assure the victory and insisted upon them, but because they were readily acceded to as the principles to which honorable and enlightened minds everywhere had been bred. They spoke the conscience of the world as well as the conscience of America, and I am happy to pay my tribute of respect and gratitude to the able, forward-looking men with whom it was my privilege to coöperate for their unfailing spirit of coöperation, their constant effort to accommodate the interests they represented to the principles we were all agreed upon. The difficulties, which were many, lay in the circumstances, not often in the men. Almost without exception the men who led had caught the true and full vision of the problem of peace as an indivisible whole, a problem, not of mere adjustments of interest, but of justice and right action.

The atmosphere in which the Conference worked seemed created, not by the ambitions of strong governments, but by the hopes and aspirations of small nations and of peoples hitherto under bondage to the power that victory had shattered and destroyed. Two great empires had been forced into political bankruptcy, and we were the receivers. Our task was not only to make peace with the Central Empires and remedy the wrongs their armies had done. The Central Empires had lived in open violation of many of the very rights for which the war had been fought, dominating alien peoples over whom they had no natural right to rule, enforcing, not obedience, but veritable bondage, exploiting those who were weak for the benefit of those who were masters and overlords only by force of arms. There could be no peace until the whole order of Central Europe was set right.

That meant that new nations were to be created,—Poland, Czecho-Slovakia, Hungary itself. No part of ancient Poland had ever in any true sense become a part of Germany, or of Austria, or of Russia. Bohemia was alien in every thought and hope to the monarchy of which she had so long been an artificial part; and the uneasy partnership between Austria and Hungary had been one rather of interest than of kinship or sympathy. The Slavs whom Austria had chosen to force into her empire on the south were kept to their obedience by nothing but fear. Their hearts were with their kinsmen in the Balkans. These were all arrangements of power, not arrangements of natural union or association. It was the imperative task of those who would make peace and make it intelligently to establish a new order which would rest upon the free choice of peoples rather than upon the arbitrary authority of Hapsburgs or Hohenzollerns.

More than that, great populations bound by sympathy and actual kin to Rumania were also linked against their will to the conglomerate Austro-Hungarian monarchy or to other alien sovereignties, and it was part of the task of peace to make a new Rumania as well as a new slavic state clustering about Serbia.

And no natural frontiers could be found to these new fields of adjustment and redemption. It was necessary to look constantly forward to other related tasks. The German colonies were to be disposed of. They had not been governed; they had been exploited merely, without thought of the interest or even the ordinary human rights of their inhabitants.

The Turkish Empire, moreover, had fallen apart, as the Austro-Hungarian had. It had never had any real unity. It had been held together only by pitiless, inhuman force. Its peoples cried aloud for release, for succor from unspeakable distress, for all that the new day of hope seemed at last to bring within its dawn. Peoples hitherto in utter darkness were to be led out into the same light and given at last a helping hand. Undeveloped peoples and peoples ready for recognition but not yet ready to assume the full responsibilities of statehood were to be given adequate guarantees of friendly protection, guidance and assistance.

And out of the execution of these great enterprises of liberty sprang opportunities to attempt what statesmen had never found the way before to do; an opportunity to throw safeguards about the rights of racial, national and religious minorities by solemn international covenant; an opportunity to limit and regulate military establishments where they were most likely to be mischievous; an opportunity to effect a complete and systematic internationalization of waterways and railways which were necessary to the free economic life of more than one nation and to clear many of the normal channels of commerce of unfair obstructions of law or of privilege; and the very welcome opportunity to secure for labor the concerted protection of definite international pledges of principle and practice.

Old-Established Relationships Had Broken Down

These were not tasks which the Conference looked about it to find and went out of its way to perform. They were inseparable from the settlements of peace. They were thrust upon it by circumstances which could not be overlooked. The war had created them. In all quarters of the world old-established relationships had been disturbed or broken and affairs were at loose ends, needing to be mended or united again, but could not be made what they were before. They had to be set right by applying some uniform principle of justice or enlightened expediency. And they could not be adjusted by merely prescribing in a treaty what should be done. New states were to be set up which could not hope to live through their first period of weakness without assured support by the great nations that had consented to their creation and won for them their independence. Ill-governed colonies could not be put in the hands of governments which were to act as trustees for their people and not as their masters if there was to be no common authority among the nations to which they were to be responsible in the execution of their trust. Future international conventions with regard to the controls of waterways, with regard to illicit traffic of many kinds, in arms as in deadly drugs, or with regard to the adjustment of many varying international administrative arrangements could not be assured if the treaty were to provide no permanent common international agency, if its execution in such matters was to be left to the slow and uncertain processes of coöperation by ordinary methods of negotiation. If the Peace Conference itself was to be the end of coöperative authority and common counsel among the governments to which the world was looking to enforce justice and give pledges of an enduring settlement, regions like the Saar basin could not be put under a temporary administrative régime which did not involve a transfer of political sovereignty and which contemplated a final determination of its political connections by popular vote to be taken at a distant date; no free city like Danzig could be created which was, under elaborate international guarantees, to accept exceptional obligations with regard to the use of its port and exceptional relations with a State of which it was not to form a part; properly safeguarded plebiscites could not be provided for where populations were at some future date to make choice what sovereignty they would live under; no certain and uniform method of arbitration could be secured for the settlement of anticipated difficulties of final decision with regard to many matters dealt with in the treaty itself; the long-continued supervision of the task of reparation which Germany was to undertake to complete within the next generation might entirely break down; the reconsideration and revision of administrative arrangements and restrictions which the treaty prescribed but which it was recognized might not prove of lasting advantage or entirely fair if too long enforced would be impracticable. The promises governments were making to one another about the way in which labor was to be dealt with, by law not only but in fact as well, would remain a mere humane thesis if there was to be no common tribunal of opinion and judgment to which liberal statesmen could resort for the influences which alone might secure their redemption. A league of free nations had become a practical necessity. Examine the treaty of peace and you will find that everywhere throughout its manifold provisions its framers have felt obliged to turn to the League of Nations as an indispensable instrumentality for the maintenance of the new order it has been their purpose to set up in the world,—the world of civilized men.

The Necessity for the League

That there should be a League of Nations to steady the counsels and maintain the peaceful understandings of the world, to make, not treaties alone, but the accepted principles of international law as well, the actual rule of conduct among the governments of the world, had been one of the agreements accepted from the first as the basis of peace with the Central Powers. The statesmen of all the belligerent countries were agreed that such a league must be created to sustain the settlements that were to be effected. But at first I think there was a feeling among some of them that, while it must be attempted, the formation of such a league was perhaps a counsel of perfection which practical men, long experienced in the world of affairs, must agree to very cautiously and with many misgivings. It was only as the difficult work of arranging an all but universal adjustment of the world's affairs advanced from day to day from one stage of conference to another that it became evident to them that what they were seeking would be little more than something written upon paper, to be interpreted and applied by such methods as the chances of politics might make available if they did not provide a means of common counsel which all were obliged to accept, a common authority whose decisions would be recognized as decisions which all must respect.

And so the most practical, the most skeptical among them turned more and more to the League as the authority through which international action was to be secured, the authority without which, as they had come to see it, it would be difficult to give assured effect either to this treaty or to any other international understanding upon which they were to depend for the maintenance of peace. The fact that the Covenant of the League was the first substantive part of the treaty to be worked out and agreed upon, while all else was in solution, helped to make the formulation of the rest easier. The Conference was, after all, not to be ephemeral. The concert of nations was to continue, under a definite Covenant which had been agreed upon and which all were convinced was workable. They could go forward with confidence to make arrangements intended to be permanent. The most practical of the conferees were at last the most ready to refer to the League of Nations the superintendence of all interests which did not admit of immediate determination, of all administrative problems which were to require a continuing oversight. What had seemed a counsel of perfection had come to seem a plain counsel of necessity. The League of Nations was the practical statesman's hope of success in many of the most difficult things he was attempting.

And it had validated itself in the thought of every member of the Conference as something much bigger, much greater every way, than a mere instrument for carrying out the provisions of a particular treaty. It was universally recognized that all the peoples of the world demanded of the Conference that it should create such a continuing concert of free nations as would make wars of aggression and spoliation such as this that has just ended forever impossible. A cry had gone out from every home in every stricken land from which sons and brothers and fathers had gone forth to the great sacrifice that such a sacrifice should never again be exacted. It was manifest why it had been exacted. It had been exacted because one nation desired dominion and other nations had known no means of defense except armaments and alliances. War had lain at the heart of every arrangement of the Europe,—of every arrangement of the world,—that preceded the war. Restive peoples had been told that fleets and armies, which they toiled to sustain, meant peace; and they now knew that they had been lied to: that fleets and armies had been maintained to promote national ambitions and meant war. They knew that no old policy meant anything else but force, force,—always force. And they knew that it was intolerable. Every true heart in the world, and every enlightened judgment demanded that, at whatever cost of independent action, every government that took thought for its people or for justice or for ordered freedom should lend itself to a new purpose and utterly destroy the old order of international politics. Statesmen might see difficulties, but the people could see none and could brook no denial. A war in which they had been bled white to beat the terror that lay concealed in every Balance of Power must not end in a mere victory of arms and a new balance. The monster that had resorted to arms must be put in chains that could not be broken. The united power of free nations must put a stop to aggression, and the world must be given peace. If there was not the will or the intelligence to accomplish that now, there must be another and a final war and the world must be swept clean of every power that could renew the terror. The League of Nations was not merely an instrument to adjust and remedy old wrongs under a new treaty of peace; it was the only hope for mankind. Again and again had the demon of war been cast out of the house of the peoples and the house swept clean by a treaty of peace; only to prepare a time when he would enter in again with spirits worse than himself. The house must now be given a tenant who could hold it against all such. Convenient, indeed indispensable, as statesmen found the newly planned League of Nations to be for the execution of present plans of peace and reparation, they saw it in a new aspect before their work was finished. They saw it as the main object of the peace, as the only thing that could complete it or make it worth while. They saw it as the hope of the world, and that hope they did not dare to disappoint. Shall we or any other free people hesitate to accept this great duty? Dare we reject it and break the heart of the world?

And so the result of the Conference of Peace, so far as Germany is concerned, stands complete. The difficulties encountered were very many. Sometimes they seemed insuperable. It was impossible to accommodate the interests of so great a body of nations,—interests which directly or indirectly affected almost every nation in the world,—without many minor compromises. The treaty, as a result, is not exactly what we would have written. It is probably not what any one of the national delegations would have written. But results were worked out which on the whole bear test. I think that it will be found that the compromises which were accepted as inevitable nowhere cut to the heart of any principle. The work of the Conference squares, as a whole, with the principles agreed upon as the basis of the peace as well as with the practical possibilities of the international situations which had to be faced and dealt with as facts.

I shall presently have occasion to lay before you a special treaty with France, whose object is the temporary protection of France from unprovoked aggression by the power with whom this treaty of peace has been negotiated. Its terms link it with this treaty. I take the liberty, however, of reserving it for special explication on another occasion.

America Has Reached Her Majority as a World Power

The rôle which America was to play in the Conference seemed determined, as I have said, before my colleagues and I got to Paris, —determined by the universal expectations of the nations whose representatives, drawn from all quarters of the globe, we were to deal with. It was universally recognized that America had entered the war to promote no private or peculiar interest of her own but only as the champion of rights which she was glad to share with free men and lovers of justice everywhere. We had formulated the principles upon which the settlement was to be made,—the principles upon which the armistice had been agreed to and the parleys of peace undertaken,—and no one doubted that our desire was to see the treaty of peace formulated along the actual lines of those principles,—and desired nothing else. We were welcomed as disinterested friends. We were resorted to as arbiters in many a difficult matter. It was recognized that our material aid would be indispensable in the days to come, when industry and credit would have to be brought back to their normal operation again and communities beaten to the ground assisted to their feet once more, and it was taken for granted, I am proud to say, that we would play the helpful friend in these things as in all others without prejudice or favor. We were generously accepted as the unaffected champions of what was right. It was a very responsible rôle to play; but I am happy to report that the fine group of Americans who helped with their expert advice in each part of the varied settlements sought in every transaction to justify the high confidence reposed in them.

And that confidence, it seems to me, is the measure of our opportunity and of our duty in the days to come, in which the new hope of the peoples of the world is to be fulfilled or disappointed. The fact that America is the friend of the nations, whether they be rivals or associates, is no new fact; it is only the discovery of it by the rest of the world that is new.

America may be said to have just reached her majority as a world power. It was almost exactly twenty-one years ago that the results of the war with Spain put us unexpectedly in possession of rich islands on the other side of the world and brought us into association with other governments in the control of the West Indies. It was regarded as a sinister and ominous thing by the statesmen of more than one European chancellery that we should have extended our power beyond the confines of our continental dominions. They were accustomed to think of new neighbors as a new menace, of rivals as watchful enemies. There were persons amongst us at home who looked with deep disapproval and avowed anxiety on such extensions of our national authority over distant islands and over peoples whom they feared we might exploit, not serve and assist. But we have not exploited them. We have been their friends and have sought to serve them. And our dominion has been a menace to no other nations. We redeemed our honor to the utmost in our dealings with Cuba. She is weak but absolutely free; and it is her trust in us that makes her free. Weak peoples everywhere stand ready to give us any authority among them that will assure them a like friendly oversight and direction. They know that there is no ground for fear in receiving us as their mentors and guides. Our isolation was ended twenty years ago; and now fear of us is ended also, our counsel and association sought after and desired. There can be no question of our ceasing to be a world power. The only question is whether we can refuse the moral leadership that is offered us, whether we shall accept or reject the confidence of the world.

The war and the Conference of Peace now sitting in Paris seem to me to have answered that question. Our participation in the war established our position among the nations and nothing but our own mistaken action can alter it. It was not an accident or a matter of sudden choice that we are no longer isolated and devoted to a policy which has only our own interest and advantage for its object. It was our duty to go in, if we were indeed the champions of liberty and of right. We answered to the call of duty in a way so spirited, so utterly without thought of what we spent of blood or treasure, so effective, so worthy of the admiration of true men everywhere, so wrought out of the stuff of all that was heroic, that the whole world saw at last, in the flesh, in noble action, a great ideal asserted and vindicated, by a Nation they had deemed material and now found to be compact of the spiritual forces that must free men of every nation from every unworthy bondage. It is thus that a new rôle and a new responsibility have come to this great Nation that we honor and which we would all wish to lift to yet higher levels of service and achievement.

The stage is set, the destiny disclosed. It has come about by no plan of our conceiving, but by the hand of God who led us into this way. We cannot turn back. We can only go forward, with lifted eyes and freshened spirit, to follow the vision. It was of this that we dreamed at our birth. America shall in truth show the way. The light streams upon the path ahead, and nowhere else.

STATEMENT TO THE MEMBERS
OF THE SENATE COMMITTEE ON FOREIGN RELATIONS,
WASHINGTON, AUGUST 19, 1919

The Nation's Business Waits upon the Senate

MR. CHAIRMAN: I have taken the liberty of writing out a little statement in the hope that it might facilitate discussion by speaking directly on some points that I know have been points of controversy and upon which I thought an expression of opinion would not be unwelcome. I am absolutely glad that the committee should have responded in this way to my intimation that I would like to be of service to it. I welcome the opportunity for a frank and full interchange of views.

I hope, too, that this conference will serve to expedite your consideration of the treaty of peace. I beg that you will pardon and indulge me if I again urge that practically the whole task of bringing the country back to normal conditions of life and industry waits upon the decision of the Senate with regard to the terms of the peace.

I venture thus again to urge my advice that the action of the Senate with regard to the treaty be taken at the earliest practicable moment because the problems with which we are face to face in the readjustment of our national life are of the most pressing and critical character, will require for their proper solution the most intimate and disinterested coöperation of all parties and all interests, and cannot be postponed without manifest peril to our people and to all the national advantages we hold most dear. May I mention a few of the matters which cannot be handled with intelligence until the country knows the character of the peace it is to have? I do so only by a very few samples.

The copper mines of Montana, Arizona and Alaska, for example, are being kept open and in operation only at a great cost and loss, in part upon borrowed money; the zinc mines of Missouri, Tennessee and Wisconsin are being operated at about one-half their capacity; the lead of Idaho, Illinois and Missouri reaches only a portion of its former market; there is an immediate need for cotton belting, and also for lubricating oil, which cannot be met—all because the channels of trade are barred by war when there is no war. The same is true of raw cotton, of which the Central Empires alone formerly purchased nearly 4,000,000 bales. And these are only examples. There is hardly a single raw material, a single important foodstuff, a single class of manufactured goods which is not in the same case. Our full, normal profitable production waits on peace.

Our military plans of course wait upon it. We cannot intelligently or wisely decide how large a naval or military force we shall maintain or what our policy with regard to military training is to be until we have peace not only, but also until we know how peace is to be sustained, whether by the arms of single nations or by the concert of all the great peoples. And there is more than that difficulty involved. The vast surplus properties of the army include not food and clothing merely, whose sale will affect normal production, but great manufacturing establishments also which should be restored to their former uses, great stores of machine tools, and all sorts of merchandise which must lie idle until peace and military policy are definitely determined. By the same token there can be no properly studied national budget until then.

The nations that ratify the treaty, such as Great Britain, Belgium and France, will be in a position to lay their plans for controlling the markets of Central Europe without competition from us if we do not presently act. We have no consular agents, no trade representatives there to look after our interests.

There are large areas of Europe whose future will lie uncertain and questionable until their people know the final settlements of peace and the forces which are to administer and sustain it. Without determinate markets our production cannot proceed with intelligence or confidence. There can be no stabilization of wages because there can be no settled conditions of employment. There can be no easy or normal industrial credits because there can be no confident or permanent revival of business.

But I will not weary you with obvious examples. I will only venture to repeat that every element of normal life amongst us depends upon and awaits the ratification of the treaty of peace; and also that we cannot afford to lose a single summer's day by not doing all that we can to mitigate the winter's suffering, which, unless we find means to prevent it, may prove disastrous to a large portion of the world, and may, at its worst, bring upon Europe conditions even more terrible than those wrought by the war itself.

Doubts about the League

Nothing, I am led to believe, stands in the way of ratification of the treaty except certain doubts with regard to the meaning and implication of certain articles of the Covenant of the League of Nations; and I must frankly say that I am unable to understand why such doubts should be entertained. You will recall that when I had the pleasure of a conference with your committee and with the committee of the House of Representatives on Foreign Affairs at the White House in March last, the questions now most frequently asked about the League of Nations were all canvassed with a view to their immediate clarification. The Covenant of the League was then in its first draft and subject to revision. It was pointed out that no express recognition was given to the Monroe Doctrine; that it was not expressly provided that the League should have no authority to act or to express a judgment on matters of domestic policy; that the right to withdraw from the League was not expressly recognized; and that the constitutional right of the Congress to determine all questions of peace and war was not sufficiently safeguarded. On my return to Paris all these matters were taken up again by the Commission on the League of Nations and every suggestion of the United States was accepted.

The views of the United States with regard to the questions I have mentioned had, in fact, already been accepted by the Commission and there was supposed to be nothing inconsistent with them in the draft of the Covenant first adopted—the draft which was the subject of our discussion in March—but no objection was made to saying explicitly in the text what all had supposed to be implicit in it. There was absolutely no doubt as to the meaning of any one of the resulting provisions of the Covenant in the minds of those who participated in drafting them, and I respectfully submit that there is nothing vague or doubtful in their wording.

The Monroe Doctrine is expressly mentioned as an understanding which is in no way to be impaired or interfered with by anything contained in the Covenant and the expression "regional understandings like the Monroe Doctrine" was used, not because any one of the conferees thought there was any comparable agreement anywhere else in existence or in contemplation, but only because it was thought best to avoid the appearance of dealing in such a document with the policy of a single nation. Absolutely nothing is concealed in the phrase.

With regard to domestic questions Article 16 of the Covenant expressly provides that, if in case of any dispute arising between members of the League the matter involved is claimed by one of the parties "and is found by the council to arise out of a matter which by international law is solely within the domestic jurisdiction of that party, the council shall so report, and shall make no recommendation as to its settlement." The United States was by no means the only Government interested in the explicit adoption of this provision, and there is no doubt in the mind of any authoritative student of international law that such matters as immigration, tariffs, and naturalization are incontestably domestic questions with which no international body could deal without express authority to do so. No enumeration of domestic questions was undertaken because to undertake it, even by sample, would have involved the danger of seeming to exclude those not mentioned.

The right of any sovereign State to withdraw had been taken for granted, but no objection was made to making it explicit. Indeed, so soon as the views expressed at the White House conference were laid before the commission it was at once conceded that it was best not to leave the answer to so important a question to inference. No proposal was made to set up any tribunal to pass judgment upon the question whether a withdrawing nation had in fact fulfilled "all its international obligations and all its obligations under the Covenant." It was recognized that that question must be left to be resolved by the conscience of the nation proposing to withdraw; and I must say that it did not seem to me worth while to propose that the article be made more explicit, because I knew that the United

States would never itself propose to withdraw from the League if its conscience was not entirely clear as to the fulfillment of all its international obligations. It has never failed to fulfill them and never will.

Article X is in no respect of doubtful meaning when read in the light of the Covenant as a whole. The council of the League can only "advise upon" the means by which the obligations of that great article are to be given effect. Unless the United States is a party to the policy or action in question, her own affirmative vote in the council is necessary before any advice can be given, for a unanimous vote of the council is required. If she is a party, the trouble is hers anyhow. And the unanimous vote of the council is only advice in any case. Each Government is free to reject it if it pleases. Nothing could have been made more clear to the conference than the right of our Congress under our Constitution to exercise its independent judgment in all matters of peace and war. No attempt was made to question or limit that right. The United States will, indeed, undertake under Article X to "respect and preserve as against external aggression the territorial integrity and existing political independence of all members of the League," and that engagement constitutes a very grave and solemn moral obligation. But it is a moral, not a legal, obligation, and leaves our Congress absolutely free to put its own interpretation upon it in all cases that call for action. It is binding in conscience only, not in law.

Article X seems to me to constitute the very backbone of the whole Covenant. Without it the League would be hardly more than an influential debating society.

The Pitfalls of Reservations

It has several times been suggested, in public debate and in private conference, that interpretations of the sense in which the United States accepts the engagements of the Covenant should be embodied in the instrument of ratification. There can be no reasonable objection to such interpretations accompanying the act of ratification provided they do not form a part of the formal ratification itself. Most of the interpretations which have been suggested to me embody what seems to me the plain meaning of the instrument itself. But if such interpretations should constitute a part of the formal resolution of ratification, long delays would be the inevitable consequence, inasmuch as all the many Governments concerned would have to accept, in effect, the language of the Senate as the language of the treaty before ratification would be complete. The assent of the German Assembly at Weimar would have to be obtained, among the rest, and I must frankly say that I could only with the greatest reluctance approach the Assembly for permission to read the treaty as we understand it and as those who framed it quite certainly understood it. If the United States were to qualify the document in any way, moreover, I am confident from what I know of the many conferences and debates which accompanied the formulation of the treaty that our example would immediately be followed in many quarters, in some instances with very serious reservations, and that the meaning and operative force of the treaty would presently be clouded from one end of its clauses to the other.

Pardon me, Mr. Chairman, if I have been entirely unreserved and plain-spoken in speaking of the great matters we all have so much at heart. If excuse is needed, I trust that the critical situation of affairs may serve as my justification. The issues that manifestly hang upon the conclusions of the Senate with regard to peace and upon the time of its action are so grave and so clearly insusceptible of being thrust on one side or postponed that I have felt it necessary in the public interest to make this urgent plea, and to make it as simply and as unreservedly as possible.

SPEECH AT PUEBLO, COLORADO,
SEPTEMBER 25, 1919

My Clients Are the Next Generation

In order to meet the present situation we have got to know what we are dealing with. We are not dealing with the kind of document which this is represented by some gentlemen to be; and inasmuch as we are dealing with a document simon-pure in respect of the very principles we have professed and lived up to, we have got to do one or other of two things—we have got to adopt it or reject it. There is no middle course. You cannot go in on a special-privilege basis of your own. I take it that you are too proud to ask to be exempted from responsibilities which the other members of the League will carry. We go in upon equal terms or we do not go in at all; and if we do not go in, my fellow citizens, think of the tragedy of that result—the only sufficient guarantee to the peace of the world withheld! Ourselves drawn apart with that dangerous pride which means that we shall be ready to take care of ourselves, and that means that we shall maintain great standing armies and an irresistible navy; that means we shall have the organization of a military nation; that means we shall have a general staff, with the kind of power that the general staff of Germany had; to mobilize this great manhood of the Nation when it pleases, all the energy of our young men drawn into the thought and preparation for war.

What of our pledges to the men that lie dead in France? We said that they went over there not to prove the prowess of America or her readiness for another war but to see to it that there never was such a war again. It always seems to make it difficult for me to say anything, my fellow citizens, when I think of my clients in this case. My clients are the children; my clients are the next generation. They do not know what promises and bonds I undertook when I ordered the armies of the United States to the soil of France, but I know, and I intend to redeem my pledges to the children; they shall not be sent upon a similar errand.

Again and again, my fellow citizens, mothers who lost their sons in France have come to me and, taking my hand, have shed tears upon it not only, but they have added, "God bless you, Mr. President!" Why, my fellow citizens, should they pray God to bless me? I advised the Congress of the United States to create the situation that led to the death of their sons. I ordered their sons overseas. I consented to their sons being put in the most difficult parts of the battle line, where death was certain, as in the impenetrable difficulties of the forest of Argonne. Why should they weep upon my hand and call down the blessings of God upon me? Because they believe that their boys died for something that vastly transcends any of the immediate and palpable objects of the war. They believe,

and they rightly believe, that their sons saved the liberty of the
world. They believe that wrapped up with the liberty of the world
is the continuous protection of that liberty by the concerted powers
of all civilized people. They believe that this sacrifice was made in
order that other sons should not be called upon for a similar gift—
the gift of life, the gift of all that died—and if we did not see this
thing through, if we fulfilled the dearest present wish of Germany
and now dissociated ourselves from those alongside whom we fought
in the war, would not something of the halo go away from the gun
over the mantelpiece, or the sword? Would not the old uniform
lose something of its significance? These men were crusaders. They
were not going forth to prove the might of the United States. They
were going forth to prove the might of justice and right, and all the
world accepted them as crusaders, and their transcendent achievement has made all the world believe in America as it believes in no
other nation organized in the modern world. There seems to me to
stand between us and the rejection or qualification of this treaty the
serried ranks of those boys in khaki, not only these boys who came
home, but those dear ghosts that still deploy upon the fields of
France.

My friends, on last Decoration Day I went to a beautiful hillside
near Paris, where was located the cemetery of Suresnes, a cemetery
given over to the burial of the American dead. Behind me on the
slopes was rank upon rank of living American soldiers, and lying
before me upon the levels of the plain was rank upon rank of de-
parted American soldiers. Right by the side of the stand where I
spoke there was a little group of French women who had adopted
those graves, had made themselves mothers of those dear ghosts by
putting flowers every day upon those graves, taking them as their
own sons, their own beloved, because they had died in the same
cause—France was free and the world was free because America had
come! I wish some men in public life who are now opposing the settlement for which these men died could visit such a spot as that. I
wish that the thought that comes out of those graves could penetrate their consciousness. I wish that they could feel the moral obligation that rests upon us not to go back on those boys, but to see

the thing through, to see it through to the end and make good their redemption of the world. For nothing less depends upon this decision, nothing less than the liberation and salvation of the world. . . .

The arrangements of this treaty are just, but they need the support of the combined power of the great nations of the world. And they will have that support. Now that the mists of this great question have cleared away, I believe that men will see the truth, eye to eye and face to face. There is one thing that the American people always rise to and extend their hand to, and that is the truth of justice and of liberty and of peace. We have accepted that truth and we are going to be led by it, and it is going to lead us, and through us the world, out into pastures of quietness and peace such as the world never dreamed of before.

MESSAGE TO JACKSON DAY DINNER
CELEBRATION, JANUARY 8, 1920

The Old Stage Set for the Old Plot

MY DEAR MR. CHAIRMAN: It is with the keenest regret that I find that I am to be deprived of the pleasure and privilege of joining you and the other loyal Democrats who are to assemble to-night to celebrate Jackson Day and renew their vows of fidelity to the great principles of our party, the principles which must now fulfill the hopes not only of our own people but of the world.

The United States enjoyed the spiritual leadership of the world until the Senate of the United States failed to ratify the treaty by which the belligerent nations sought to effect the settlements for which they had fought throughout the war.

It is inconceivable that at this supreme crisis and final turning point in the international relations of the whole world, when the results of the Great War are by no means determined and are still questionable and dependent upon events which no man can foresee or count upon, the United States should withdraw from the concert of progressive and enlightened nations by which Germany was defeated, and all similar Governments (if the world be so unhappy as to contain any) warned of the consequences of any attempt at a like iniquity, and yet that is the effect of the course which the United States has taken with regard to the Treaty of Versailles.

Germany is beaten, but we are still at war with her, and the old stage is reset for a repetition of the old plot. It is now ready for a resumption of the old offensive and defensive alliances which made settled peace impossible. It is now open again to every sort of intrigue.

The old spies are free to resume their former abominable activities. They are again at liberty to make it impossible for Governments to be sure what mischief is being worked among their own people, what internal disorders are being fomented.

Without the Covenant of the League of Nations there may be as many secret treaties as ever, to destroy the confidence of Governments in each other, and their validity cannot be questioned.

None of the objects we professed to be fighting for has been secured, or can be made certain of, without this Nation's ratification of the treaty and its entry into the Covenant. This Nation entered the Great War to vindicate its own rights and to protect and preserve free government. It went into the war to see it through to the end, and the end has not yet come. It went into the war to make an end of militarism, to furnish guarantees to weak nations, and to make a just and lasting peace. It entered it with noble enthusiasm. Five of the leading belligerents have accepted the treaty and formal ratifications soon will be exchanged. The question is whether this country will enter and enter whole-heartedly. If it does not do so, the United States and Germany will play a lone hand in the world.

The maintenance of the peace of the world and the effective execution of the treaty depend upon the whole-hearted participation of the United States. I am not stating it as a matter of power. The point is that the United States is the only Nation which has sufficient moral force with the rest of the world to guarantee the substitution of discussion for war. If we keep out of this agreement, if we do not give our guarantees, then another attempt will be made to crush the new nations of Europe.

I do not believe that this is what the people of this country wish or will be satisfied with. Personally, I do not accept the action of the Senate of the United States as the decision of the Nation.

I have asserted from the first that the overwhelming majority of the people of this country desire the ratification of the treaty, and my impression to that effect has recently been confirmed by the unmistakable evidence of public opinion given during my visit to seventeen of the States.

I have endeavored to make it plain that if the Senate wishes to say what the undoubted meaning of the League is I shall have no objection. There can be no reasonable objection to interpretation accompanying the act of ratification itself. But when the treaty is acted upon, I must know whether it means that we have ratified or rejected it.

A Great and Solemn Referendum

We cannot rewrite this treaty. We must take it without changes which alter its meaning, or leave it, and then, after the rest of the world has signed it, we must face the unthinkable task of making another and separate treaty with Germany.

But no mere assertions with regard to the wish and opinion of the country are credited. If there is any doubt as to what the people of the country think on this vital matter, the clear and single way out is to submit it for determination at the next election to the voters of the Nation, to give the next election the form of a great and solemn referendum, a referendum as to the part the United States is to play in completing the settlements of the war and in the prevention in the future of such outrages as Germany attempted to perpetrate.

We have no more moral right to refuse now to take part in the execution and administration of these settlements than we had to refuse to take part in the fighting of the last few weeks of the war which brought victory and made it possible to dictate to Germany what the settlements should be. Our fidelity to our associates in the war is in question and the whole future of mankind. It will be heartening to the whole world to know the attitude and purpose of the people of the United States.

I spoke just now of the spiritual leadership of the United States, thinking of international affairs. But there is another spiritual leadership which is open to us and which we can assume.

The world has been made safe for democracy, but democracy has not been finally vindicated. All sorts of crimes are being committed in its name, all sorts of preposterous perversions of its doctrines and practices are being attempted.

This, in my judgment, is to be the great privilege of the democracy of the United States, to show that it can lead the way in the solution of the great social and industrial problems of our time, and lead the way to a happy, settled order of life as well as to political liberty. The program for this achievement we must attempt to formulate, and in carrying it out we shall do more than can be done in any other way to sweep out of existence the tyrannous and arbitrary forms of power which are now masquerading under the name of popular government.

Whenever we look back to Andrew Jackson we should draw fresh inspiration from his character and example. His mind grasped with such a splendid definiteness and firmness the principles of national authority and national action. He was so indomitable in his purpose to give reality to the principles of the Government, that this is a very fortunate time to recall his career and to renew our vows of faithfulness to the principles and the pure practices of democracy.

Chapter Seventeen

EPILOGUE

An ARTICLE wrung out word by word in sickness was Wilson's only major statement in the years of retirement. He returns to the preoccupation with social justice which had fired his vision of the New Freedom.

"THE ATLANTIC MONTHLY,"
AUGUST 1923

The Road Away from Revolution

In these doubtful and anxious days, when all the world is at unrest and, look which way you will, the road ahead seems darkened by shadows which portend dangers of many kinds, it is only common prudence that we should look about us and attempt to assess the causes of distress and the most likely means of removing them.

There must be some real ground for the universal unrest and perturbation. It is not to be found in superficial politics or in mere economic blunders. It probably lies deep at the sources of the spiritual life of our time. It leads to revolution; and perhaps if we take the case of the Russian Revolution, the outstanding event of its kind in our age, we may find a good deal of instruction for our judgment of present critical situations and circumstances.

What gave rise to the Russian Revolution? The answer can only be that it was the product of a whole social system. It was not in fact a sudden thing. It had been gathering head for several generations. It was due to the systematic denial to the great body of Russians of the rights and privileges which all normal men desire and must have if they are to be contented and within reach of happiness. The lives of the great mass of the Russian people contained no opportunities, but were hemmed in by barriers against which they were constantly flinging their spirits, only to fall back bruised and dispirited. Only the powerful were suffered to secure their rights or even to gain access to the means of material success.

It is to be noted as a leading fact of our time that it was against 'capitalism' that the Russian leaders directed their attack. It was capitalism that made them see red; and it is against capitalism under one name or another that the discontented classes everywhere draw their indictment.

There are thoughtful and well-informed men all over the world who believe, with much apparently sound reason, that the abstract thing, the system, which we call capitalism, is indispensable to the industrial support and development of modern civilization. And yet everyone who has an intelligent knowledge of social forces must know that great and widespread reactions like that which is now unquestionably manifesting itself against capitalism do not occur without cause or provocation; and before we commit ourselves irreconcilably to an attitude of hostility to this movement of the time, we ought frankly to put to ourselves the question, Is the capitalistic system unimpeachable? which is another way of asking, Have capitalists generally used their power for the benefit of the countries in which their capital is employed and for the benefit of their fellow men?

Material Survival Dependent on Spiritual Redemption

Is it not, on the contrary, too true that capitalists have often seemed to regard the men whom they used as mere instruments of profit, whose physical and mental powers it was legitimate to exploit with as slight cost to themselves as possible, either of money or of sympathy? Have not many fine men who were actuated by the highest principles in every other relationship of life seemed to hold that generosity and humane feeling were not among the imperative mandates of conscience in the conduct of a banking business, or in the development of an industrial or commercial enterprise?

And, if these offenses against high morality and true citizenship have been frequently observable, are we to say that the blame for the present discontent and turbulence is wholly on the side of those who are in revolt against them? Ought we not, rather, to seek a way to remove such offenses and make life itself clean for those who will share honorably and cleanly in it?

The world has been made safe for democracy. There need now be no fear that any such mad design as that entertained by the insolent and ignorant Hohenzollerns and their counselors may prevail against it. But democracy has not yet made the world safe against irrational revolution. That supreme task, which is nothing less than the salvation of civilization, now faces democracy, insistent, imperative. There is no escaping it, unless everything we have built up is presently to fall in ruin about us; and the United States, as the greatest of democracies, must undertake it.

The road that leads away from revolution is clearly marked, for it is defined by the nature of men and of organized society. It therefore behooves us to study very carefully and very candidly the exact nature of the task and the means of its accomplishment.

The nature of men and of organized society dictates the maintenance in every field of action of the highest and purest standards of justice and of right dealing; and it is essential to efficacious thinking in this critical matter that we should not entertain a narrow or technical conception of justice. By justice the lawyer generally means the prompt, fair, and open application of impartial rules; but we call ours a Christian civilization, and a Christian conception of justice must be much higher. It must include sympathy and helpfulness and a willingness to forego self-interest in order to promote the welfare, happiness, and contentment of others and of the community as a whole. This is what our age is blindly feeling after in its reaction against what it deems the too great selfishness of the capitalistic system.

The sum of the whole matter is this, that our civilization cannot survive materially unless it be redeemed spiritually. It can be saved only by becoming permeated with the spirit of Christ and being made free and happy by the practices which spring out of that spirit. Only thus can discontent be driven out and all the shadows lifted from the road ahead.

Acknowledgments and Sources

In preparing this book I have had the sympathetic support and encouragement of Mrs. Woodrow Wilson, who has given her permission to use material of which she holds the copyright as well as a small amount of manuscript material appearing here for the first time. The Woodrow Wilson Foundation of New York has given me additional support; and I am indebted to Mr. Frank Altschul, president of the Foundation 1952–1954, who not only urged me to undertake the work but at the River House on his farm at Stamford, Connecticut, provided agreeable calm for writing the Introduction. My son, Stephen A. Heckscher, helped me with the burdensome task of reproducing by photographic process the printed pages of the Wilson texts. Mr. Alexander P. Clark, curator of manuscripts at the Princeton University Library, showed me every courtesy in making available to my inspection the Wilson manuscripts and other material in that collection.

To the following publishers I am grateful for permission to reproduce Wilson material which has appeared under their imprint: Harper & Brothers, New York; Houghton Mifflin Company, Boston; Columbia University Press, New York; Princeton University Press, Princeton, New Jersey; Doubleday & Company, Inc., New York.

Wilson's speeches, messages, and occasional papers have been collected in six volumes: *The Public Papers of Woodrow Wilson*, edited by Ray Stannard Baker and William E. Dodd (New York and London: Harper & Brothers, 1925). The main body of this selection is taken from that source, now out of print. In this book I have given at the head of each passage the date and place of its delivery (if it was a speech) or its first appearance in print as it appears in the table of contents in the above volumes. The reader will thus be able to identify readily the full source of the selections reprinted here. The following notes refer only to passages from other sources. I have followed the printed texts, correcting typographical errors or obvious errors in reporting, occasionally breaking up longer paragraphs, and indicating deletions I have made within sections.

CHAPTER ONE

Page 1. *Congressional Government* (Boston: Houghton Mifflin Company, 1885). The selections included here can be found beginning at pp. 5, 53, 94, 254, 278, 331.

Page 17. *Constitutional Government in the United States* (New York: The Columbia University Press, 1908). The selections included here can be found beginning at pp. 20, 65, 77.

CHAPTER TWO

Page 25. *The Forum*, February 1894. Reprinted from *Mere Literature and Other Essays* (Boston: Houghton Mifflin and Company, 1896), pp. 199–200.

Page 26. Address before the New Jersey Historical Society, Newark, New Jersey, May 16, 1895. *Ibid.*, pp. 224–228, 231, 232–238, 240–246.

CHAPTER THREE

Page 55. *The Atlantic Monthly*, September 1897. This article was reprinted under the title *On Being Human* (New York and London: Harper & Brothers, 1916). This text, with deletions as shown, is from that source.

Page 63. *The Century Magazine*, June 1901. Reprinted under the title *When a Man Comes to Himself* (New York and London: Harper & Brothers, 1915). The text is from that source.

Page 70. Address at the University of Tennessee, Knoxville, June 17, 1890. This address was printed for the first time in 1952 as *Leaders of Men*, edited with introduction and notes, by T. H. Vail Motter (Princeton, New Jersey: Princeton University Press). Passages here are from that source.

CHAPTER FOUR

Page 83. Address at the Hartford Theological Seminary, Hartford, Conn., May 26, 1909. Reprinted here from a pamphlet, "The Present Task of the Ministry," Hartford, 1909, in the Princeton University Library.

Page 86. Baccalaureate Address, Princeton University, June 7, 1908. This and the Baccalaureate Address of June 13, 1909, beginning on page 93 are taken from manuscripts in the Princeton University Library, and are printed here by permission.

CHAPTER FIVE

Page 137. Founders Day Address at Carnegie Institute, Pittsburgh, November 5, 1903. These passages are taken from a pamphlet,

"The Statesmanship of Letters," in the library of the Woodrow Wilson Foundation, New York.

CHAPTER SEVEN

Page 177. *The New Freedom* (Garden City and New York: Doubleday Page and Company, 1913), pp. 80–84.

CHAPTER NINE

Page 220. Letter to Joseph R. Wilson, April 22, 1913. This is from *Woodrow Wilson, Life and Letters*, by Ray Stannard Baker (Garden City and New York: Doubleday, Doran and Company, Inc., 1931), Vol. IV, p. 50.

DATE

GAYLORD